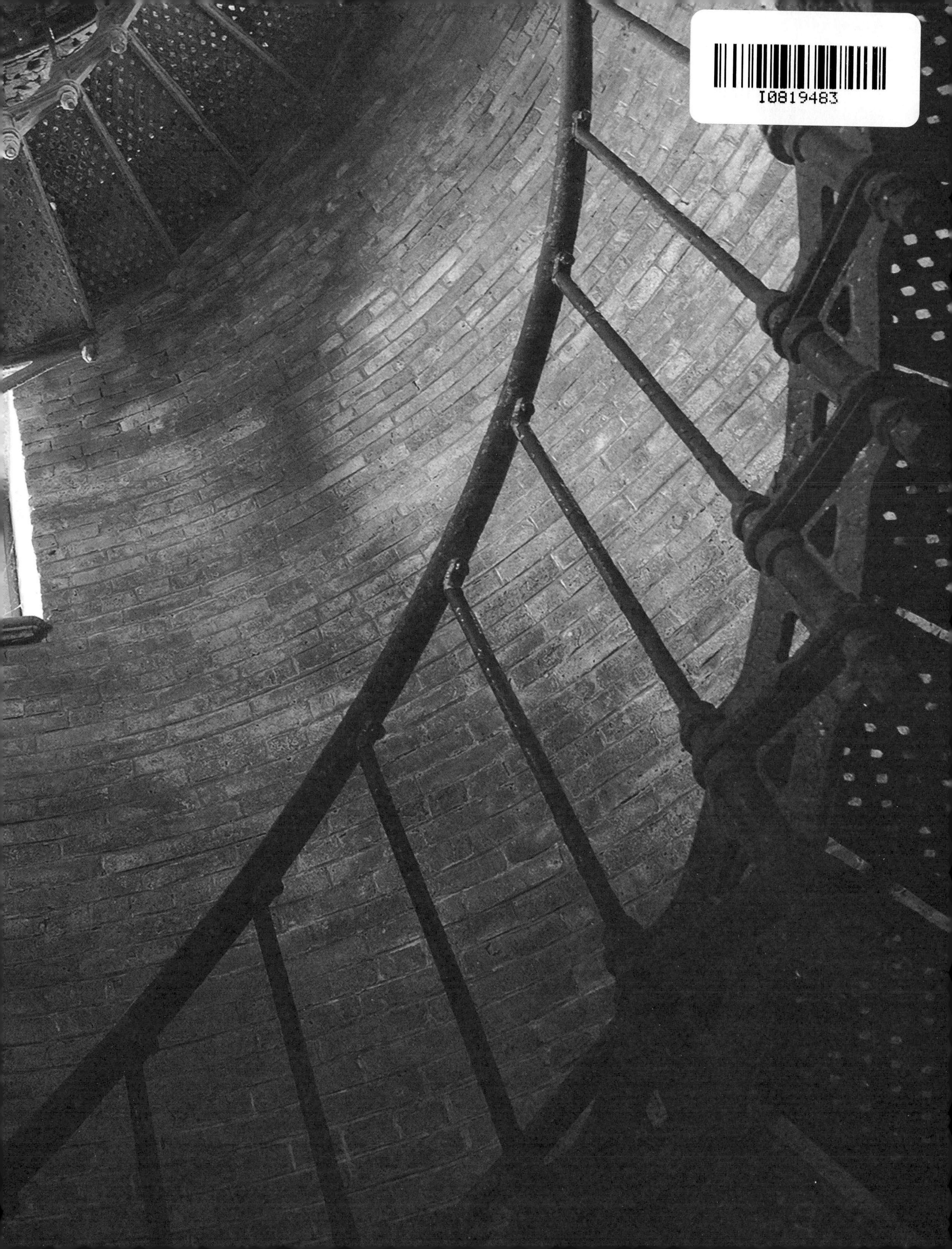
I0819483

Arthur P. Richmond

LIGHTHOUSES & LIGHTSHIPS OF RHODE ISLAND

Past & Present

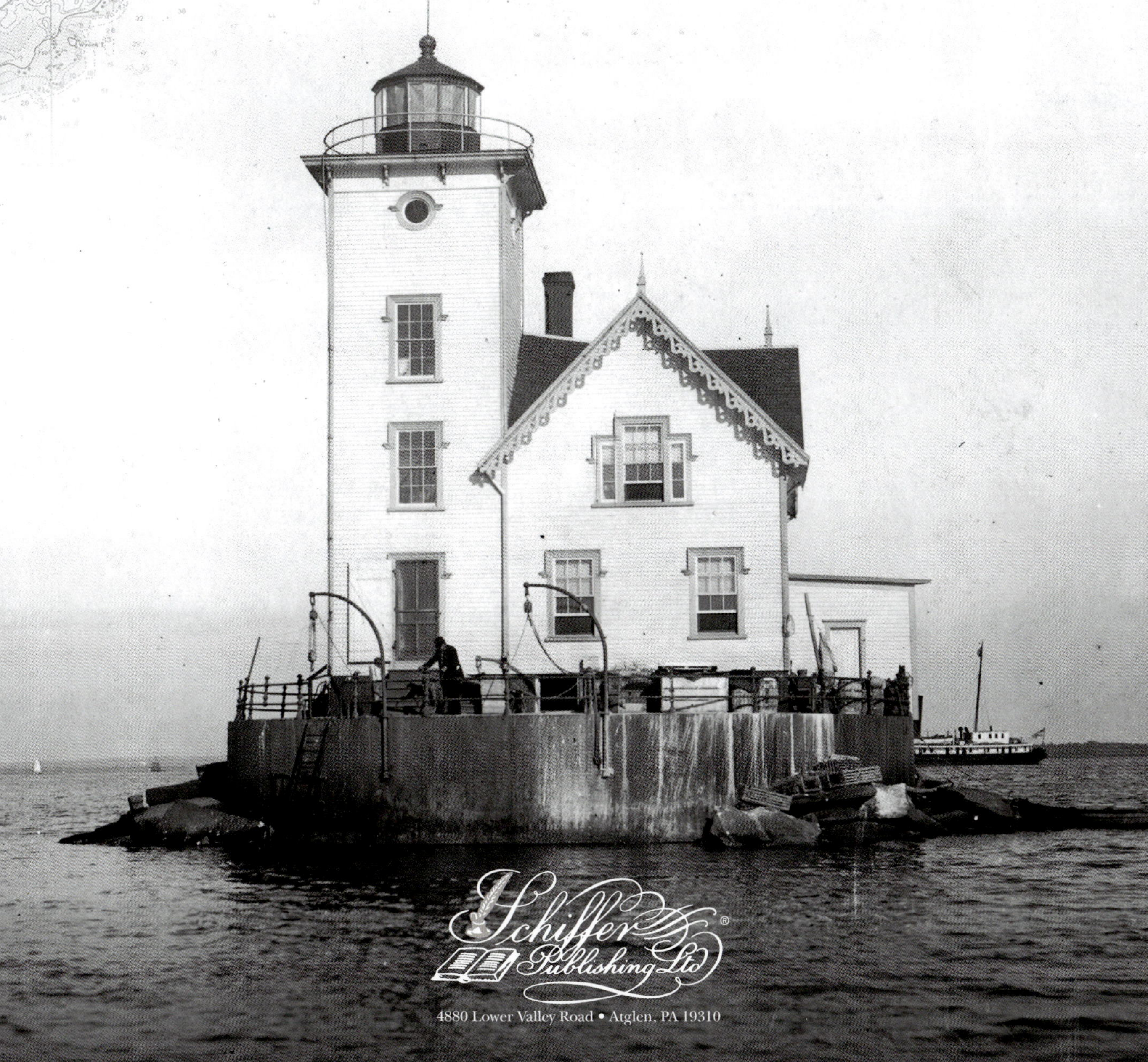

Schiffer Publishing Ltd

4880 Lower Valley Road • Atglen, PA 19310

Other Schiffer Books by the Author:

Cape Cod Lighthouses and Lightships, 978-0-7643-3545-7

Cape Cod Wide, 978-0-7643-2776-6

Provincetown Perspectives, 978-0-7643-2959-3

Martha's Vineyard Wide, 978-0-7643-3555-6

The Evolution of the Cape Cod House: An Architectural History, 978-0-7643-3848-9

Lighthouses of Cape Cod & the Islands Postcards, 978-0-7643-2460-4

Massachusetts Lighthouses: Past & Present, 978-0-7643-4305-6

Library of Congress Control Number: 2014948366

Designed by Brenda McCallum
Type set in Caslon Pro
Cover design by Molly Shields

ISBN: 978-0-7643-4782-5

Printed in China

Published by Schiffer Publishing, Ltd.
4880 Lower Valley Road
Atglen, PA 19310
Phone: (610) 593-1777; Fax: (610) 593-2002
E-mail: Info@schifferbooks.com

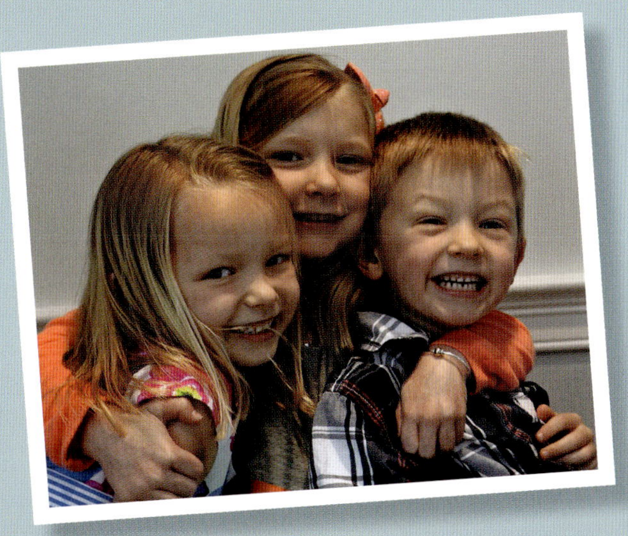

This book is dedicated to
Charlotte Rose, Ava Elizabeth, and Charles Douglas.

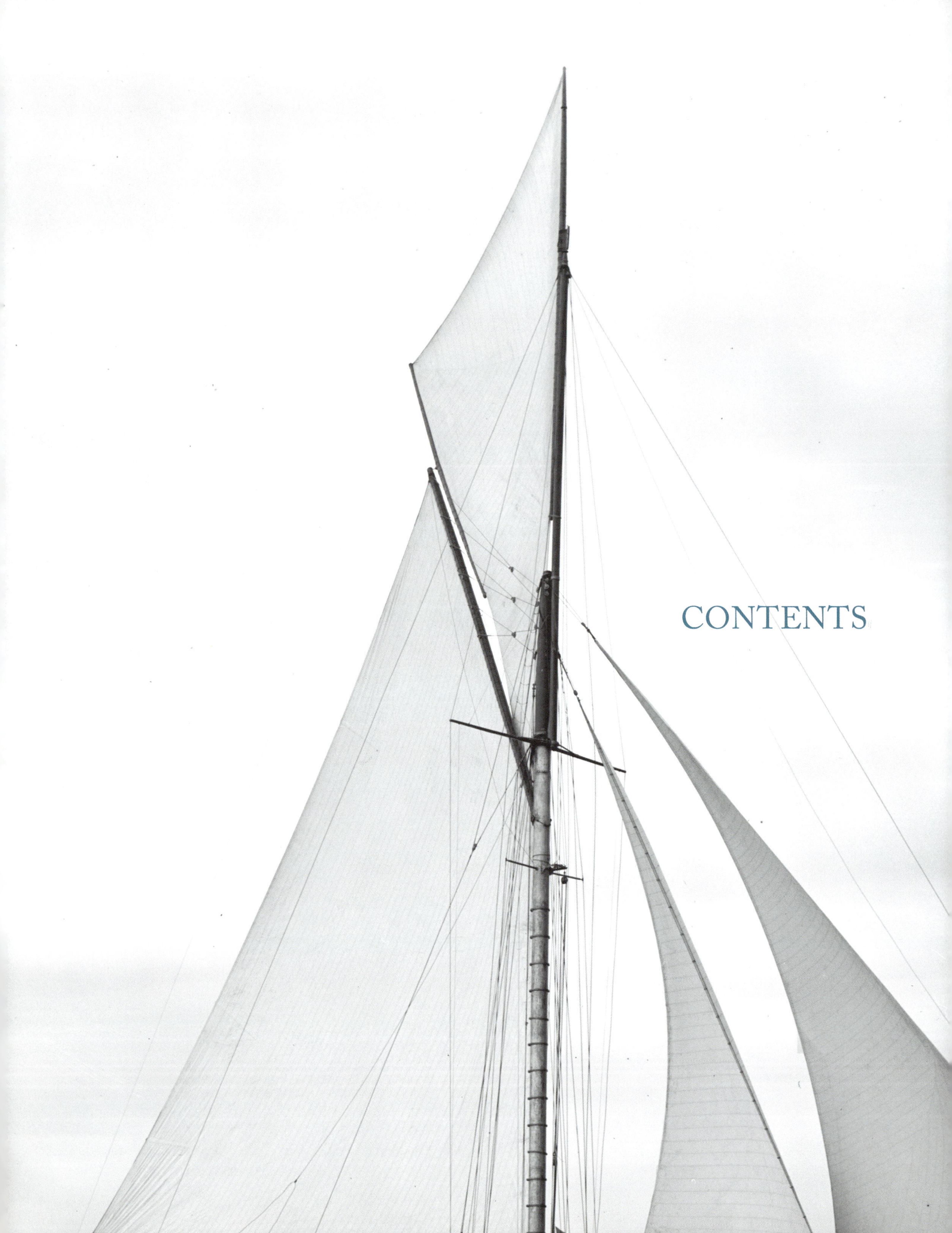

CONTENTS

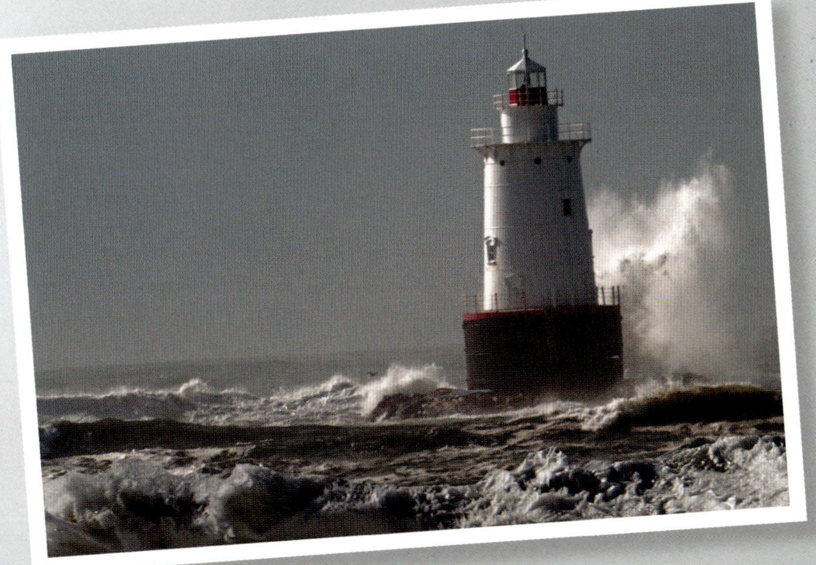

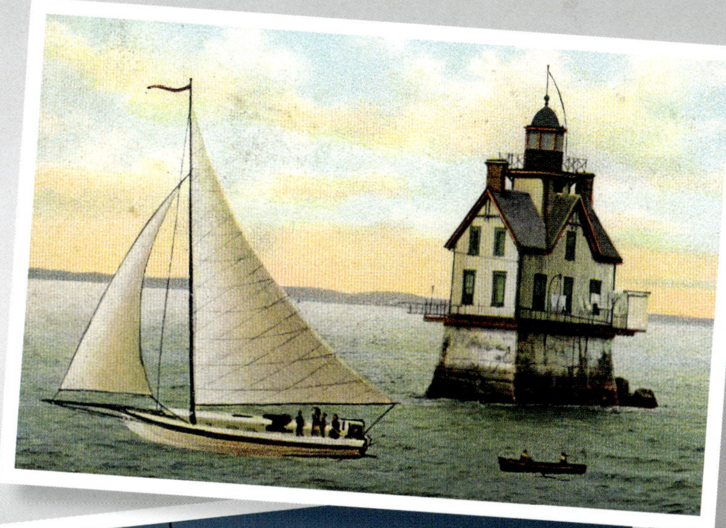

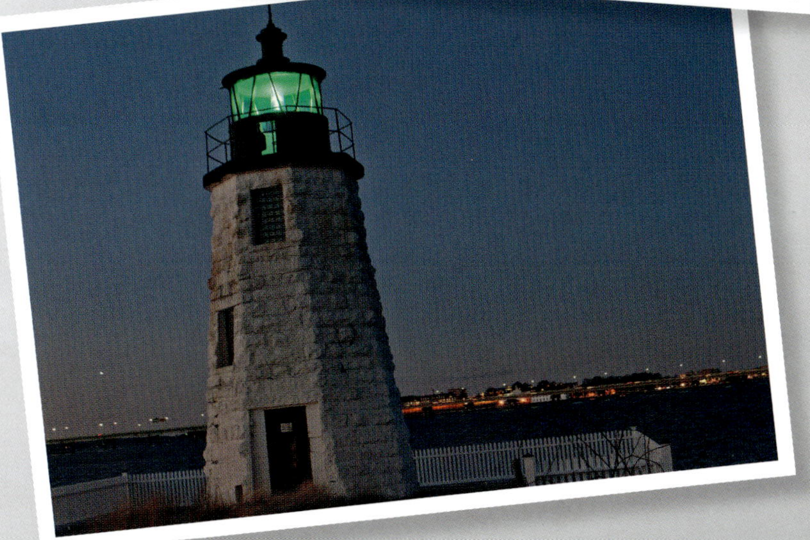

INTRODUCTION

For more than 300 years, lighthouses and lightships along the coast of Rhode Island have guided mariners. Beginning with Beavertail Light, the third built in the New World in the early 1700s, more than thirty aids were built along the coast and along inland waterways. Now, many of these lighthouses and lightships no longer exist, many are private aids to navigation, and many are still maintained by the United States Coast Guard; but whatever their status, these beacons evoke an interest and a fascination.

This pictorial guide is a survey with extensive images of every lighthouse station in Rhode Island, past and present. It also includes the two lightship stations: Hog Island Shoal, in existence for only fifteen years at the end of the nineteenth century, and Brenton Reef, the only offshore station from 1853 to 1962.

This is the fourth book that I have completed on lighthouses, the first about these Rhode Island aids to navigation. It reflects various useful comments I've received from readers of my previous publications, and offers you a rapid reference guide with numerous images that show the development and changes of these lighthouses and lightships through the years. One goal of this guide is to expand your knowledge and to stimulate an interest in lighthouses.

Along with the salient information, archival images, and significant historical information in these pages, the bibliography lists numerous well-written books that can be used to find more history, background, and stories about these aids to navigation.

The information here has been collected from a variety of sources, collated, and presented in a reader-friendly format. Many of the beacons mentioned in this book are listed on the National Register of Historic Places (NRHP). Archival photographs have been primarily collected from the National Archives (NA) in College Park, Maryland and the United States Coast Guard Historians Office (USCG) in Washington, DC. I have tried to include as many germane and significant facts as possible; latitude and longitude have been added and charts, some archival, have been used to show the location of these aids to navigation. For some of the lighthouses that are no longer in existence, historical data is missing, lost, or just hidden away in some archive.

Ranges of the lights, when available, are given in nautical miles; these have been taken from the latest USCG Light List. Most of these lights are now solar-powered with the energy being stored in batteries during the day and used by the lamp in the dark.

Images and information about the two lightship stations found in Rhode Island waters, Hog Island Shoal and Brenton Reef, lend insight into some of the maritime history of Rhode Island. Interestingly, many of the lighthouses and lightships cited in this book were, during the eighteenth century, privately owned by shipping companies whose vessels sailed through Narragansett and Mount Hope bays. In the nineteenth century, The Lighthouse Establishment made a determined and rigorous effort to provide navigators with an organized system of navigational aids. At the zenith of the shipping era, there were thirty lighthouses and one lightship (there had been two).

Now in the twenty-first century, nine of these towers no longer exist. In fact, the original location of Sassafras Point doesn't exist. Several old stations are now private residences, one is a significant feature of a yacht club, and many are owned by an organization dedicated to maintaining these historical treasures. The U.S. Coast Guard has only four lighthouse stations in Rhode Island.

Enjoy your opportunity to get to know Rhode Island's thirty lighthouses and two lightships, past and present.

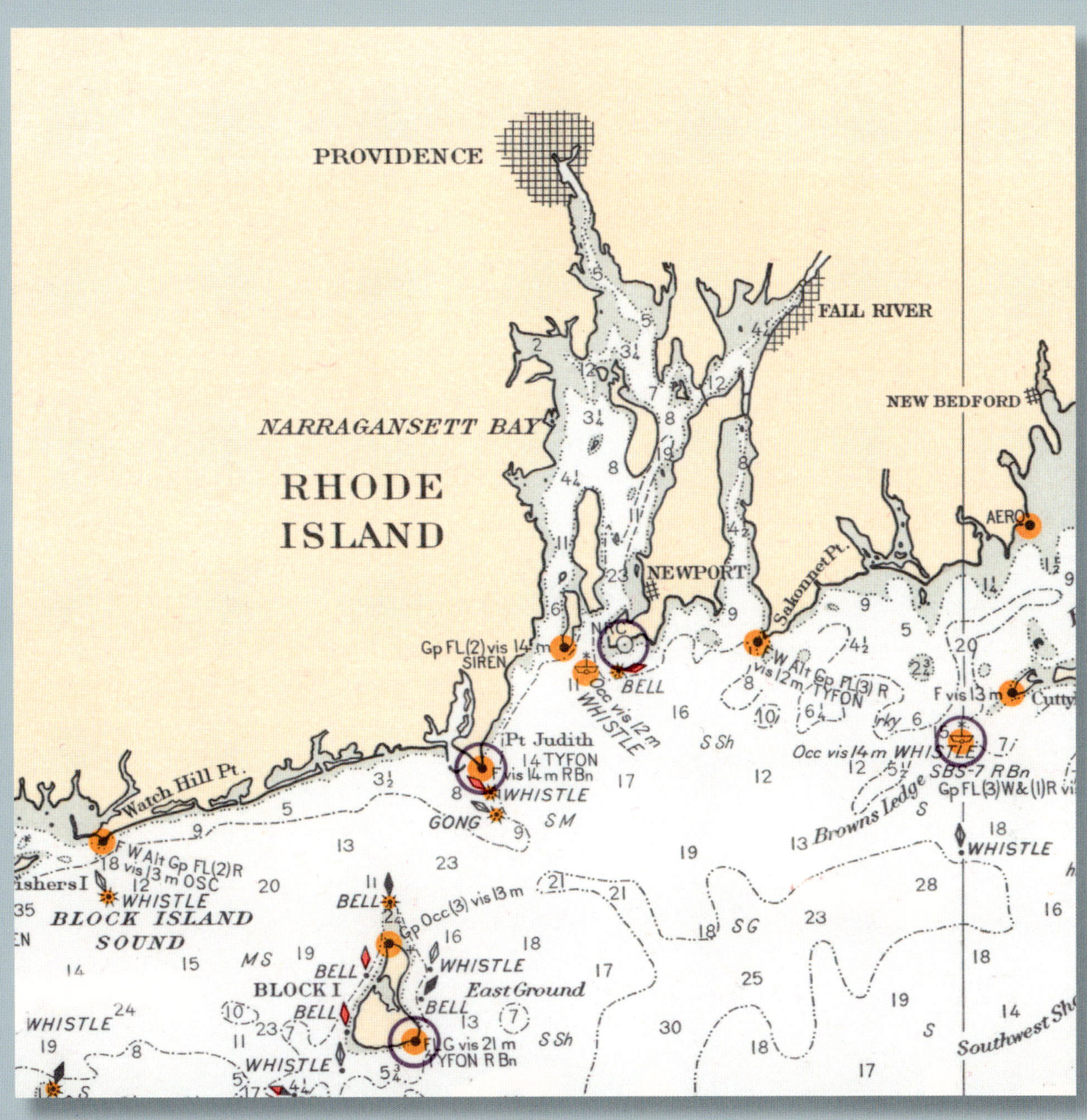

This portion of a 1941 chart shows a part of the area between New Bedford and Block Island, Rhode Island. Of note are the three identifiable aids to navigation on the chart: lighthouses, lightships, and large, offshore, navigational buoys. The yellow rings represent stations or sites with radio beacons; the distinctive characteristic signal of each beacon is indicated on the chart. Navigators would also have access to the light and sound characteristics of each aid that didn't have a radiobeacon. This chart, intended to be used only for offshore navigation, has a scale of 1:625,000 meaning that 1 inch is equal to 9.86 miles. Many of the charts used for illustrative purposes in this book have a scale of 1:40,000 where 1 inch equals .63 miles. Smaller-scale charts, with more detail, would be used when ships are closer to the harbors along the coast. Note that as improvements are made to navigation and technologies become outdated, those changes are either included or deleted as future charts are printed. *(Courtesy of NOAA)*

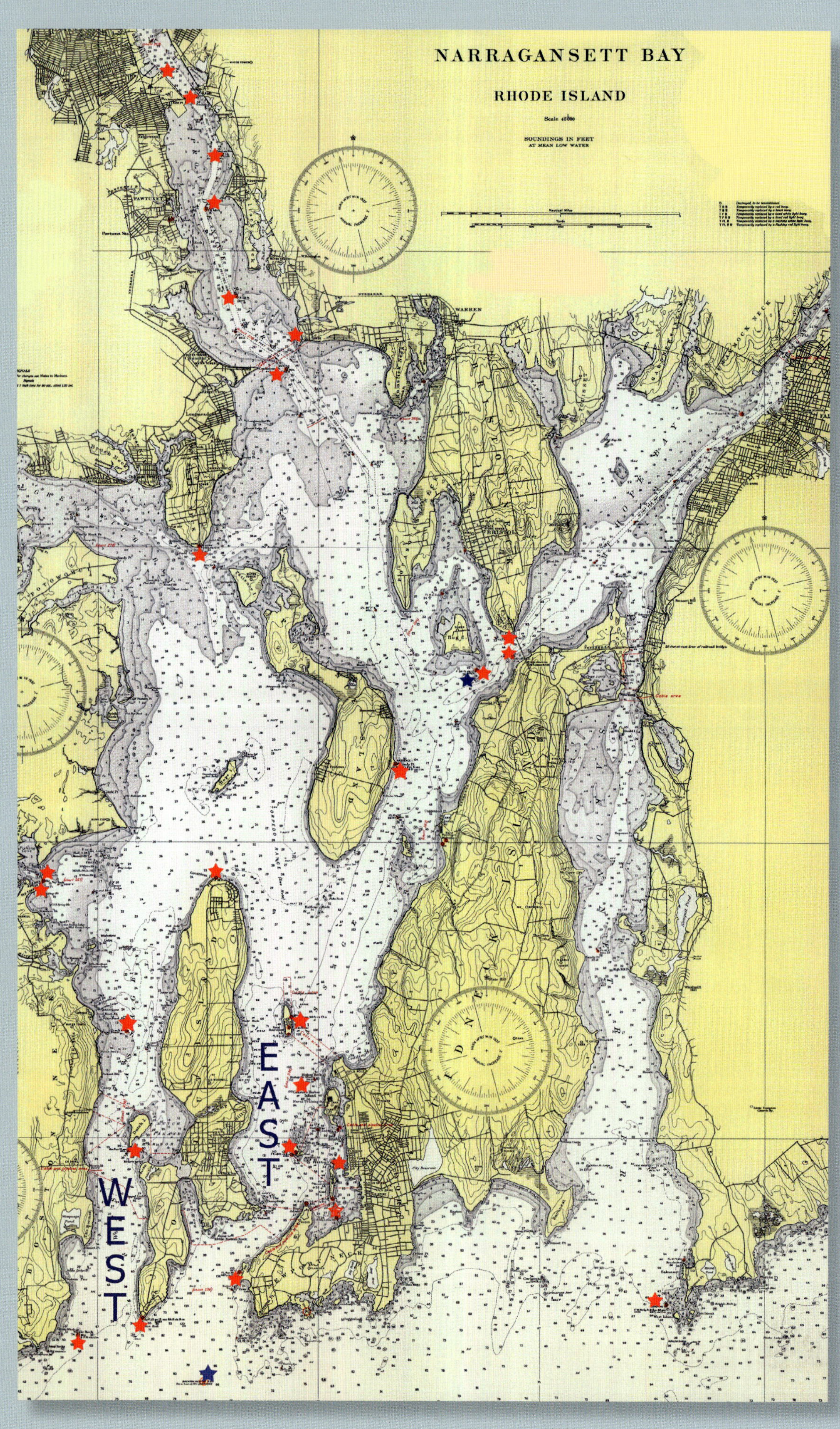
NARRAGANSETT BAY
RHODE ISLAND
SOUNDINGS IN FEET
AT MEAN LOW WATER
EAST
WEST

Opposite: This chart, with a scale of 1:40,000, identifies the locations of the twenty-six Rhode Island lighthouses past and present. Each red star indicates the position of a specific aid. Providence, at the top left of the chart, was/is a major destination for shipping; two passages as indicated here, West and East, are the routes vessels would take to reach this port. The two blue stars represent the locations of the lightships, Hog Island Shoal near the top and Brenton Reef offshore close to the bottom of the chart. Not located on this chart, but still active aids to navigation, are Point Judith, Watch Hill, and the two lighthouses on Block Island. *(Courtesy of NOAA)*

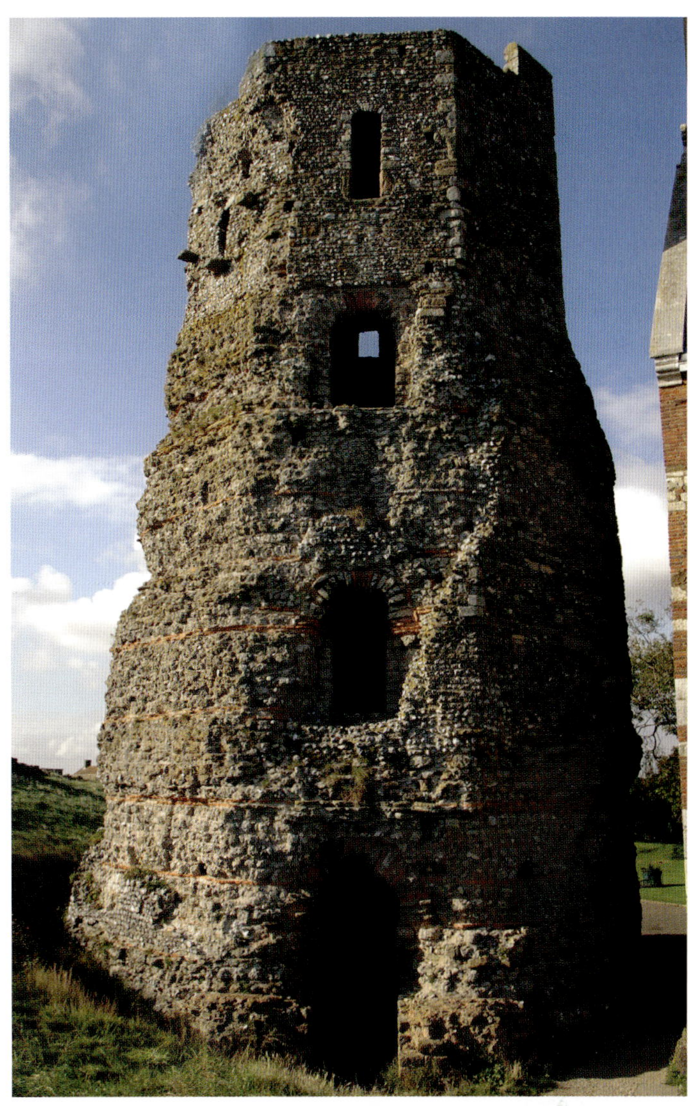

Right: Built almost two millennia ago, this pharos erected by the Romans stands on the grounds of Dover Castle in England and is one of the oldest towers in existence. It was originally twice this height. Fires would be lit at the top to guide mariners.

Below: Designed by Augustin Fresnel and first used in a lighthouse in France in 1823, the Fresnel lens captured more light from the source than did previous lenses, and produced a beam that was visible over greater distances. Built in several categories of size, the lenses were identified by order, 1st being the largest and 6th the smallest. The three lenses seen here (left to right) are the large 1st order which was, and is today, used in a location for offshore navigation, and the smaller 4th order and 5th order which were used in bays and harbors. All three of these sizes were and are used in Rhode Island. Presently there is a 1st order lens at Southeast Point, Block Island; many of the smaller Fresnel lenses have been replaced with modern plastic aero beacons.

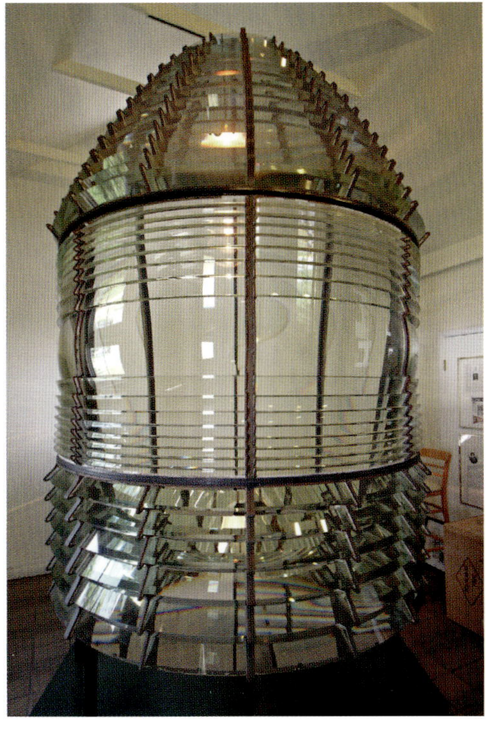

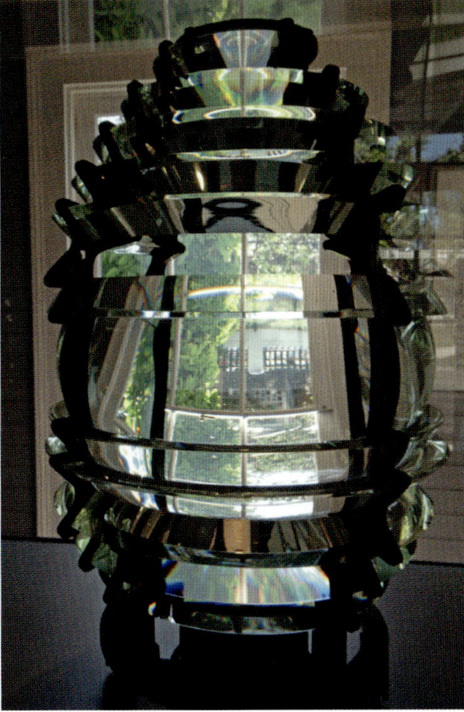

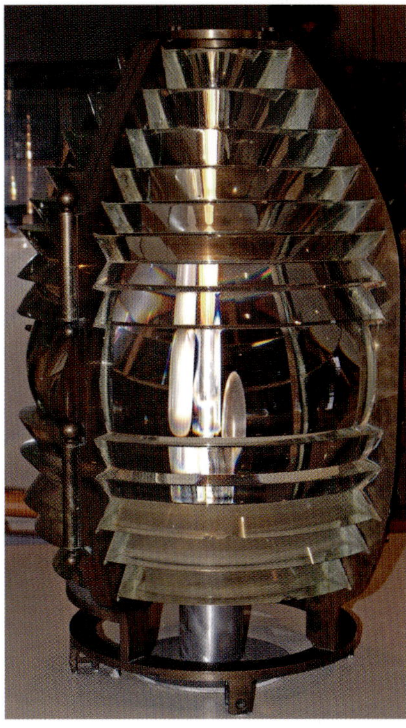

BLOCK ISLAND

About twelve miles south of Point Judith and fourteen miles northeast of Montauk Point, New York, Block Island has two lighthouses, at opposite ends of the island. Southeast Light with its large 1st order Fresnel lens and with a range of twenty nautical miles guides mariners in the Atlantic Ocean; North Light with its smaller 4th order Fresnel lens and a range of only thirteen nautical miles directs ships in Block Island Sound.

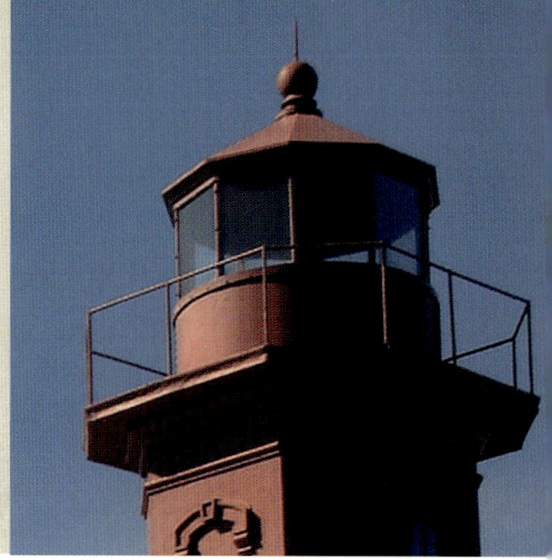

BLOCK ISLAND NORTH

(Sandy Point Light)

Location: Block Island, Sandy Point, northwest point, N41°13′40″, W71°34′33″

Appropriation: $5,500 in March 1829; $5,000 in March 1837; $9,000 in August 1856; $15,000 in July 1866

Established: 1829

Automated: 1956

Deactivated: 1970–1989

Relit: 2003 on a skeleton tower

Relit: 2010, lighthouse maintained as a private aid to navigation

Tower, original: Two towers 58 feet high, 25 feet apart and separated by keeper's house

Rebuilt 1837: Granite with two towers on keeper's house

Rebuilt 1857: Single tower 65 feet high

Rebuilt 1867: Present-day station, white octagonal tower, 55 feet, on granite keeper's house, black lantern room

Other Structures: Two storage buildings

Original Optics: 1829, 7 oil lamps with 16-inch parabolic reflectors, fixed white (FW)

Original Lens: 1857, 4th order Fresnel lens, fixed white (FW)

Present Lens: 4th order Fresnel lens, focal plane 61 feet

Light Characteristics: Flashing white every 5 seconds (Fl w 5s)

Range: 13 nm

Fog Signal: None

Status: Private aid to navigation

Access: Grounds open year-round; museum on first floor open during summer season; tower closed at present.

Comments: Owned and maintained by the North Light Commission, New Shoreham; restoration on upper floors underway to provide for overnight guests; listed in NHRP.

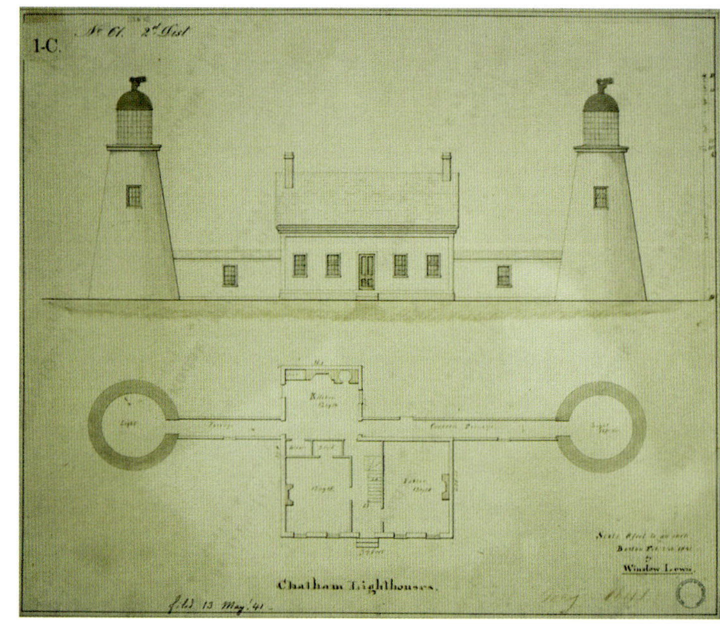

No photographs (although maybe somebody had painted a picture) exist of the first Sandy Point/Block Island North Light; this plan, dated 13 May 1841, of the original twin lights at Chatham, Massachusetts, may be what they looked like. Centuries ago when a lighthouse was first erected, design plans would be used for multiple stations. *(Courtesy of NA)*

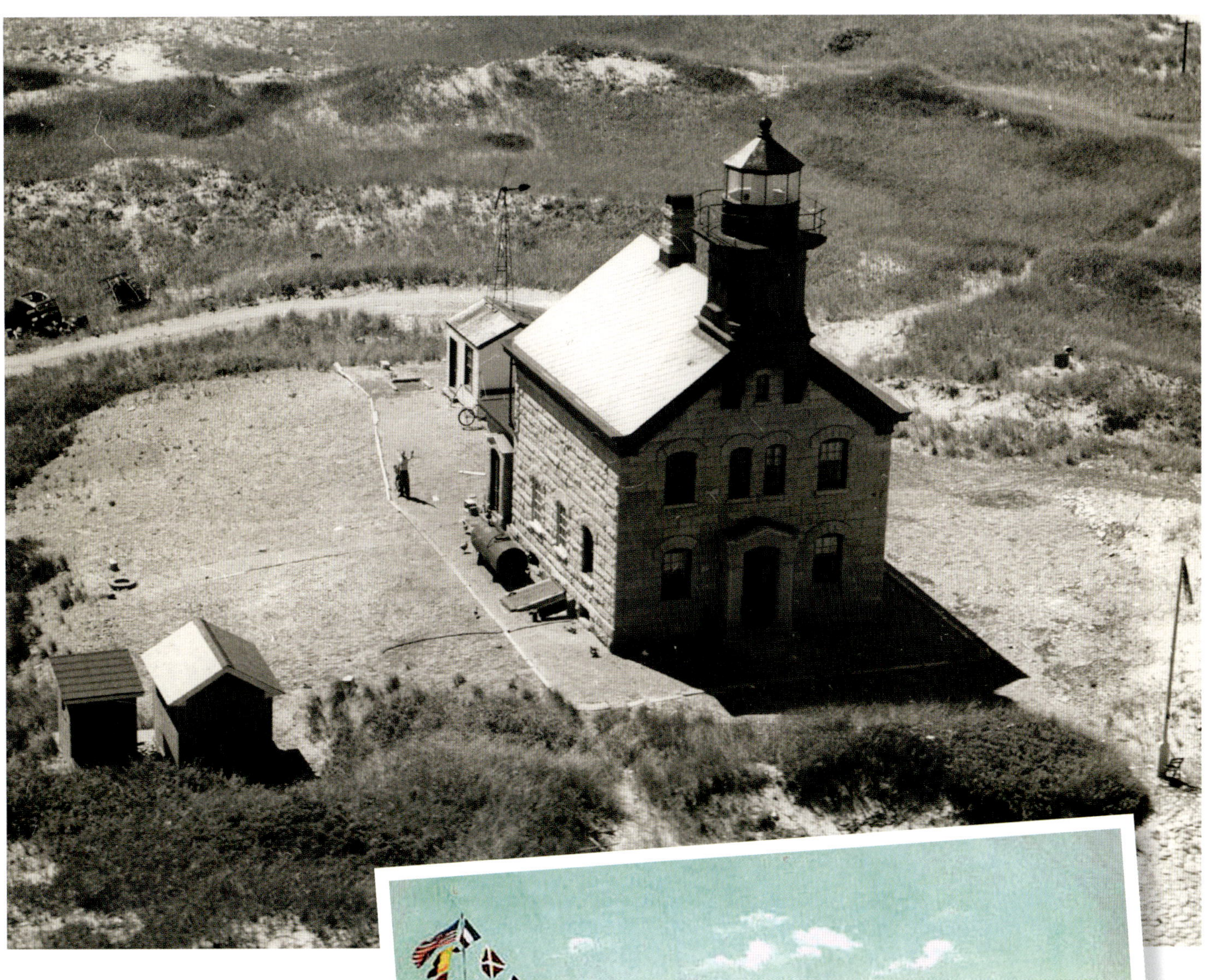

Above: An aerial view of the station captured about a half century ago. *(Courtesy of USCG)*

Right: A postcard of the Life Saving Station with the lighthouse in the background.

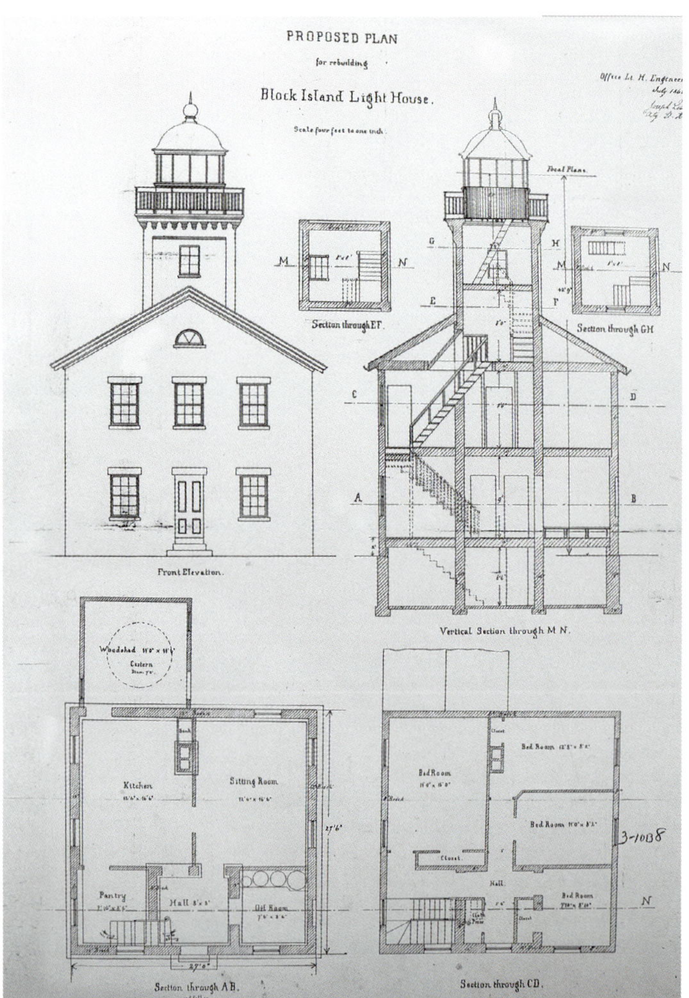

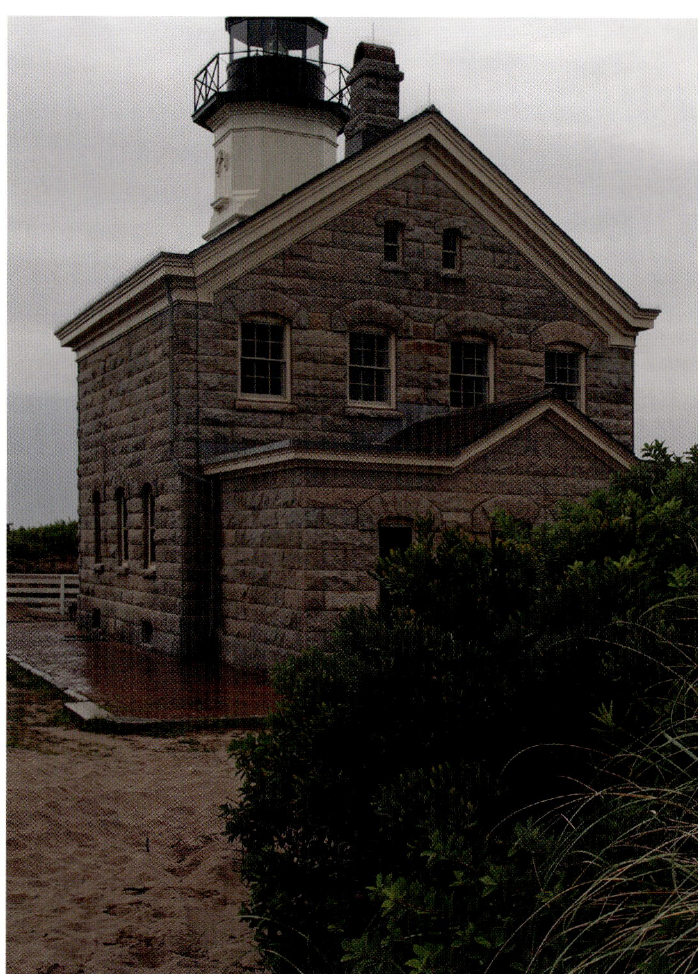

Above left: Dated July 1865, these are the proposed plans for the present-day Block Island North Lighthouse. *(Courtesy of BINLA)*

Above right: A view from the rear of the station; the one-story addition as well as the first floor houses a museum detailing its history and chronicling significant events.

Right: An early photograph of the North Light with part of the Life Saving Station in the background. *(Courtesy of NA)*

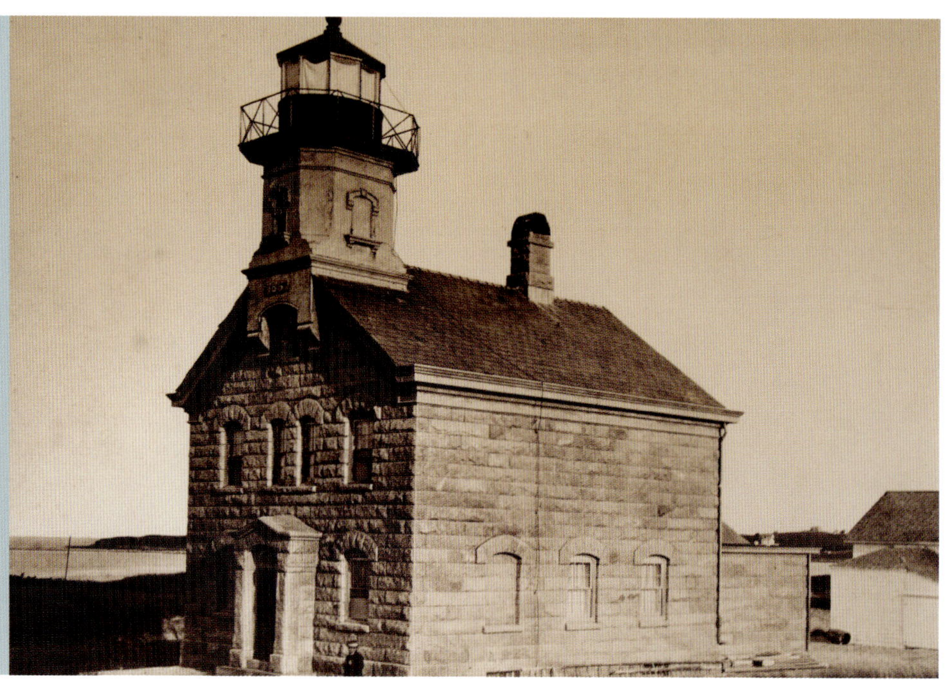

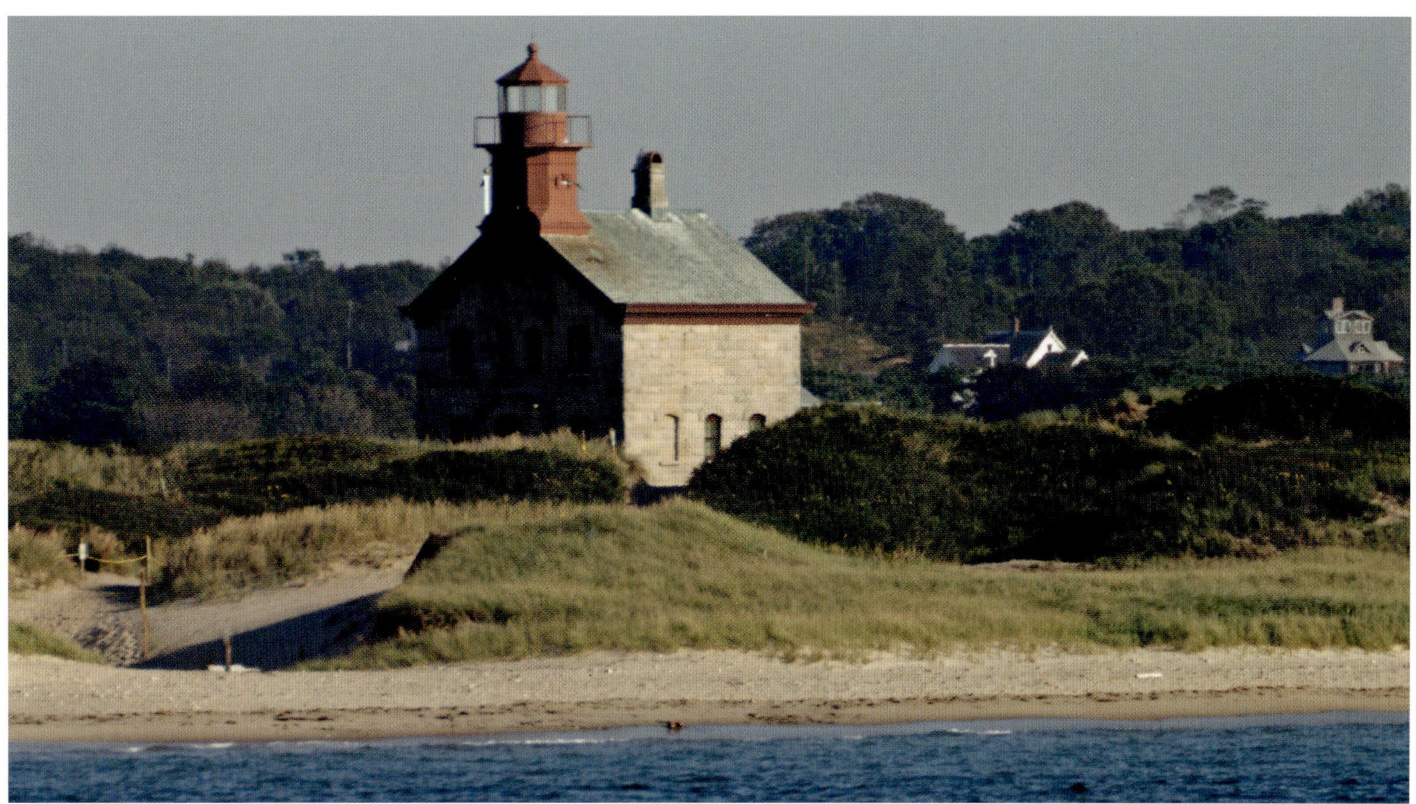

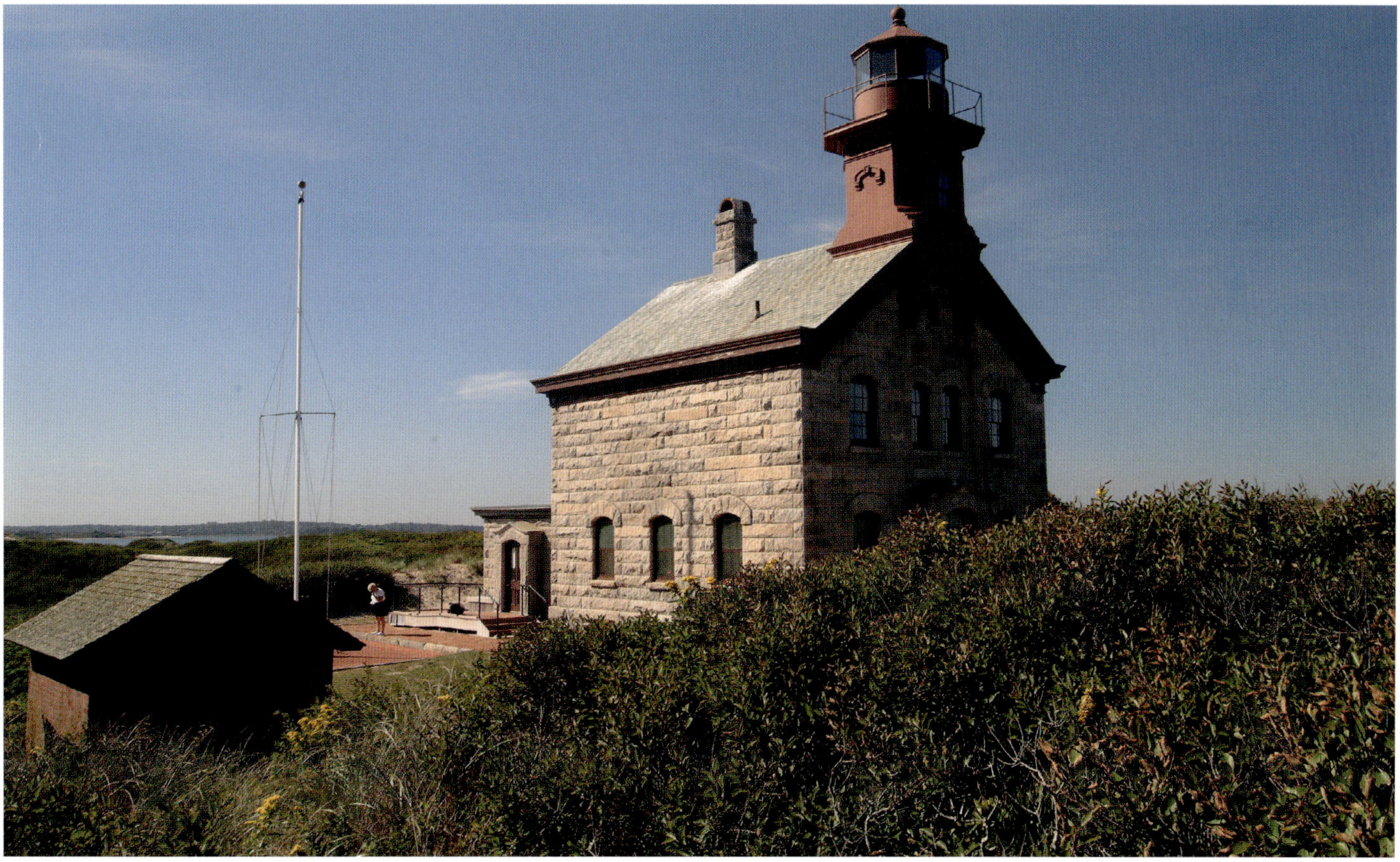

Taken several years ago, these images from the water and the land show the tower before it was repainted.

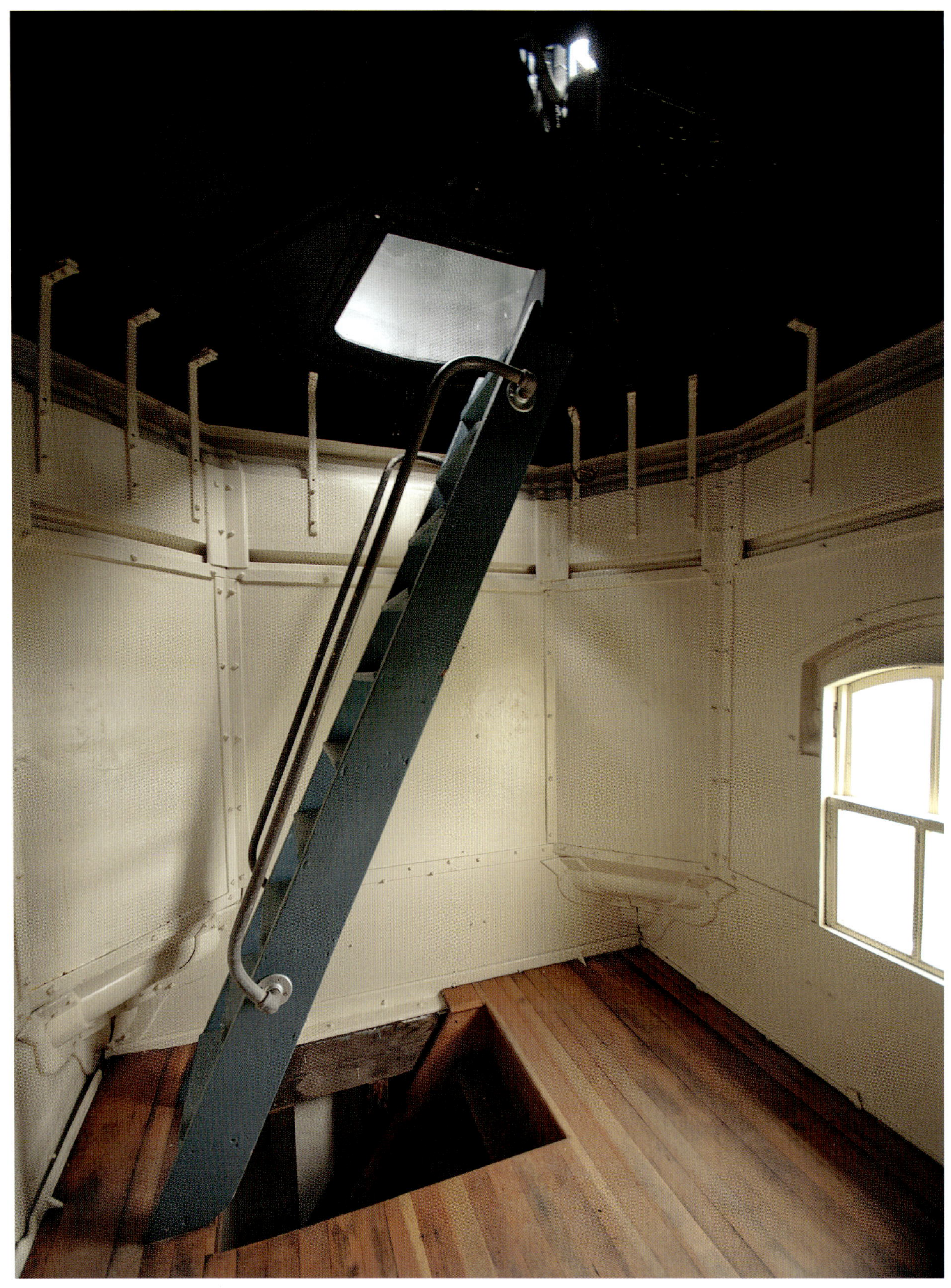

A short flight of stairs leads to the lantern room.

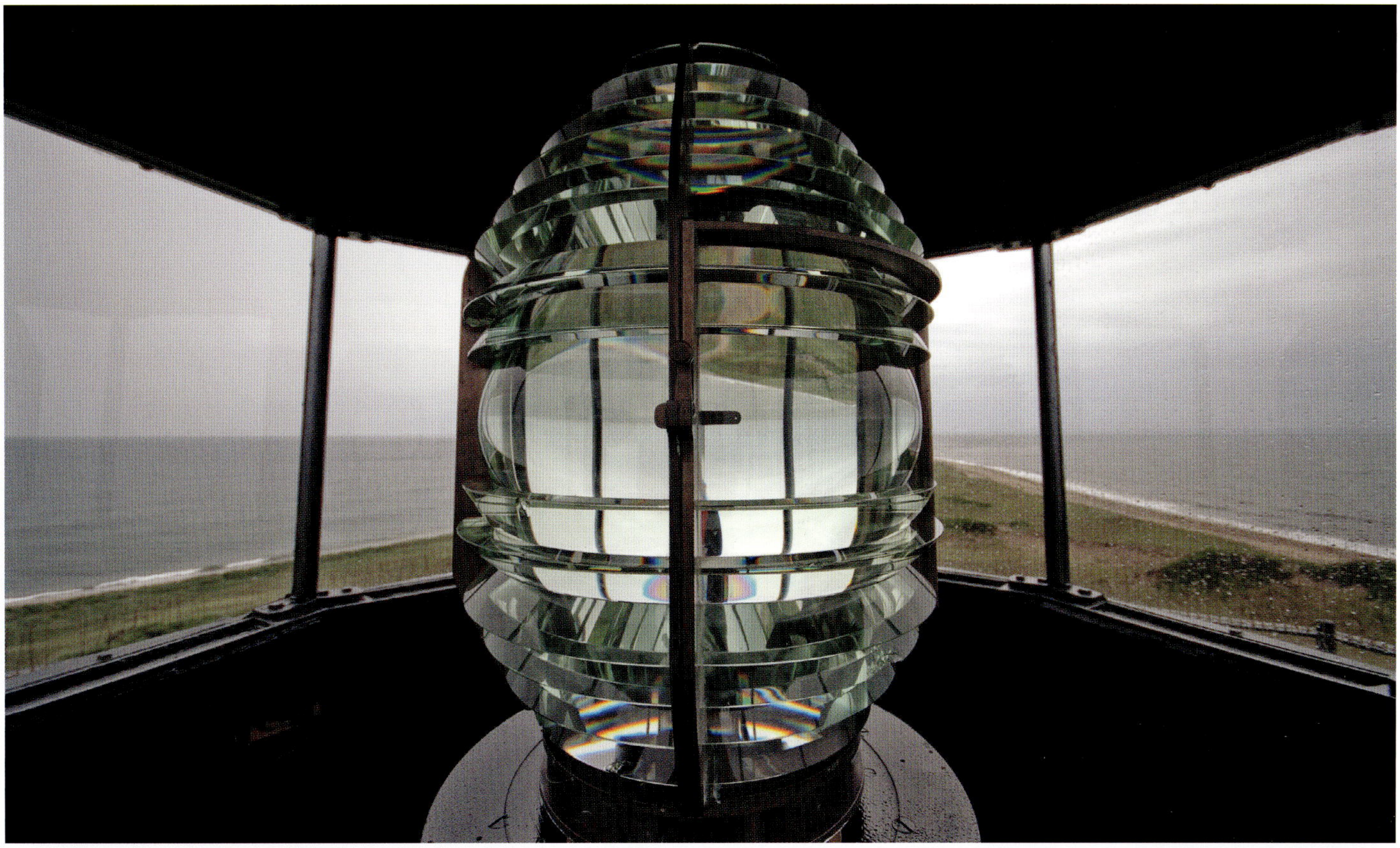

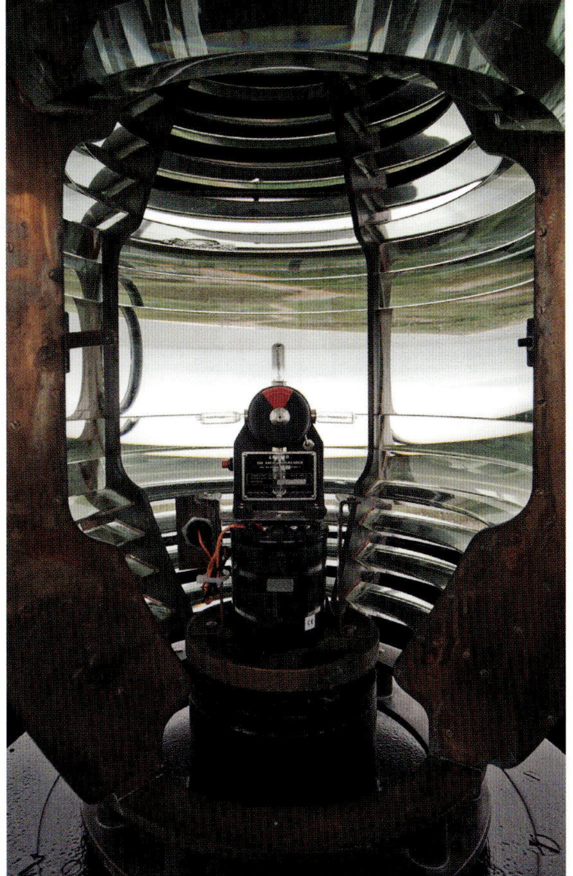

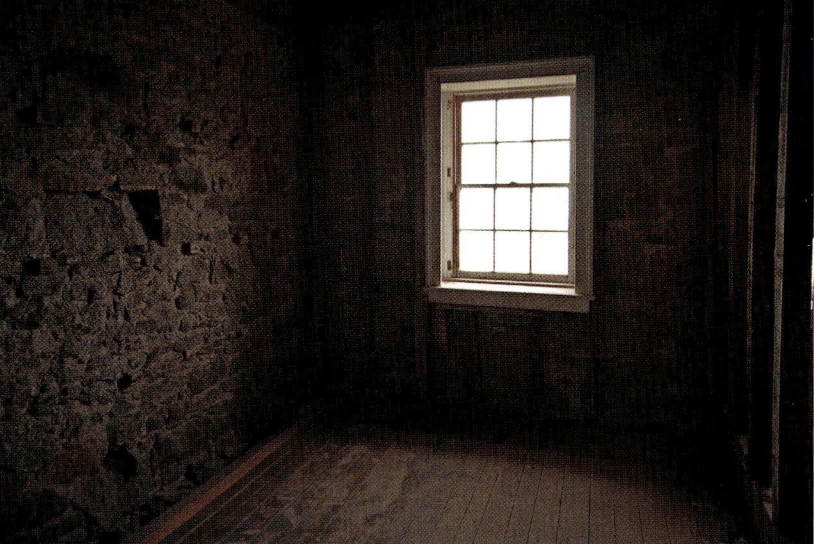

Top and left: Two views of the 4th order Fresnel lens; one perspective is the entire lens looking north toward the point, and the other is a close-up of the lamp.

Above: Undergoing restoration, this is one of the rooms that may eventually house guests.

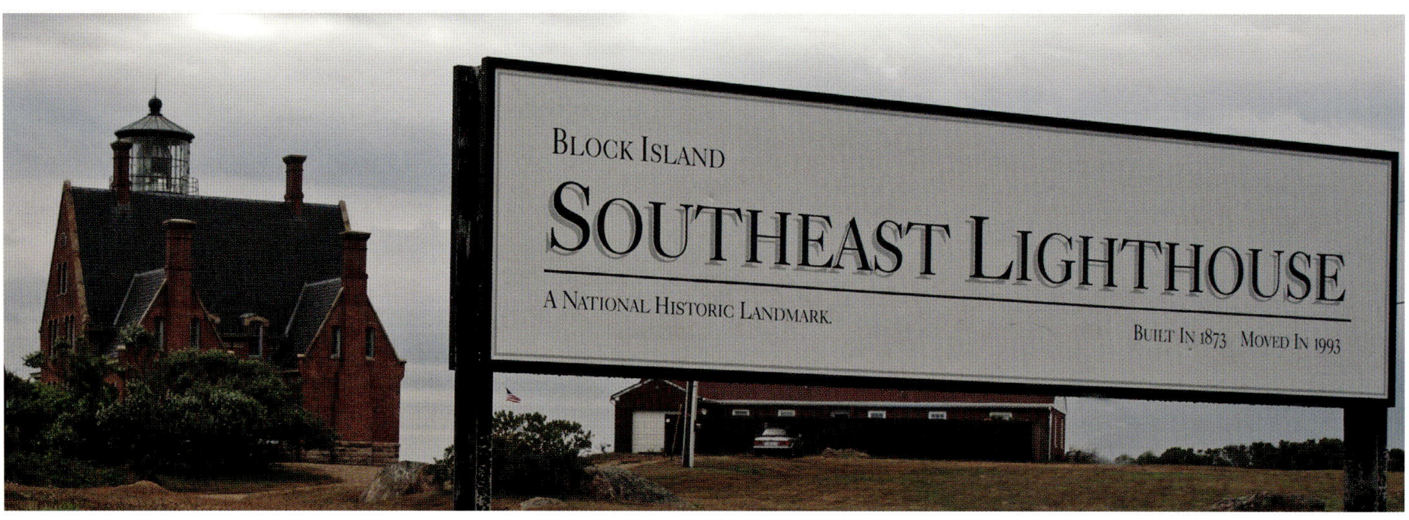

BLOCK ISLAND SOUTHEAST

Location: Block Island, southeast point, N41°09′10″, W71°33′04″

Appropriation: $75,000 in June 1872

Established: 1875

Deactivated: 1990–1994

Relit: August 1994

Automated: 1994

Tower: Brick red, octagonal, pyramidal (rear wall opens into keeper's house), 67 feet, black lantern room (16-sided)

Other Structures: Keeper's house, fog signaling building, garage

Original Lens: 1875, 1st order Fresnel lens, fixed white (FW)

Present Lens: 1st order Fresnel lens (from Cape Lookout, North Carolina), focal plane 261 feet

Light Characteristics: Flashing green every 5 seconds (FG 5s)

Range: 20 nm

Fog Signal: 1874, first class steam siren, 6-second blast, 20-second interval. 1907, 4-second blast, 30-second interval. Present, 1-second blast every 30 seconds

Status: Active U.S. Coast Guard aid to navigation

Access: Grounds and tower open during season; guides provide tours of tower.

Comments: Owned and maintained by Southeast Lighthouse Foundation; fog signal activated (1874) before lighthouse finished (1875); last lighthouse manned in Rhode Island (1988); moved 300 feet back from cliff in 1993; listed in NHRP; restoration underway to provide for overnight guests; highest light in New England.

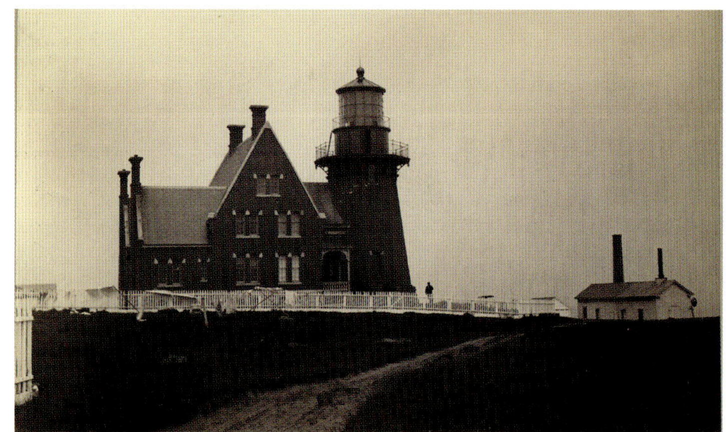

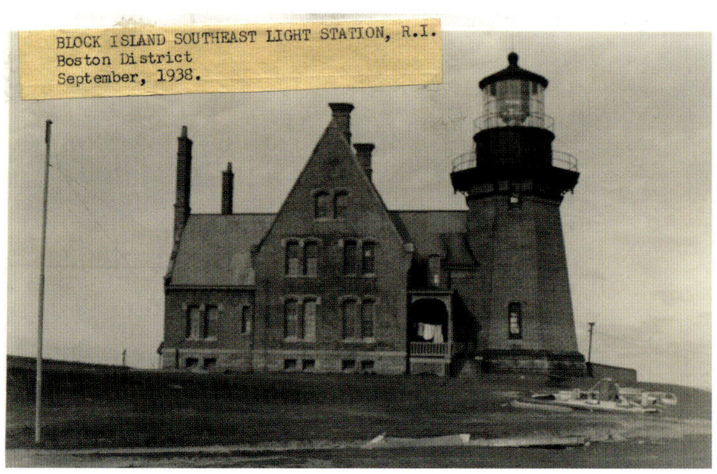

Top: With the lighthouse in the background, a sign welcomes visitors to the grounds.

Center: This image, dated 1884, upon close examination shows the fog signaling building to the right, the keeper (?) just to the right of the tower, and the lantern room door open. *(Courtesy of NA)*

Bottom: After the hurricane of 21 September 1938, a survey was done of all aids to navigation. Unlike other stations, this tower received little damage. *(Courtesy of USCG)*

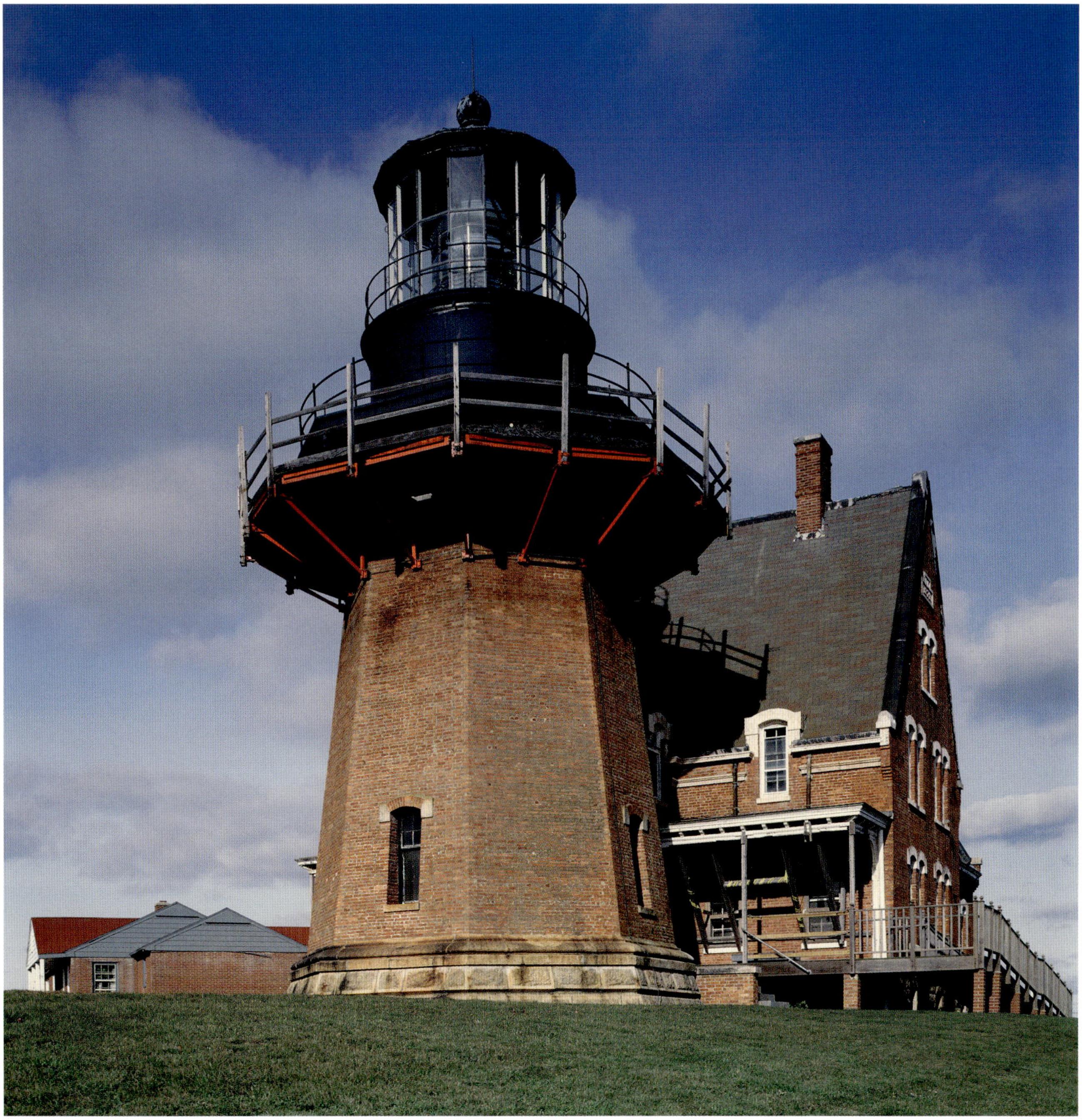

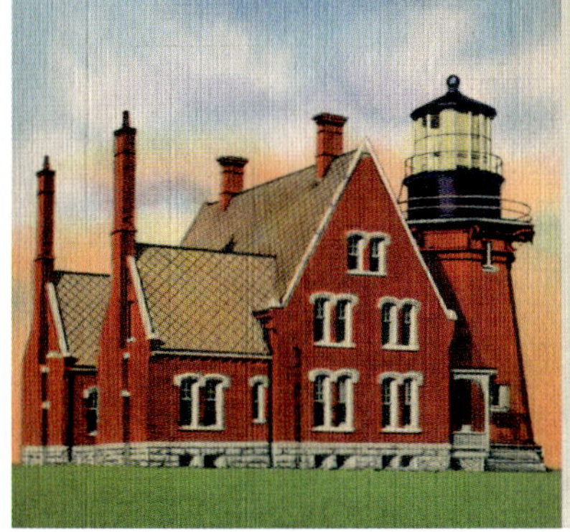

Two views of Southeast Light captured more than a half century apart. *(Color photograph courtesy of LOC)*

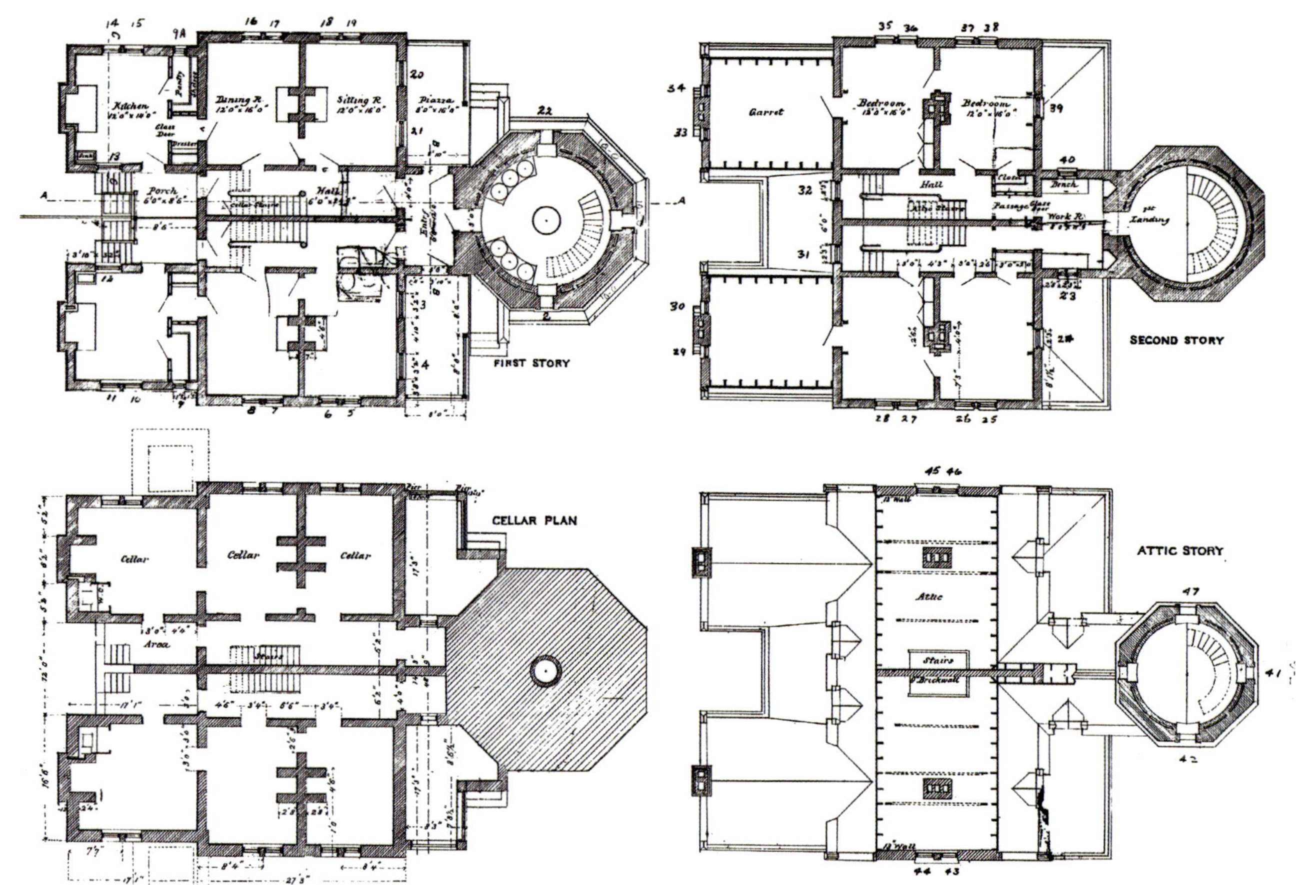

Plans, dated 1873, of the keeper's house and tower. *(Courtesy of LOC)*

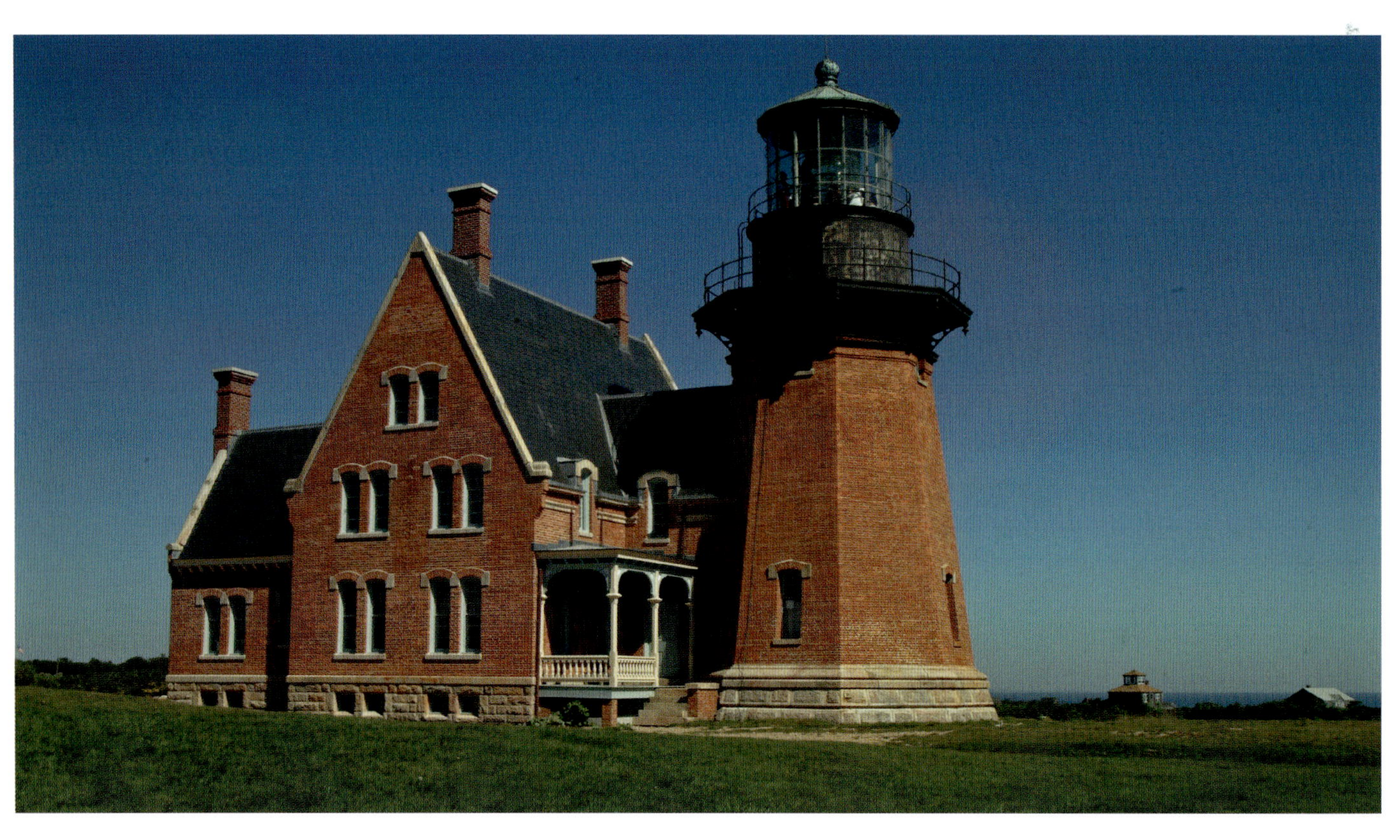

A relatively recent photograph of Southeast Light taken on a bright, clear day.

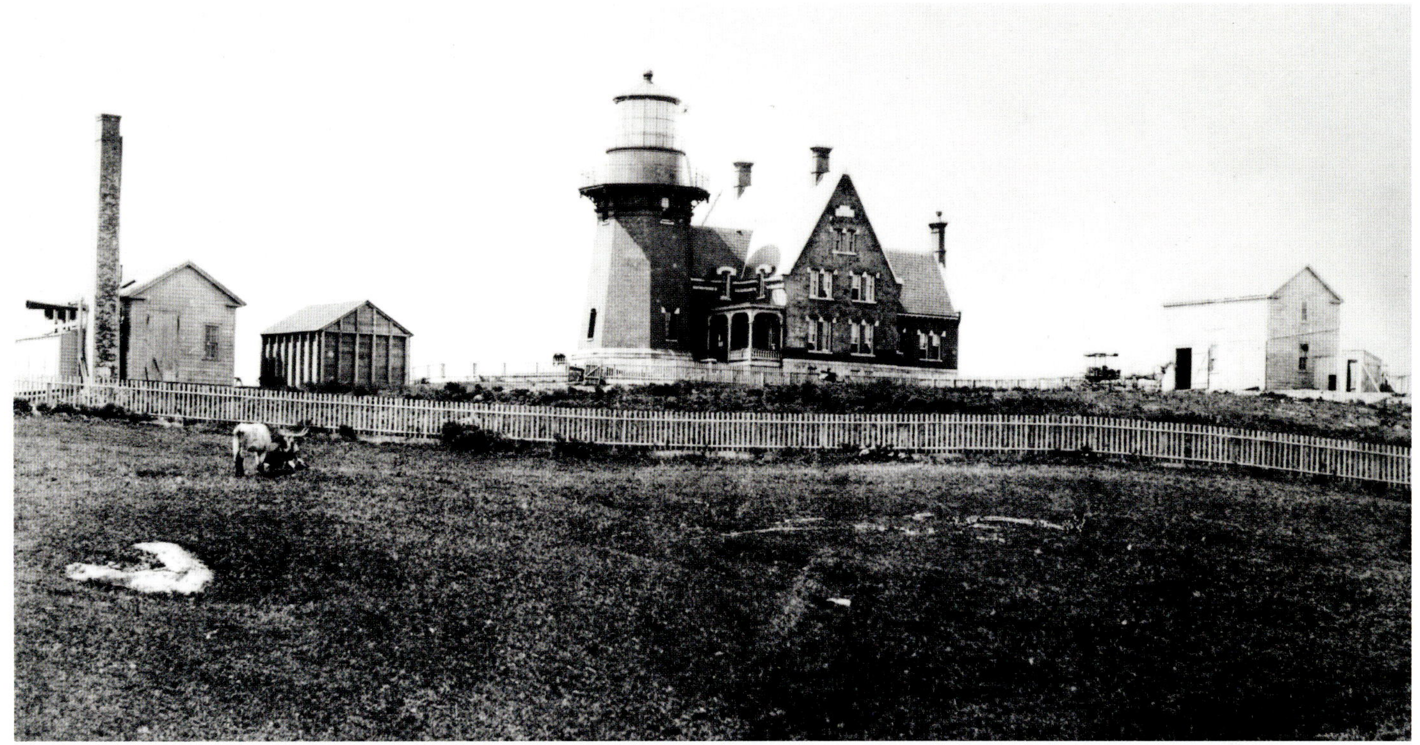

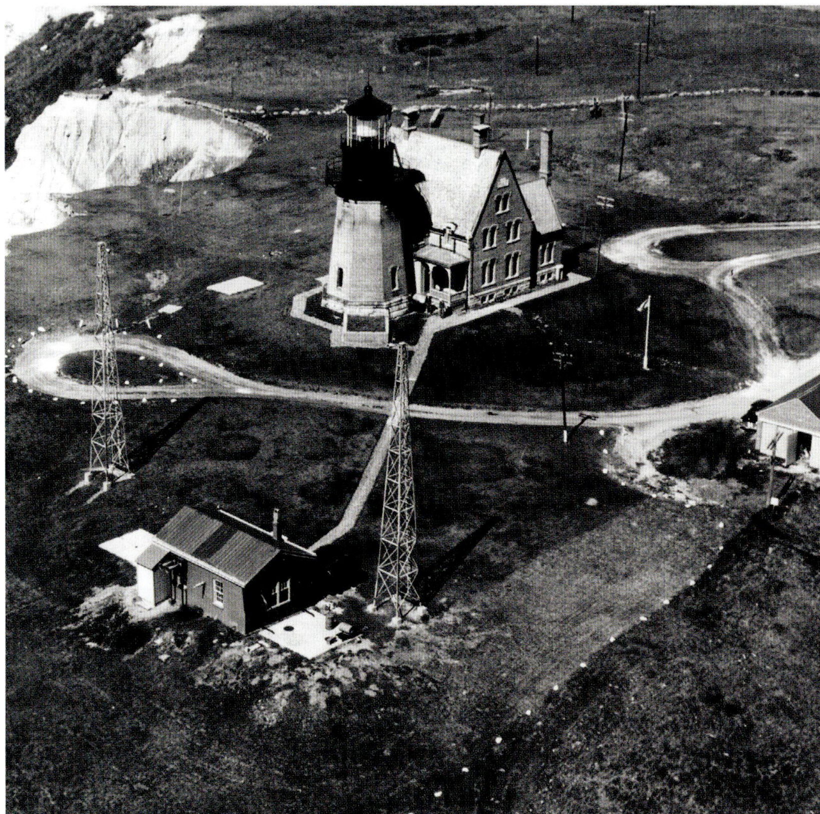

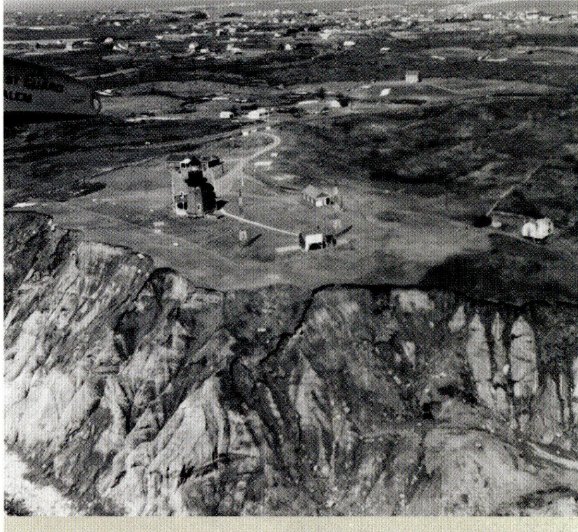

Top: The same vintage as the 1884 photograph on page 16, this photograph is a different view of the lighthouse. *(Courtesy of LOC)*

Bottom left and right: These two aerial images of the station were taken by the U.S.C.G. in the mid 1900s. *(Courtesy of USCG)*

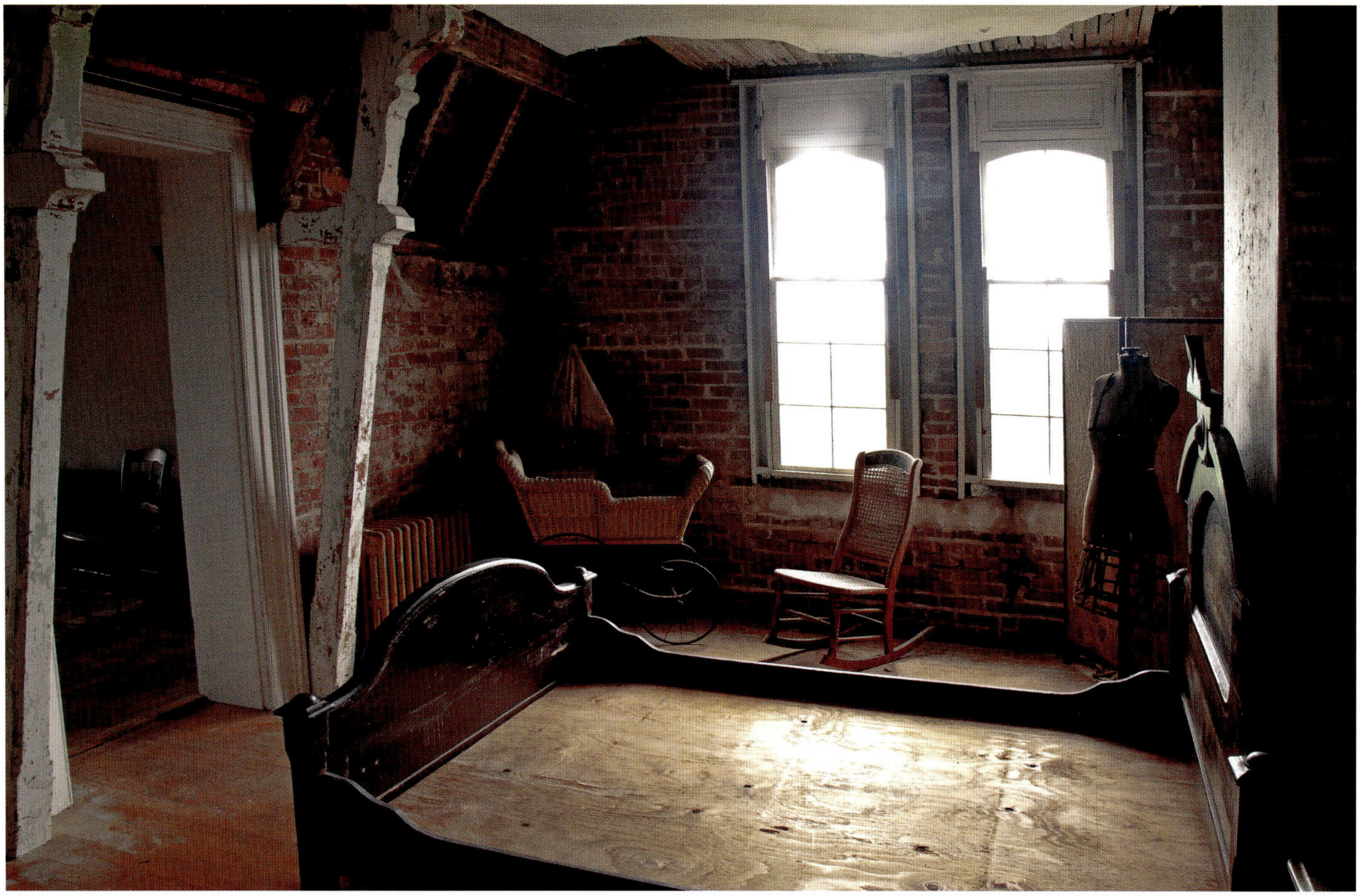

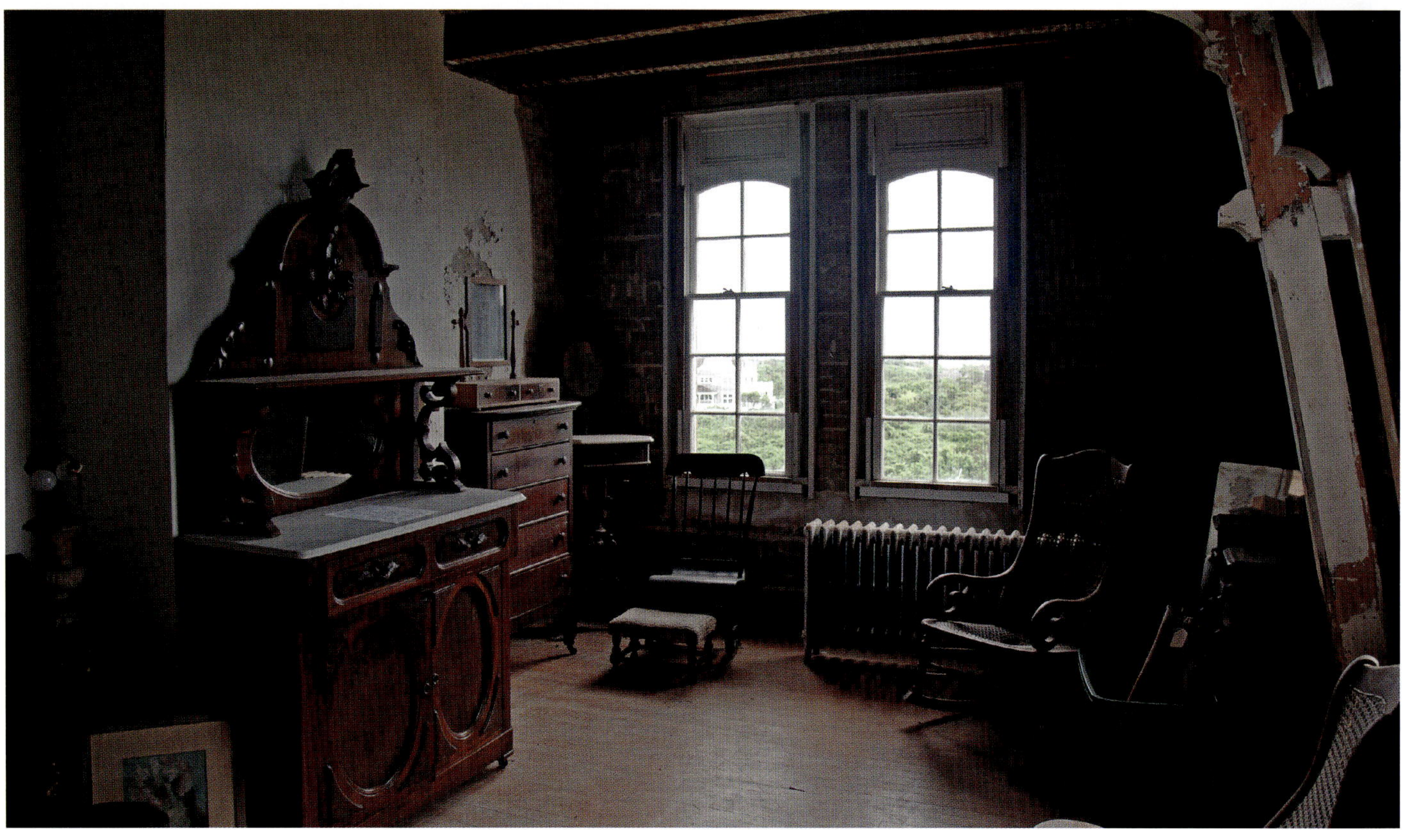

Opposite: On the second level of the keeper's house are the partially restored bedrooms. These are planned to be available in the future to overnight guests.

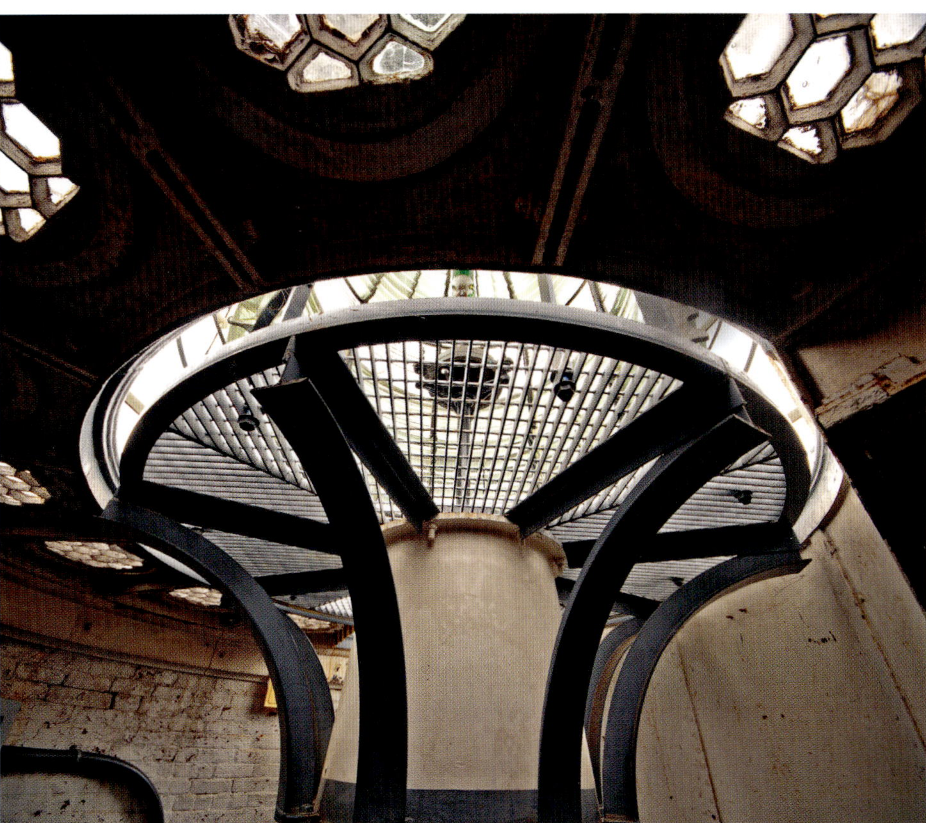

Right: The base under the lantern room floor.

Below: Looking down the stairs; the entryway is at the bottom.

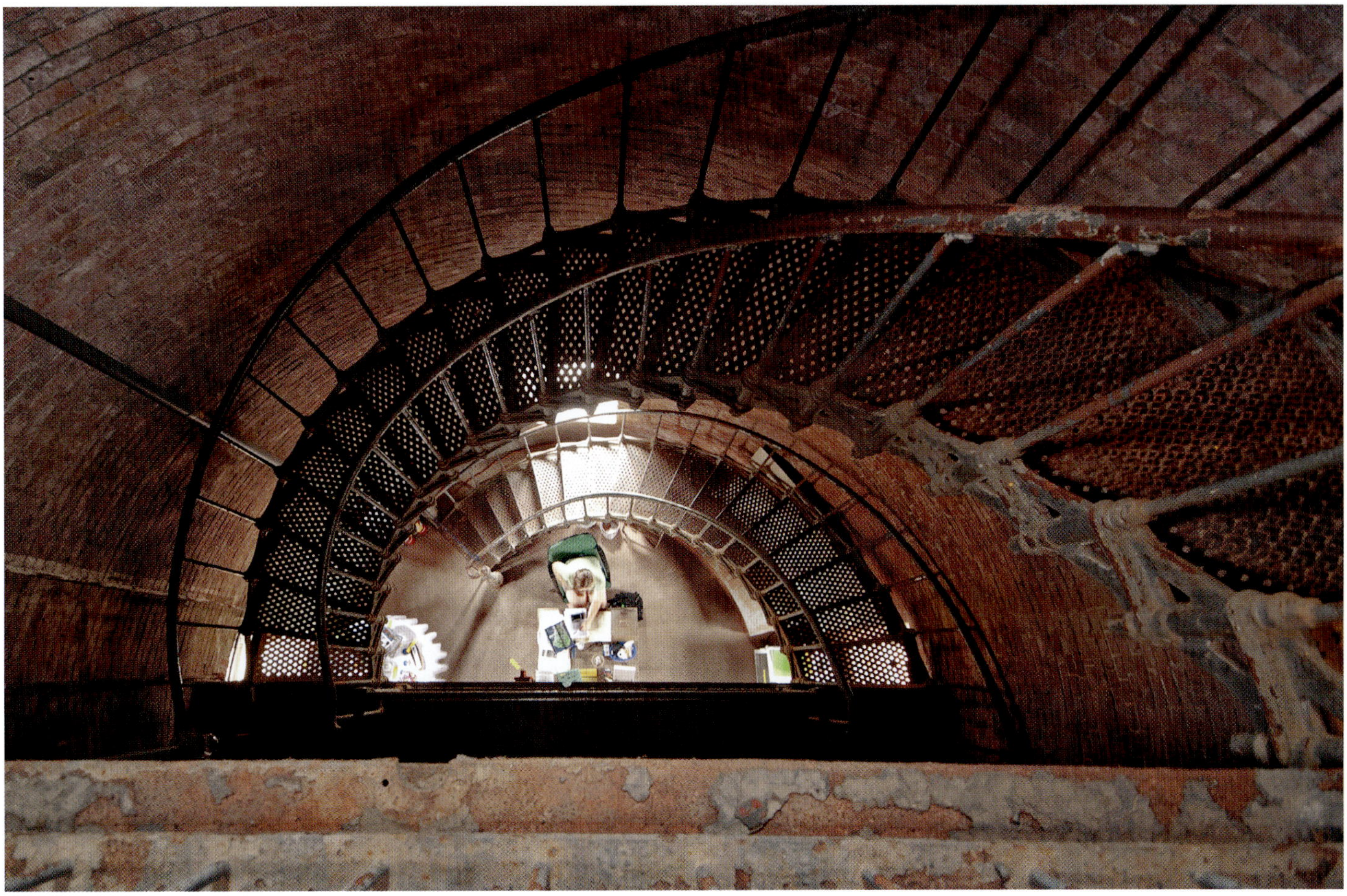

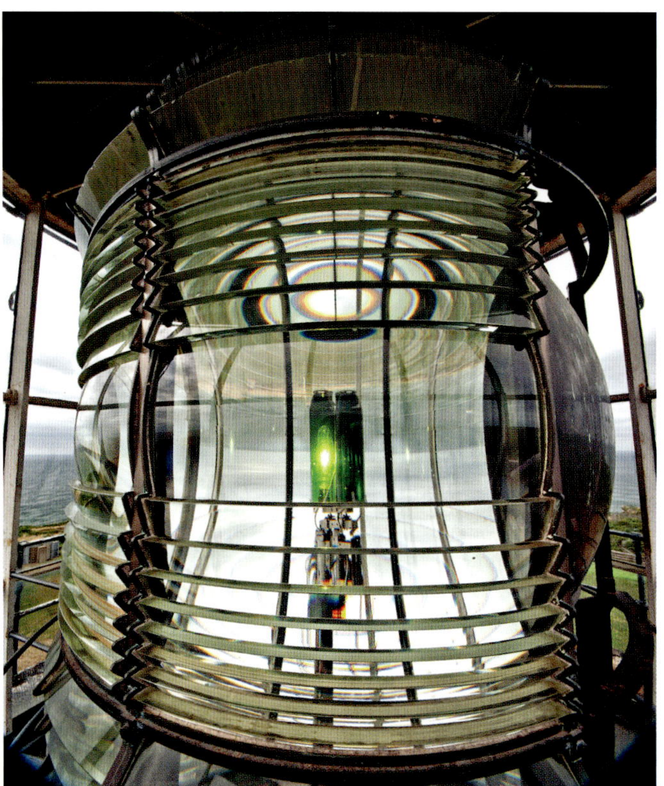

Left: A view of the 1st order Fresnel lens and the green light source.

Below: A vista, looking southwest, out the walkway door.

Bottom: This view, from almost the opposite direction as the previous picture, shows the constantly eroding cliffs.

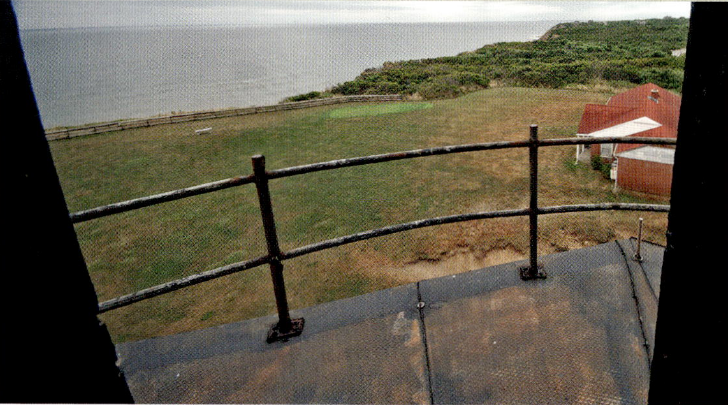

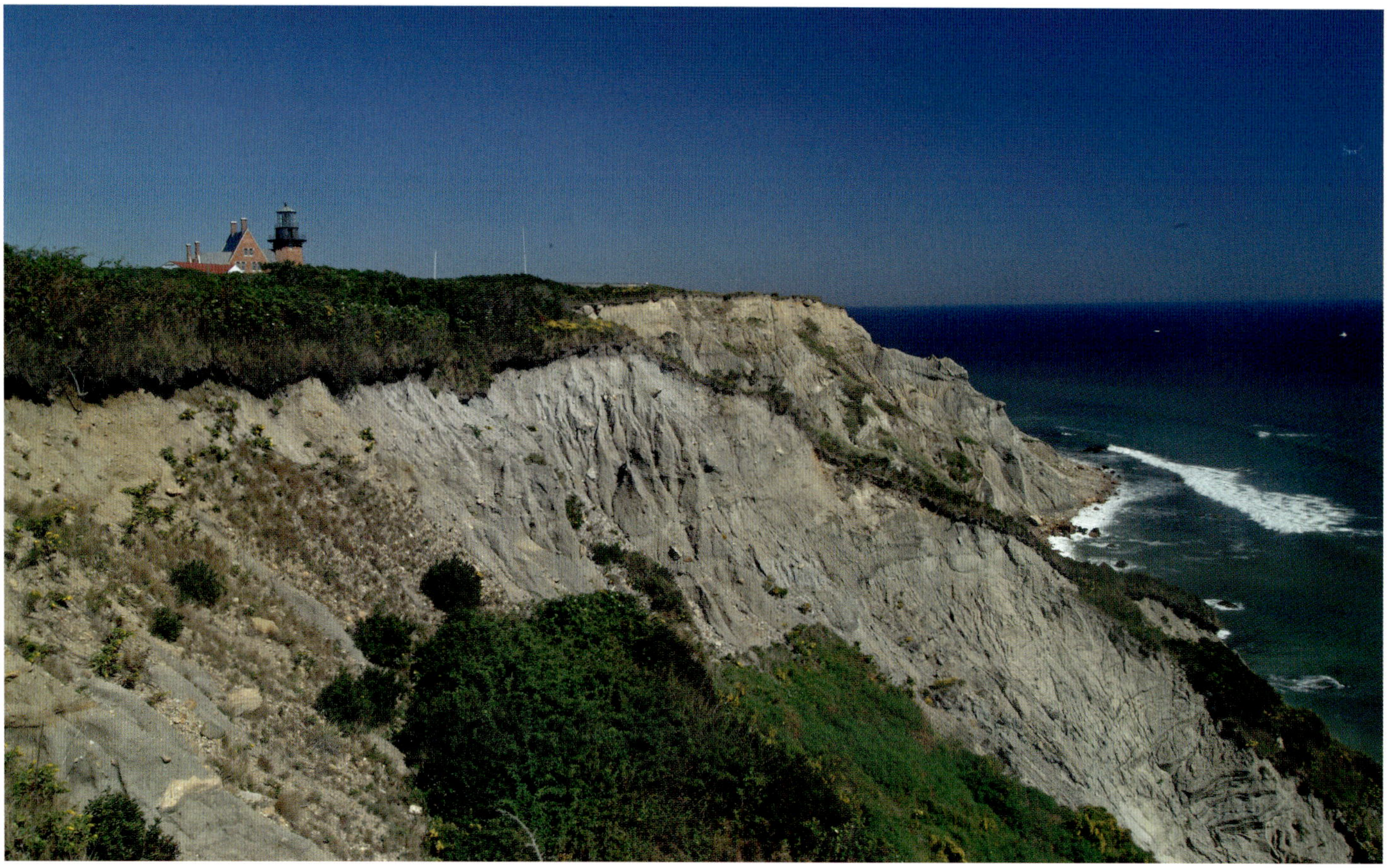

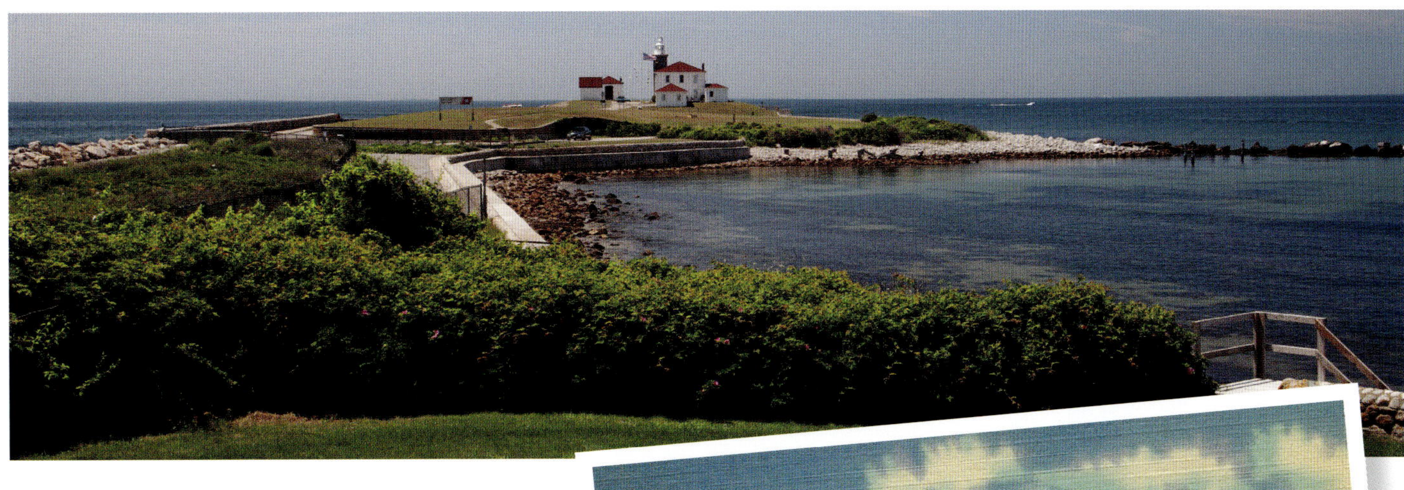

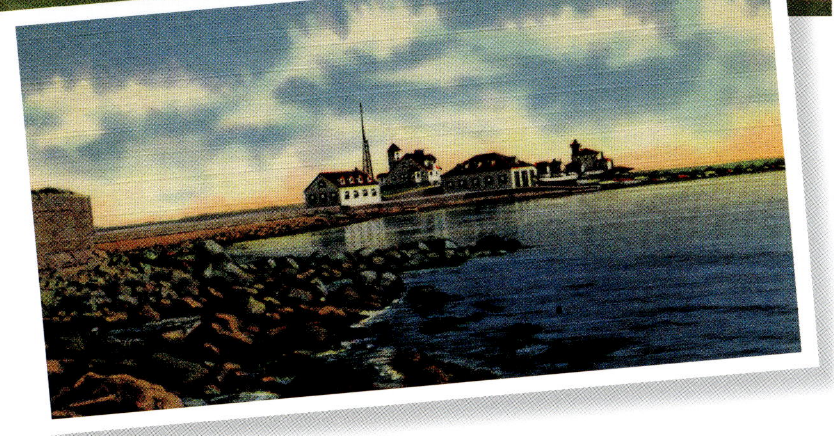

Above: Compare and contrast these two images, one a postcard of the lighthouse station that also includes the lifesaving station, the other a present-day panorama.

WATCH HILL

Location: Westerly, N41°18′12″, W71°51′30″

Appropriation: $6,000 in 1806; $1,000 in 1808; $8,300 in 1854

Established: 1807

Automated: August 1986

Tower, original: Wood frame, 30 feet

Tower, present: 1855, granite, natural, square, brick-lined, attached to keeper's house, black lantern room, 45 feet

Other Structures: Oil house, 2 other buildings

Original Optics: 1838, 10 lamps with parabolic reflectors, revolving white light

Original Lens: 1857, 4th order Fresnel lens, fixed white (FW), focal plane 61 feet

Present Lens: VRB-25

Light Characteristics: Alternating red and white flash every 2.5 seconds (AL WR 5s), lighted 24 hours

Range: White 16 nm, red 14 nm

Fog Signal, original: 1924, second-class reed horn, 5-second blast, 25-second interval

Fog Signal, present: One blast every 30 seconds

Status: Active U.S. Coast Guard aid to navigation

Access: Tower not open; renovated oil house, now a museum, open Tuesday and Thursday during the summer.

Comments: Sensor detects fog at 5 miles and activates horn; keeper's house residence for CG personnel.

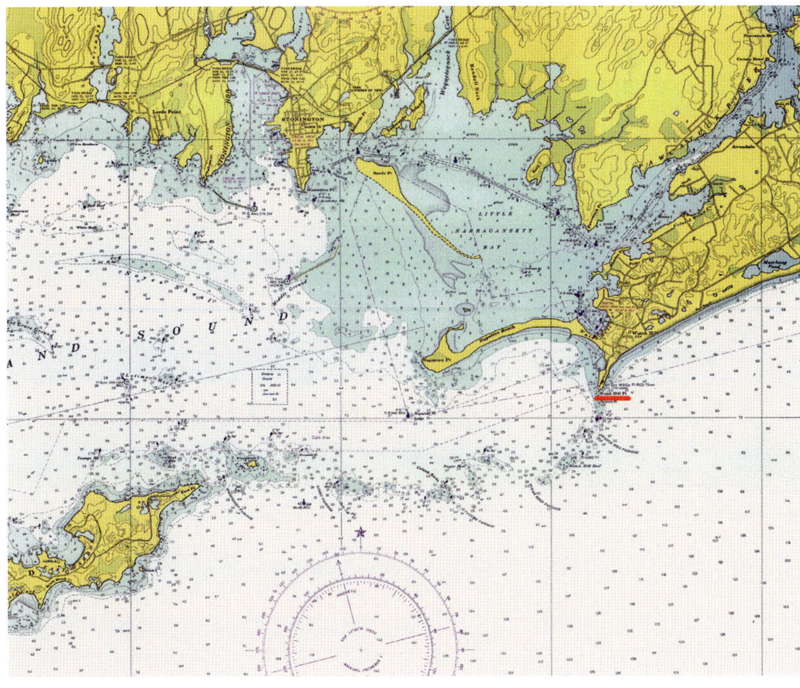

This 1974 chart shows the location of the Watch Hill Lighthouse underlined in red. Stonington, Connecticut, is to the northwest; Fisher's Island, New York, is to the southwest. *(Courtesy of NOAA)*

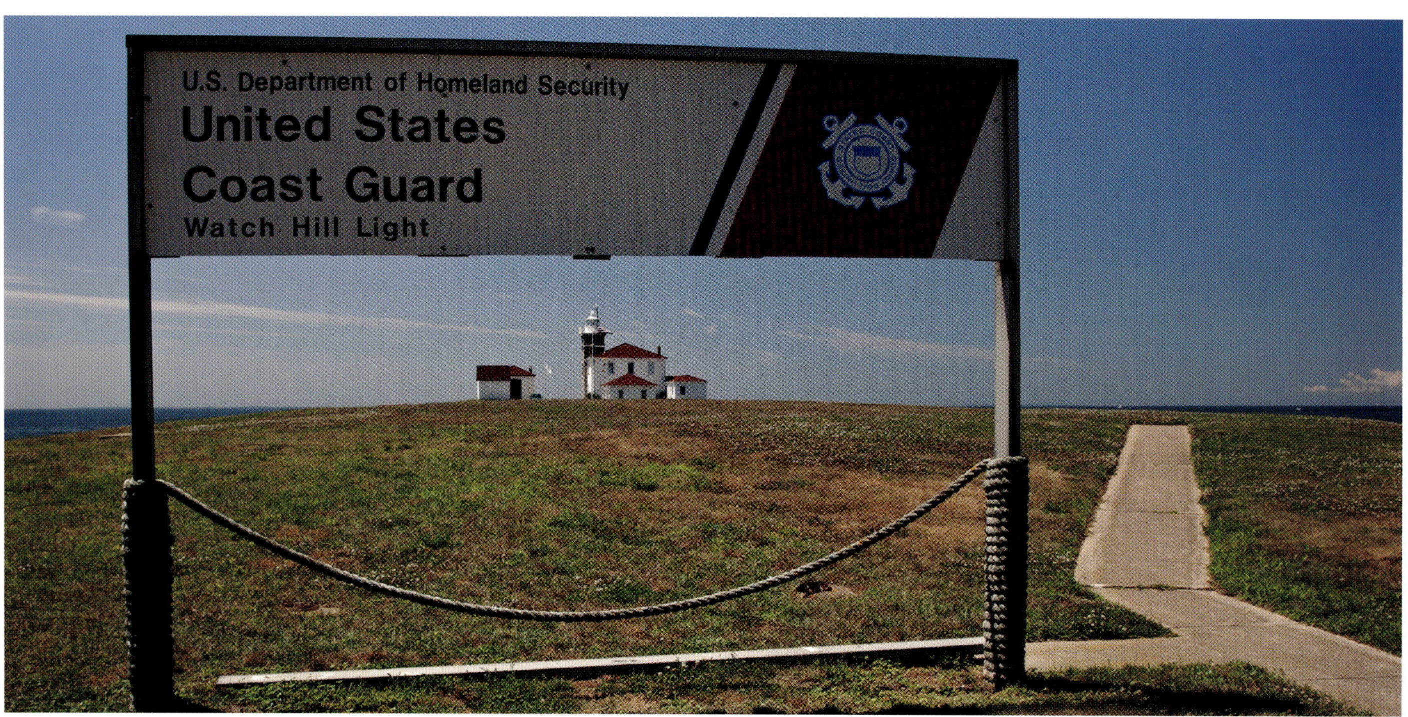

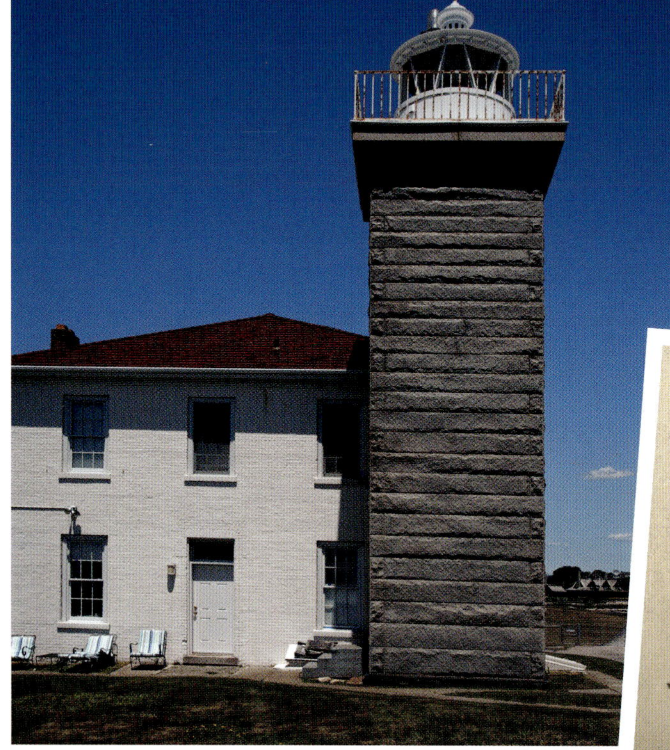

With the lighthouse in the background, a distinctive sign welcomes visitors.

Compare these two photographs of the Watch Hill Light tower and keeper's house; the black-and-white was taken in the 19th century and the color is a shot from the 21st century. *(Black-and-white image courtesy of USCG)*

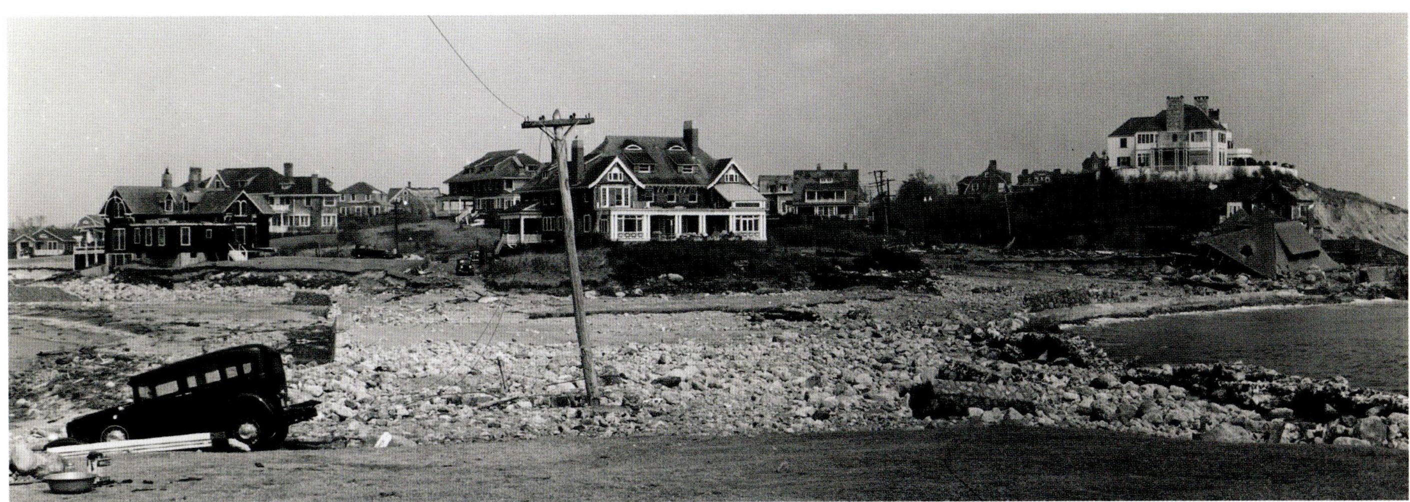

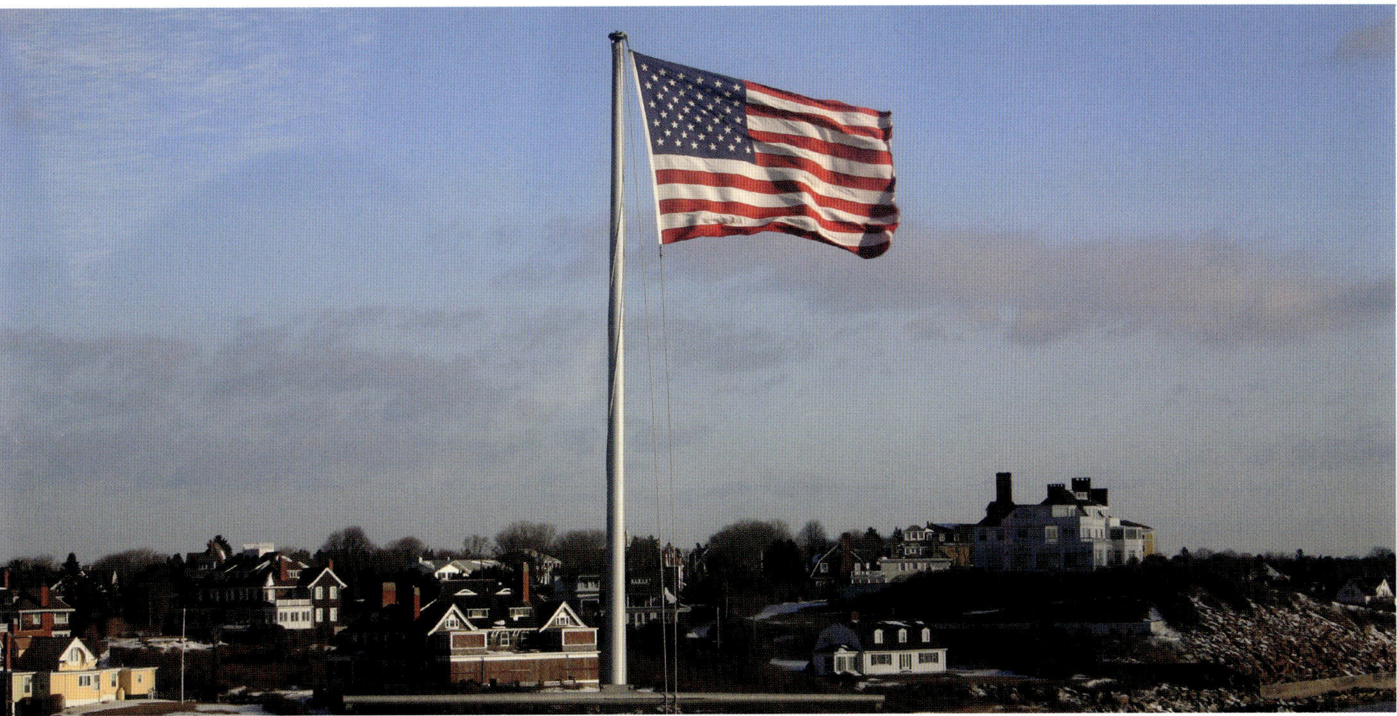

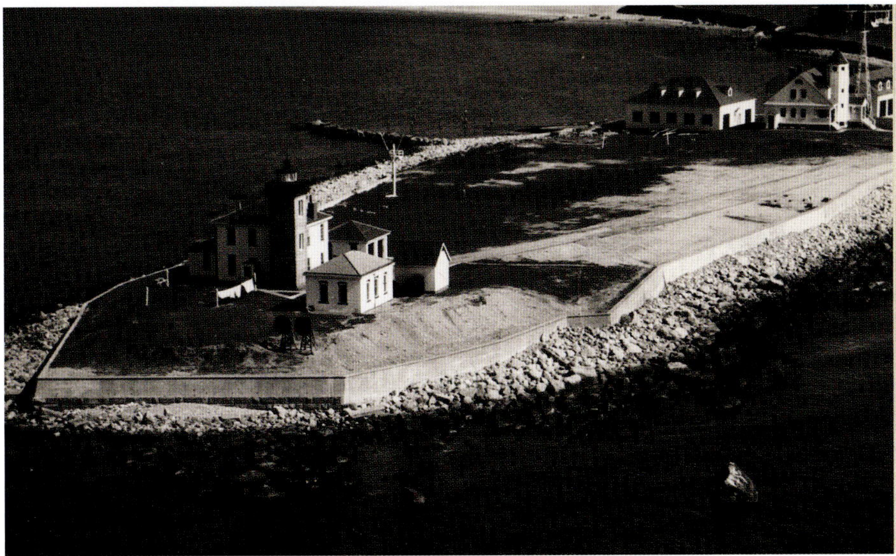

Top: This archival image, looking north, with the lighthouse station to the rear, shows some of the damage as a result of the hurricane in September 1938. *(Courtesy of NA)*

Center: A view from the lantern room looking toward the town; compare this picture with the black-and-white hurricane shot. *(Courtesy of J. D'Entremont)*

Bottom: An aerial image shows Watch Hill Light as well as the Life Saving Station, shot sometime before 1963 when the Life Saving Station was razed. *(Courtesy of USCG)*

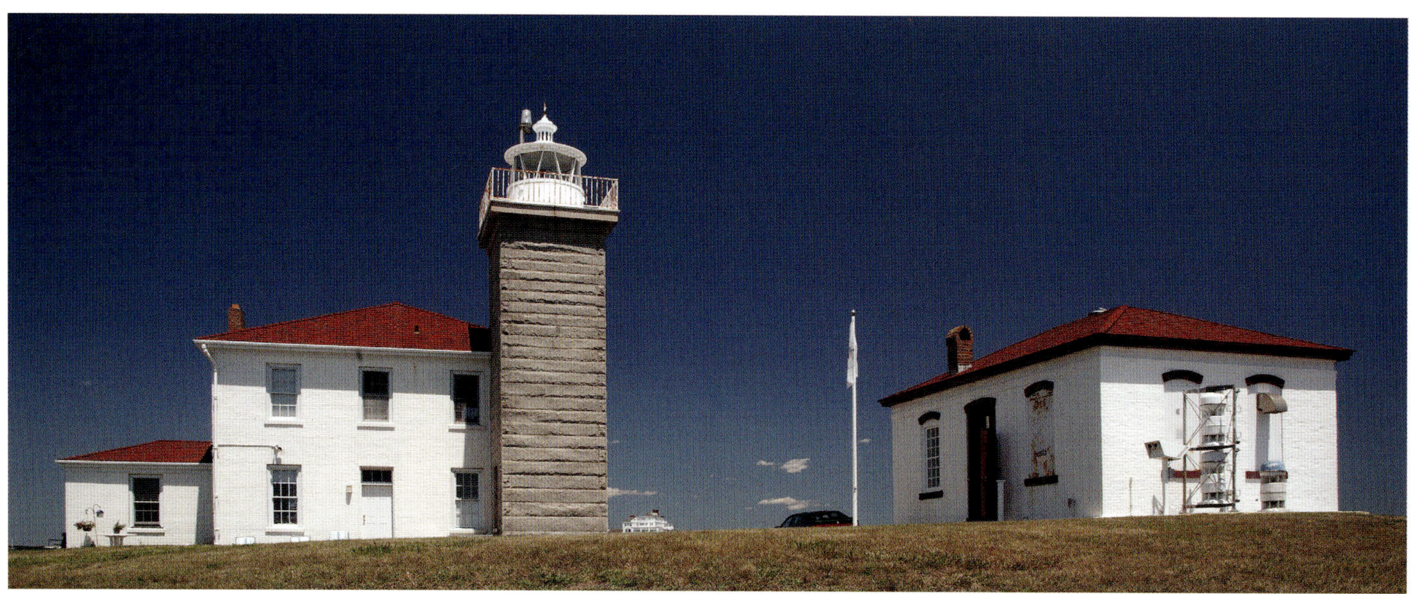

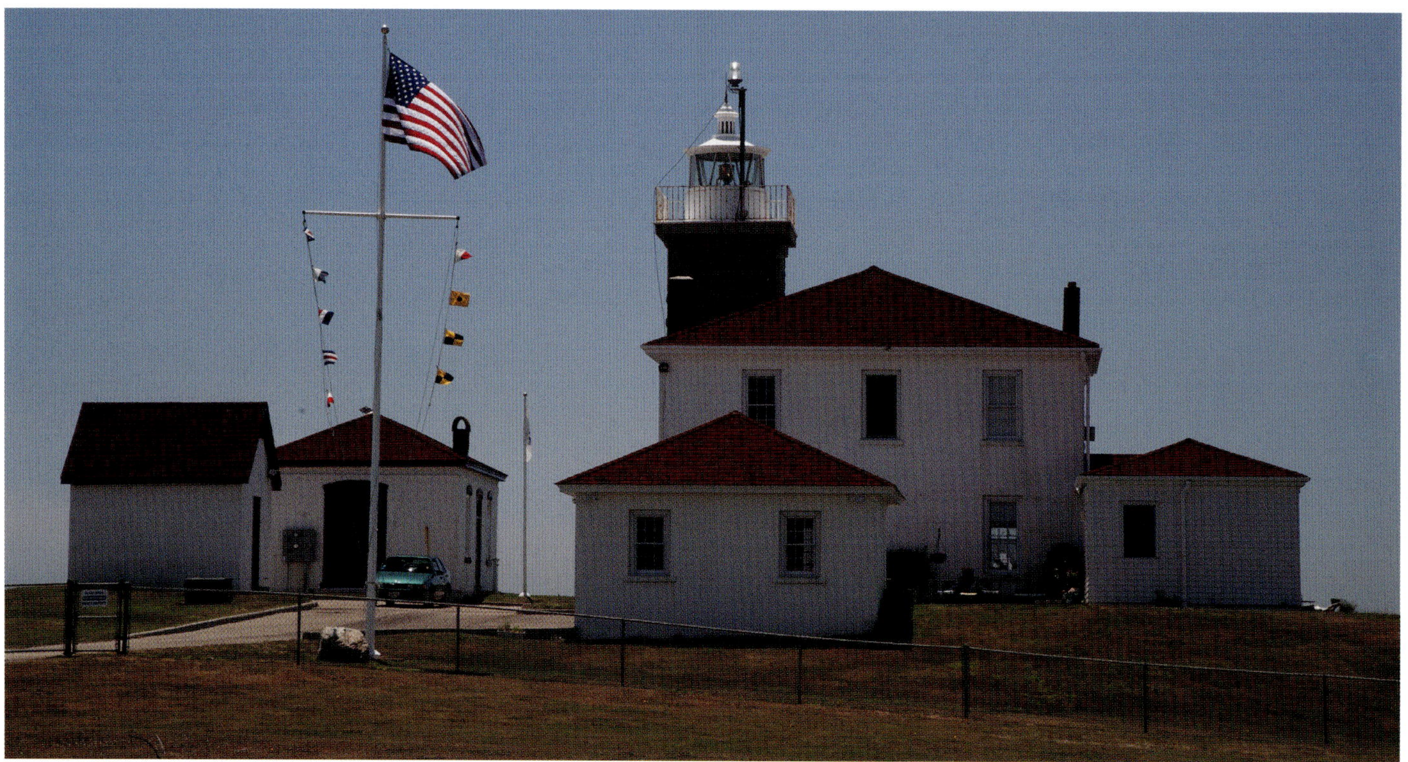

Two present-day images of the front and rear of Watch Hill Light Station.

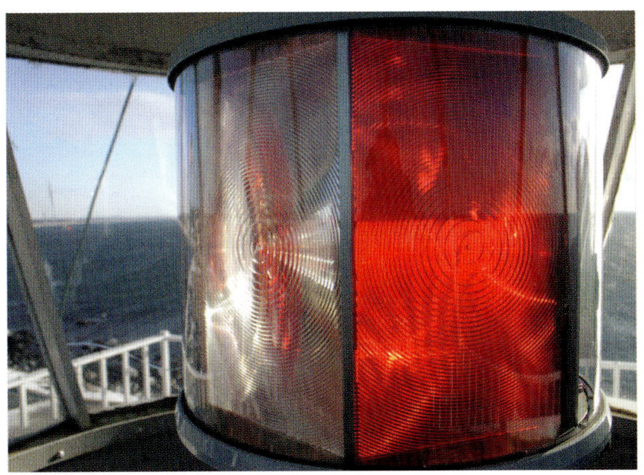

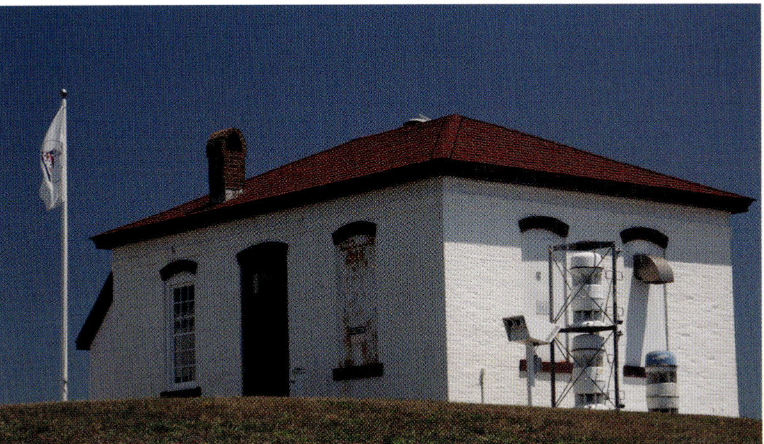

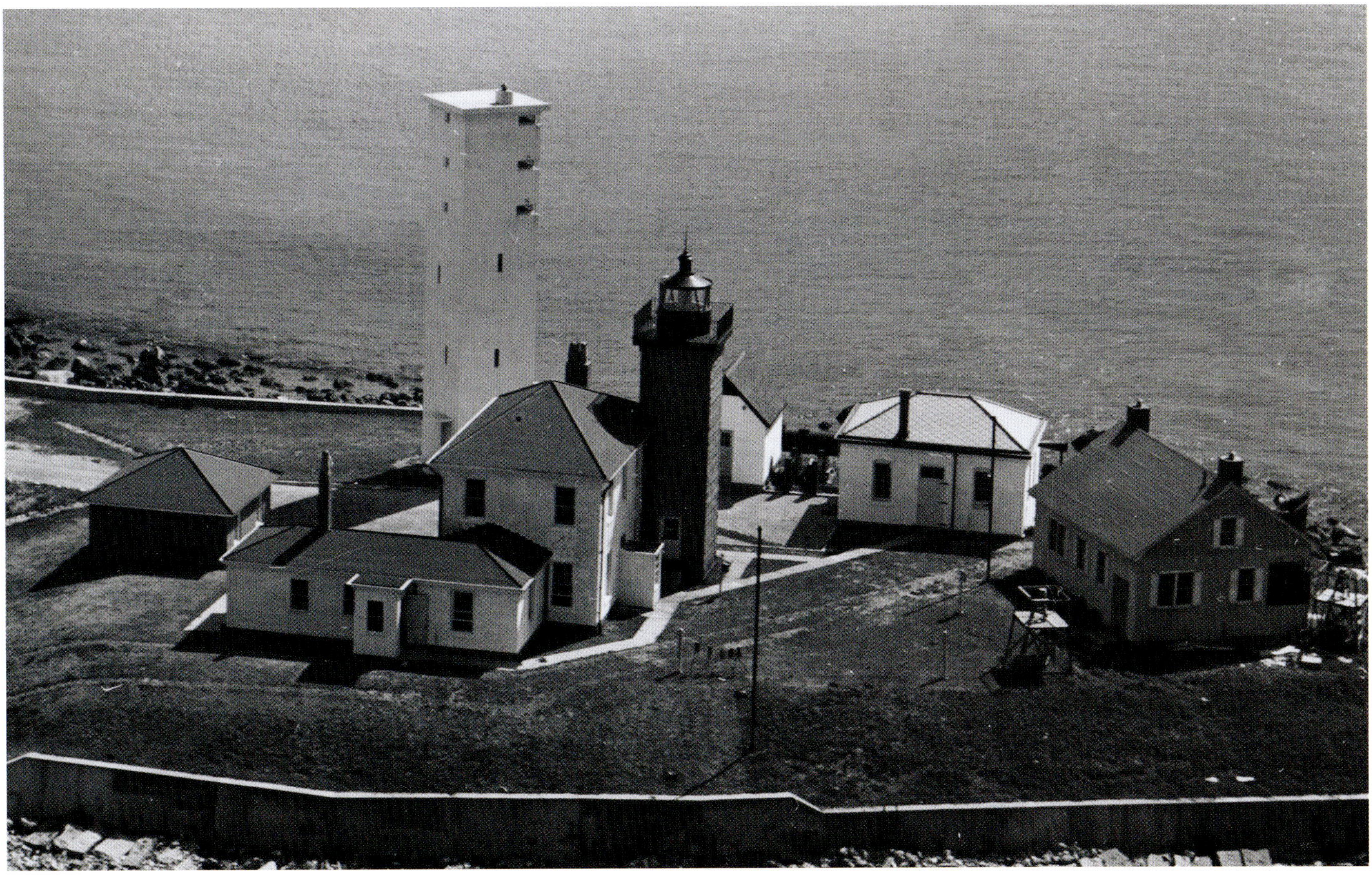

Top left: The modern plastic aero beacon. *(Courtesy of J. D'Entremont)*

Top right: In addition to a light, fog signaling devices were a necessity for many coastal stations; this image shows the building in the present day. Open during the summer, the house now serves as a museum.

Bottom: An aerial photograph shows the observation tower. *(Courtesy of USCG)*

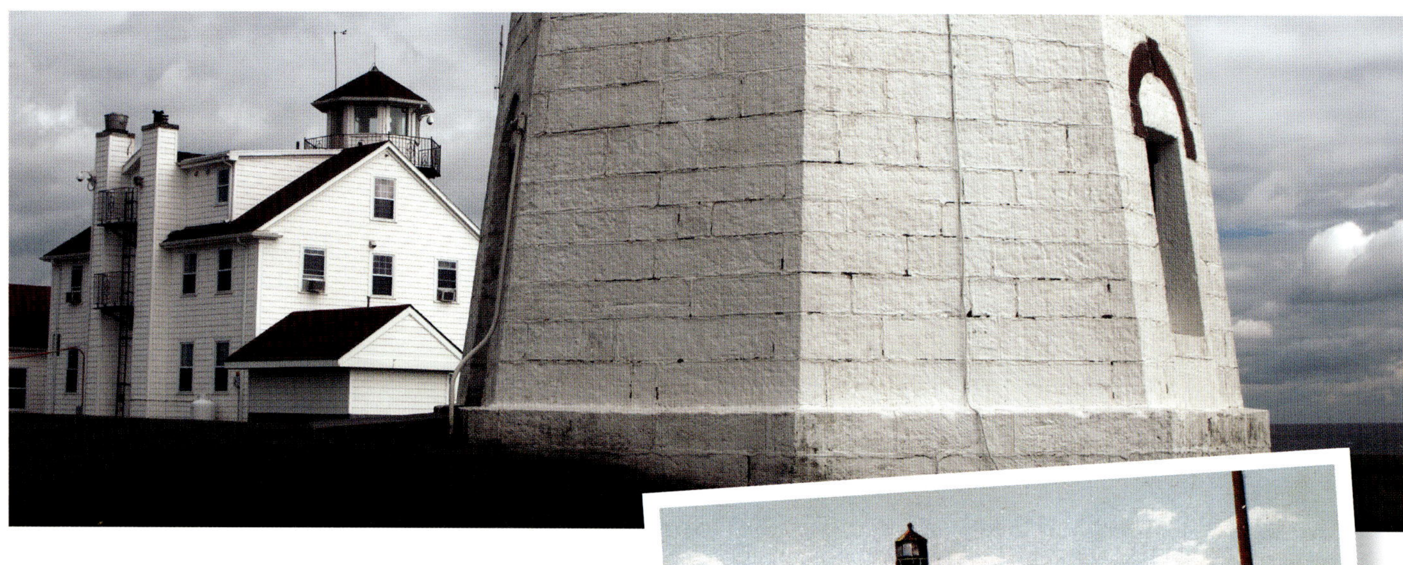

POINT JUDITH

Location: Galilee, Narragansett, N41°21′42″, W71° 28′54″

Appropriation: $5,000 in 1808; $200 in 1810; $7,500 in 1816

Established: 1810

Tower, 1810: Octagonal wood, 12 fixed lights; destroyed by gale of 17 September 1815

Rebuilt 1816: Stone, octagonal, 35 feet, with 10 revolving lamps

Rebuilt 1857: Present tower, octagonal, brownstone, top half brown, bottom half white, 51 feet, black lantern room

Other Structures: CG station, oil house, fog signaling building

Original Optics: 10 lamps with 8.5-inch reflectors, revolving white

Original Lens: 1857 4th order Fresnel lens, revolving white

Present Lens: Original 4th order Fresnel lens, focal plane 65 feet

Light Characteristics: White light eclipsed every 15 seconds; 5 seconds on, 2 seconds off, 2 on, 2 off, 2 on, 2 off (Oc 3 W 15s)

Range: 16 nm

Fog Signal: One 2-second blast every 15 seconds

Status: Active U.S. Coast Guard aid to navigation

Access: Grounds open daytime year-round, tower closed.

Comments: Radiobeacon established November 1931.

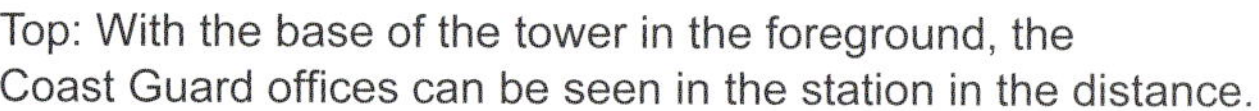

Top: With the base of the tower in the foreground, the Coast Guard offices can be seen in the station in the distance.

Above: A popular vista for a postcard, and a common view of the Point Judith Light Station.

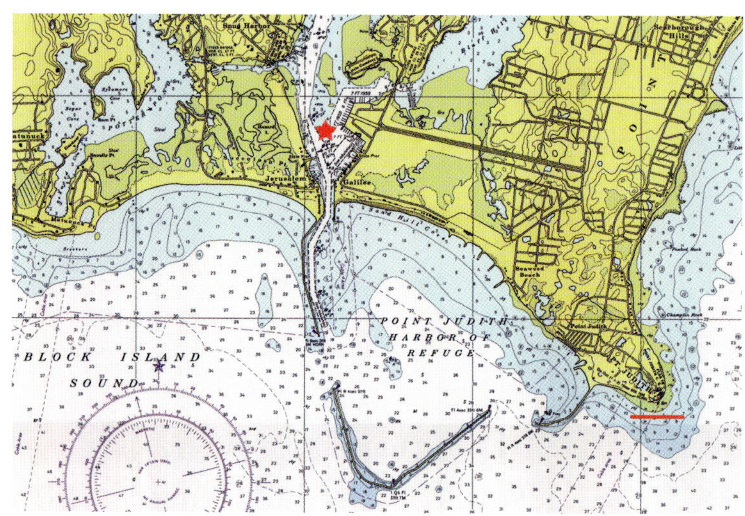

This section of a 1976 chart of coastal Rhode Island shows the lighthouse Point Judith at the bottom right; the star is at the hectic Galilee Harbor with its ferries, fishing boats, and recreational craft. *(Courtesy of NOAA)*

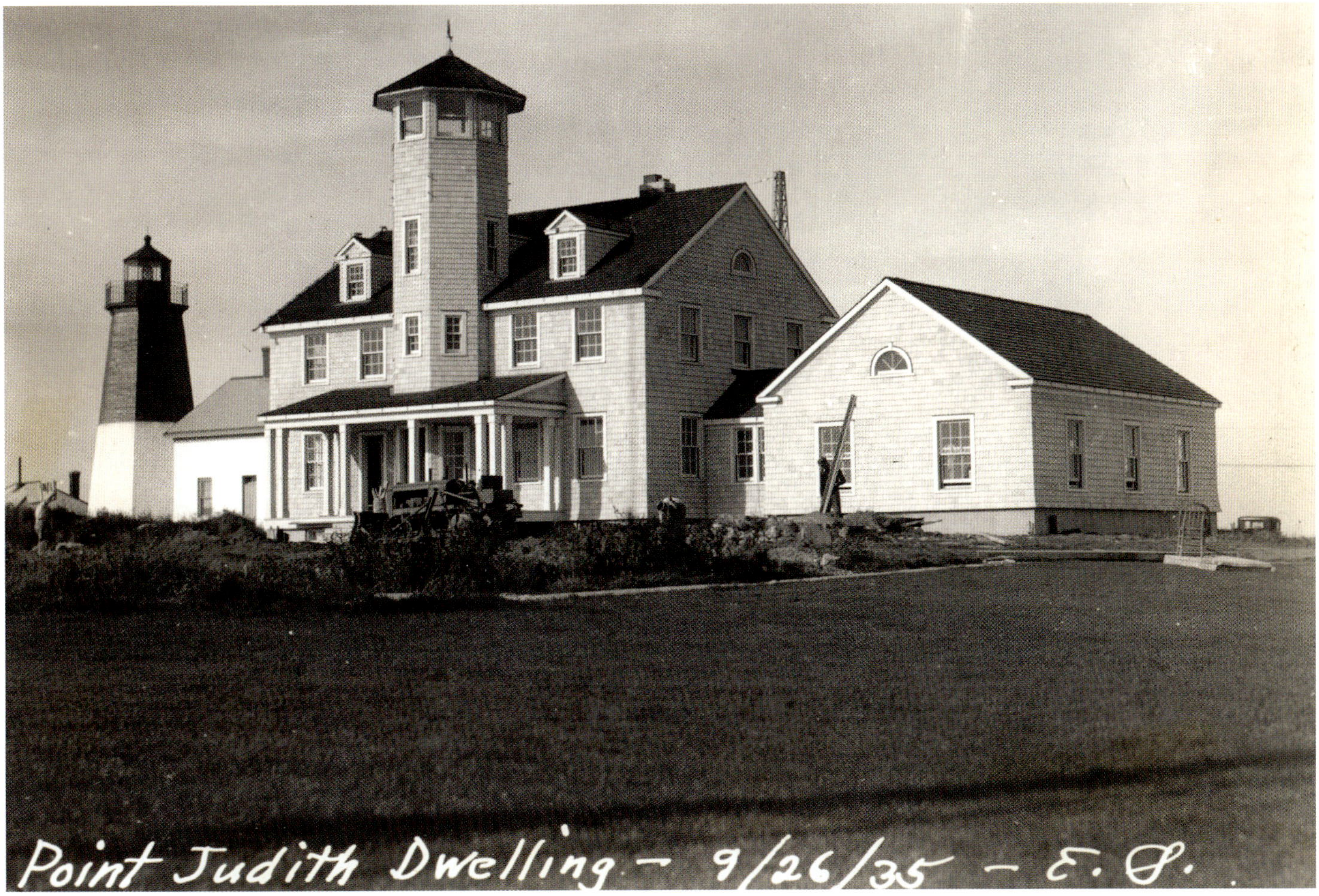

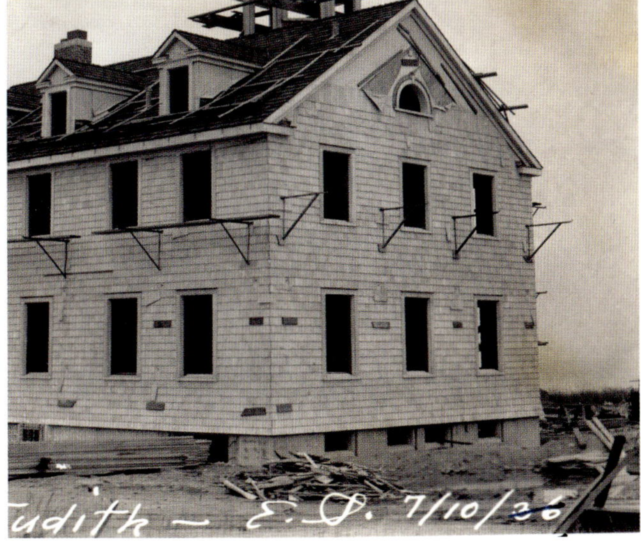

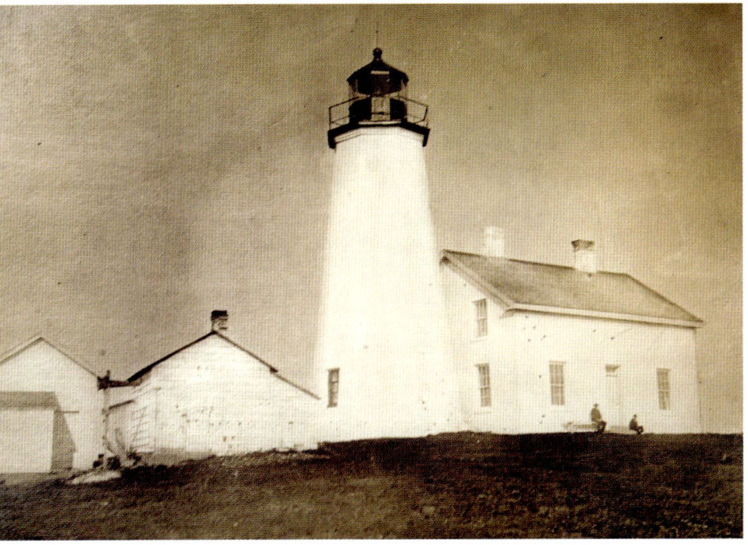

Top and bottom left: In 1935, the station was renovated and the windows replaced. *(Courtesy of USCG)*

Bottom right: An archival image of Point Judith. *(Courtesy of NA)*

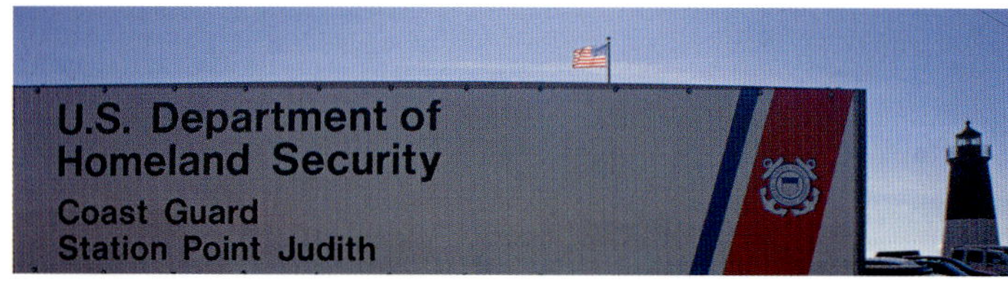

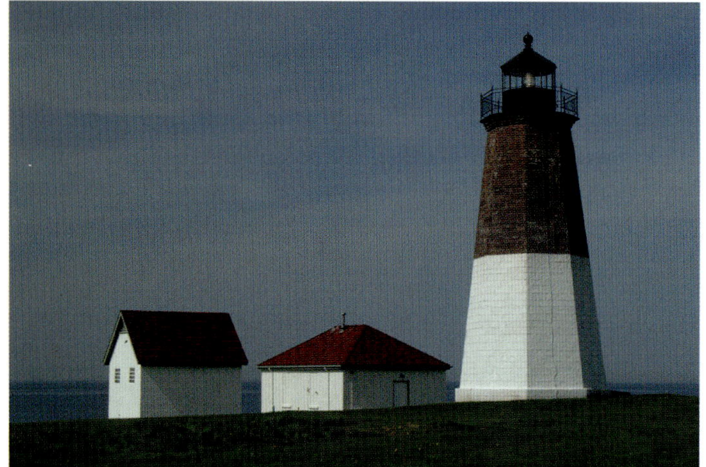

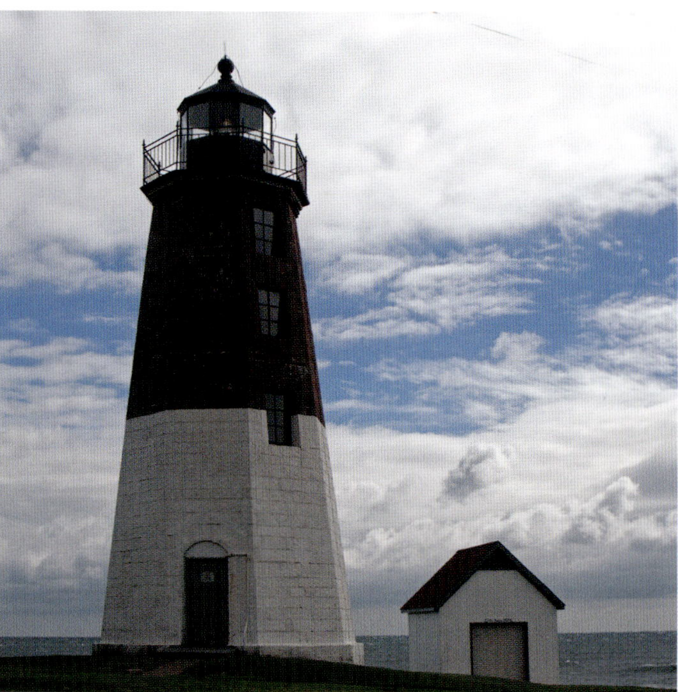

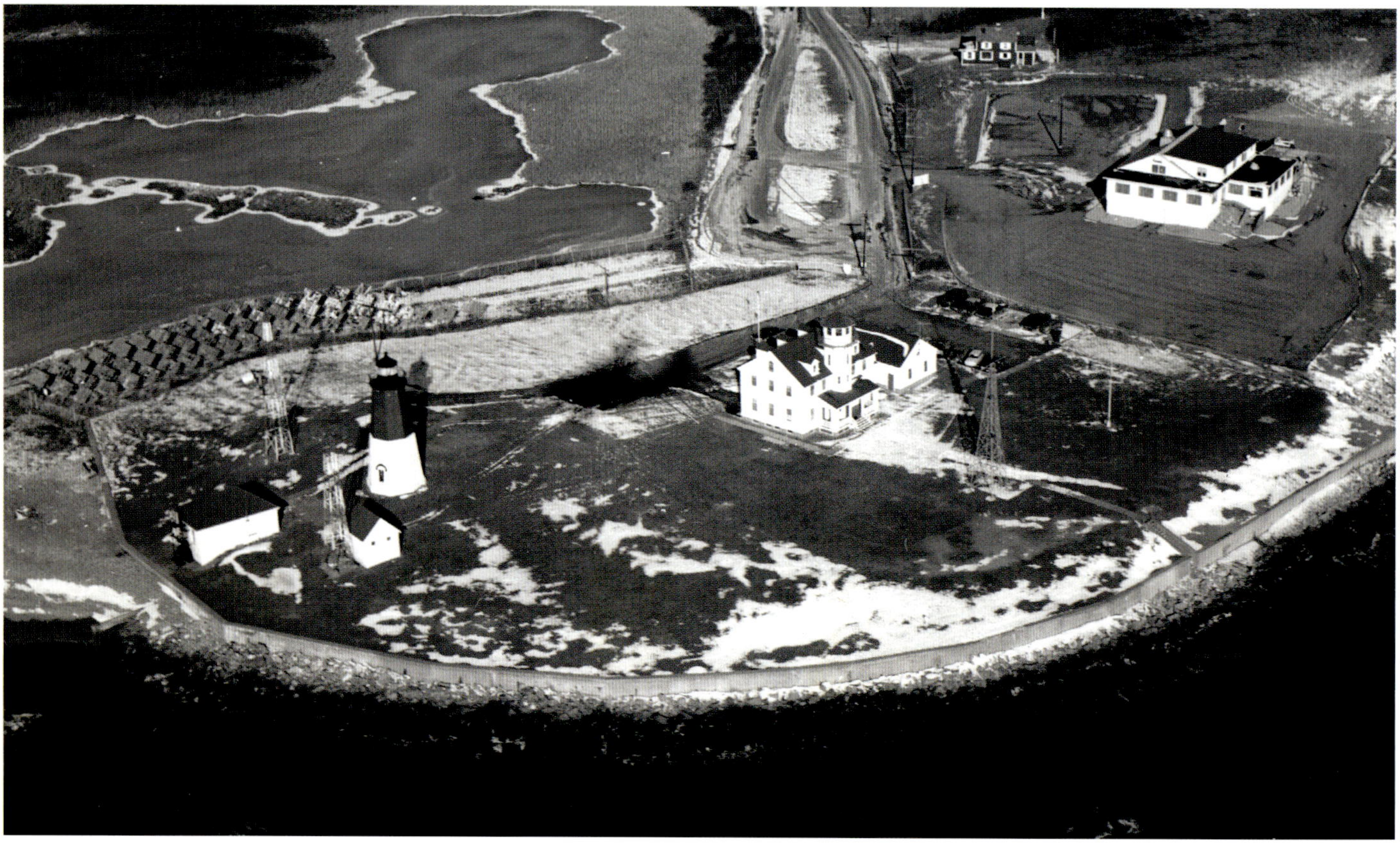

Top left: With the tower in the background, a sign identifies the station.

Center and top right: Two present-day views of the tower from slightly different angles.

Bottom: Taken in the mid 1900s, this is an aerial view of the station. *(Courtesy of USCG)*

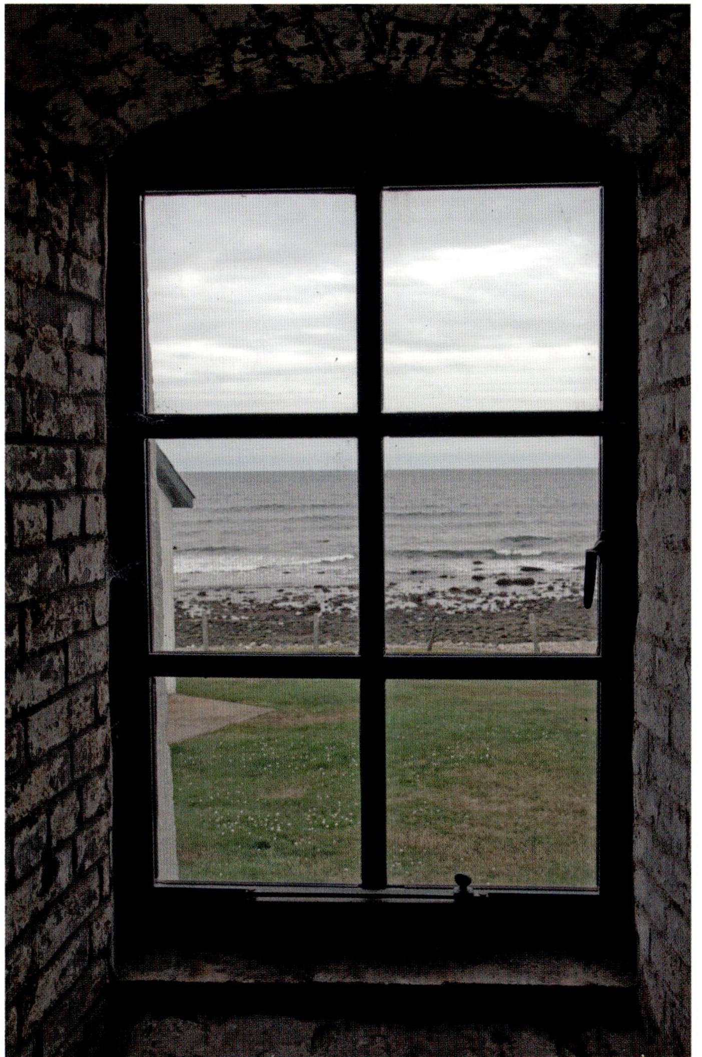

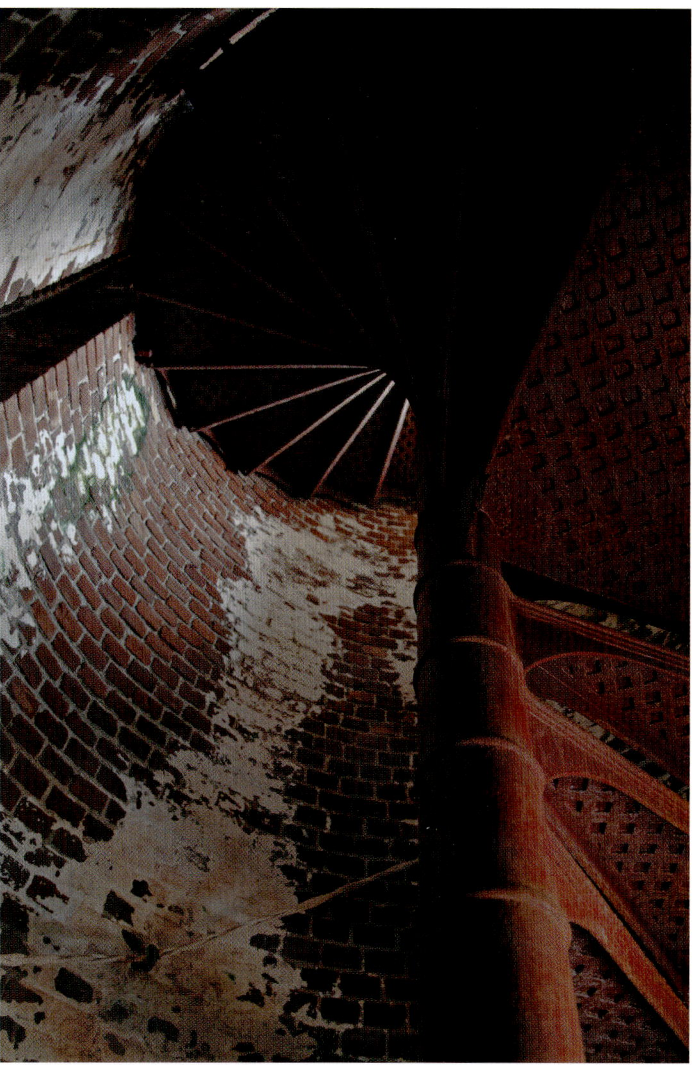

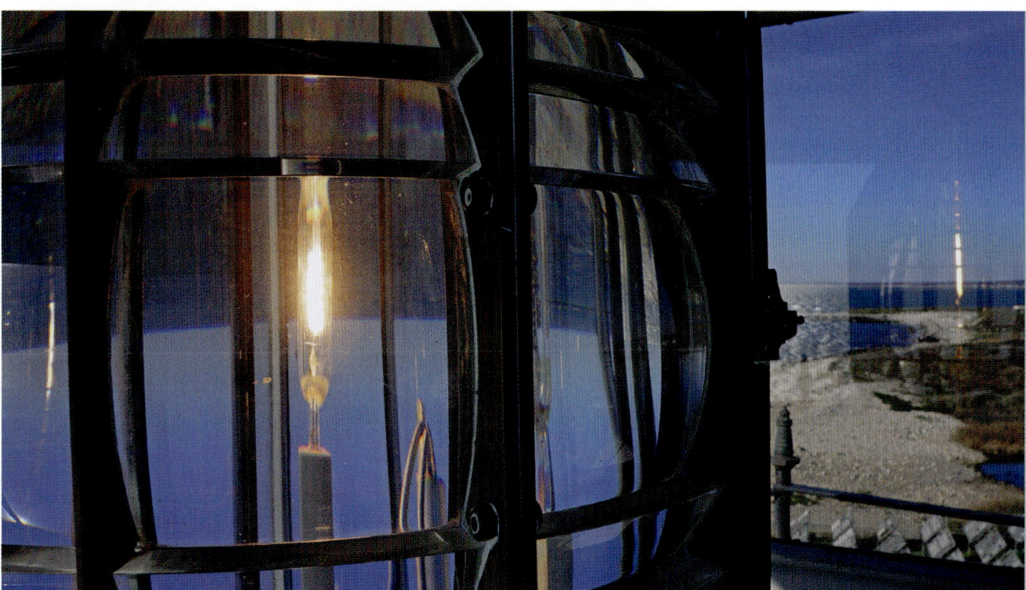

Above left: Looking south from a window inside the tower; note the thickness of the walls.

Above right: With a central post for support, cast-iron stairs lead to the lantern room.

Left: Looking west from the lantern room, with the Galilee Harbor entrance in the distance.

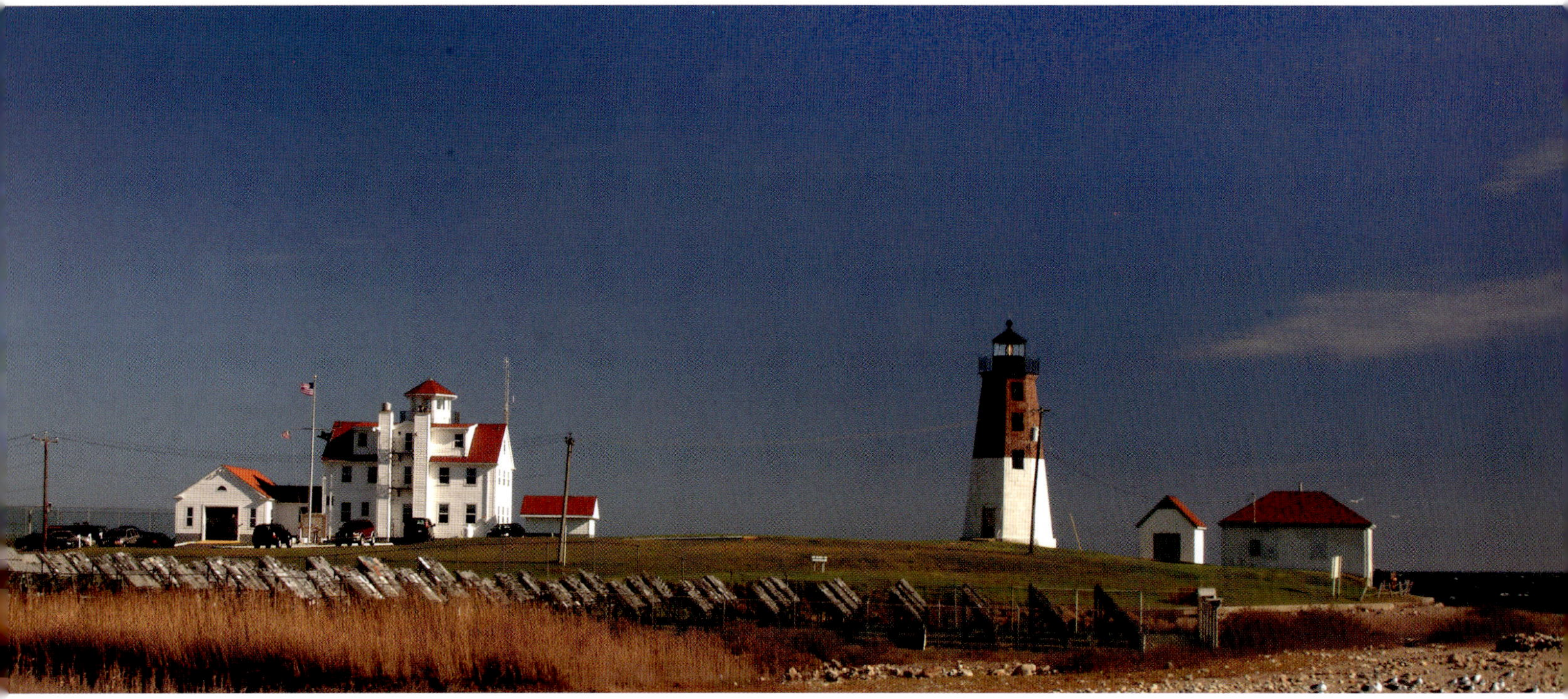

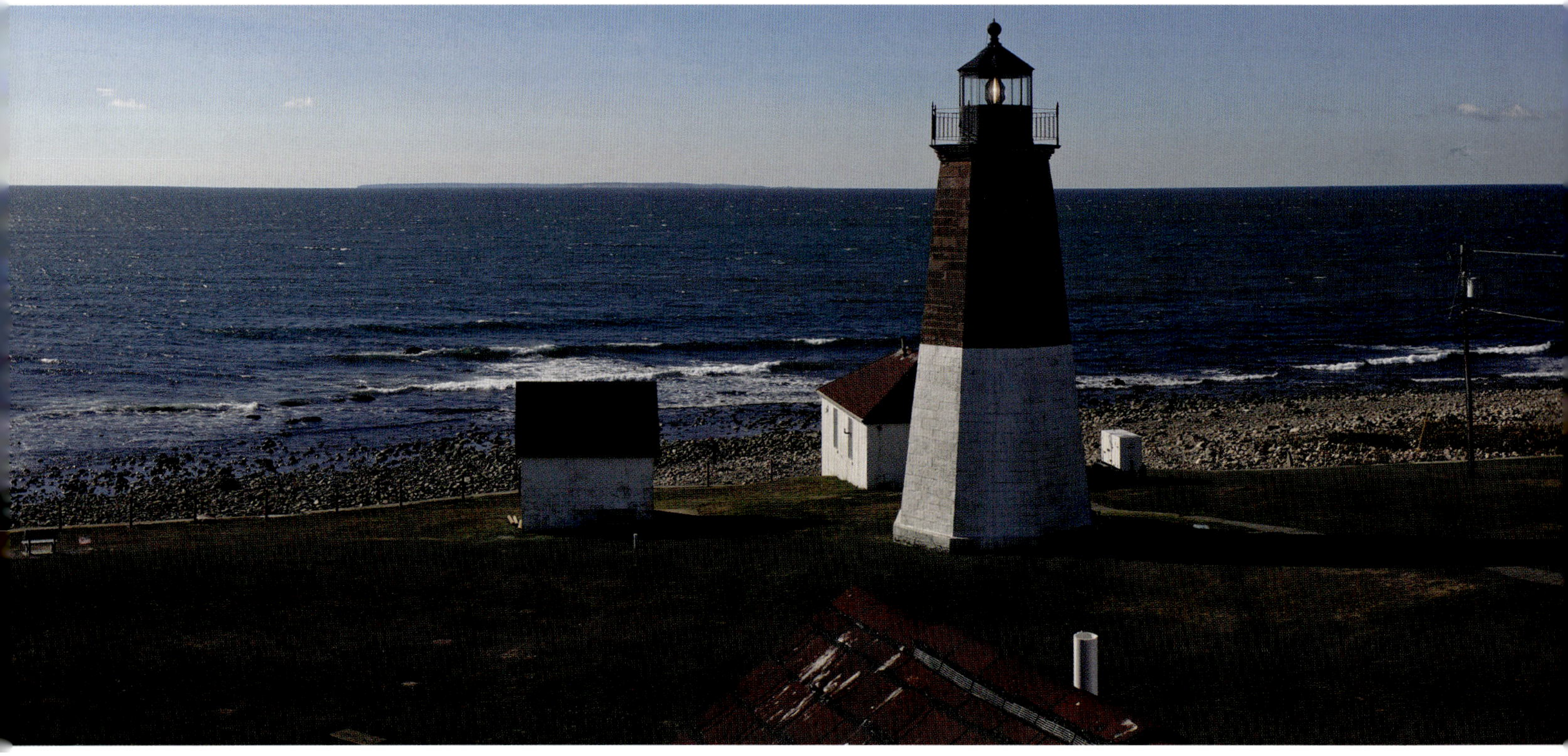

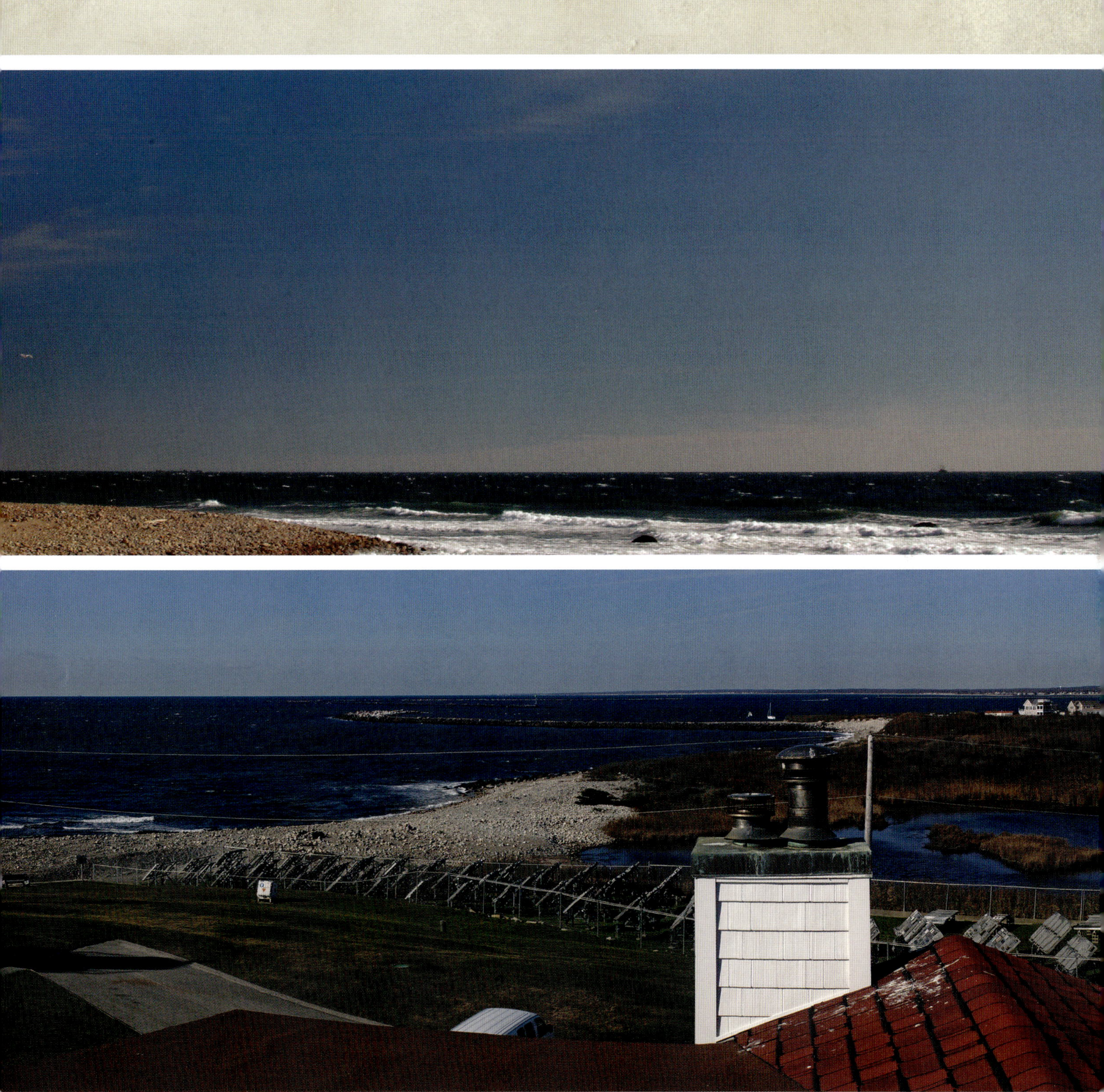

Top: Looking east, a view of the Point Judith Lighthouse Station. Look at the chart and determine where this picture was taken.

Bottom: From the cupola in the station, a view of the tower.

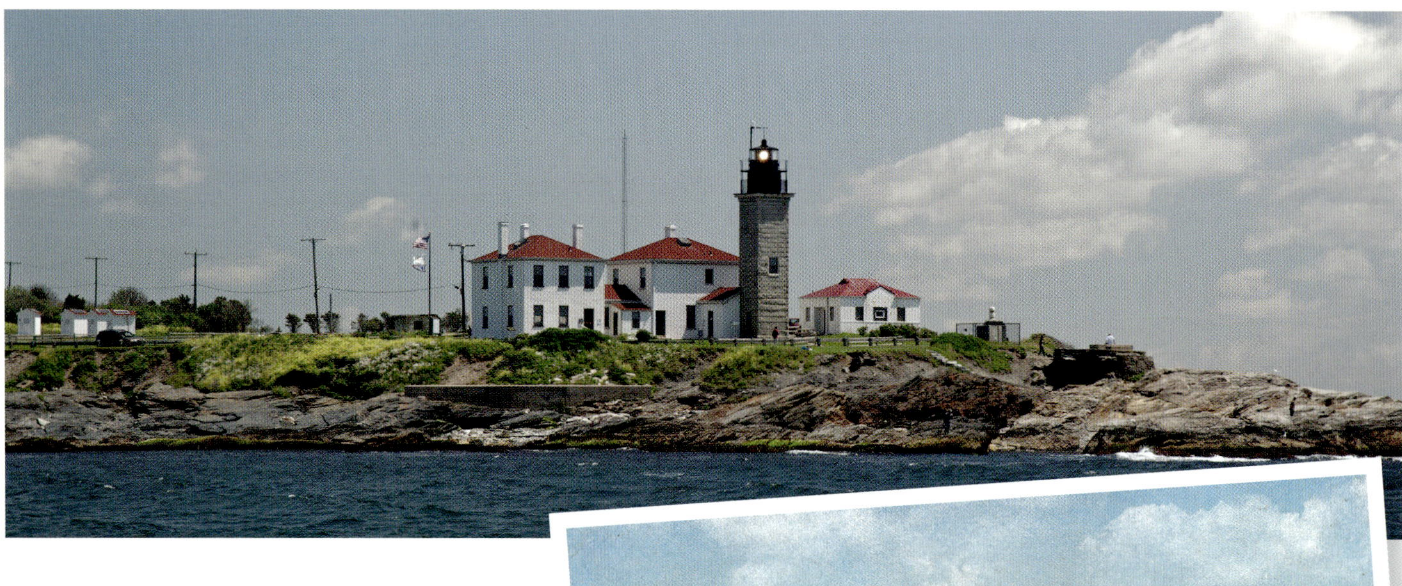

BEAVERTAIL

Location: Conanicut Island, Jamestown, Beavertail Point, N41°26′57″, W71°23′57″

Appropriation: $14,500 in 1854

Established: 1749

Automated: 1972

Tower, original: Wood, 69 feet high, 24-foot diameter base, destroyed by fire 1753

Rebuilt: 1754, brick and stone, 64 feet high, damaged by British in 1779

Rebuilt: Present tower, 1856, square, granite, brick-lining, 52 feet, black lantern room, with attached keeper's house

Other Structures: Assistant keeper's house and several outbuildings

Original Optics: 15 lamps, 9-inch reflectors, fixed white

Original Lens: 1856, 3rd order Fresnel lens, fixed white; 1907, 4th order Fresnel lens, 8 white flashes with interval of 15 seconds

Present Optic: DCB 24

Light Characteristics: Flashing white (FL W) every 10 seconds, lighted 24 hours, obscured 175° to 215°, focal plane 64 feet

Range: 15 nm

Fog Signal: One 3-second blast every 30 seconds

Status: Active U.S. Coast Guard aid to navigation

Access: Grounds open year-round; tower open during scheduled summer hours for tours.

Comments: Third lighthouse established in America; testing site for fog signals, more than 10 tested from 1829 till 1901; listed in NRHP; nearby park popular with visitors.

Above: Compare these two images captured more than a century apart. The postcard, undated, shows the station when the tower had two distinctive bands, probably white over red/brown. Relate this view with the present-day photograph (top), taken from almost the same perspective, and identify the buildings.

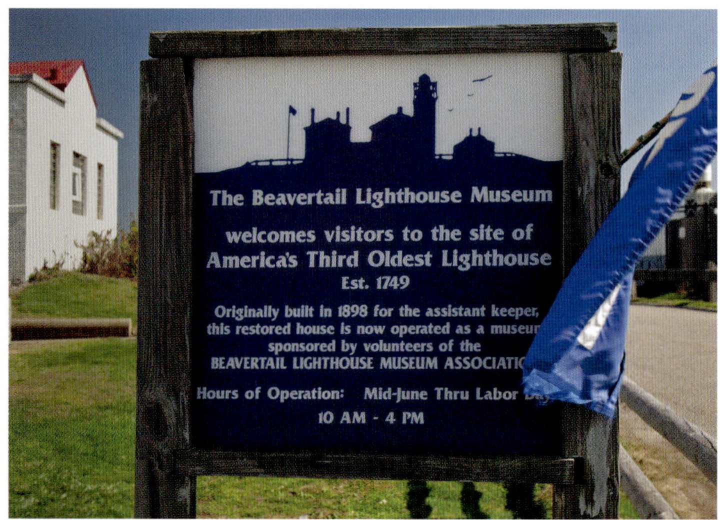

As the sign explains, the assistant keeper's house is open as a museum; on selected dates during the summer, the tower is also open to visitors.

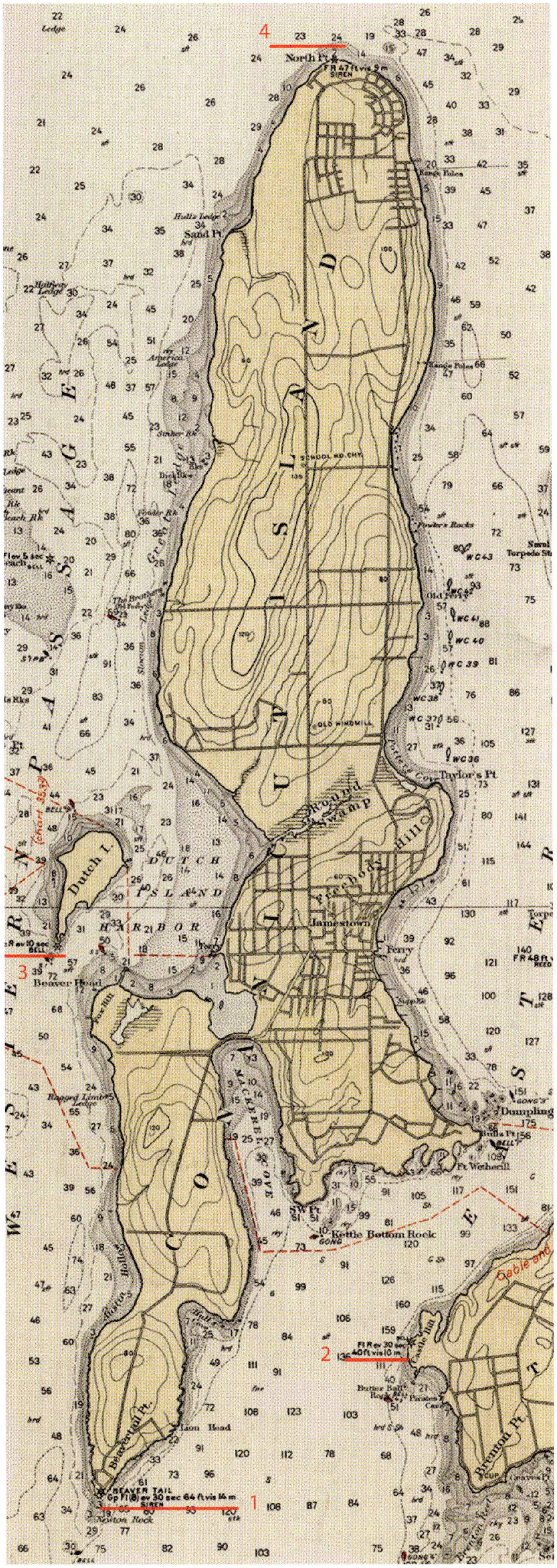

Left: Available to mariners, this section of a 1930 chart shows Conanicut Island in Narragansett Bay. To the left of the island is the waterway referred to as the West Passage, and to the right the East Passage. Identified as number 1, Beavertail Light is at the southern tip of the island; when it is sighted, the ship's captain will then determine which course the ship will sail. If he heads east, the next aid, Castle Hill, 2, will be on his starboard side to the northeast. If he sails west, Dutch Island, 3, is almost due north. Number 4, Conanicut Light, marks the north end of the island. *(Courtesy of NOAA)*

Below: This image was taken sometime in the 1880s. Curtains in the lantern room protect the lens. *(Courtesy of USCG)*

Bottom: Plans for the tower that was built in 1754. *(Courtesy of R. Holmes)*

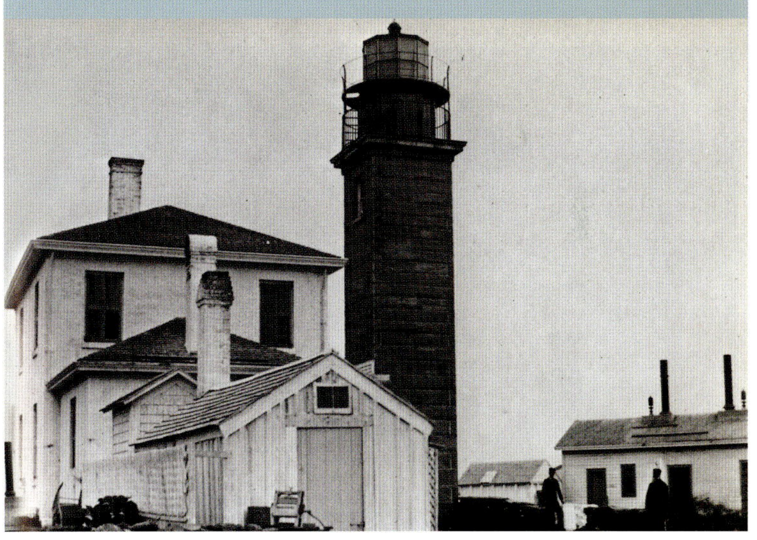

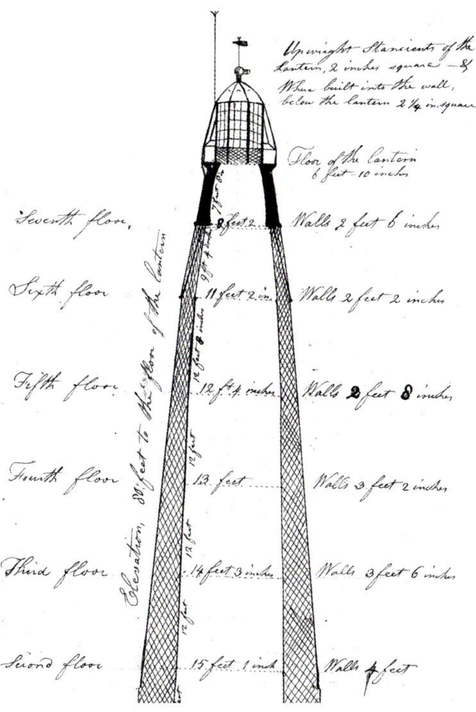

Right: Many of the lighthouses in Rhode Island were damaged or destroyed by the September hurricane of 1938. This image shows the destruction that occurred to Beavertail Light. *(Courtesy of USCG)*

Far Right: A rainbow behind the Beavertail lantern room. *(Courtesy of D. Zapatka)*

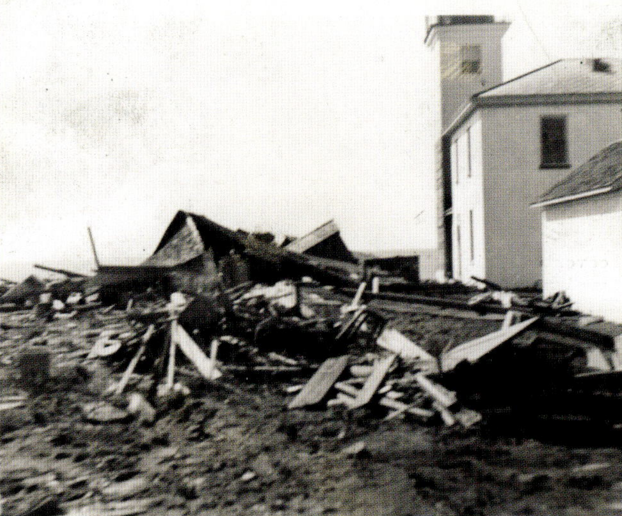

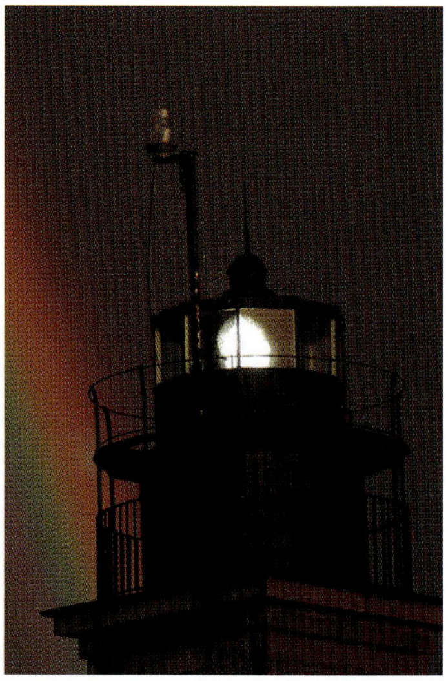

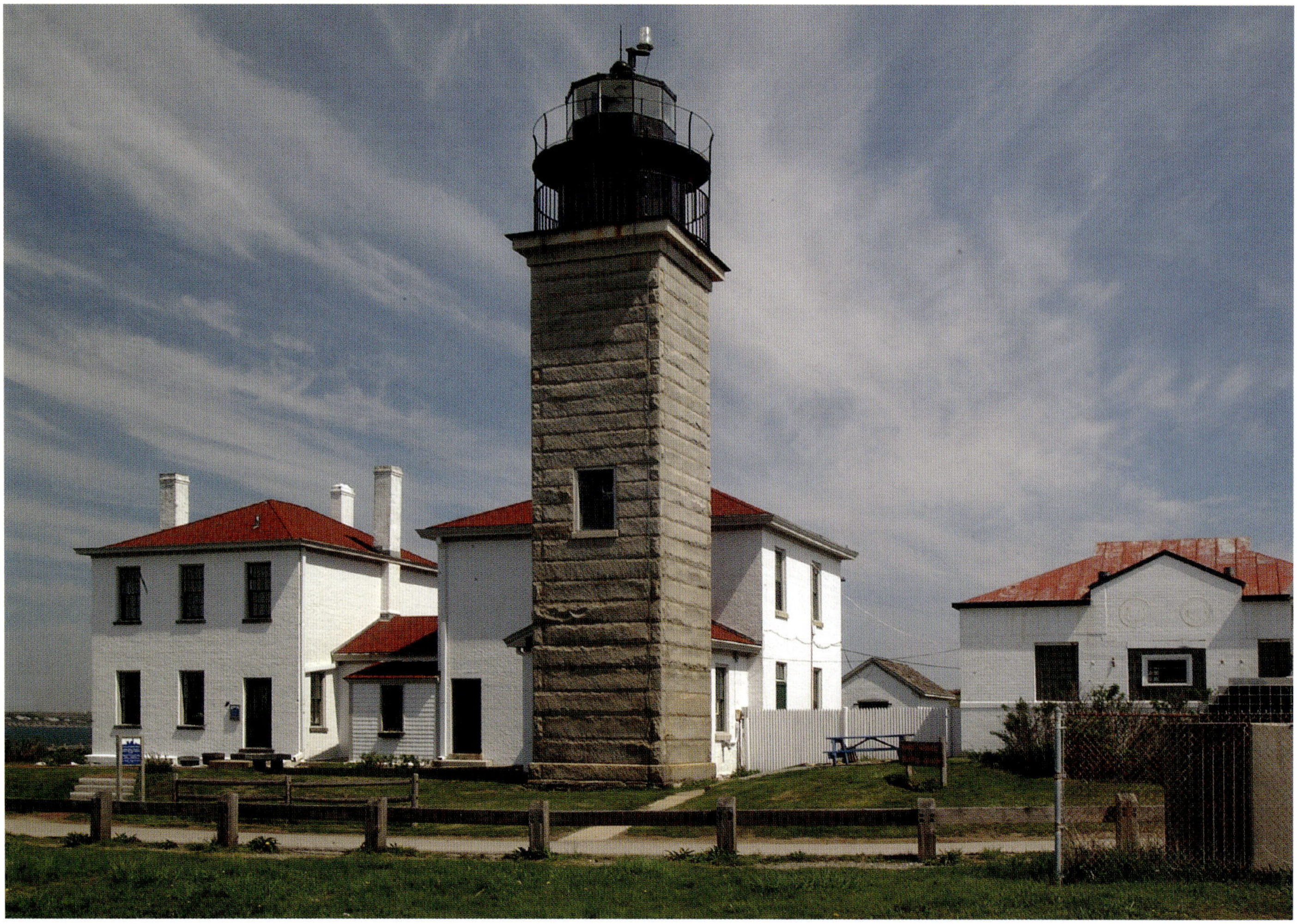

Above: A view, looking north, of the station; note the fog-signaling machinery to the right. Compare this photograph to the present-day aerial on page 39, and try to determine where the shot was taken from.

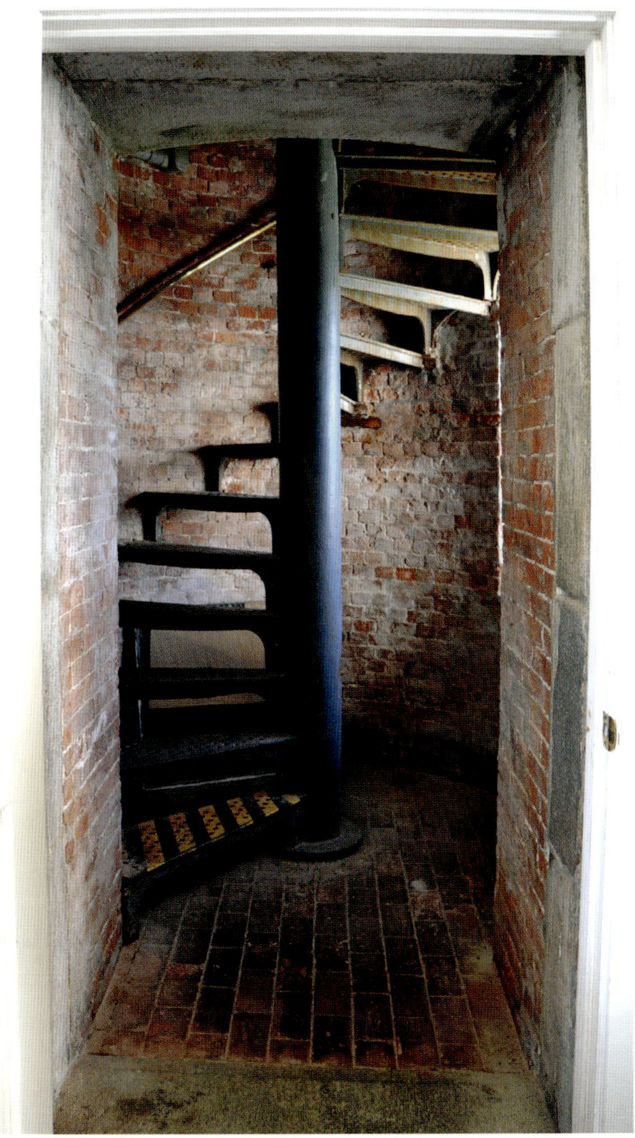

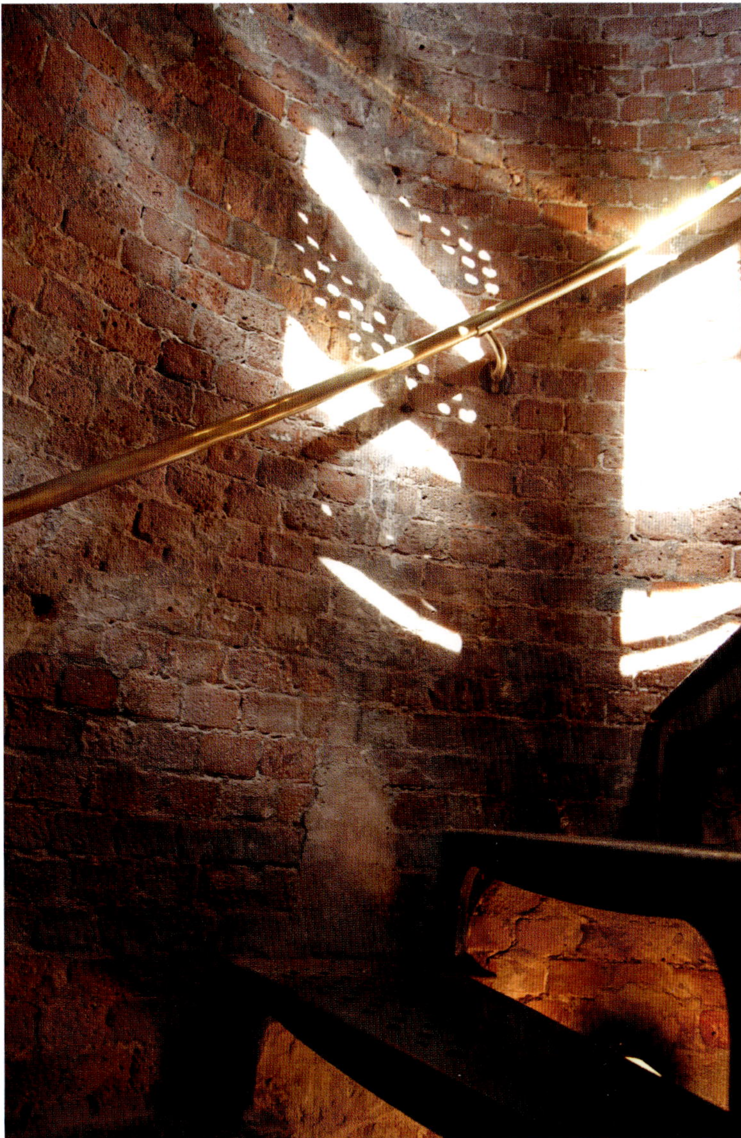

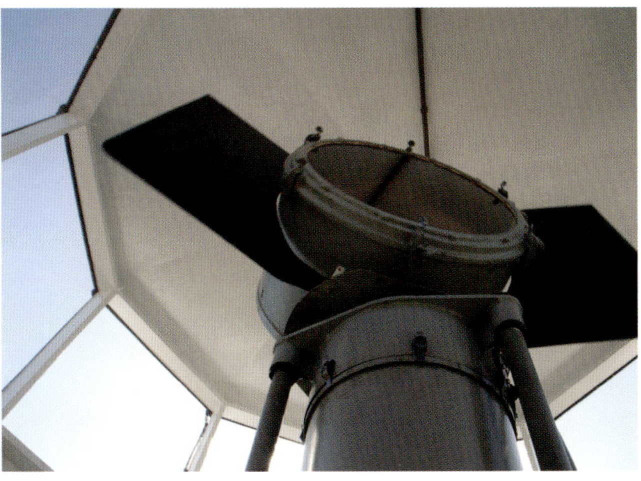

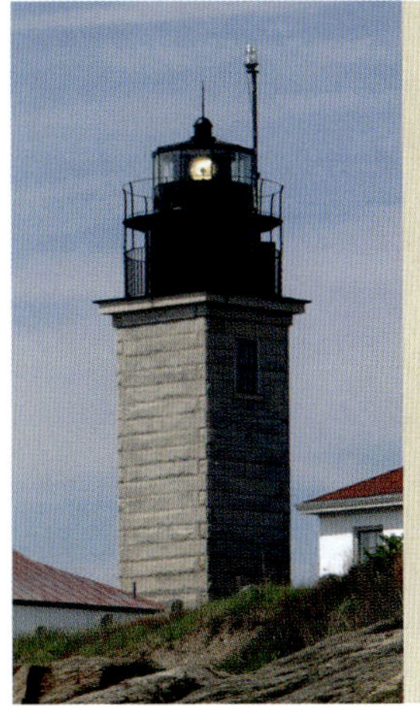

Above left: Enter the first-floor door, and you see circular stairs that lead to the lantern room.

Above right: Stairs and a brass handrail in the brick-lined tower.

Far left: The present-day DCB-24 in the lantern room.

Left: A present-day view of the tower.

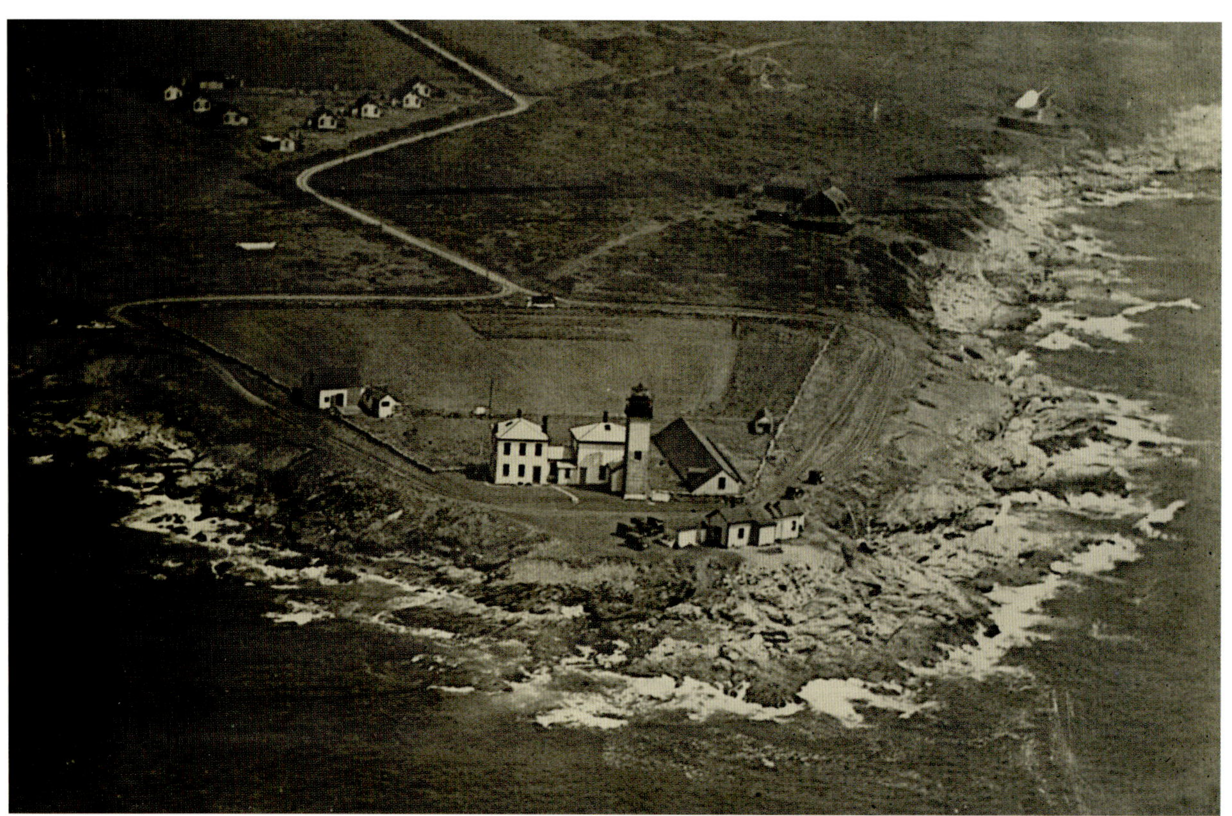

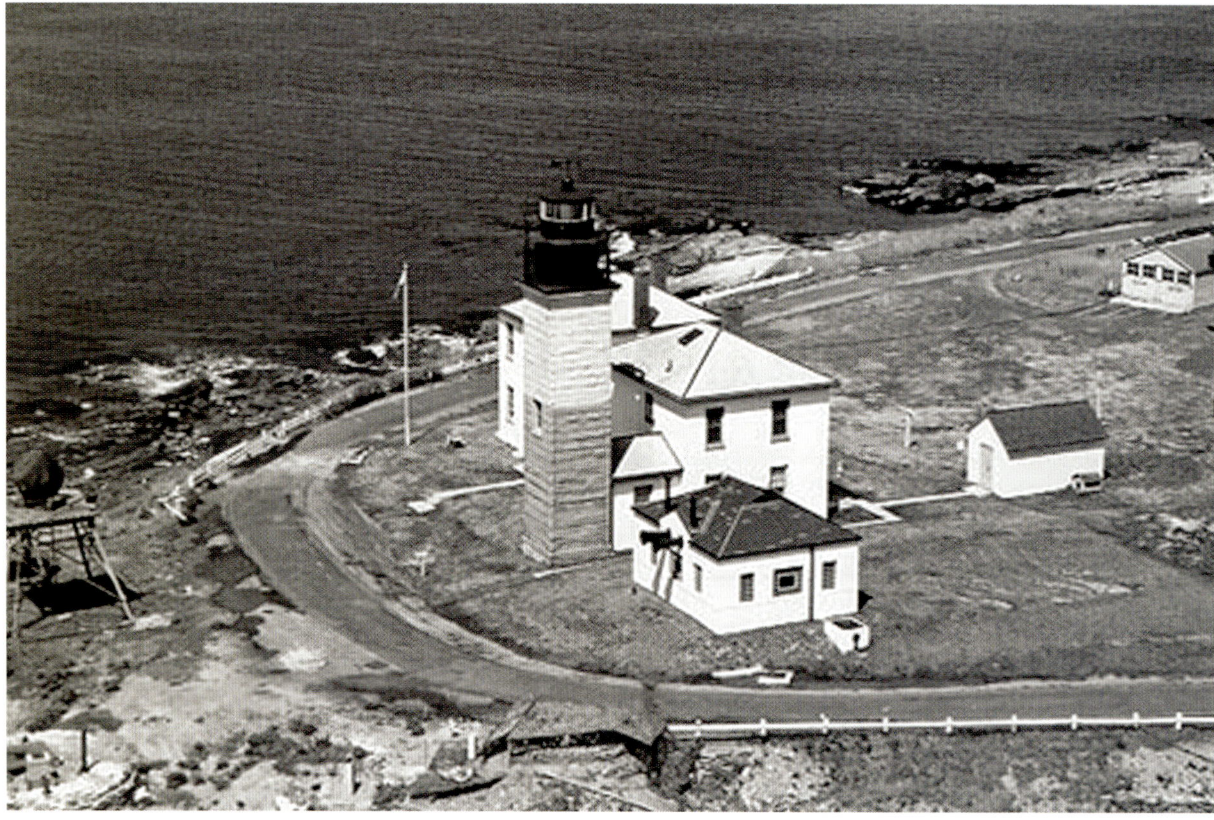

Compare these two archival aerial images of Beavertail Light with the next present-day view. *(Courtesy of USCG)*

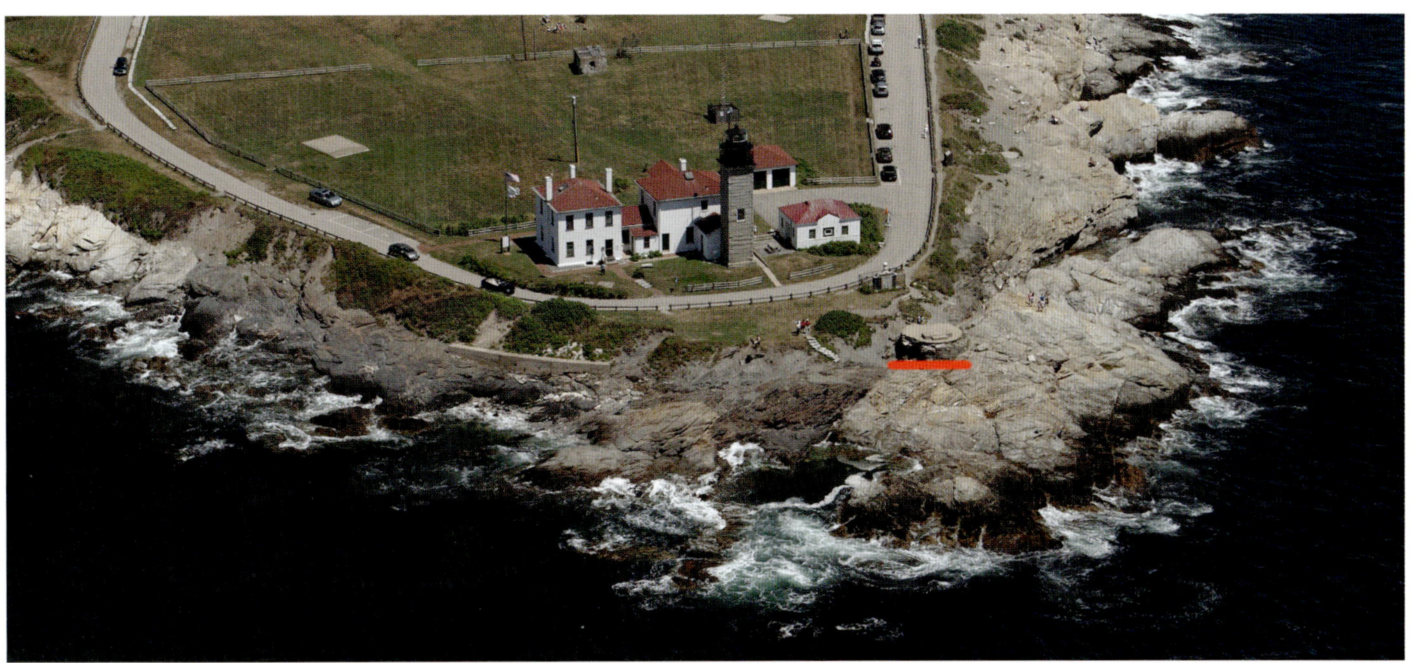

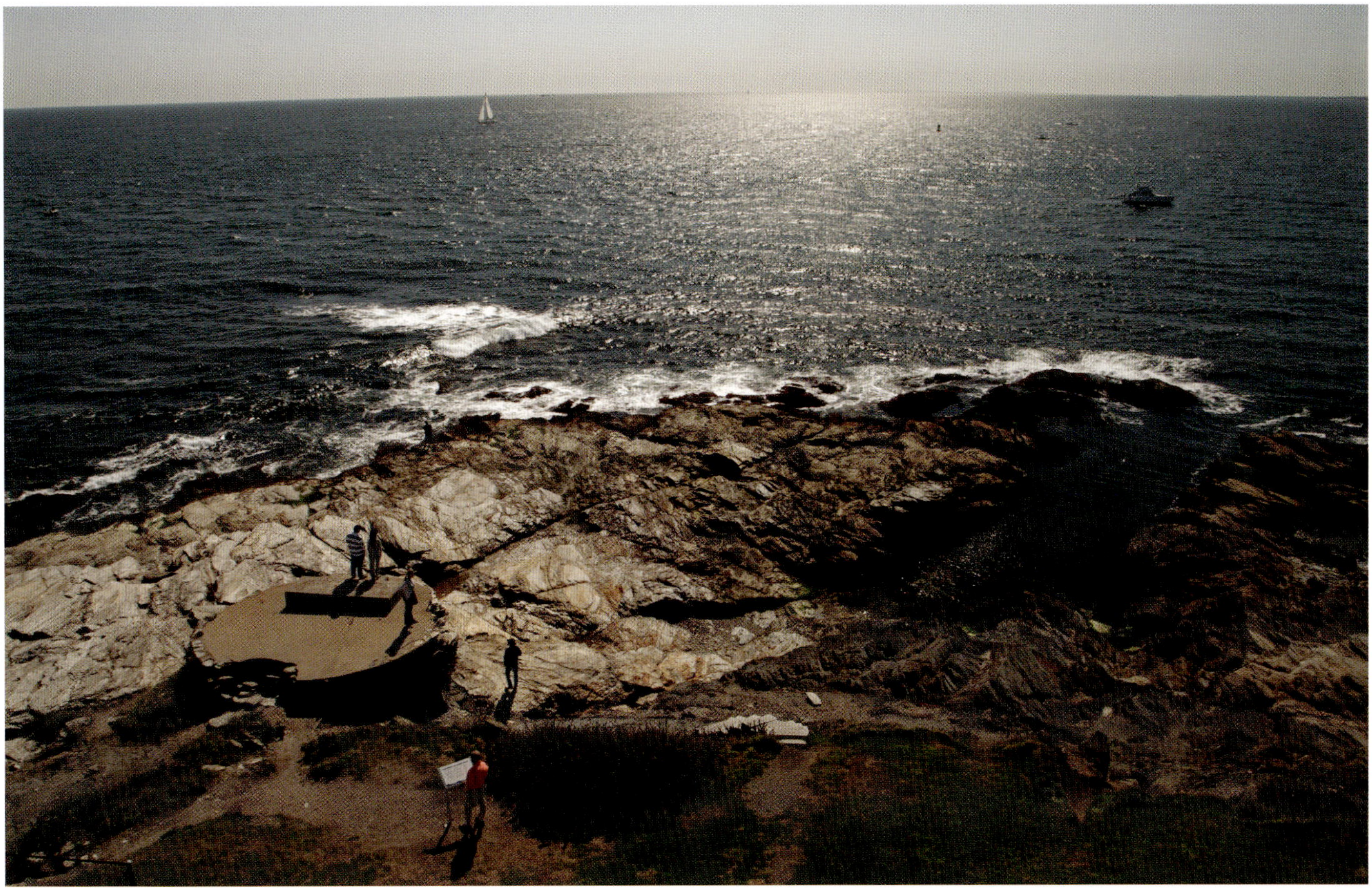

Top: A current aerial image of the Beavertail Light Station. Underlined in red, in front of the present station, is the location of the 1754 tower. Just to the rear is the fog-signaling device.

Bottom: Looking south from the lantern room.

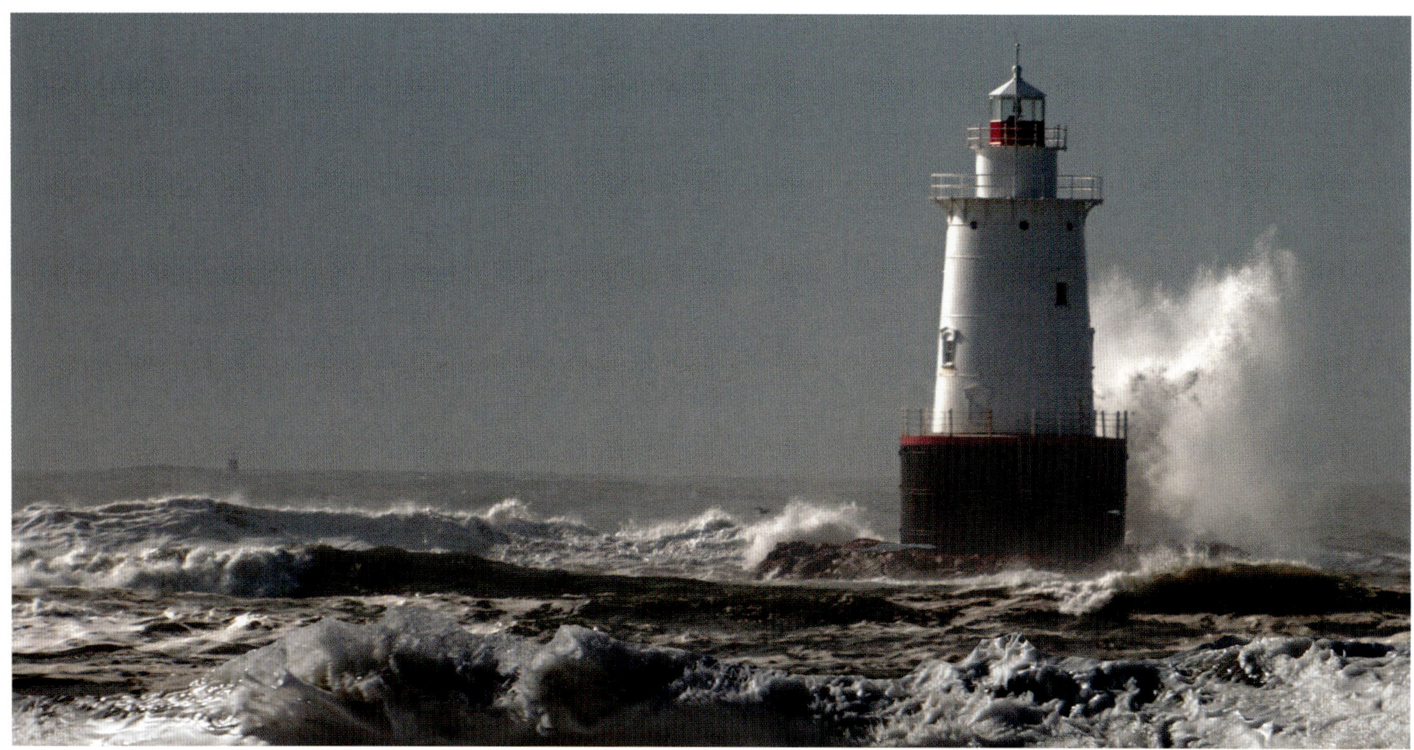

SAKONNET POINT

Location: Sakonnet, Little Compton, about half-mile offshore, N41°27′11″, W71°12′09″

Appropriation: $20,000 in August 1882

Established: 1884

Deactivated: 1955–1997

Reactivated and Automated: March 1997

Tower: White conical cast-iron tower, red band around lantern room, 66 feet

Other Structures: None

Original Lens: 1891 4th order, fixed white for 30 seconds, 3 red flashes at 10-second interval

1939: 4th order Fresnel lens, fixed white alternating with flashing red, focal plane 58 feet

Present Lens: 300 mm, solar-powered

Light Characteristics: Flashing white/red every 6 seconds (Fl WR 6s), red sector 195° to 350°

Range: 7 nm white, 5nm red

Fog Signal: 1939 air-diaphragm horn

Status: Private aid to navigation; maintained by The Friends of Sakonnet Point Lighthouse, Inc.

Access: Island; tower restricted; best views from boat.

Comments: Tower has been totally restored; original lens on display at Shore Village Museum, Rockland, Maine; listed in NHRP.

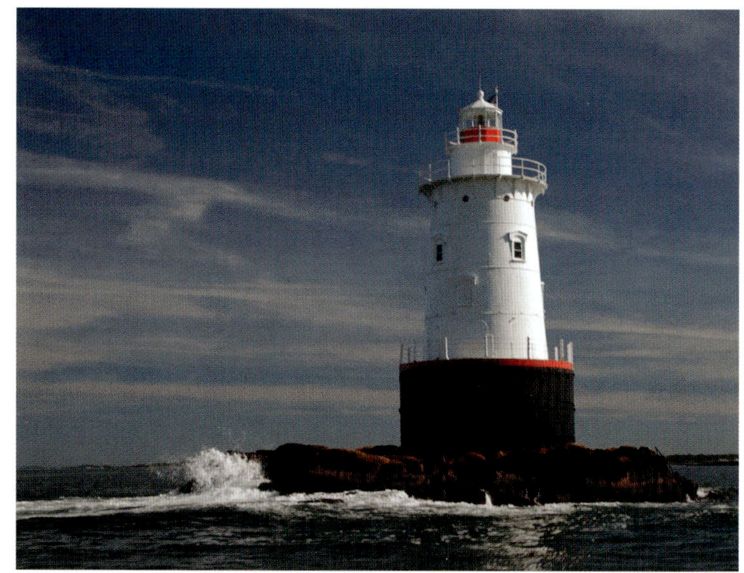

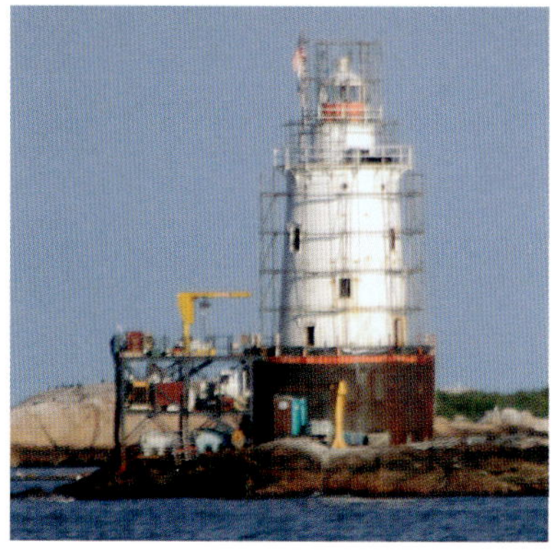

Above: Two images of the restored tower, one from a boat in calm conditions and the other during a storm.

Left: Money was raised and the tower was totally restored in 2005.

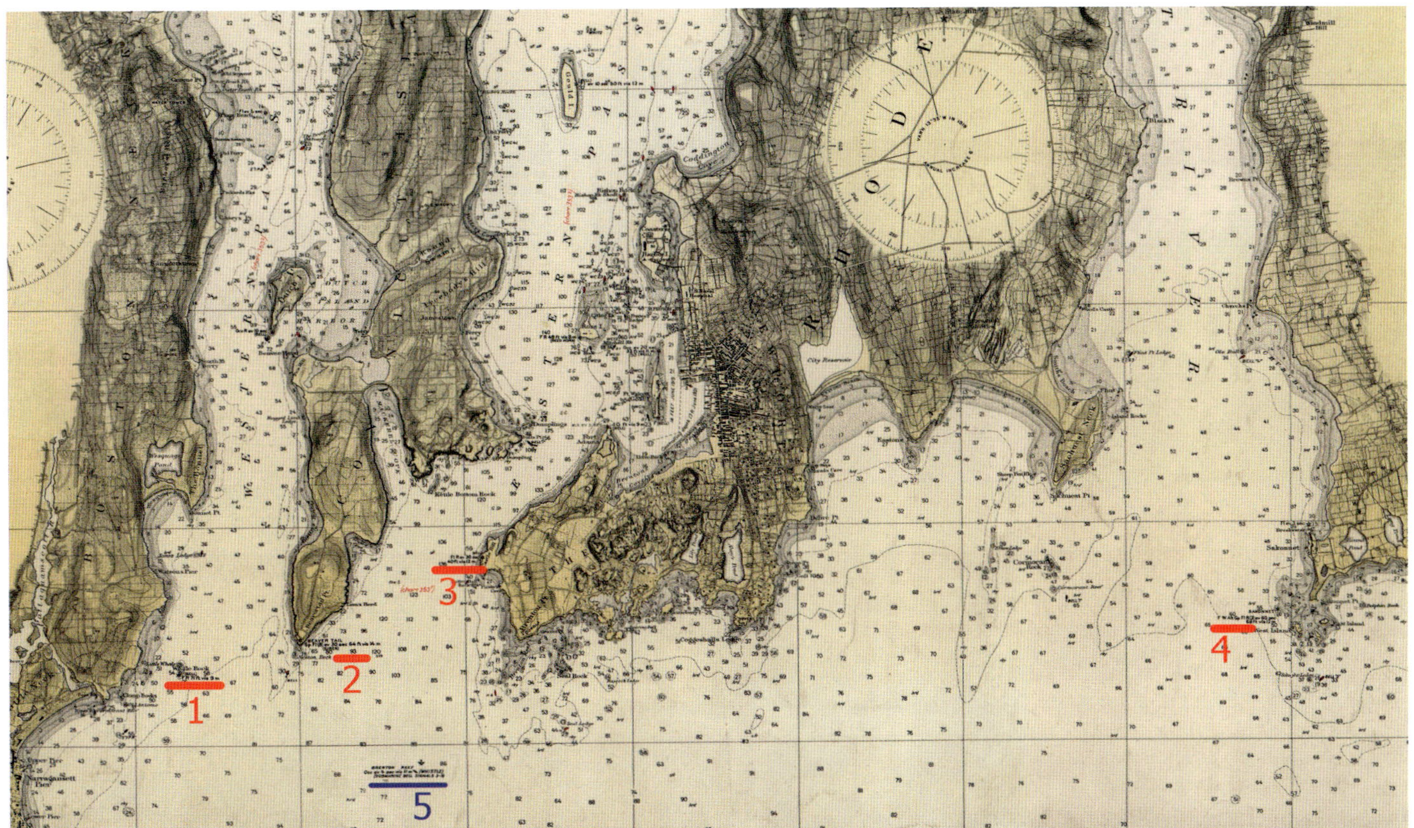

Above: This 1921 chart indicates, at that time, the major coastal lighthouses and lightship in Rhode Island. Number 1, Whale Rock, no longer exists; it was destroyed by the hurricane in September 1938. Number 2 is Beavertail, previously discussed; number 3 is Castle Hill. Travelling east, the last lighthouse in Rhode Island is Sakonnet, number 4. No lightship stations presently exist in the United States; in 1921, there was a lightship assigned to mark Brenton Reef, marked here as 5. *(Courtesy of NOAA)*

Right: This Coast Guard aerial image was probably taken more than a half century ago. *(Courtesy of USCG)*

Far right: A present-day image of the restored Sakonnet Light Tower.

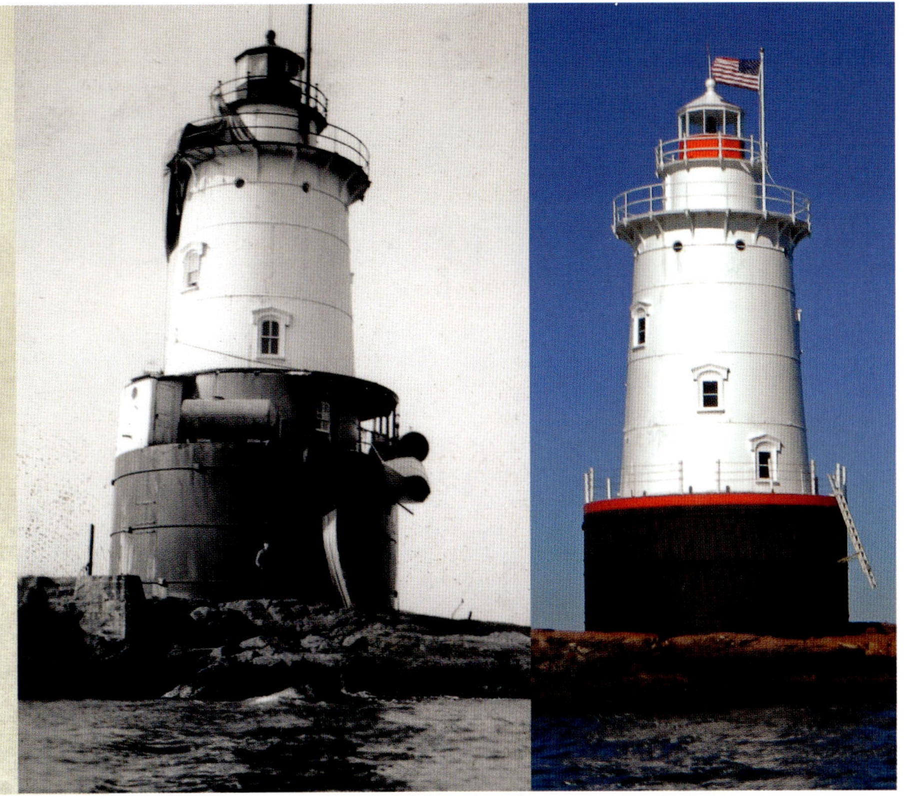

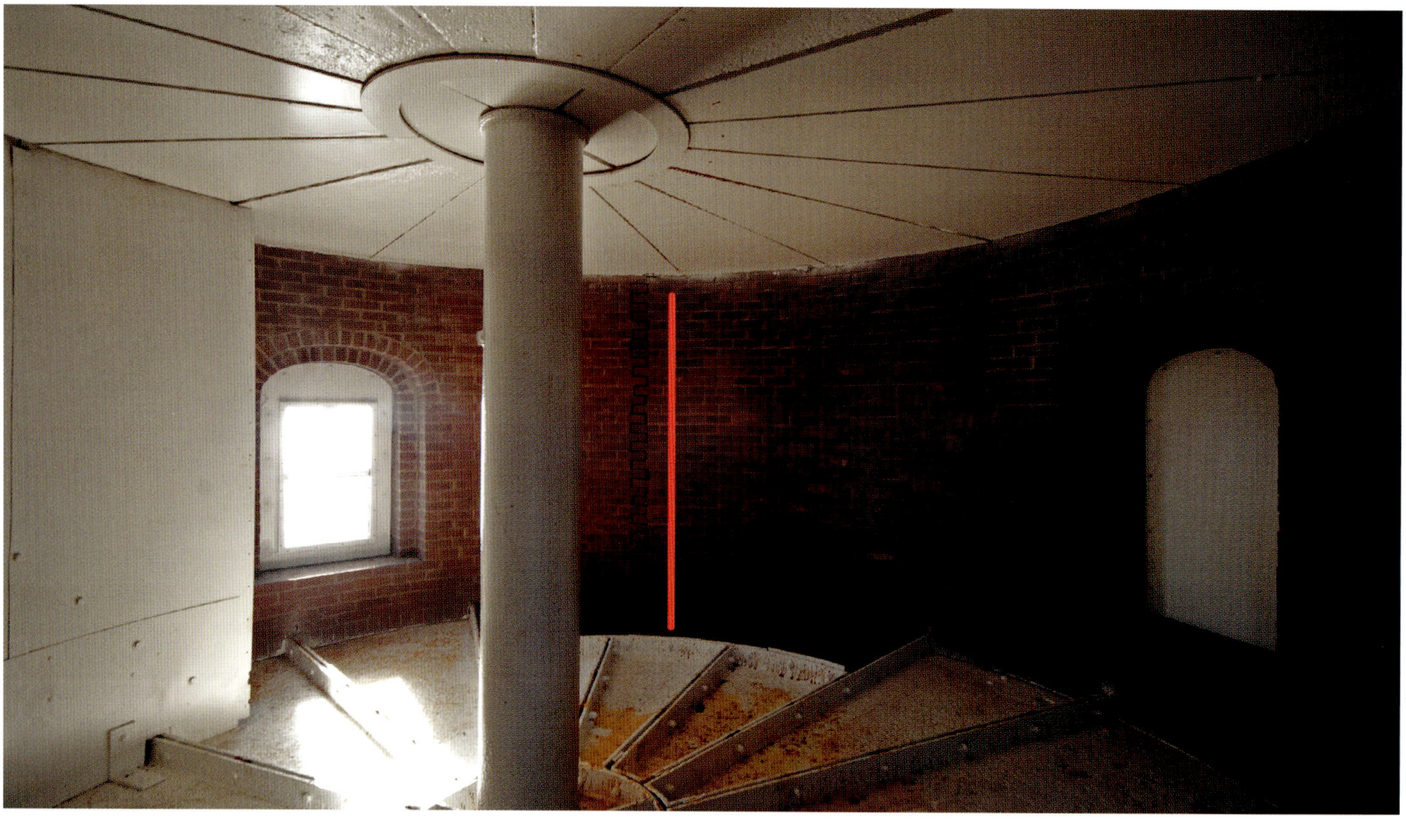

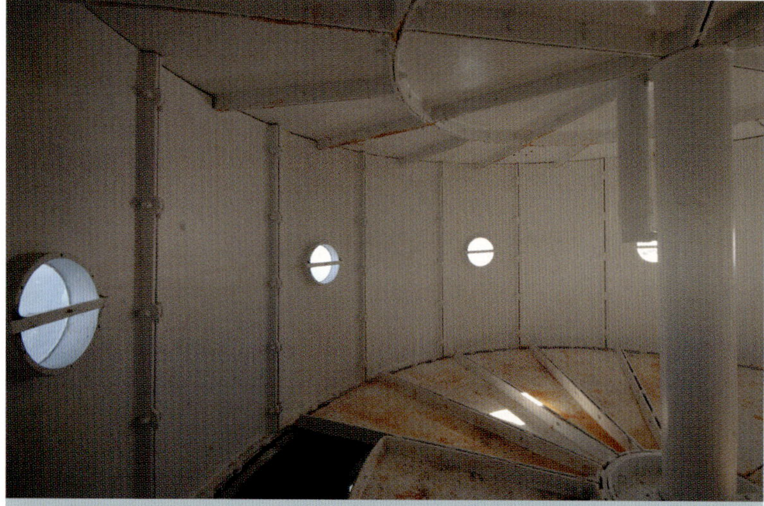

Top: This is a view of the second floor of the restored tower; just to the left of the red vertical line is an expansion joint in the bricks.

Above: This is the fourth level; note the portholes, which can be seen on the exterior view images of the tower.

Right: Also on the fourth level, metal stairs lead to lower levels.

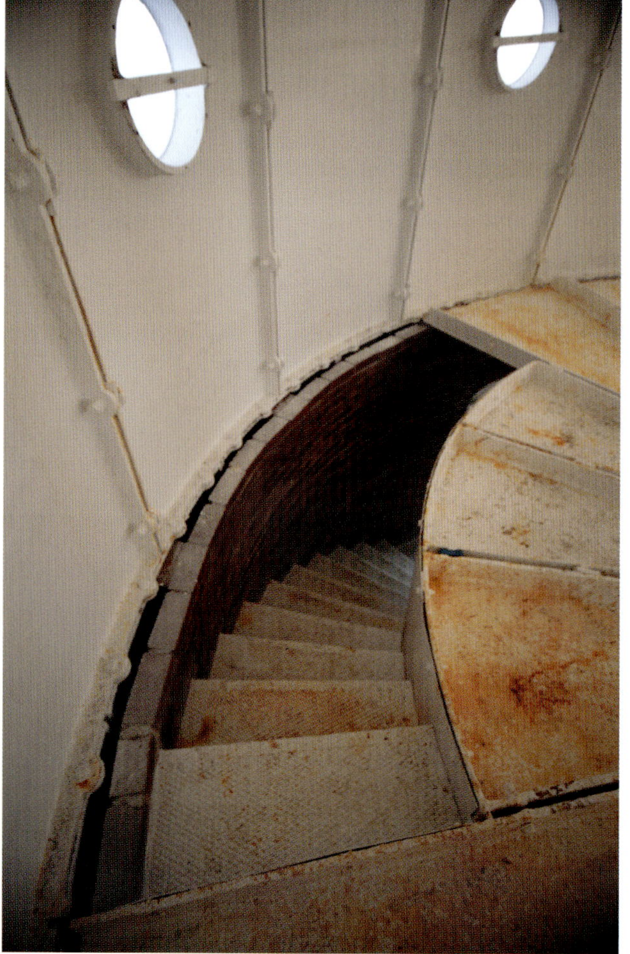

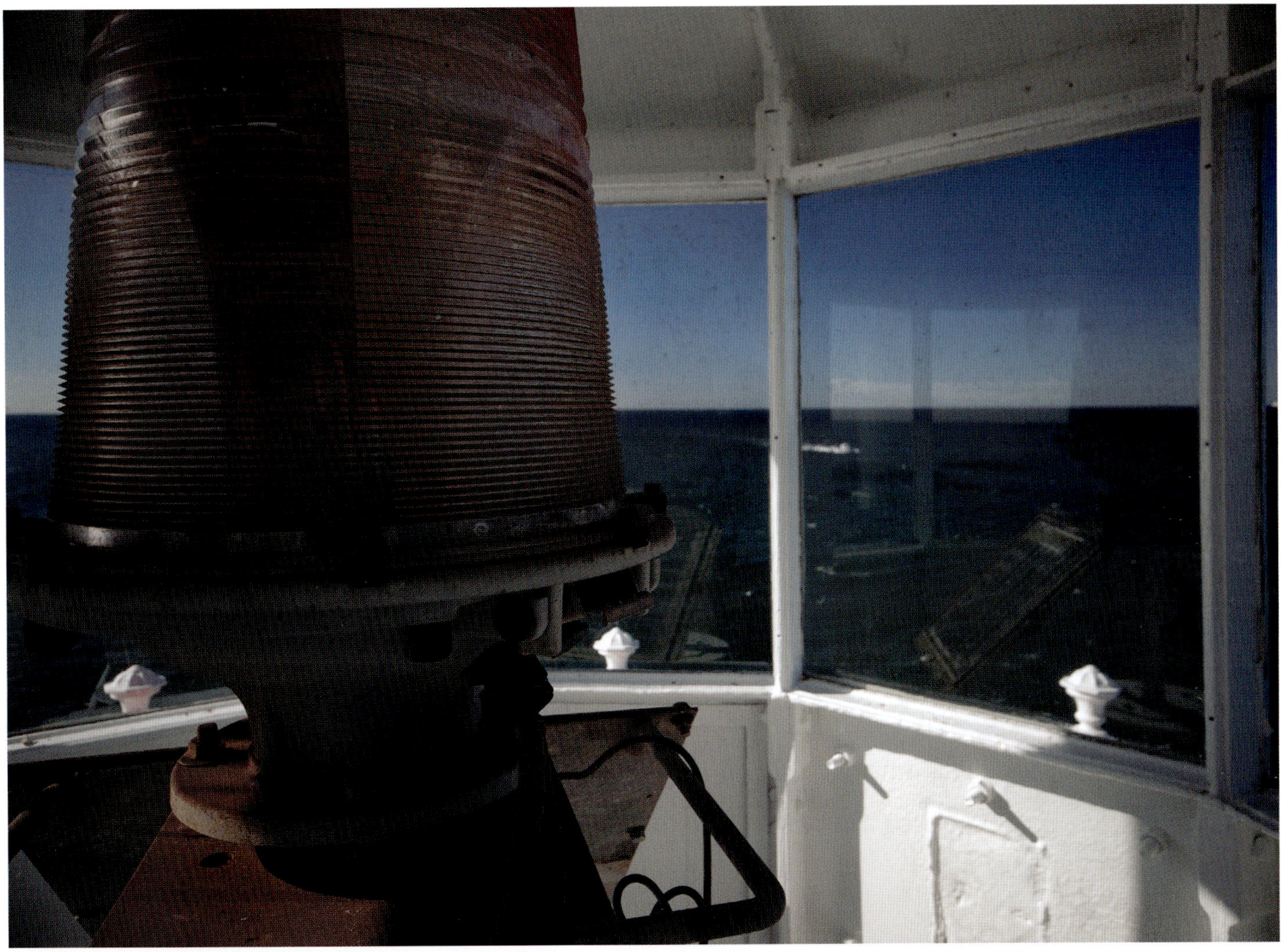

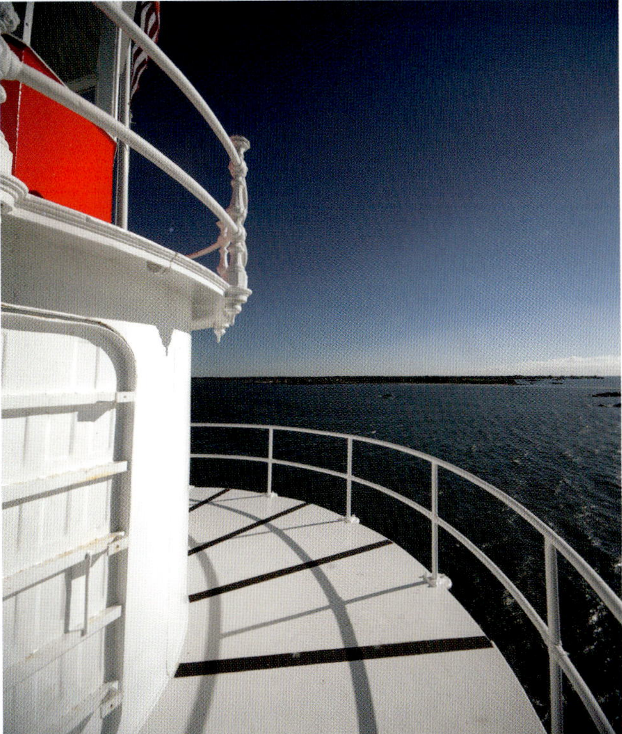

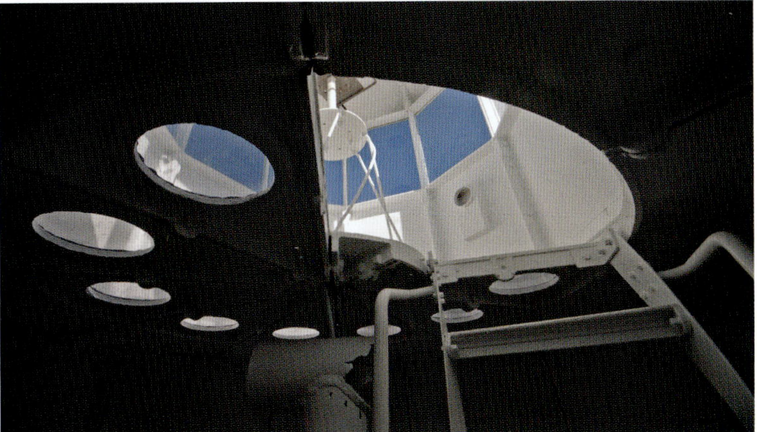

Top: Looking south. A boat can be seen returning to harbor; the solar-powered panel can be seen in the reflection in the glass.

Left: Looking east. The islands in the distance once housed an exclusive fishing club. Compare this view with the previous old map.

Above right: Looking up the stairs that lead to the lantern room.

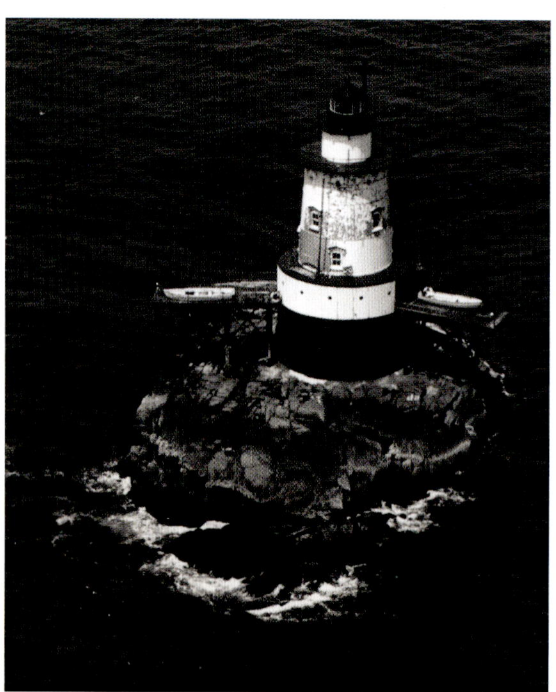

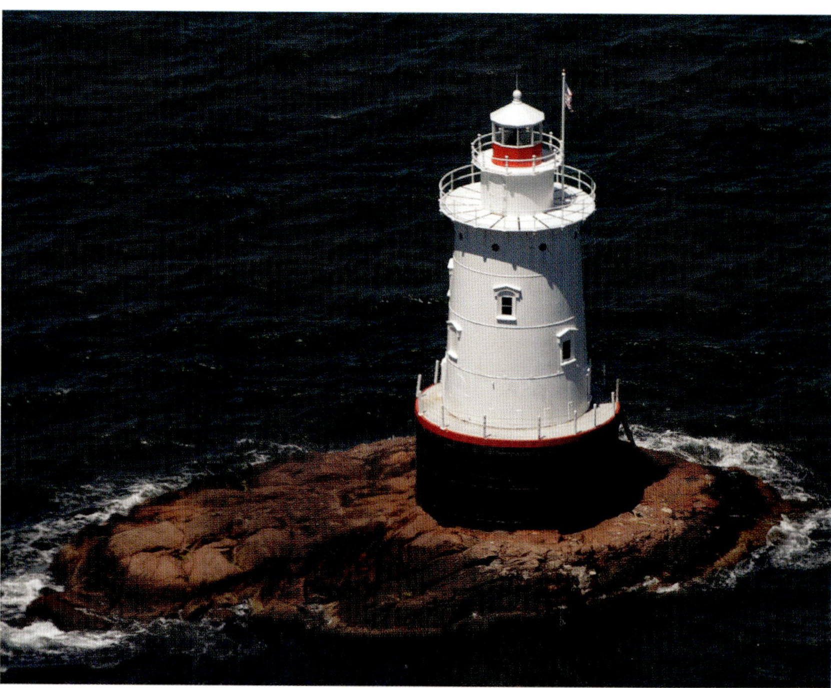

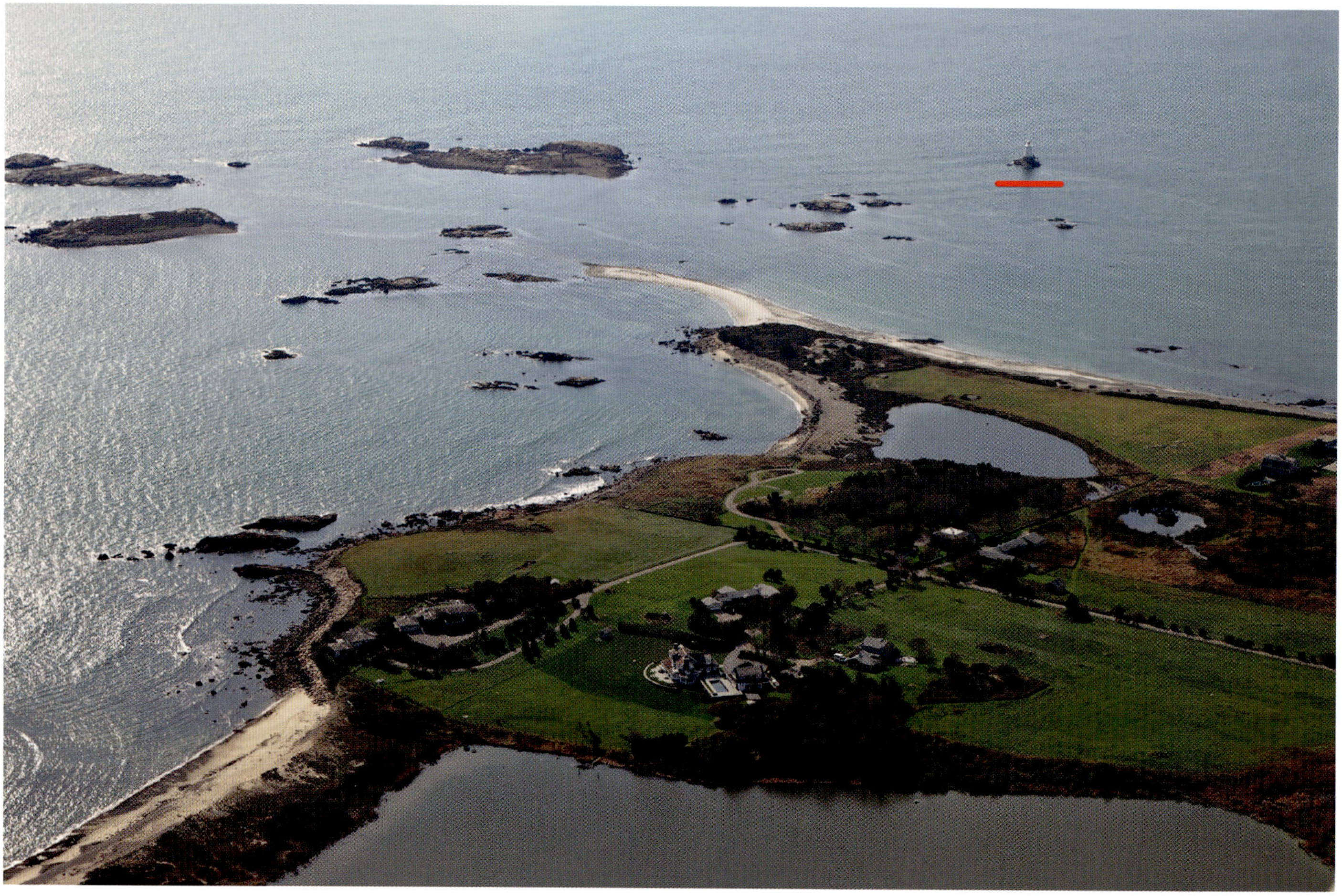

Top left and right: These two aerial images were captured more than a half century apart; note the differences when the tower was an active station. *(Black-and-white image courtesy of USCG)*

Bottom: Locate the lighthouse in this aerial image of the tip of Sakonnet.

WEST PASSAGE

Ships sailing to Providence had two choices; to the left of Conanicut Island was/is the West Passage and to the right of the island was/is the East Passage. The West Passage passes three harbors: Dutch, Wickford, and Warwick. In the past, this channel would have been busy with ferries from Wickford, Providence, and Fall River carrying tourists to their destinations. Now pleasure craft and commercial shipping boats ply the waterway.

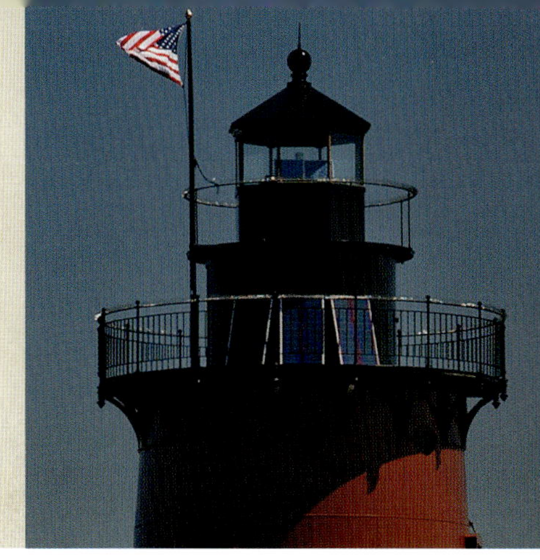

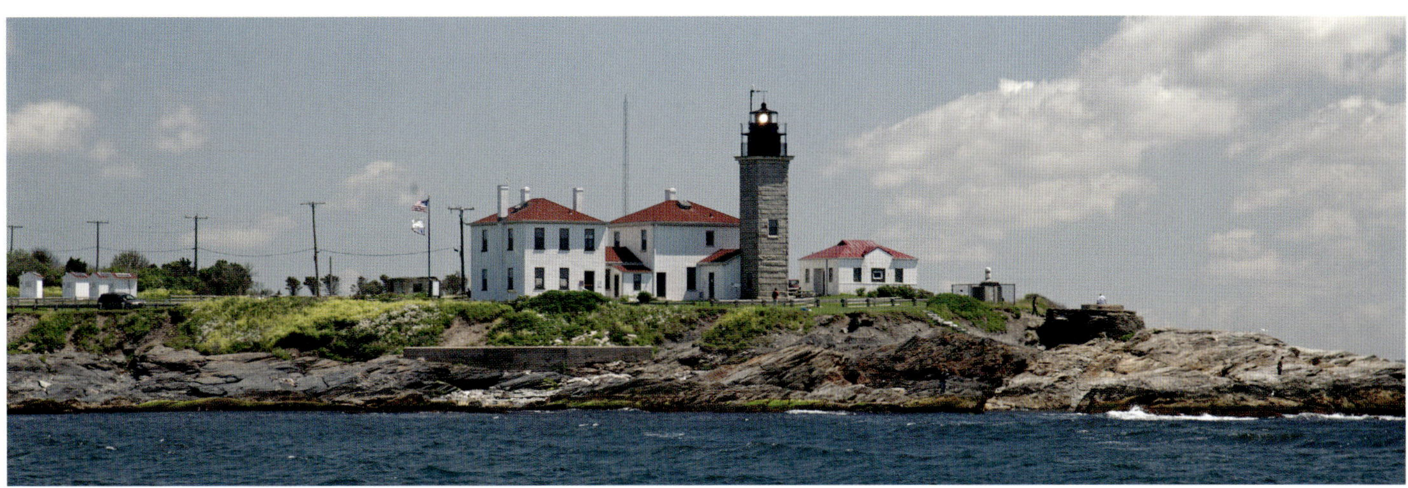

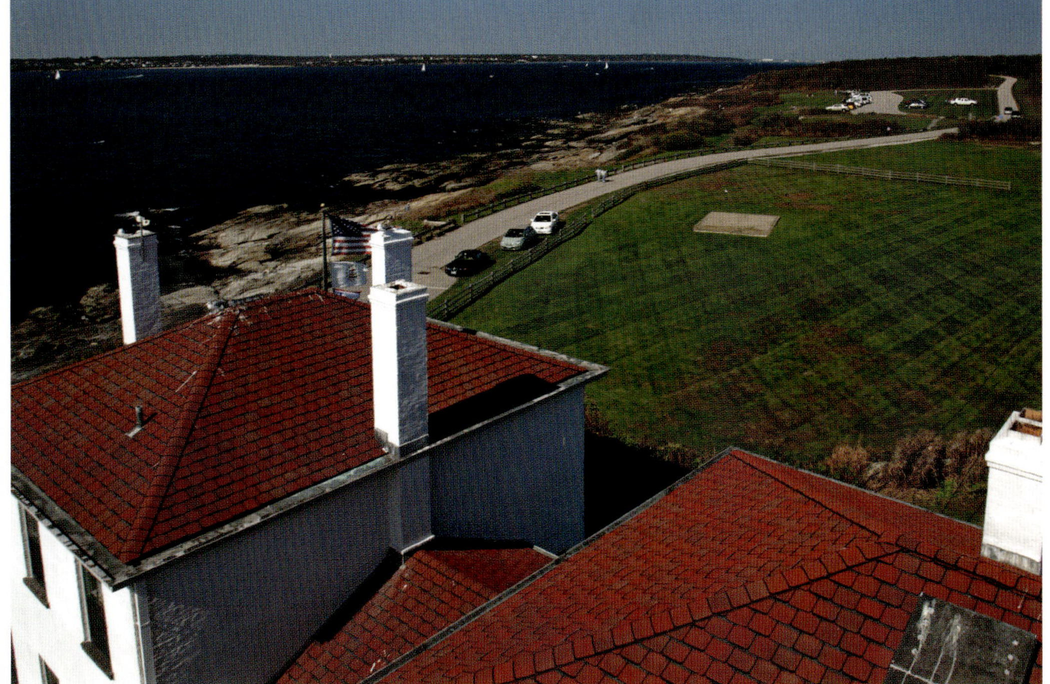

Above: Beavertail Light at the southern tip of Conanicut Island provides mariners with a signal that will determine their course to navigate; if the vessel sails to the left, it enters the West Passage.

Left: Taken from the lantern room at Beavertail Light, this is a view, looking west of north, in the direction that vessels would sail to reach, for instance, Wickford Harbor. Whale Rock Light, before 1938, would have been farther to the left and is not visible in this perspective. Narragansett is on the far shore.

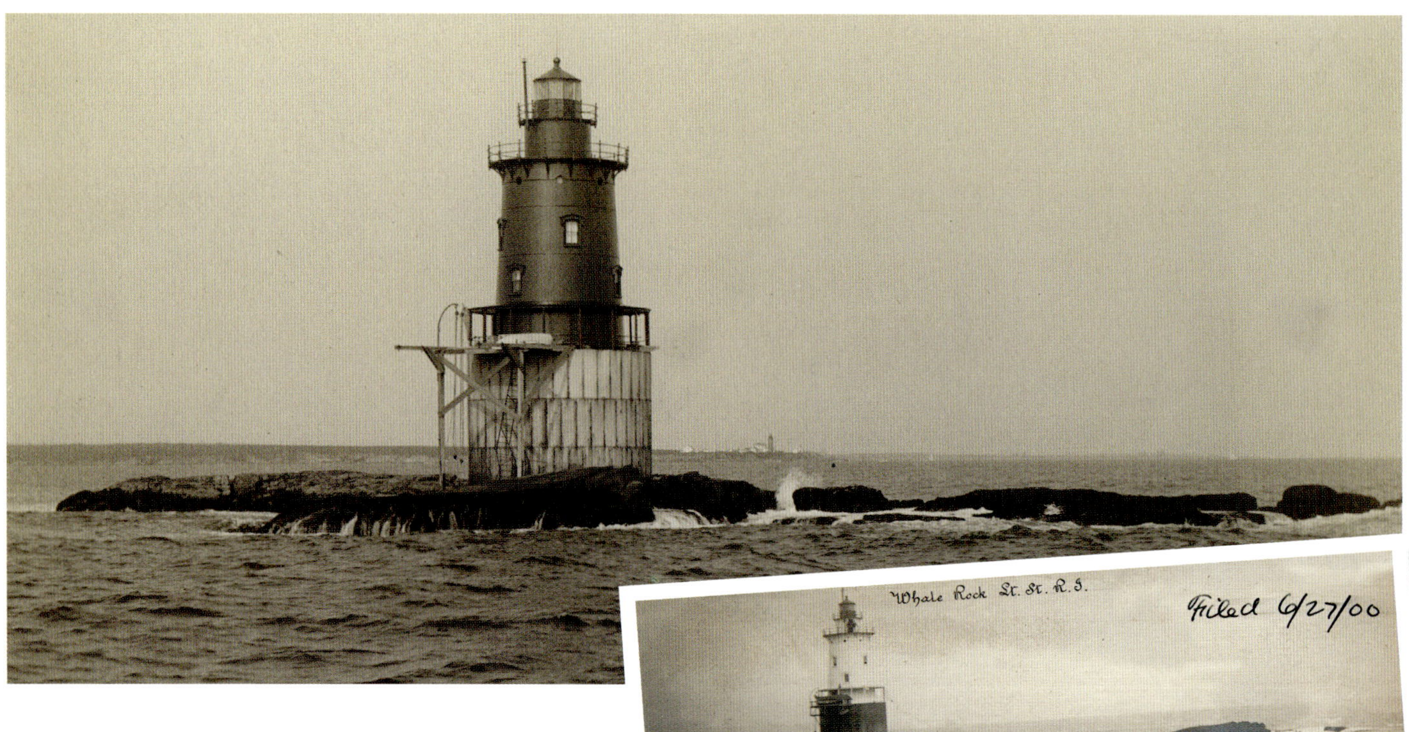

Top: This photograph, like the bottom postcard's, is undated. The view taken by the photographer is due east; Beavertail Light can be seen in the distance. *(Courtesy of NA)*

Above: Many archival images lack pertinent data; but in this case we know the identity of the aid as well as an approximate date the photograph was captured. In some cases, the identity of the photographer is also known. *(Courtesy of NA)*

WHALE ROCK

Location: Rocky ledge, offshore from Narragansett, N41°26′38″, W71°25′23″. Station no longer exists

Appropriation: Unknown, March 1881

Established: October 1892

Destroyed: Hurricane of 21 September 1938 toppled tower

Replaced: Lighted gong buoy, flashing green every 4 seconds (Fl G 4s)

Tower: White, conical, cast-iron, black lantern room

Other Structures: None

Original Lens: 1883 4th order Fresnel lens, fixed red (FR), focal plane 73 feet

Present Lens: N/A

Light Characteristics: N/A

Fog Signal, original: Machine struck bell, double blow every 20 seconds

Status: Only base remains on rocky ledge

Access: Base, rocky ledge best seen from boat.

Comments: In 2004, archeological divers discovered the remnants of the tower littered across the sea floor.

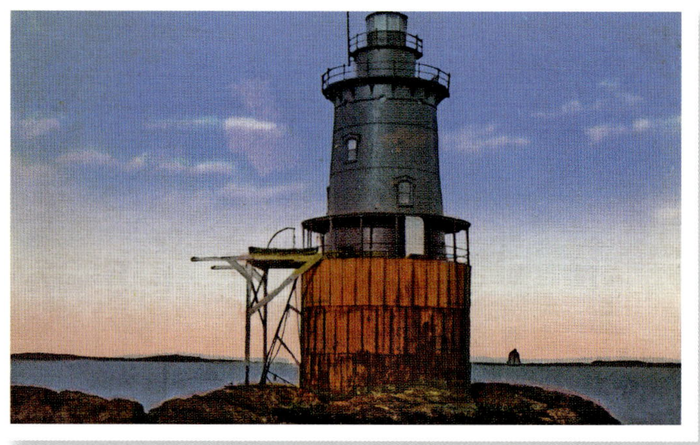

This image, on an unused postcard, was probably taken after the previous image. Early in the 20th century, towers were painted dark colors to serve as better day markers. But, because of excessive condensation and the increase of interior temperatures, it was decided to paint the towers white.

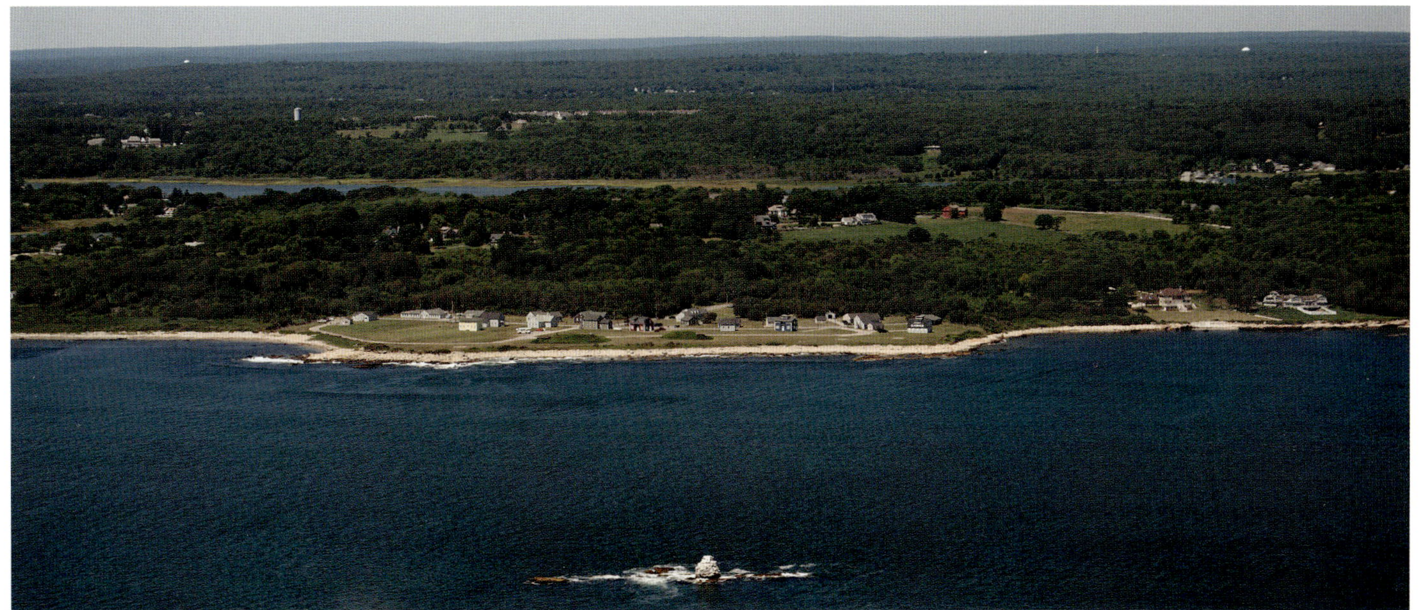

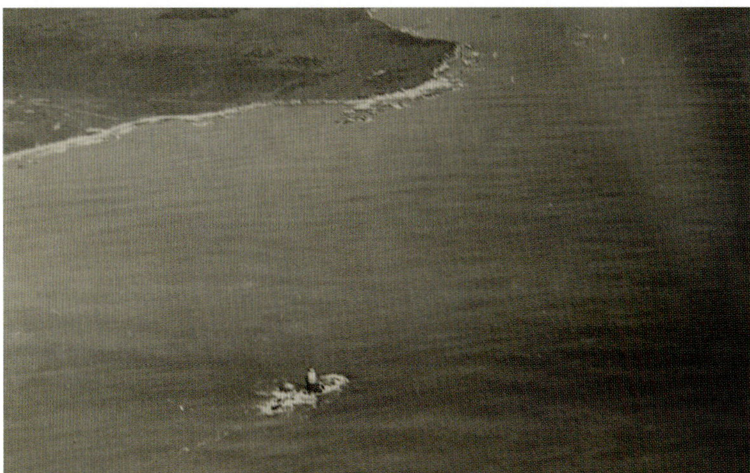

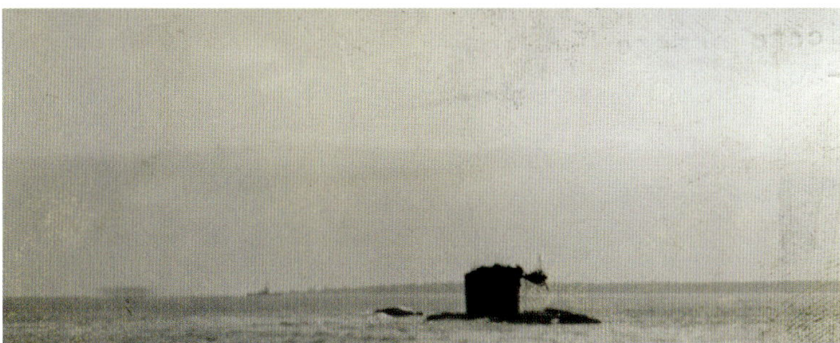

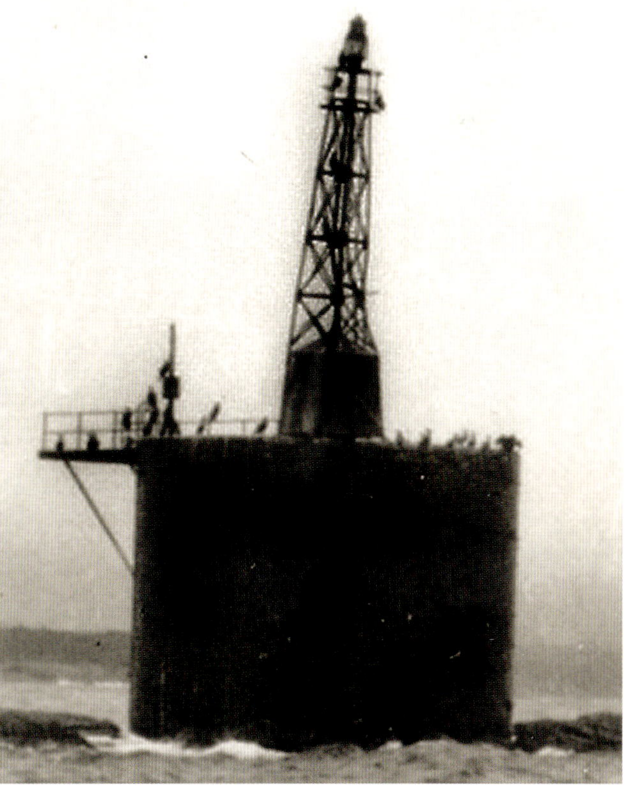

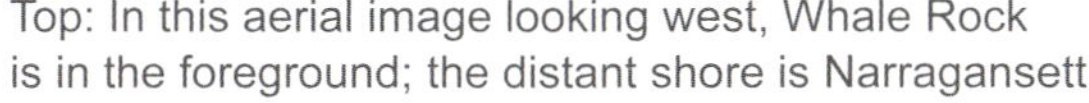

Top: In this aerial image looking west, Whale Rock is in the foreground; the distant shore is Narragansett.

Center left: An aerial view of Whale Rock Light captured before the hurricane of September 1938. *(Courtesy of USCG)*

Bottom left: Shortly after the hurricane, all that remained of Whale Rock Light was the base. *(Courtesy of USCG)*

Bottom right: After the hurricane and with only the base remaining, a skeleton tower was erected and, using acetylene as a fuel, a light provided an aid to mariners. *(Courtesy of USCG)*

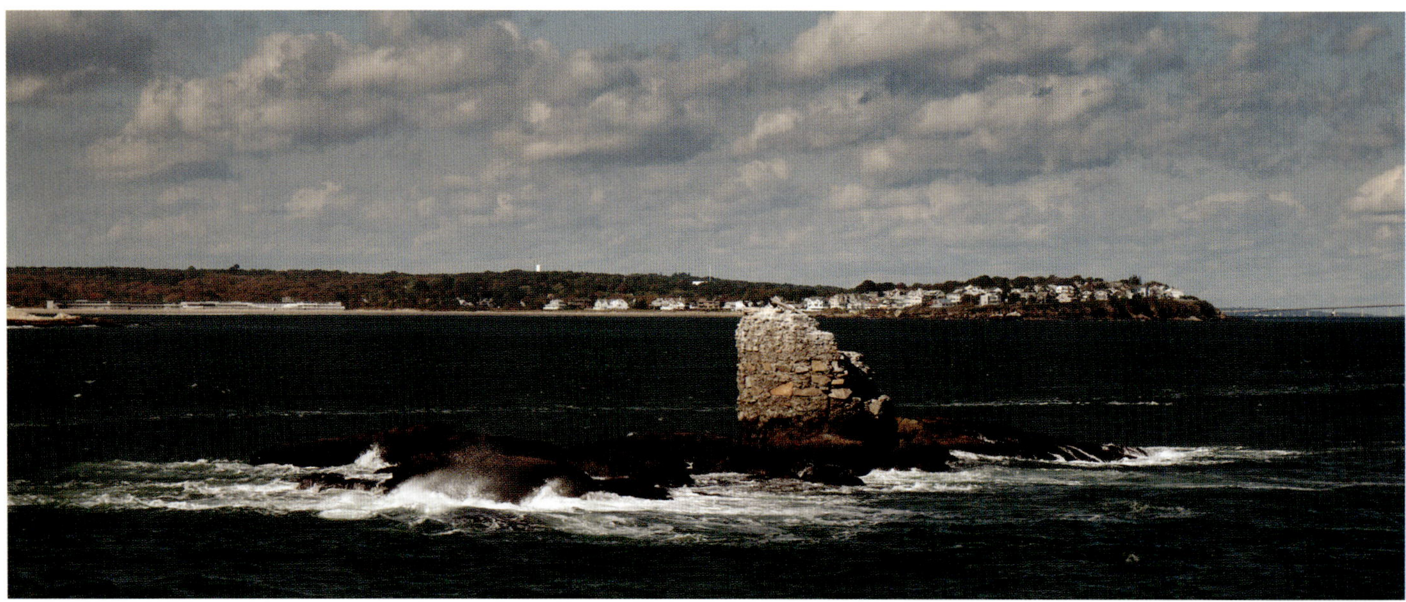

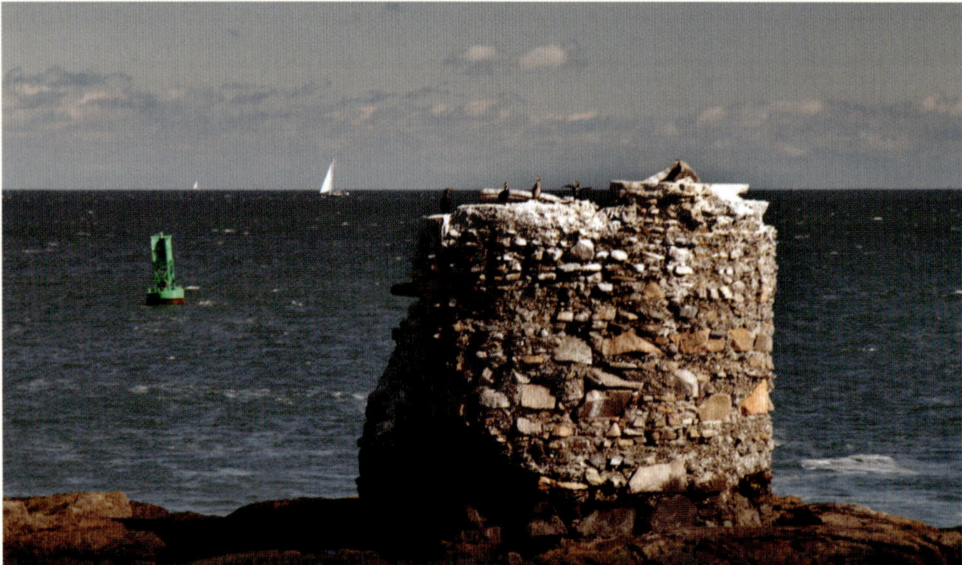

Top: Looking north, only the base remains of Whale Rock Light. Note, barely visible, the Jamestown-Verrazano Bridge in the background.

Center: Looking south at the slowly crumbling base of the Whale Rock Light. Note the present-day buoy in the background; also, the sailboats common in these waters.

Bottom: A present-day close-up aerial image; the rocky ledge remains a hazard to navigation.

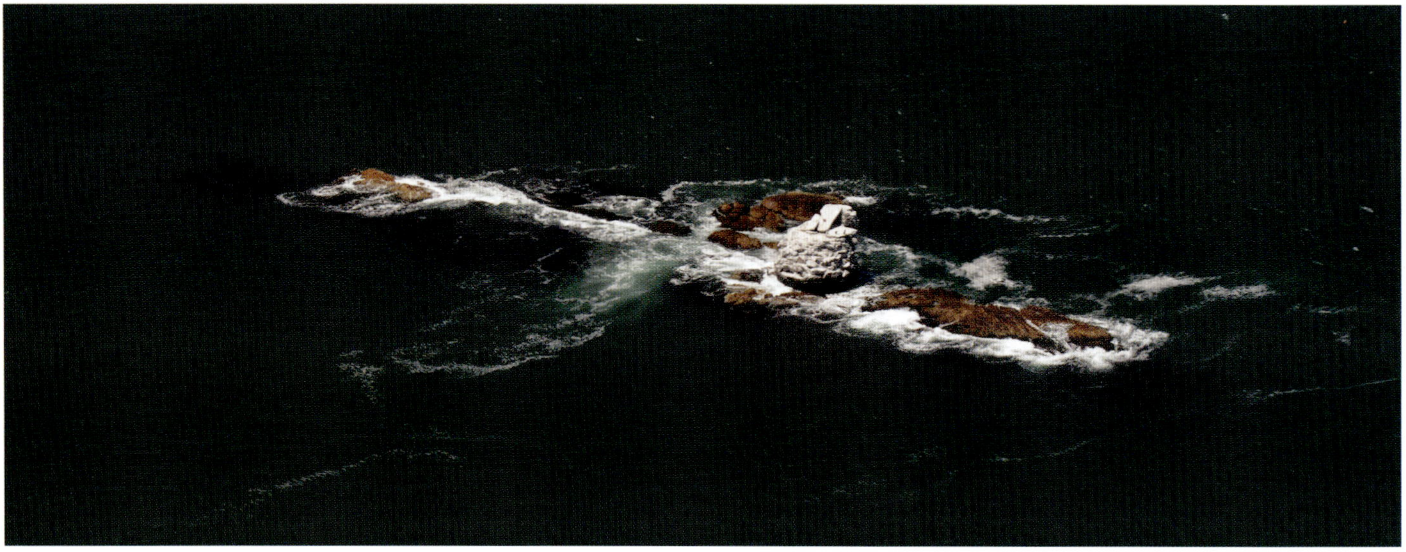

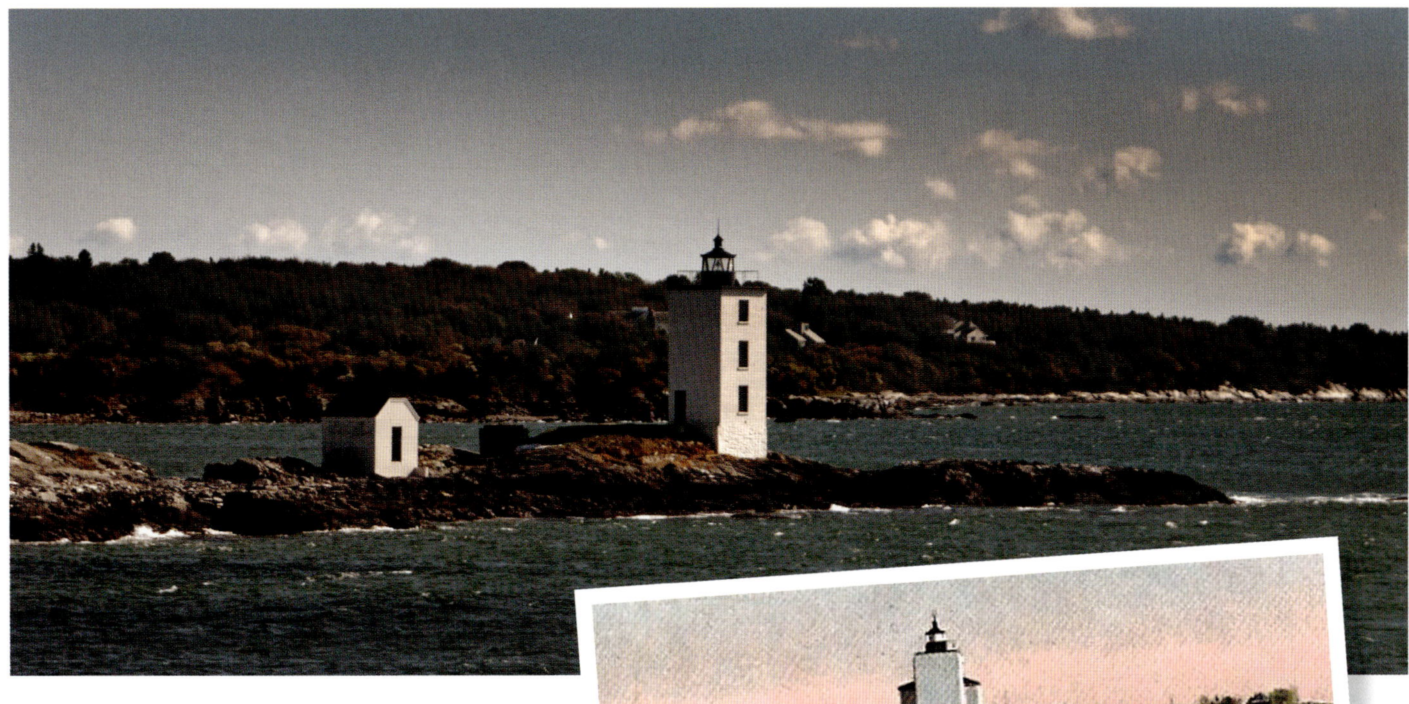

DUTCH ISLAND

Location: Dutch Island, Narragansett Bay, between Saunderstown and Jamestown, N41°29′48″, W71°24′16″

Appropriation: \$3,000 in March 1825; \$2,000 in March 1826

Established: 1826

Rebuilt: 1857

Disestablished: 1979

Rebuilt: 2007

Tower: Brick, square, white, 42 feet, black lantern room

Other Structures: Oil house; all others razed

Original Optics: 8 lamps and 14-inch reflectors

Original Lens: 1857, 4th order Fresnel lens, fixed white (FW), focal plane 56 feet

Present Lens: LED

Light Characteristics: Red, two seconds on, four seconds off (ALR 6s)

Range: 6–8 nm

Fog Signal: 1891, fog bell struck by machine every 15 seconds

Status: Private aid to navigation

Access: Not open to the public.

Comments: Maintained by Dutch Island Lighthouse Society, a chapter of the American Lighthouse Foundation.

Top: Looking southeast; all that remains of the original station are the tower and the oil house.

Above: An old postcard of the station. Now, the houses in the background no longer exist and that area is mostly treed.

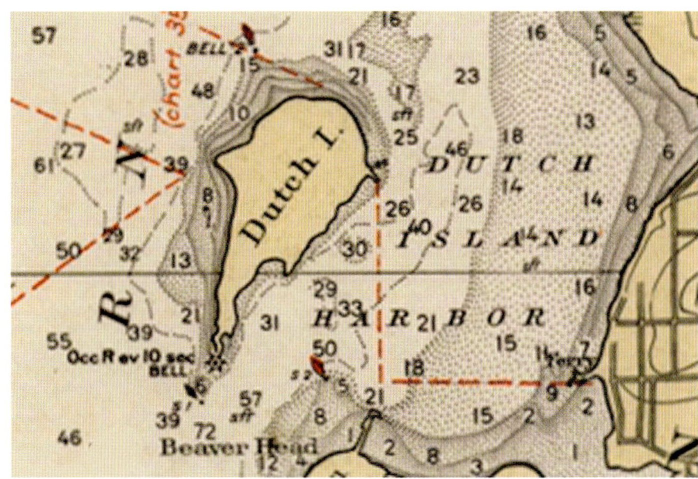

This 1930 chart of Dutch Island and the nearby harbor designates the light at the southern tip. The light characteristic is occluded red every 10 seconds; a bell is also present. *(Courtesy of NOAA)*

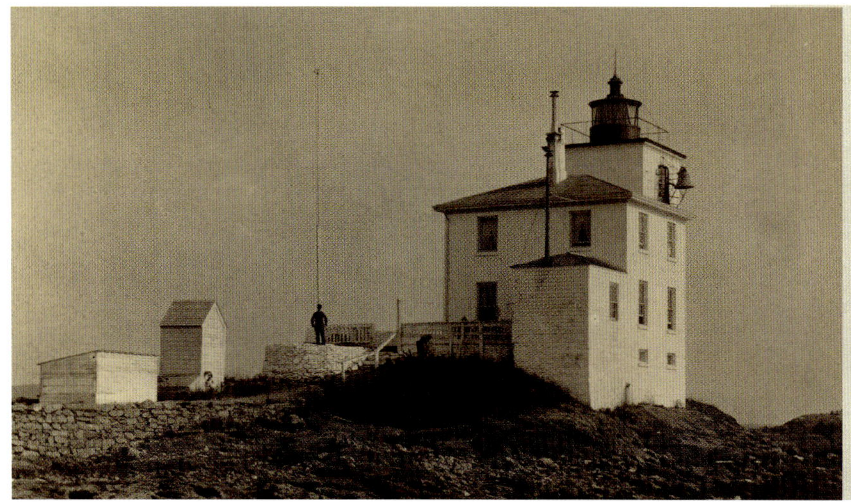

Top: The lighthouse station in 1884.
Is that the keeper on the walkway?
(Courtesy of NA)

Center: The Dutch Island station in 1939.
(Courtesy of DILS)

Bottom: Before restoration,
the Dutch Island tower and oil house.
(Courtesy of D. Zapatka)

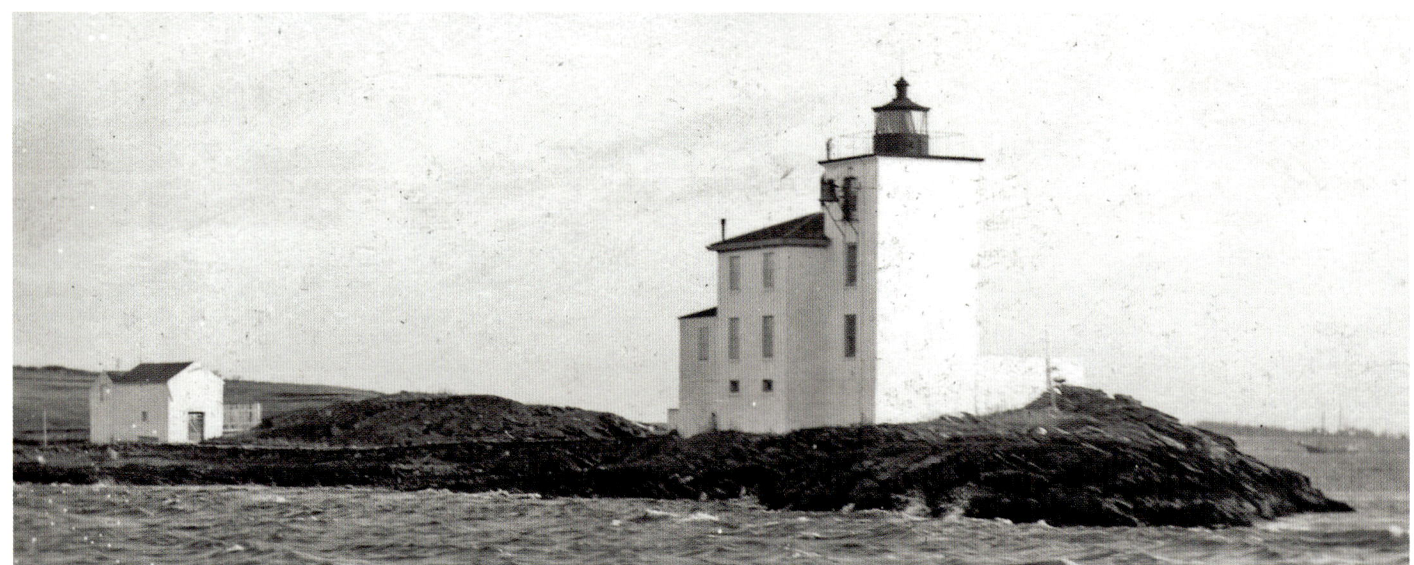

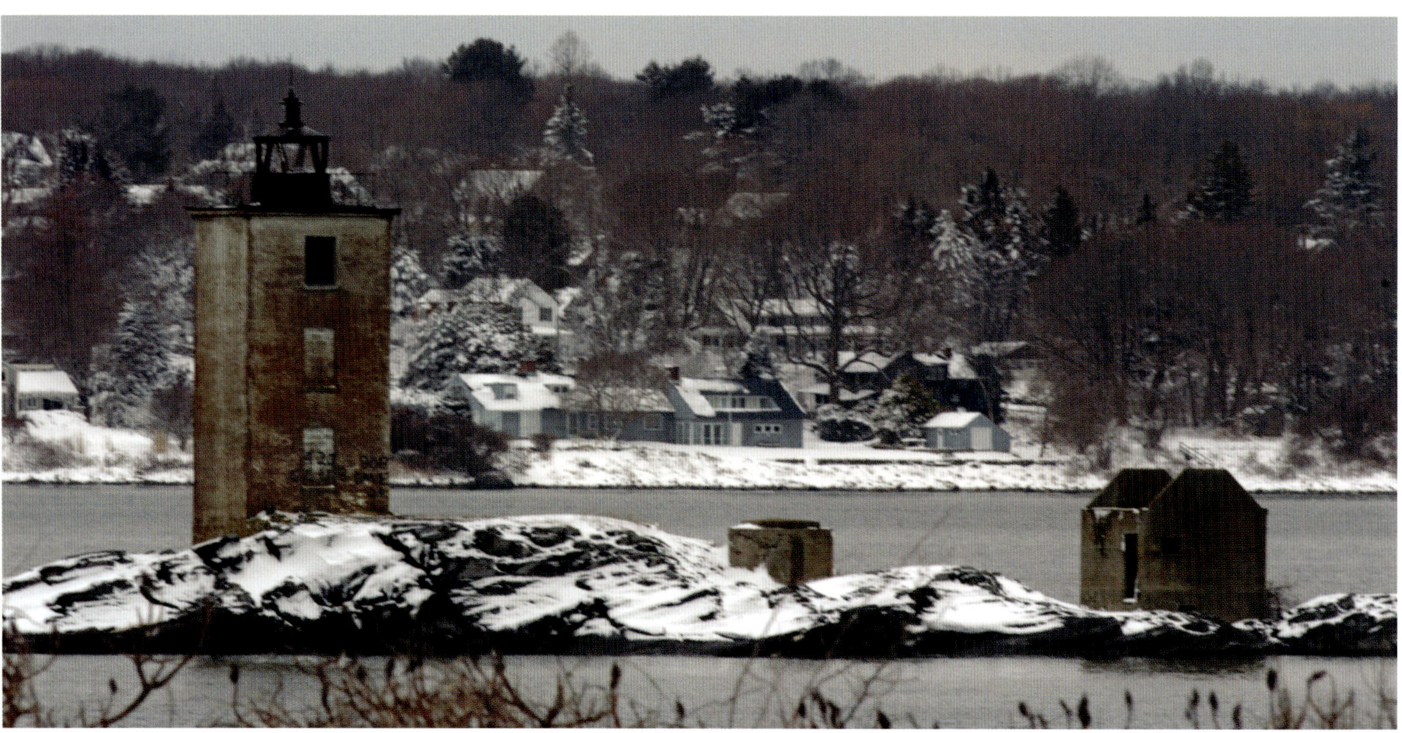

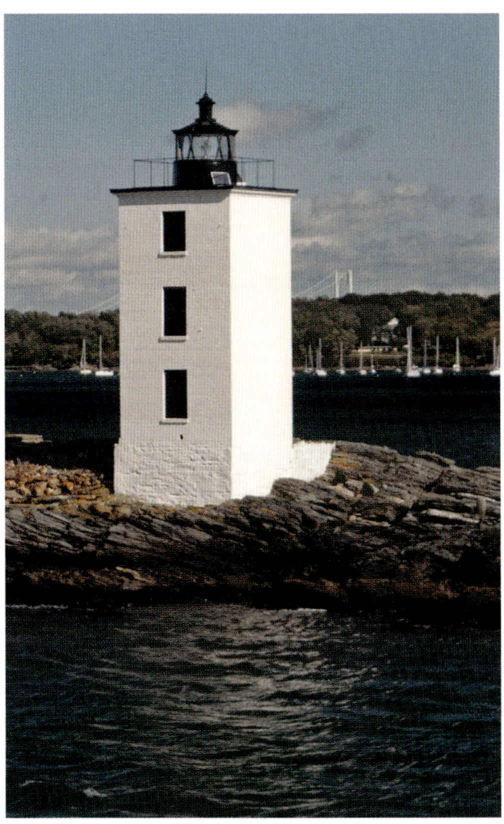

Top: A view of the tower with the harbor in the background.

Center left: Looking north from the tower with the oil house in the foreground. *(Courtesy of D. Zapatka)*

Center right: An aerial view of the tower and oil house; find their location on the previous chart.

Bottom: Looking north towards Wickford, the Dutch Island tower is in the foreground. In the background is the Jamestown-Verrazano Bridge; to the left is Plum Beach Light. Navigators would plot their course and sail from one aid to the next. Compare this shot with the previous postcard, which showed houses and cleared land.

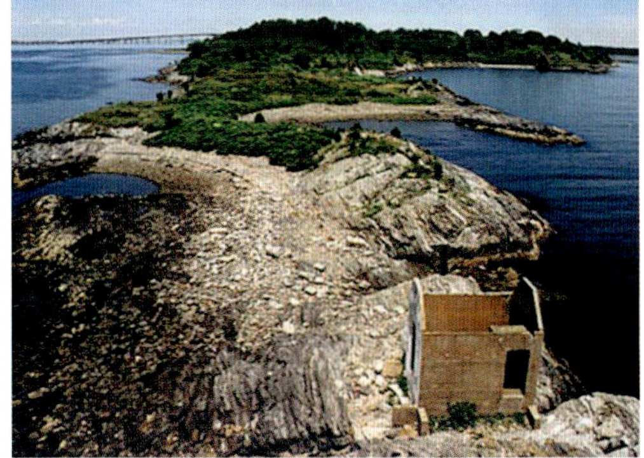

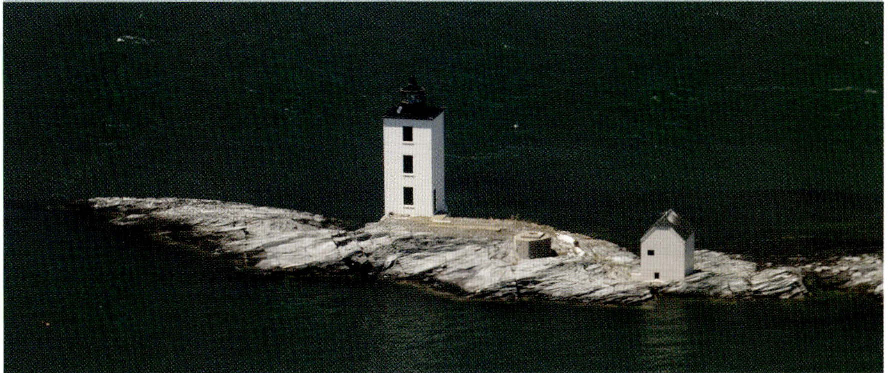

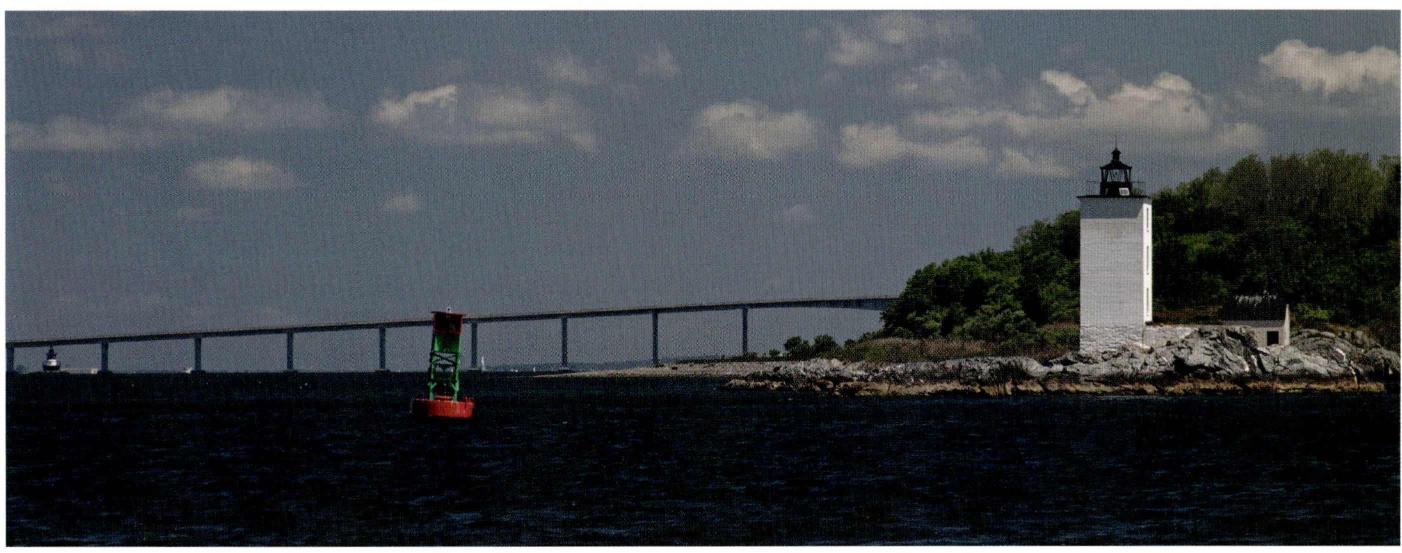

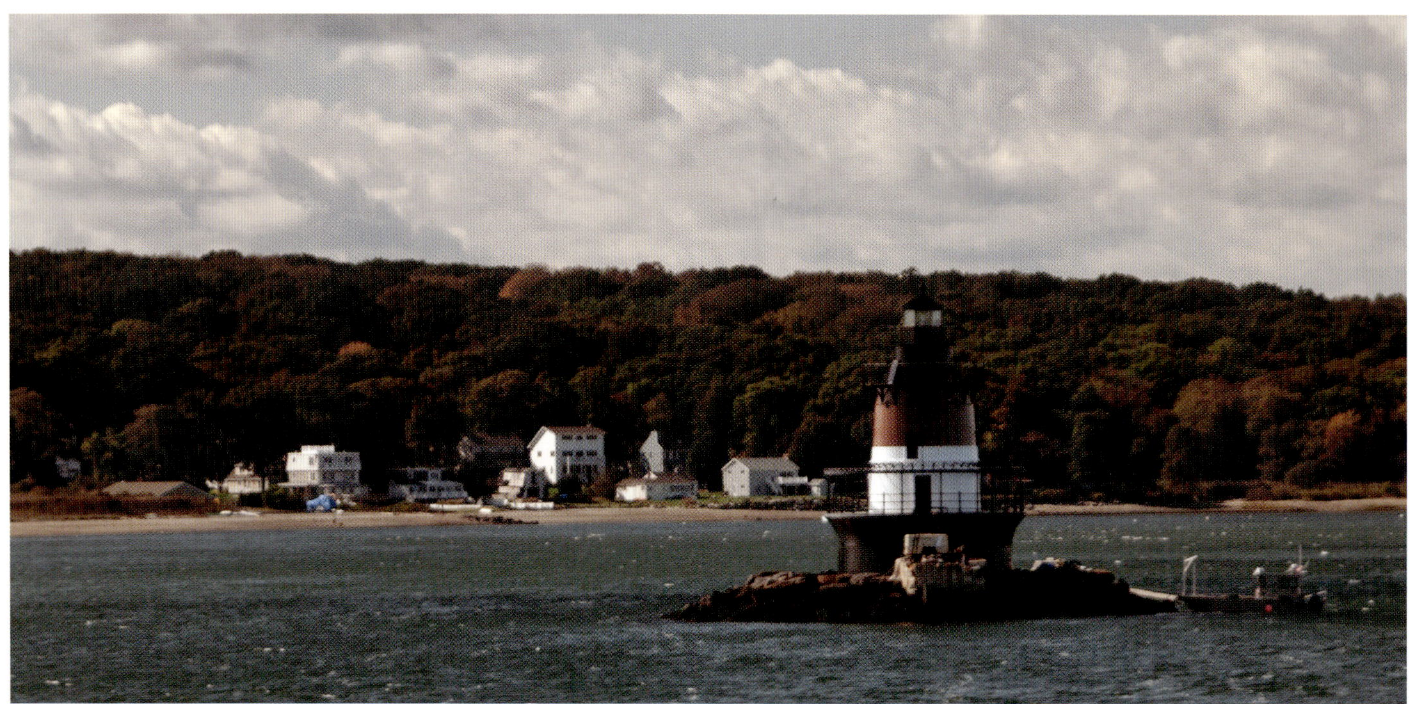

PLUM BEACH

Location: Offshore between Saunderstown and Jamestown, N41°31′49″, W71°24′19″

Appropriation: $20,000 in 1895; $40,000 in 1896; $9,000 in 1898

Established: February 1897

Disestablished: 1941, replaced by Jamestown-Verrazano Bridge lights

Relit: 2003

Tower: Conical, red over white band, spark plug design, 53 feet, black lantern room

Original Lens: 1899 4th order Fresnel lens, focal plane 54 feet

Present Lens: LED, solar-powered

Light Characteristics: Flashing white every 5 seconds (Fl W 5s)

Range: 4 nm

Fog Signal, original: Machine struck bell

Status: Private aid to navigation

Access: None; best seen by boat.

Comments: Owned and maintained by Friends of Plum Beach Lighthouse, Inc.; featured on a state motor vehicle license plate.

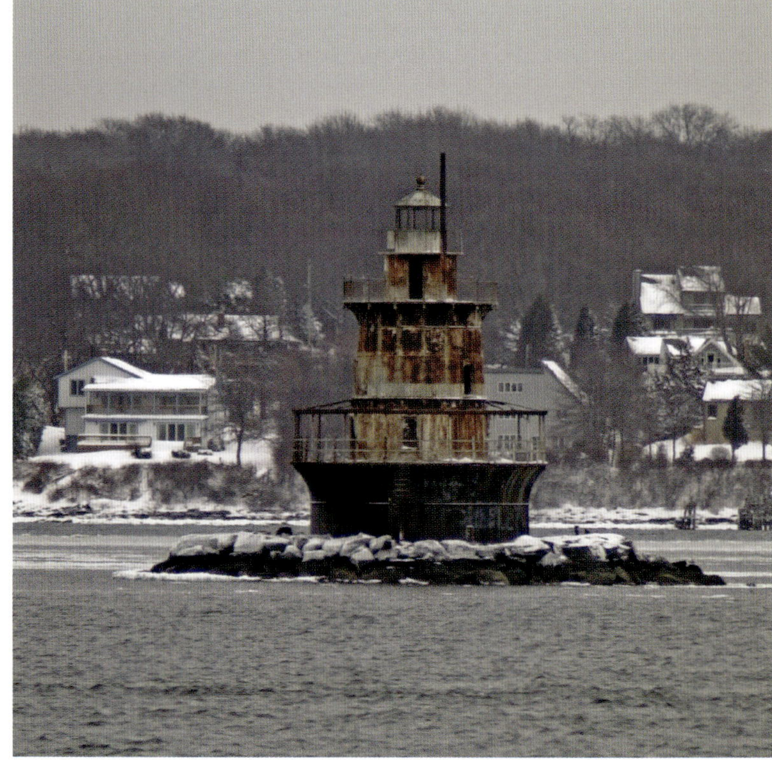

Two views, two seasons, before and after restoration, with Plum Beach in the background. *(Pre-restoration image courtesy of D. Zapatka)*

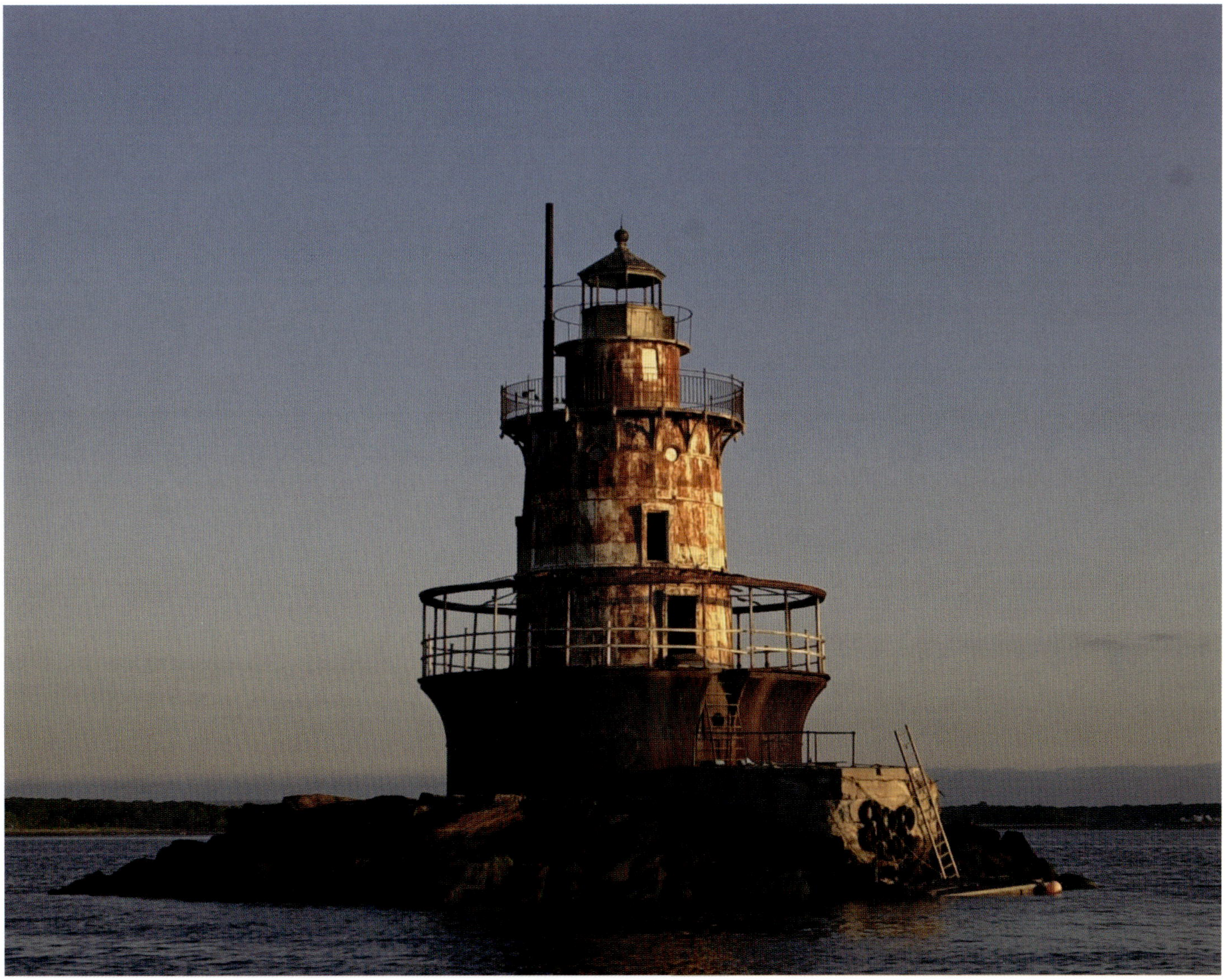

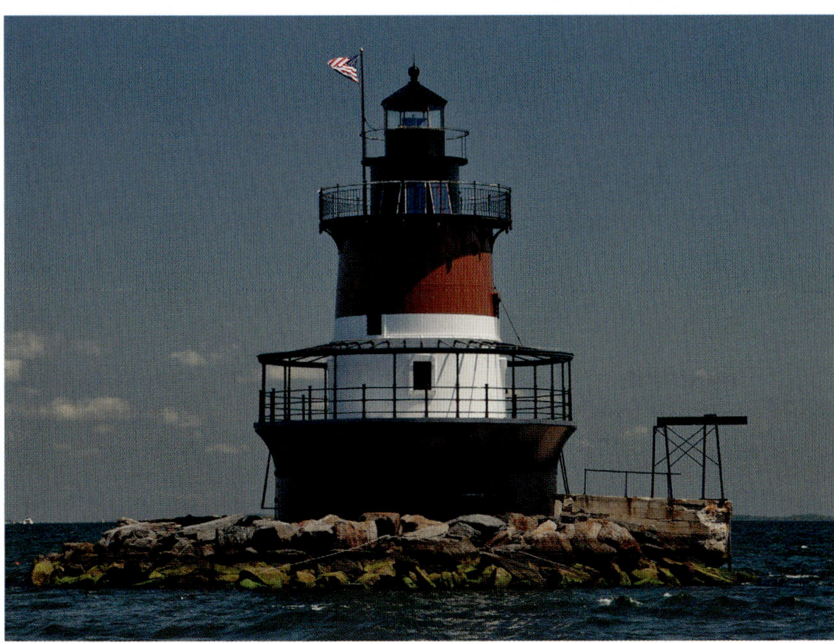

Compare these two images: *Above* Disestablished and abandoned in 1939 when the first bridge was built, the tower was in serious need of restoration. *Below* Now shown fully refurbished. *(Early image courtesy of D. Zapatka)*

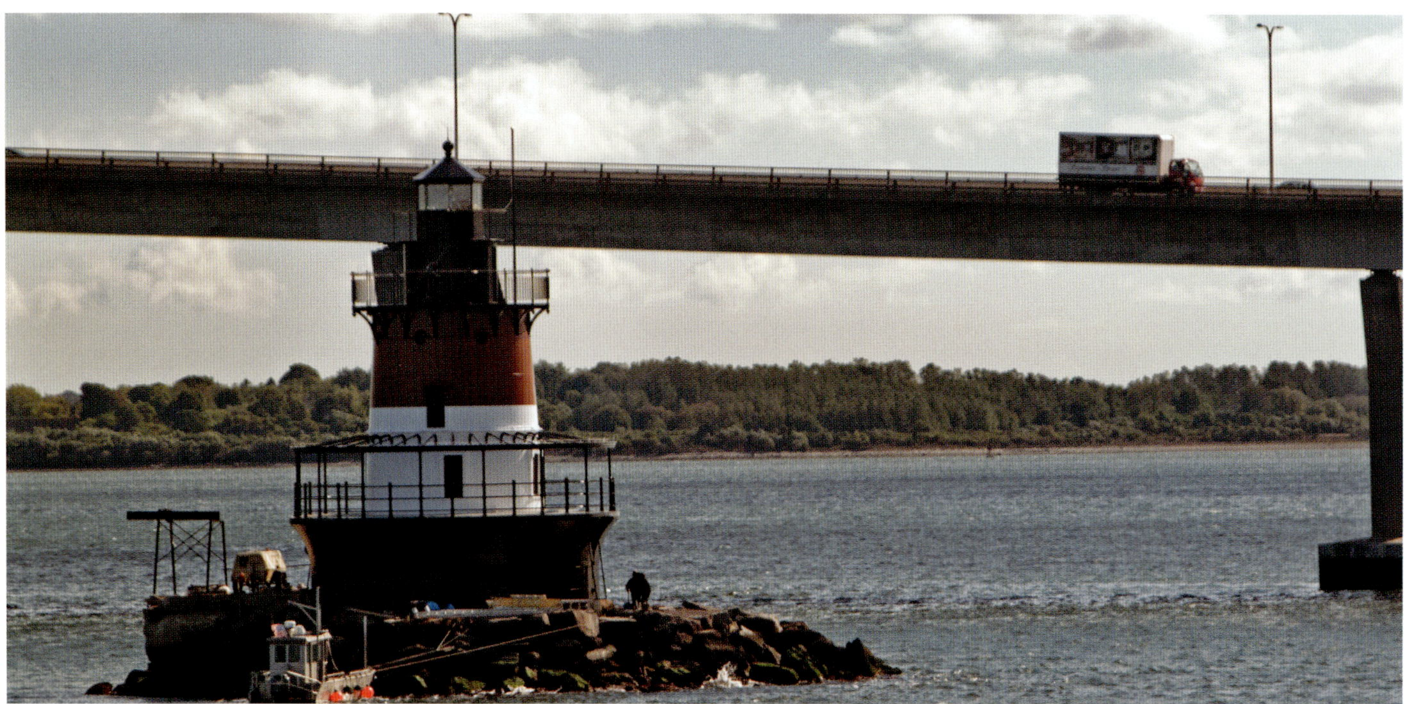

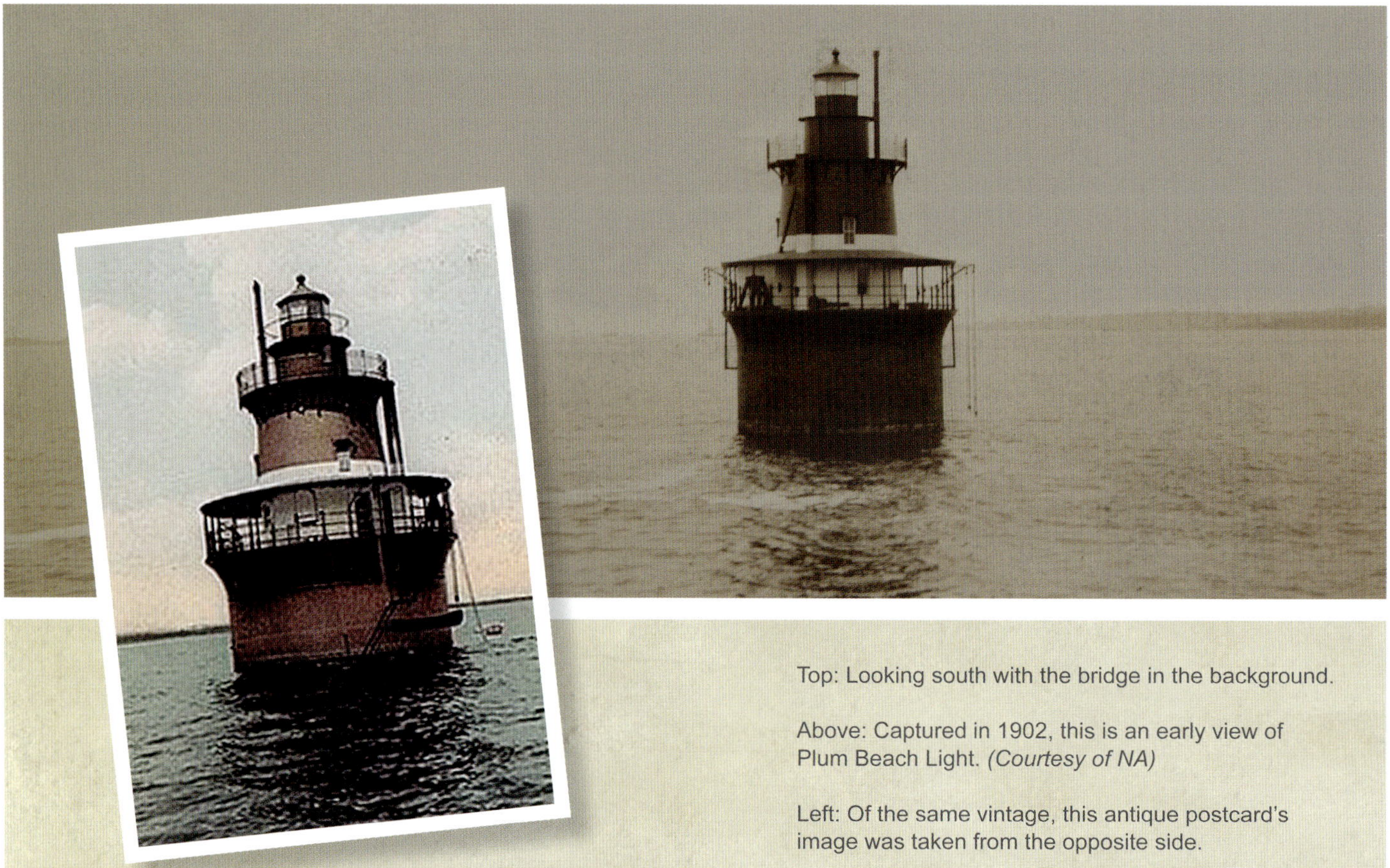

Top: Looking south with the bridge in the background.

Above: Captured in 1902, this is an early view of Plum Beach Light. *(Courtesy of NA)*

Left: Of the same vintage, this antique postcard's image was taken from the opposite side.

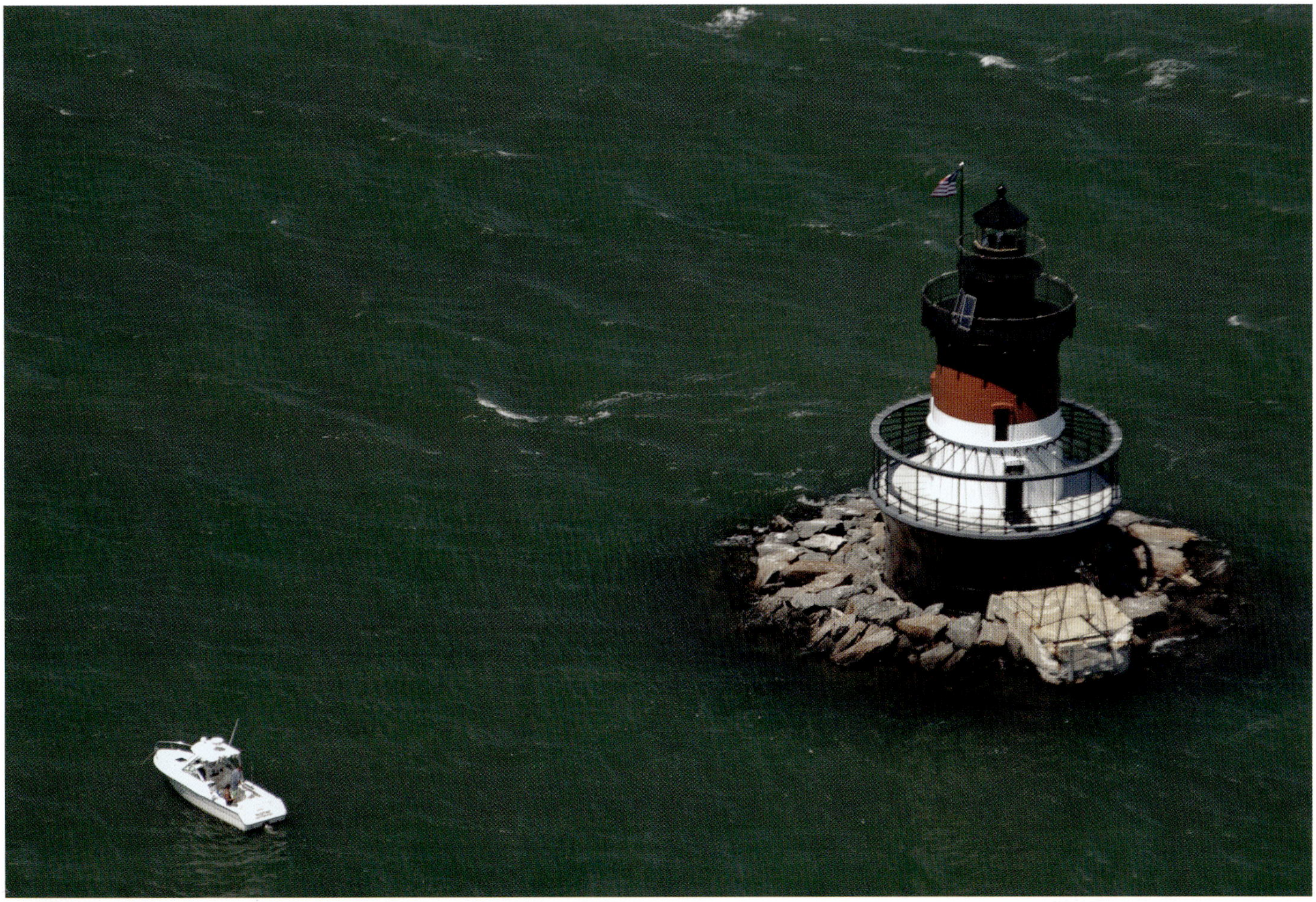

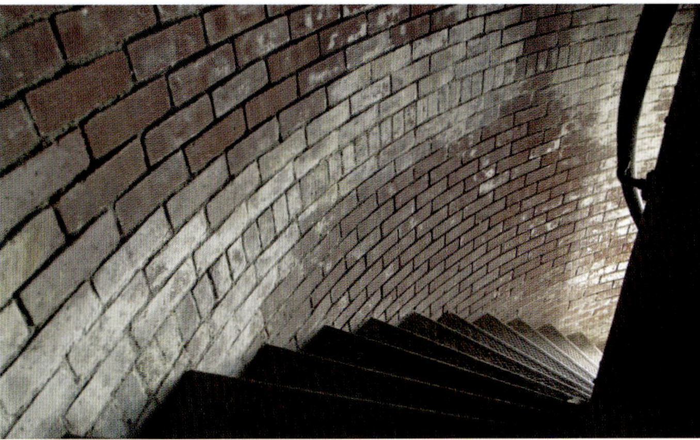

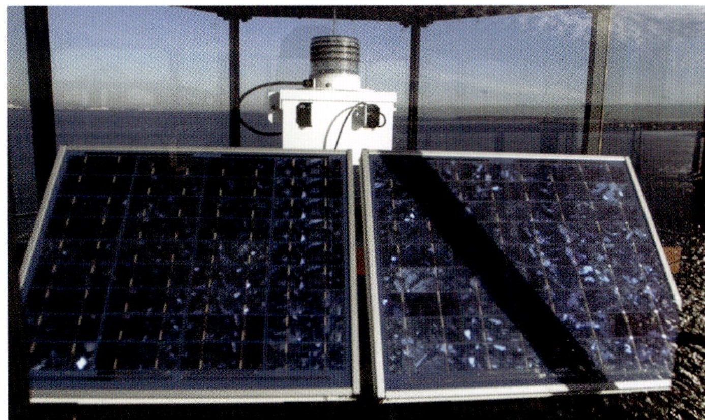

Top: A present-day aerial view; the rip-rap around the tower is popular with fishermen.

Left: Inside the brick-lined tower, a view looking down the stairs. *(Courtesy of D. Zapatka)*

Right: Inside the lantern room with the solar-powered lamp. A reflection of the bridge can be seen in the glass. *(Courtesy of D. Zapatka)*

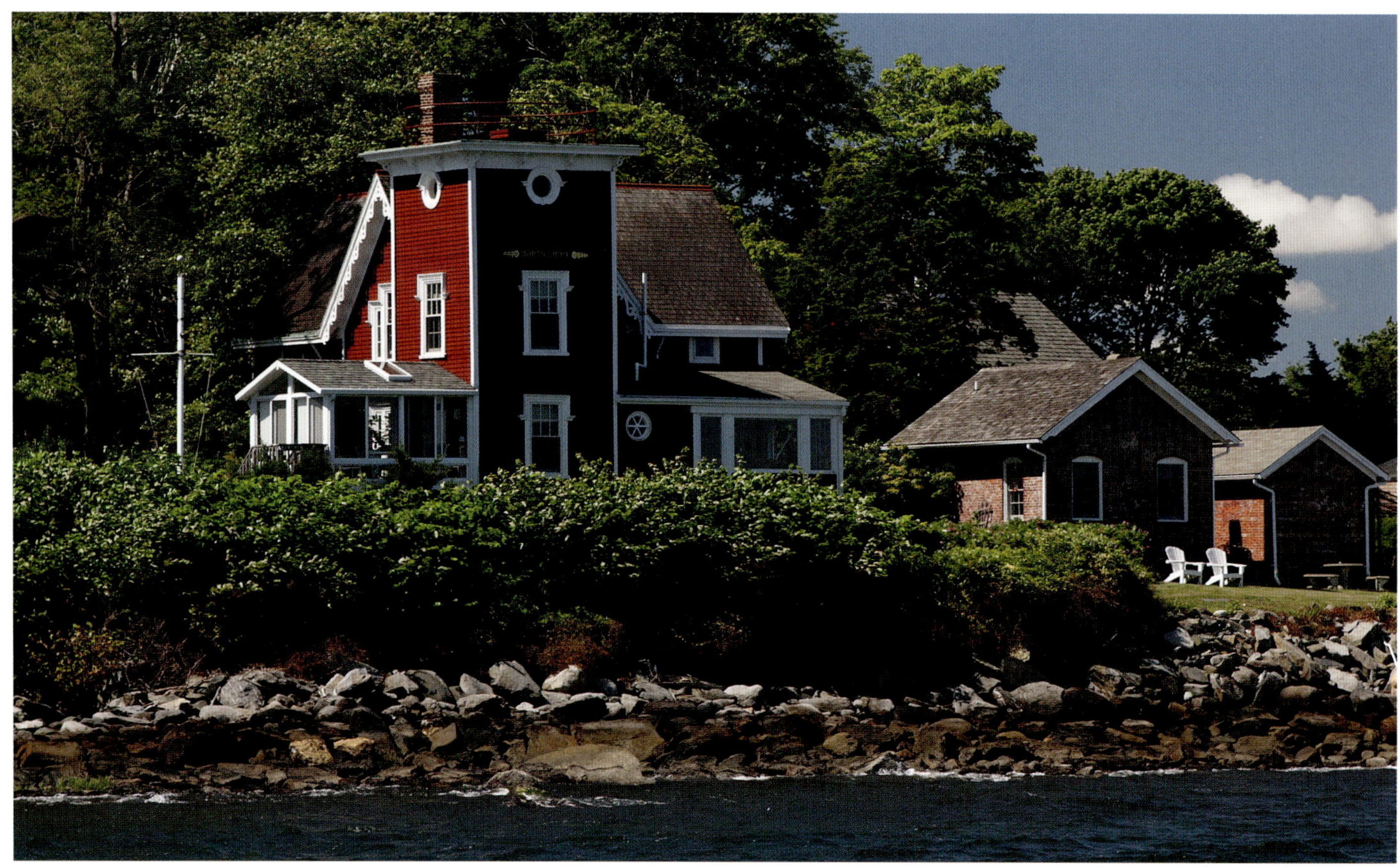

Several lighthouse cruises tour Narragansett Bay; this is a view from one of those.

CONANICUT

Location: Conanicut Island, northern tip, N41°34′25″, W71°22′18″

Appropriation: $18,000 in 1884

Established: April 1886

Disestablished: 1933

Tower: Square, wood tower, 30 feet, an integral part of six-room Victorian keeper's house

Other Structures: Oil house, fog signaling building, garage

Original Lens: 1891, 5th order Fresnel lens, fixed white (FW), focal plane 47 feet, range 8 miles; 1907, 5th order Fresnel lens, fixed red (FW)

Present Lens: N/A

Light Characteristics: N/A

Range: N/A

Fog Signal, original: 1891, double blow every 30 seconds; 1903, compressed air siren, 3-second blast, 17-second interval

Status: No longer active station; private residence; tower present; no lantern room; no optics

Access: None.

Comments: Replaced by skeleton tower in 1933, fixed red (FR), which was torn down in 1982.

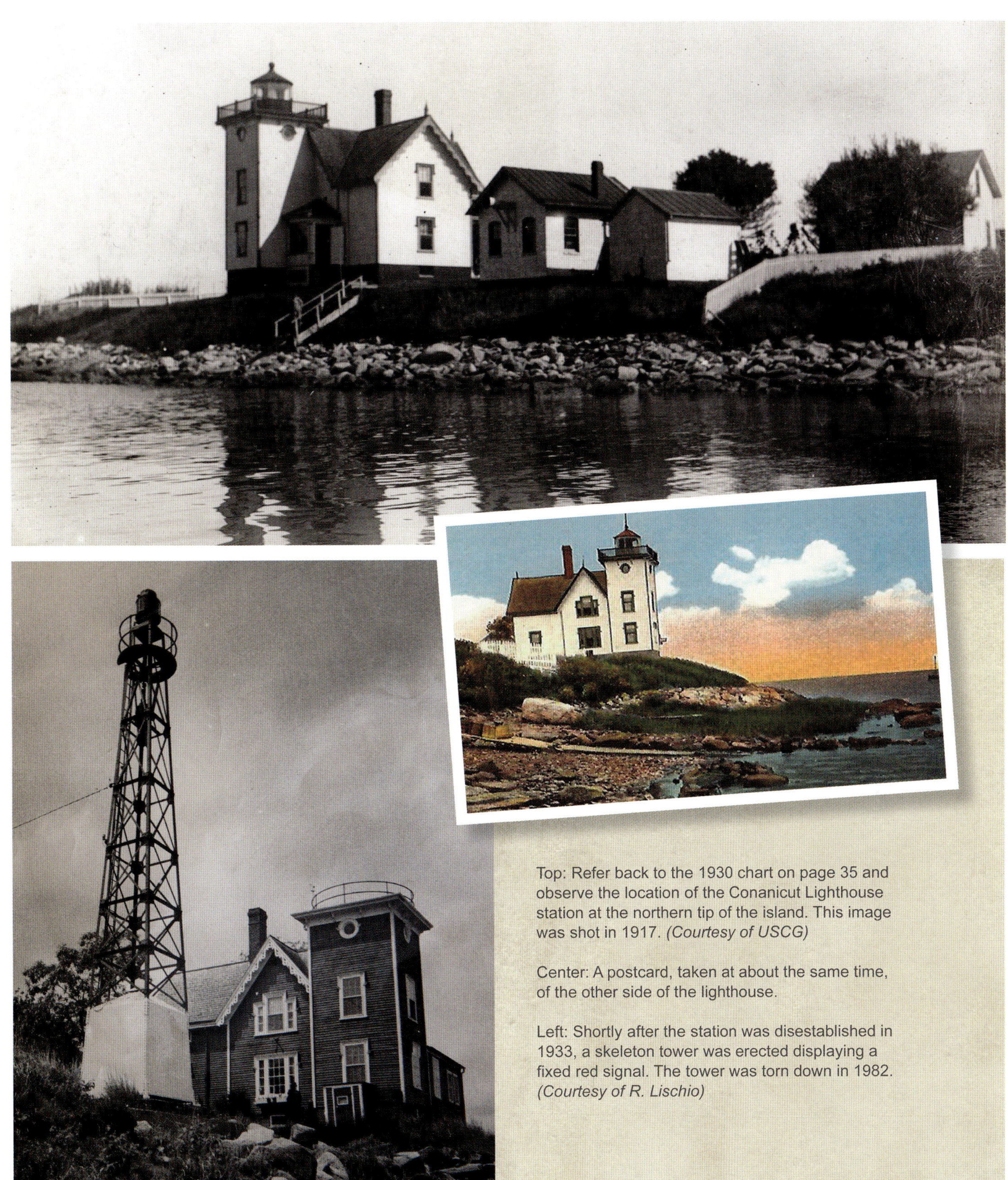

Top: Refer back to the 1930 chart on page 35 and observe the location of the Conanicut Lighthouse station at the northern tip of the island. This image was shot in 1917. *(Courtesy of USCG)*

Center: A postcard, taken at about the same time, of the other side of the lighthouse.

Left: Shortly after the station was disestablished in 1933, a skeleton tower was erected displaying a fixed red signal. The tower was torn down in 1982. *(Courtesy of R. Lischio)*

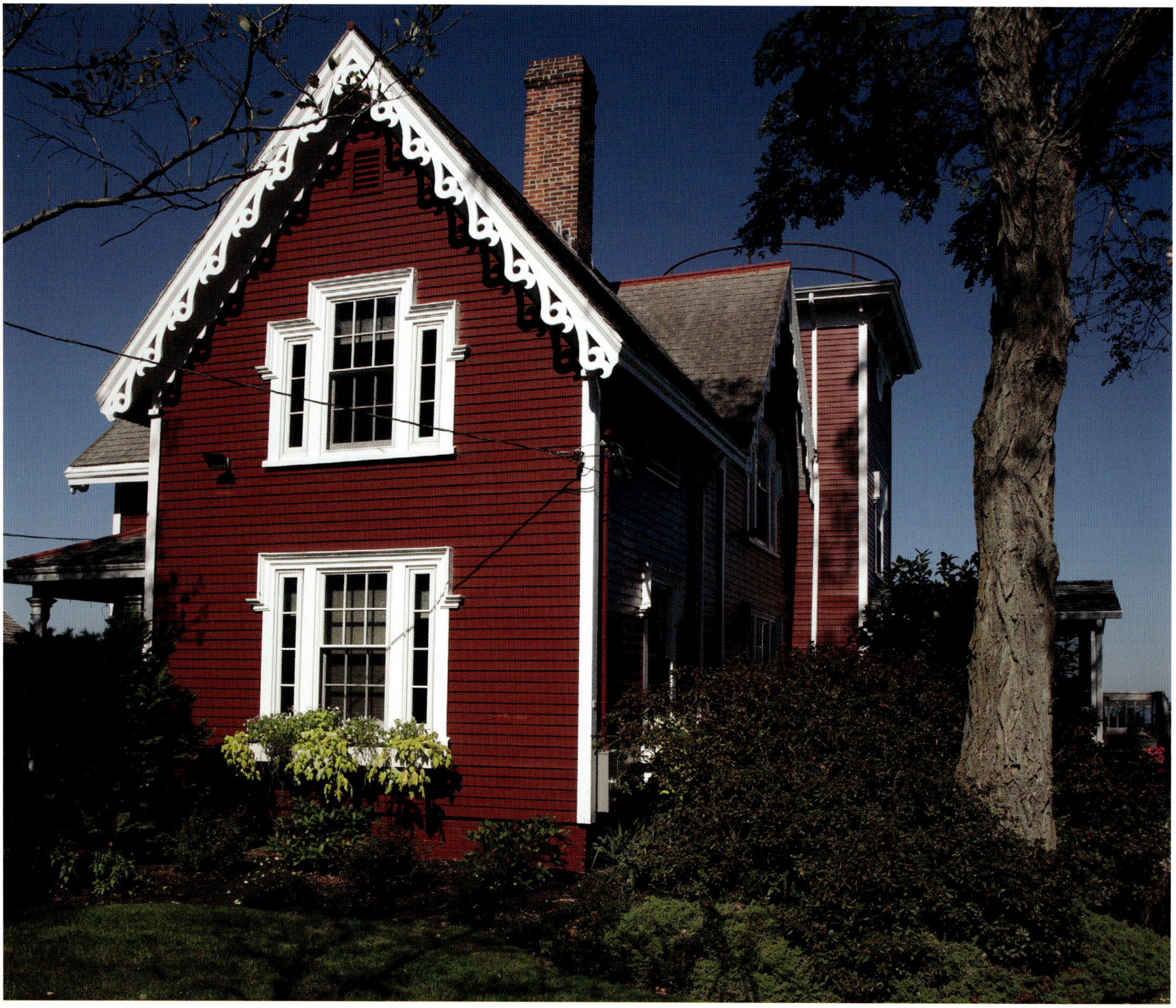

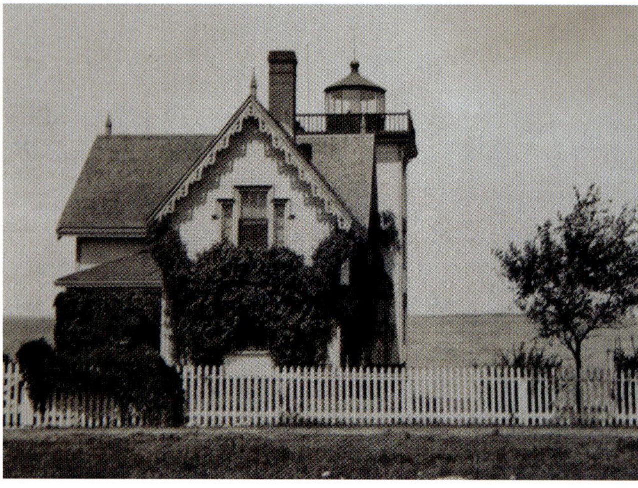

Compare these two views of Conanicut when it was an active light (pre-1933) and now. *(Black-and-white image courtesy of R. Lischio)*

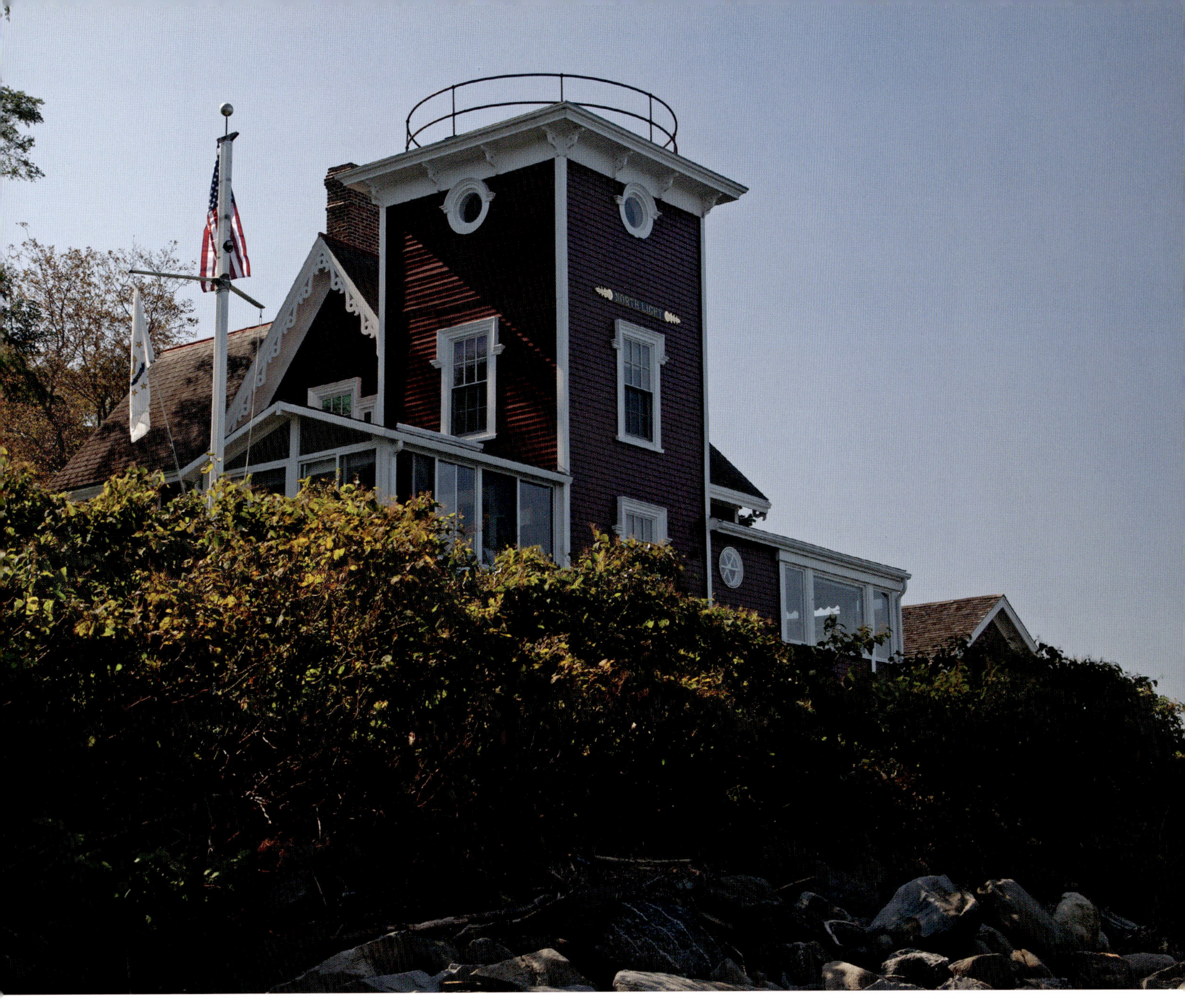

A view of the tower from the rocky shoreline.

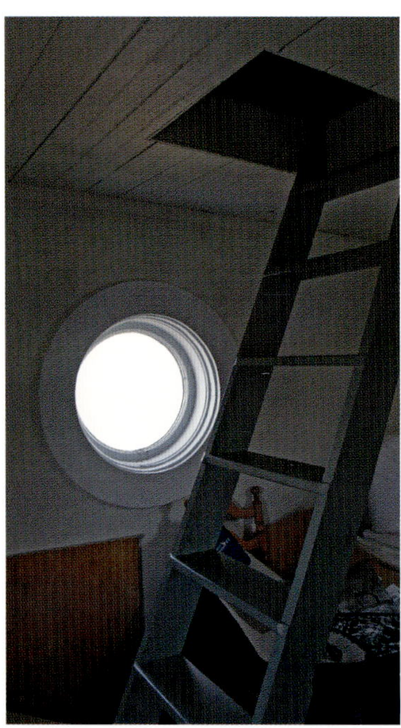

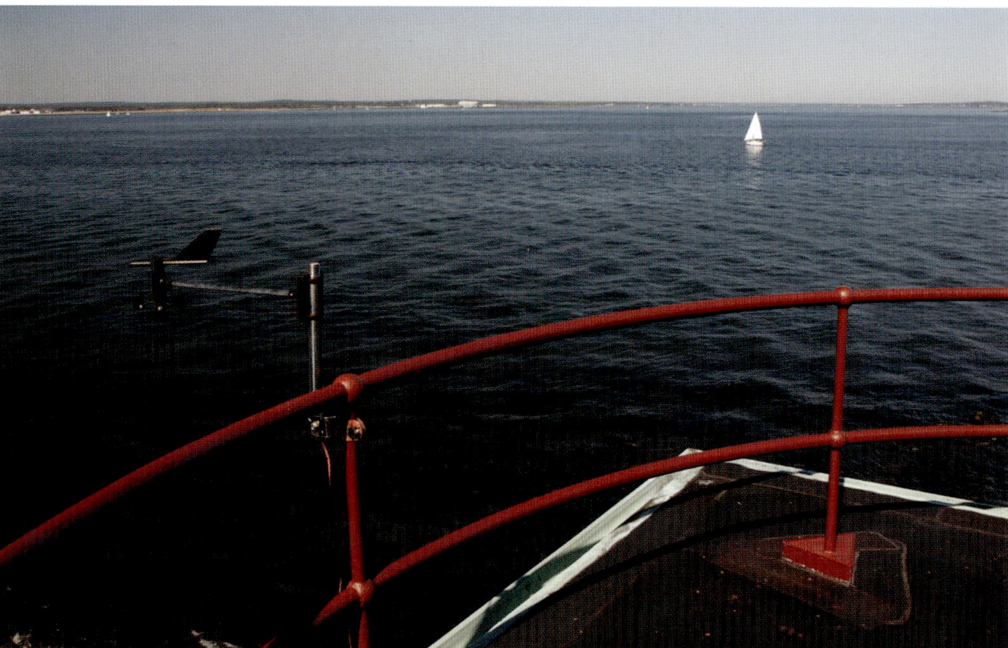

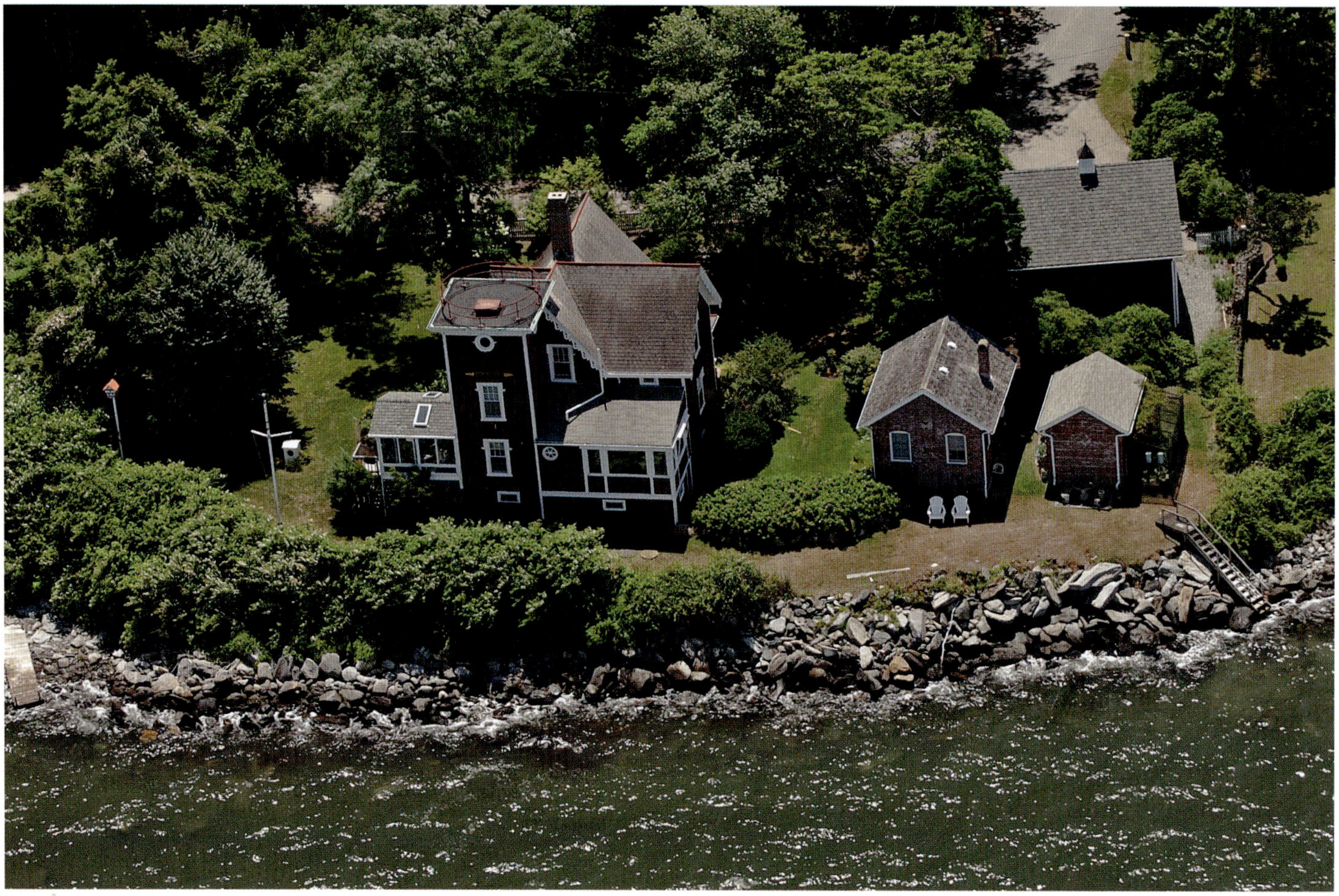

Top left: Wooden stairs lead to the roof (former lantern room).

Top right: A vista from the roof; Quonset Point is in the distance to the left.

Bottom: An aerial view of the property.

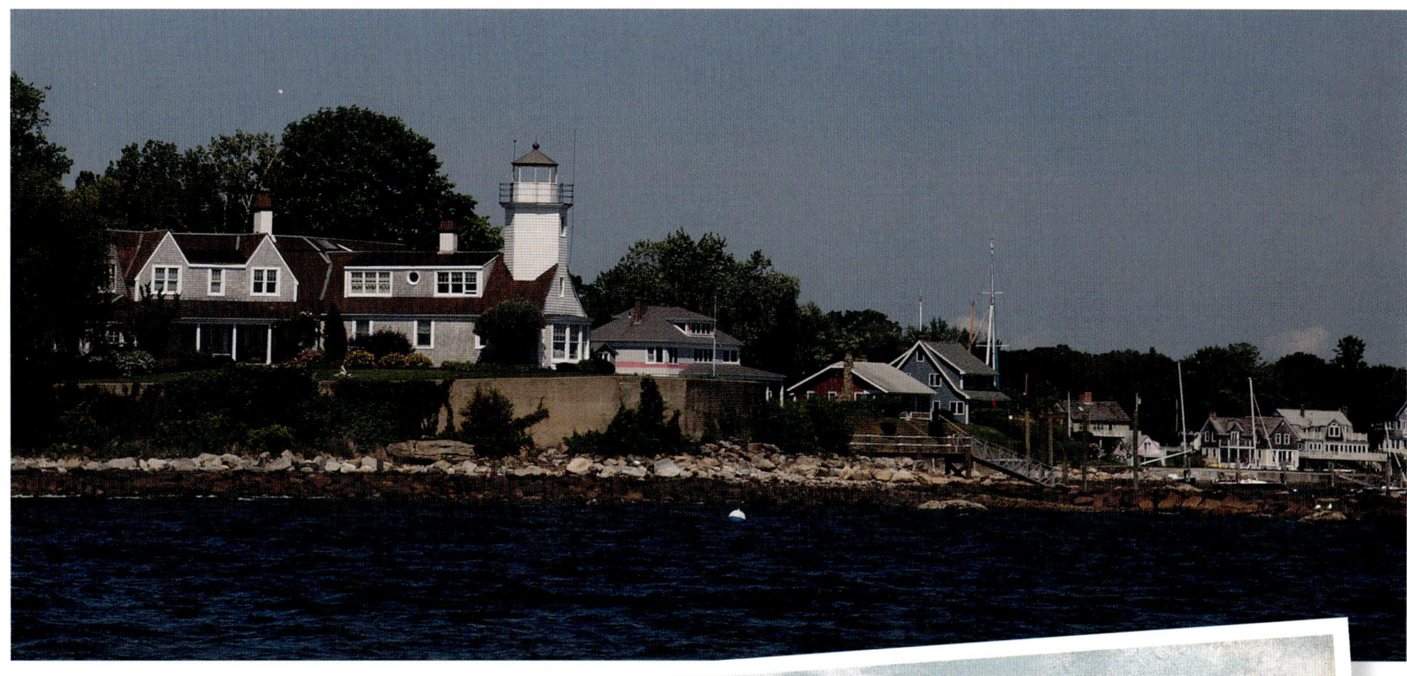

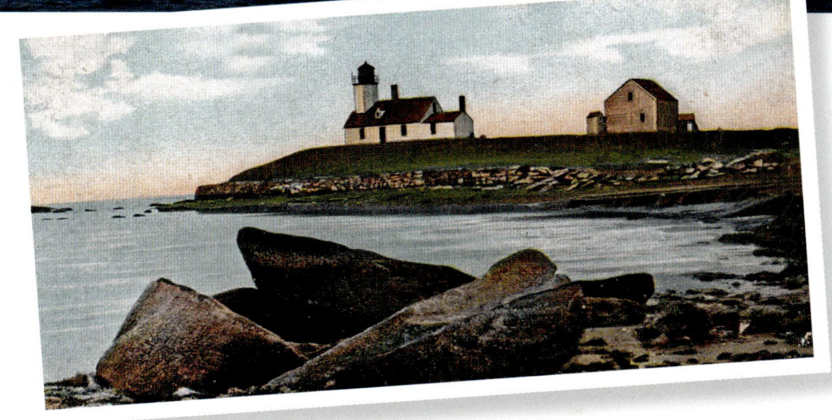

Top: A panorama of Poplar Point today.

Above: A vintage postcard of Poplar Point.

POPLAR POINT

Location: Wickford Harbor, N41°34′16″, W71°26′21″

Appropriation: $3,000 in March 1831

Established: 1831

Disestablished: 1882

Tower: Octagonal, wood, white, 26 feet high, integral part of keeper's house, black lantern room

Other Structures: Keeper's house includes several additions

Original Optics: 8 lamps, 14.5-inch reflectors

Original Lens: 1855, 5th order Fresnel lens, fixed white (FW)

Present Lens: None

Light Characteristics: N/A

Range: N/A

Fog Signal: None

Status: No longer active station, private residence, tower and lantern room present, no optics present

Access: None; private residence since 1884.

Comments: Replaced by Wickford Harbor Light; best views of Poplar Point are from boat.

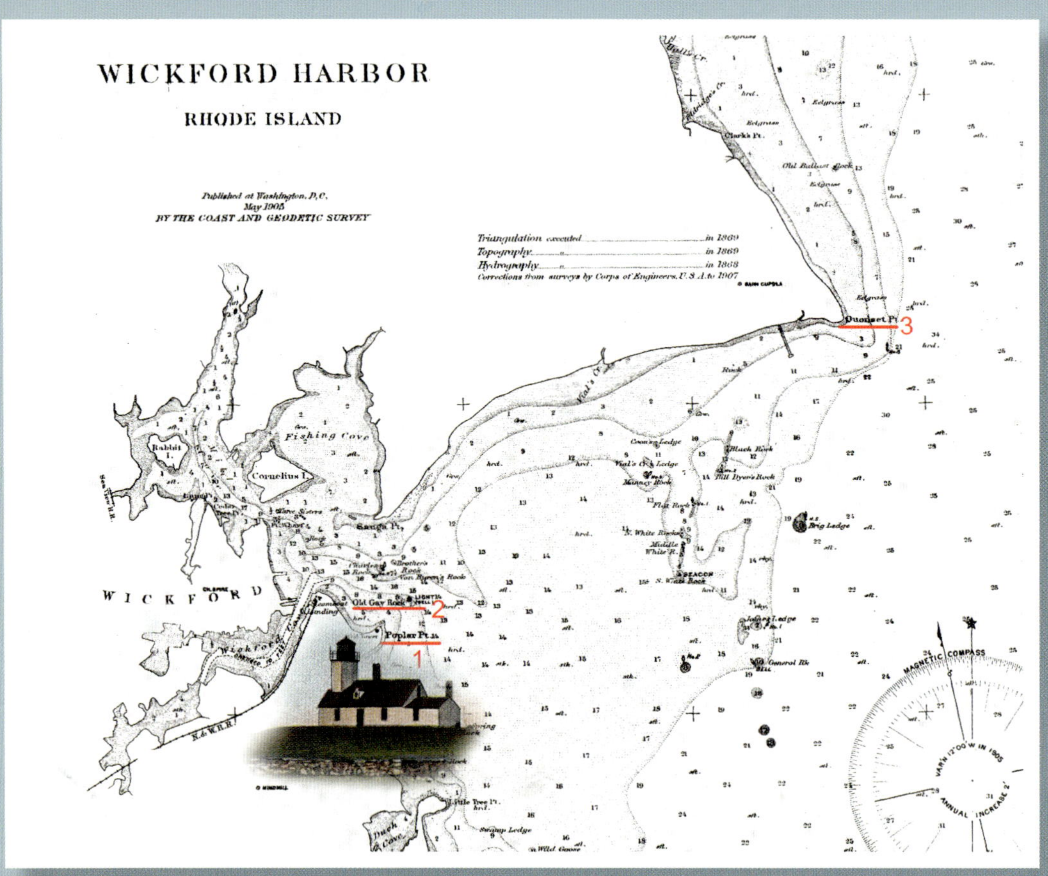

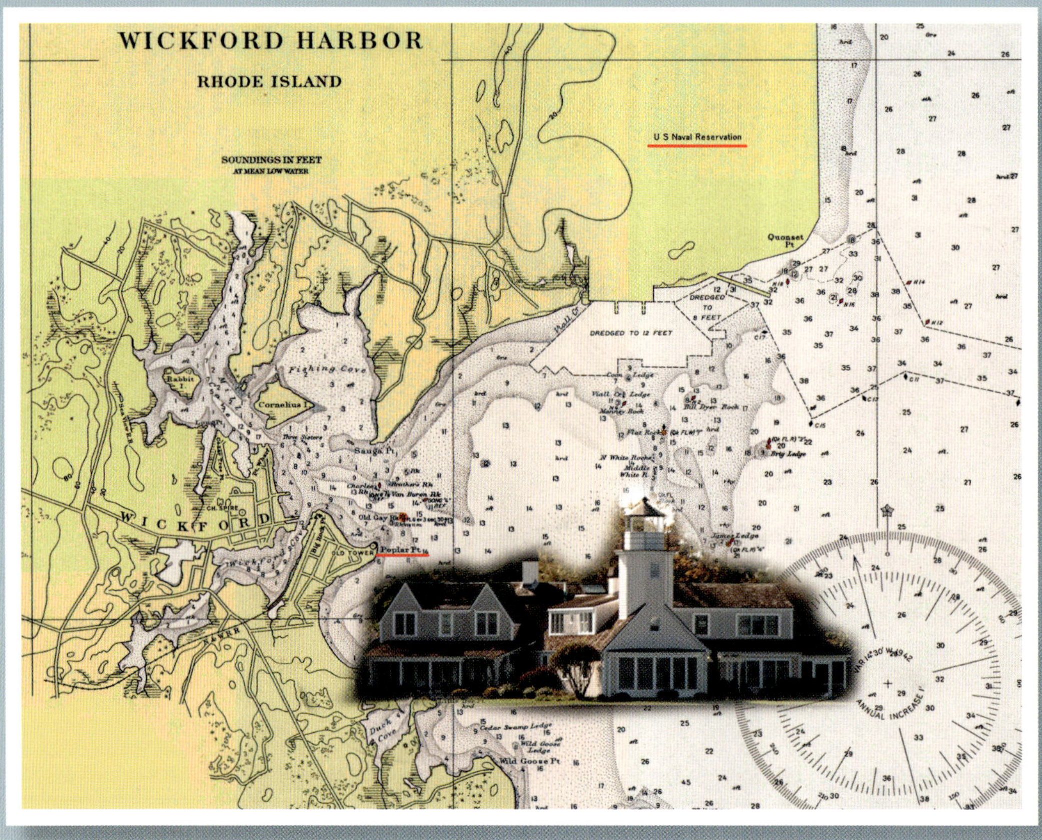

Two charts, 1903 and 1942, of Wickford Harbor. Poplar Point was active from 1831 to 1882; Wickford Harbor was active from 1882 to 1930.

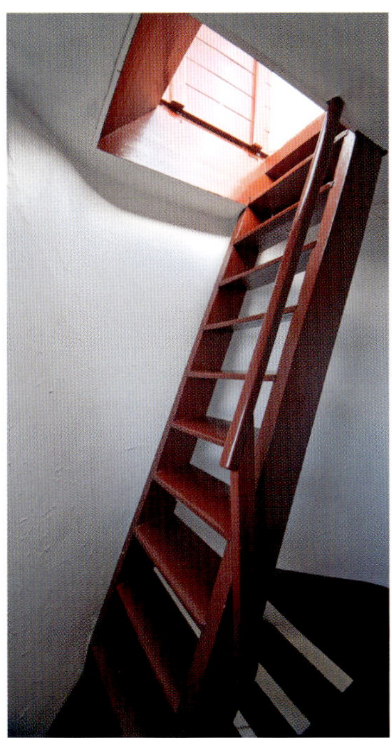

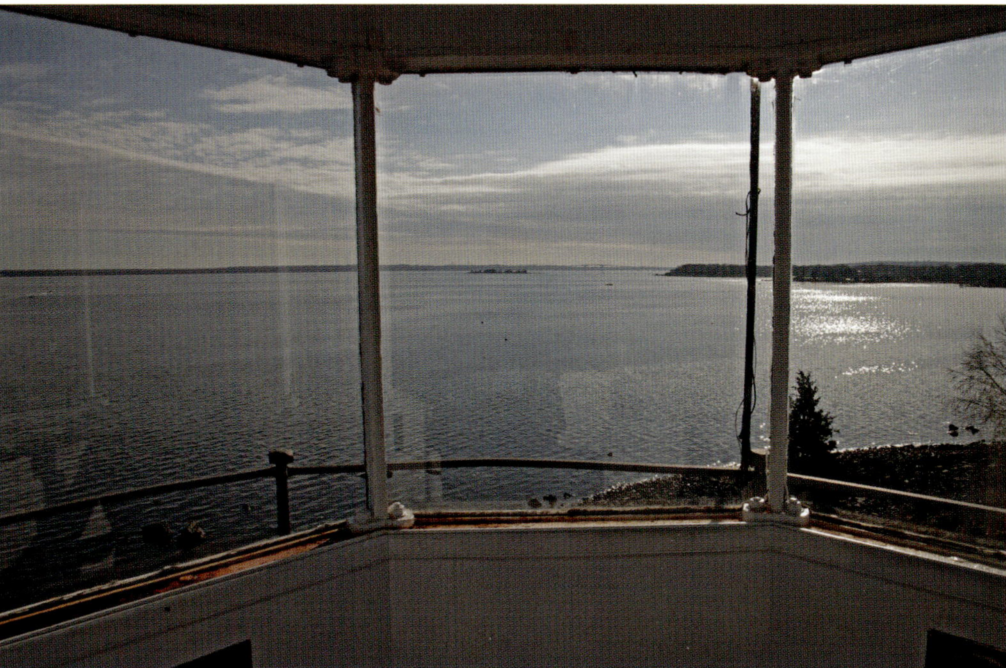

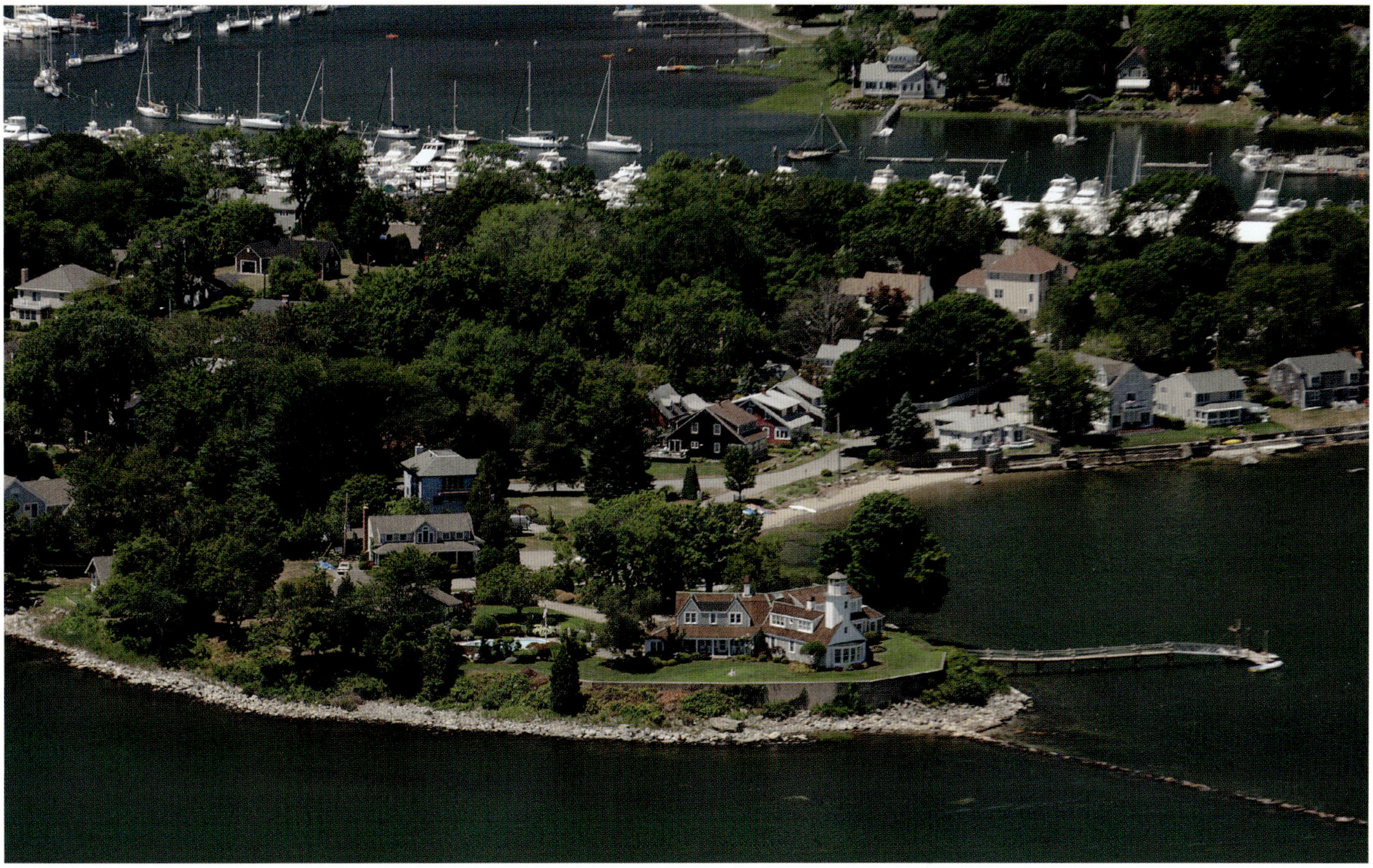

Top left: Red wooden stairs lead to the lantern room.

Top right: Looking east from the lantern room; Conanicut Light is on the tip of land in the center panel.

Bottom: An aerial image of Poplar Point.

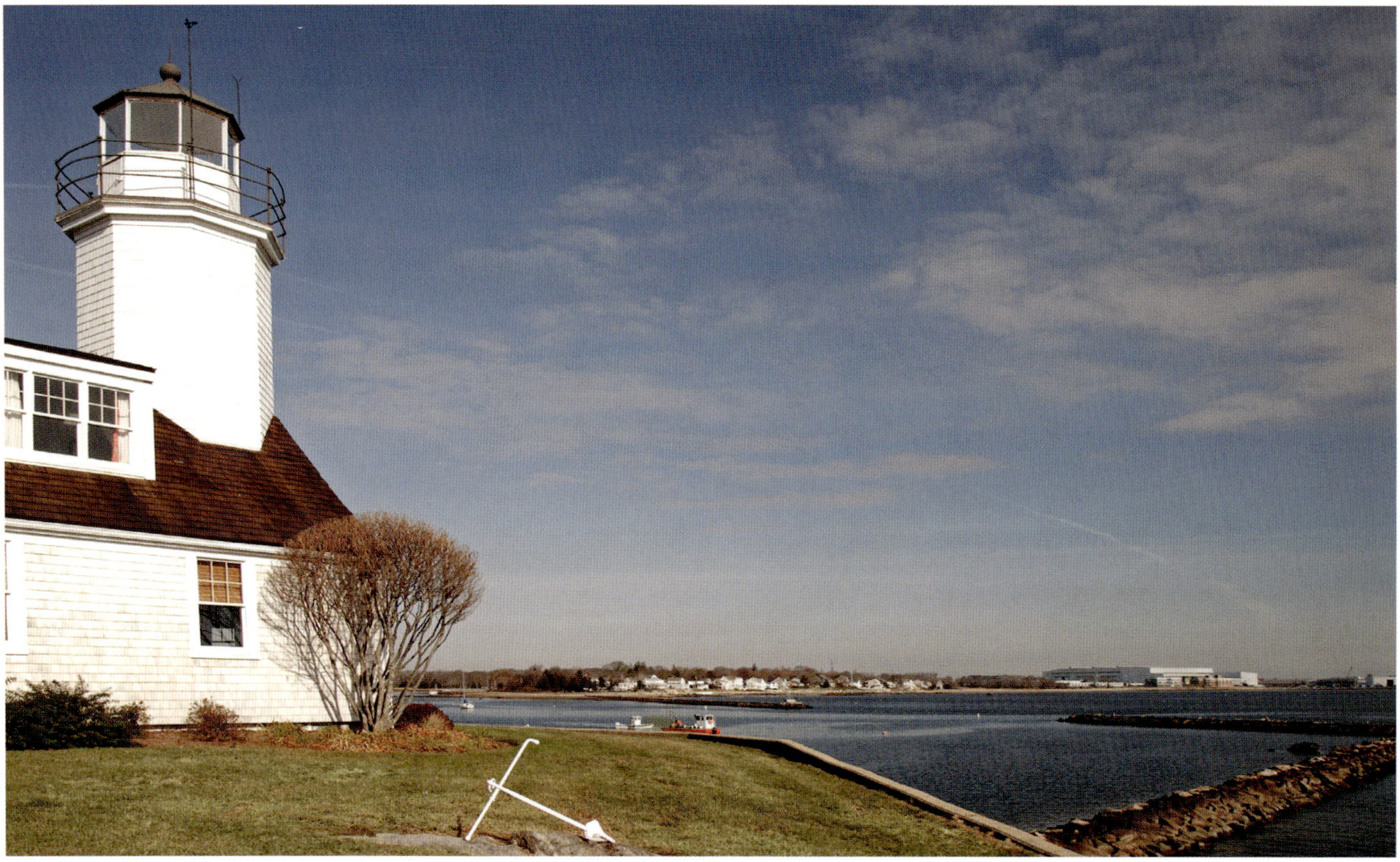

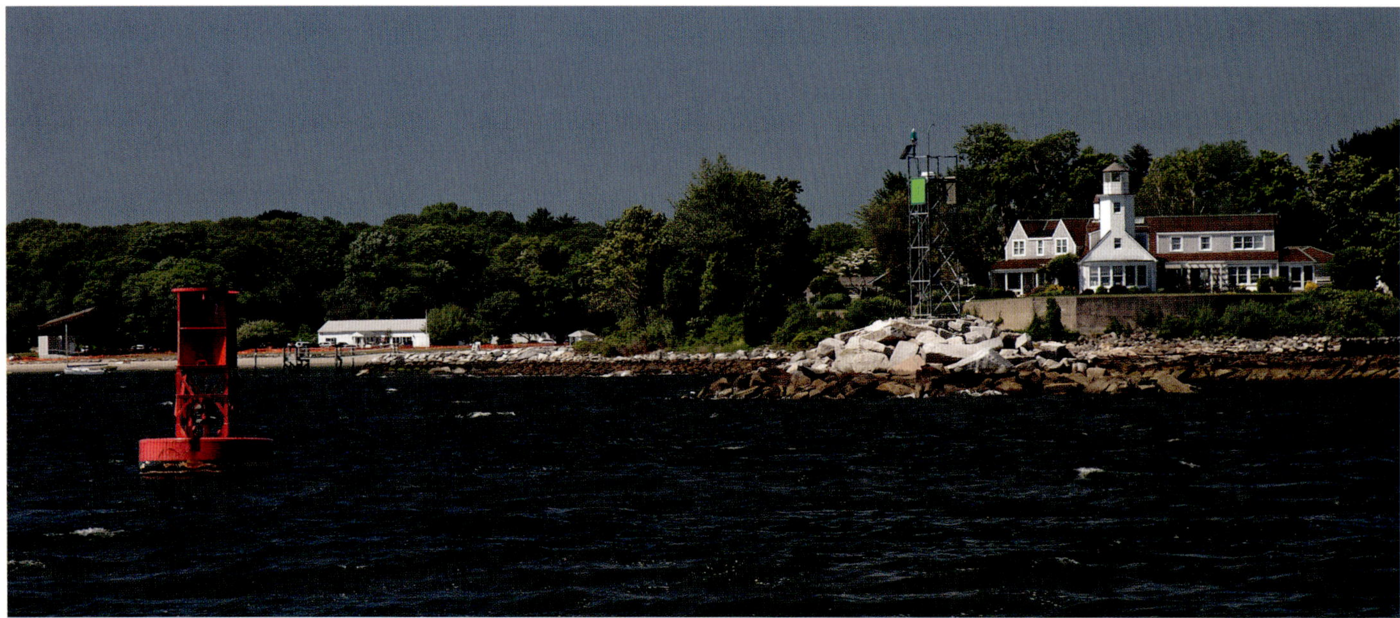

Top: Looking north across the harbor; Wickford Harbor Light would have been seen in the distance.

Bottom: A panorama of Poplar Point from the water.

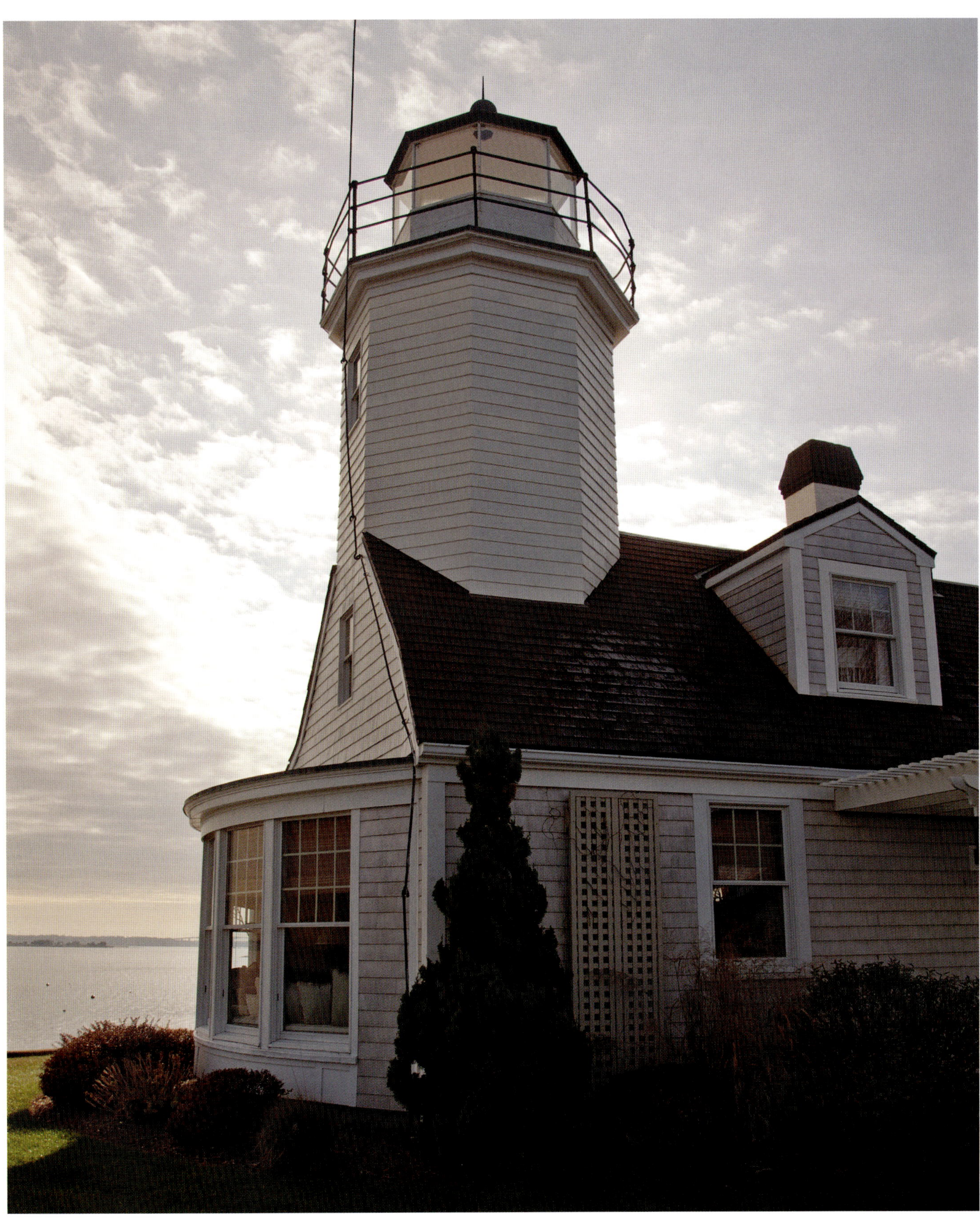

A view of the other side of the tower.

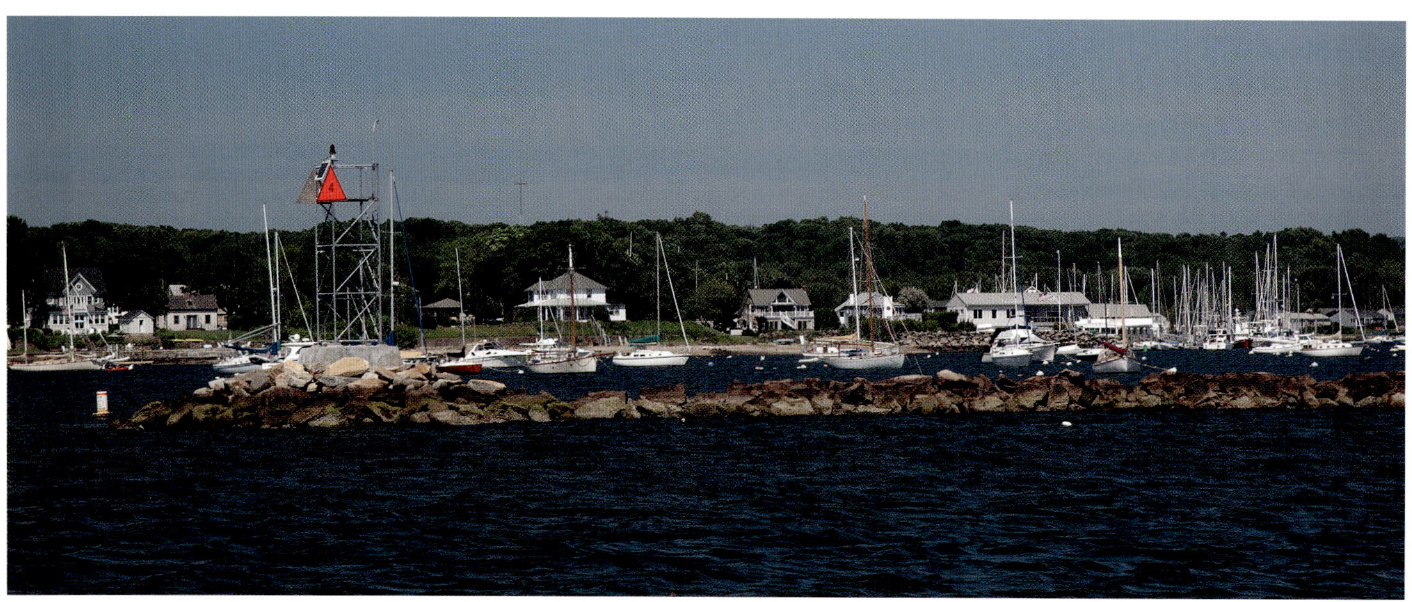

WICKFORD HARBOR

Location: Wickford Harbor, Gay Rocks, N41°34′22″, W71°26′10″, original station no longer exists

Appropriation: $45,000 in June 1880

Established: November 1882

Disestablished: 1930

Tower: Eight-room keeper's house with tower on roof, wood, 52 feet, black lantern room

Other Structures: None

Original Lens: 5th order Fresnel lens, fixed white (FW), focal plane 52 feet

Present Lens, skeleton Tower: 375 mm lens, 1939 flashing white (Fl W)

Light Characteristics, skeleton Tower: Flashing green every six seconds (FL G 6s)

Range: 6 nm

Fog Signal: None

Status: Active U.S. Coast Guard aid to navigation

Access: None.

Comments: Station razed in 1930, replaced by skeleton tower.

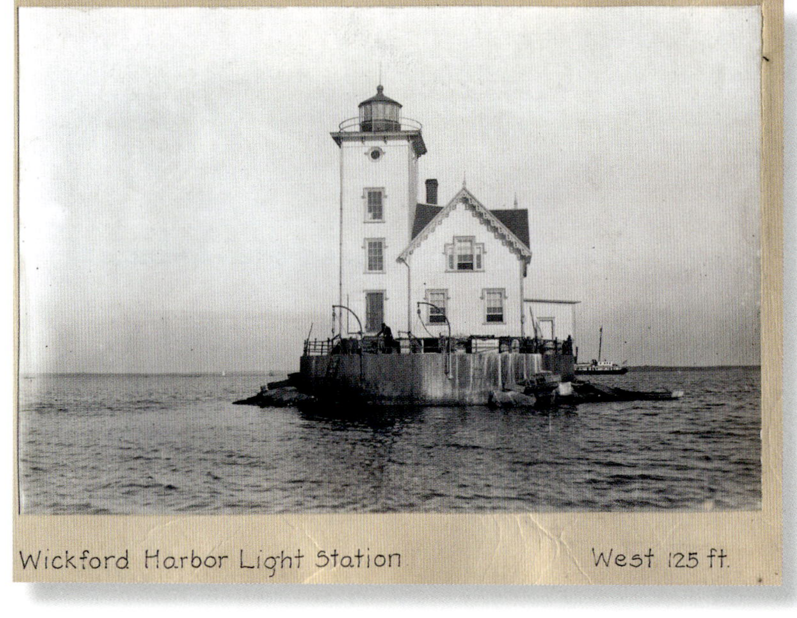

Top: This is the right jetty that leads into Wickford Harbor.

Below: This photograph of Wickford Harbor was shot by J. T. Yates on 11 September 1917; the location was also identified. *(Courtesy of USCG)*

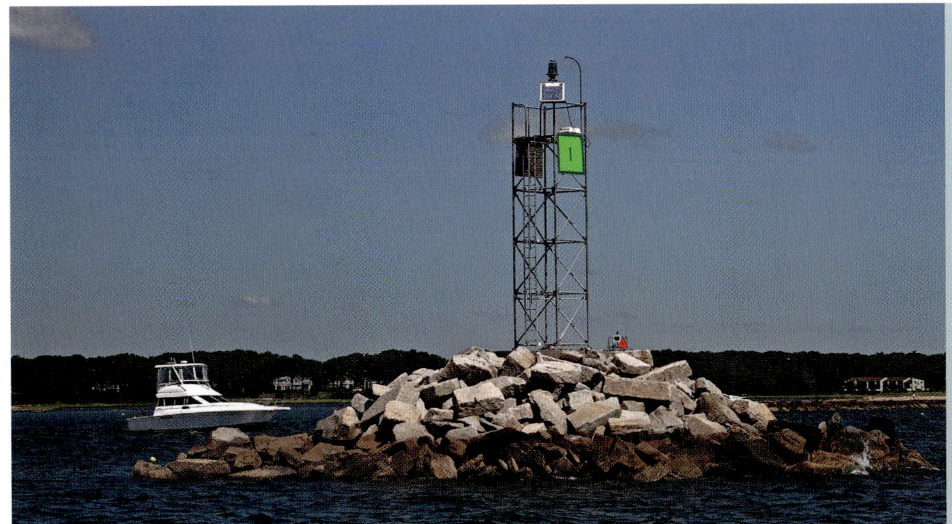

Left: A present-day view of where the original lighthouse was.

Below: An aerial view of outer Wickford harbor; Poplar Point is to the left, with the former Wickford Harbor location in the foreground.

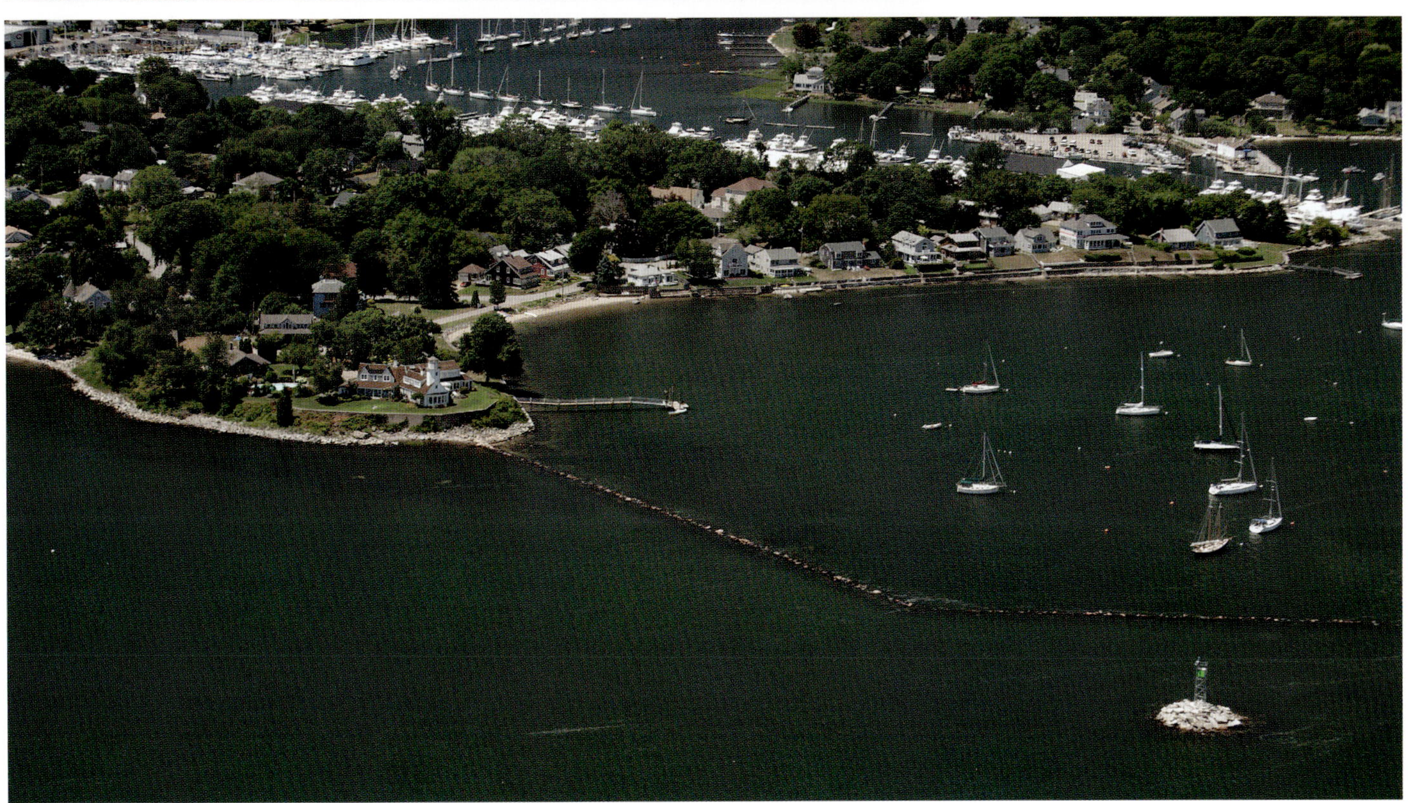

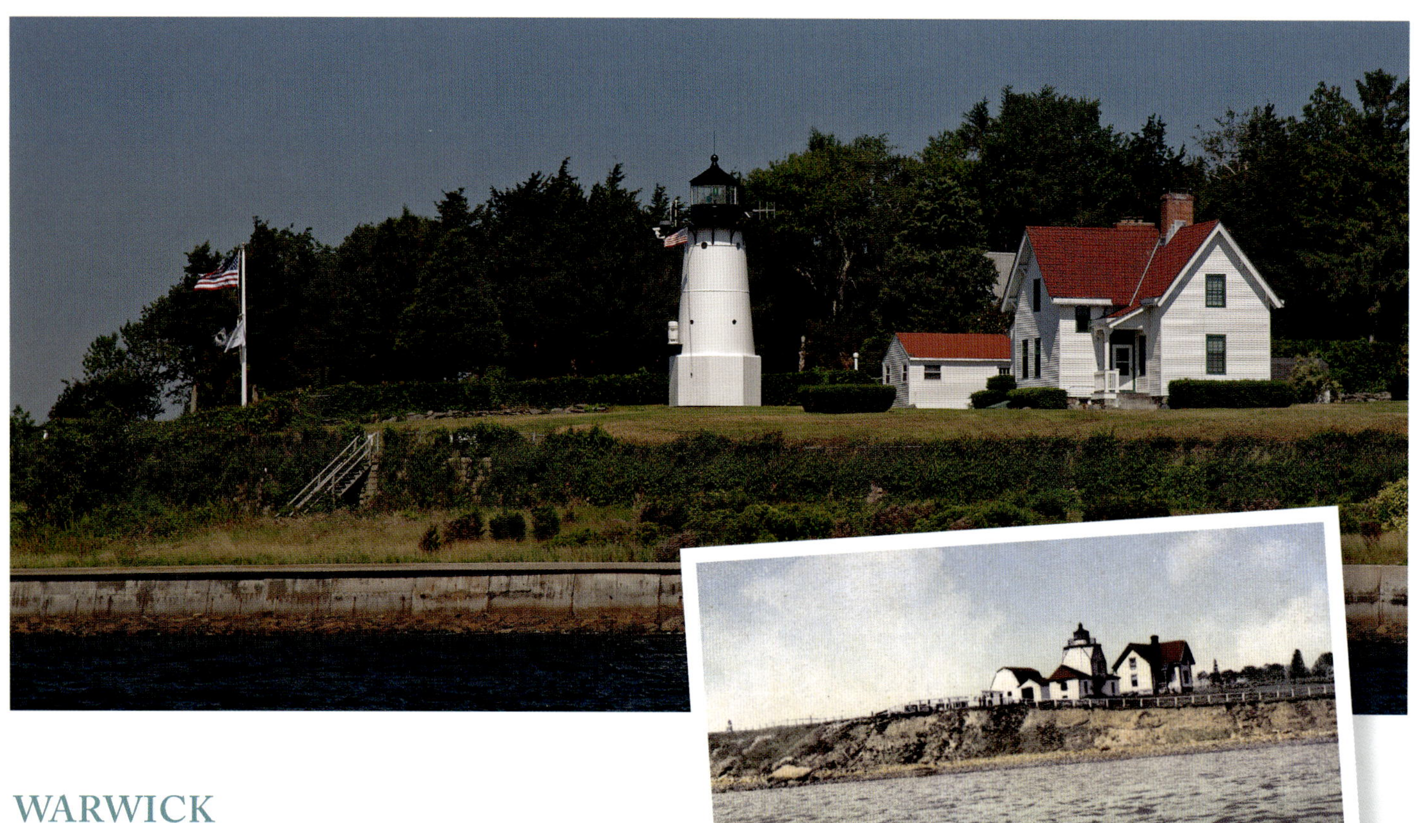

WARWICK

Location: Warwick Neck, N41°40′01″, W71°22′42″
Appropriation: \$1,000 in 1825; \$2,000 in 1826
Established: 1826
Tower, original: White 2-room stone house with white, square tower on roof, 30 feet
Rebuilt: 1932 white cast-iron, cylindrical, 51 feet, black lantern room
Other Structures: Keeper's house, garage
Original Optics: 1838, 8 lamps with 9-inch reflectors, fixed white (FW)
Original Lens: 1856, 4th order Fresnel lens FW; 1891, 4th order Fresnel lens FW; 1939, 4th order fixed green (FG)
Present Lens: 250 mm (1985)
Light Characteristics: Green eclipsed every 4 seconds (Oc G 4s), focal plane 66 feet
Range: 12 nm
Fog Signal: 1882 fog bell; compressed air siren 3-second blast, 3-second interval; 1939 horn
Status: Active U. S. Coast Guard aid to navigation
Access: None; keeper's house private, U.S. Coast Guard personnel housing.
Comments: 1939 tower moved 50 feet inland as a result of hurricane of 1938.

Top: Lighthouse cruises sail close to Warwick Light.

Above: A postcard, mailed in 1911, of Warwick Light from the water.

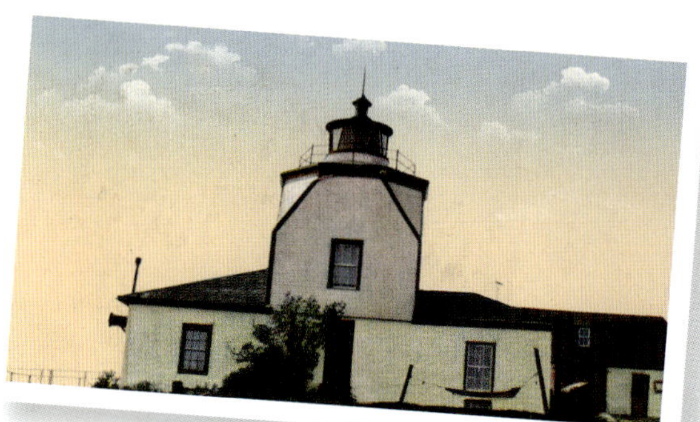

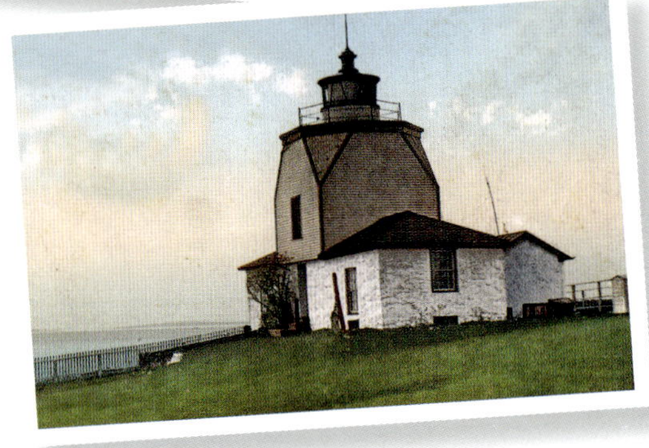

Two archival postcards of the first Warwick Light.

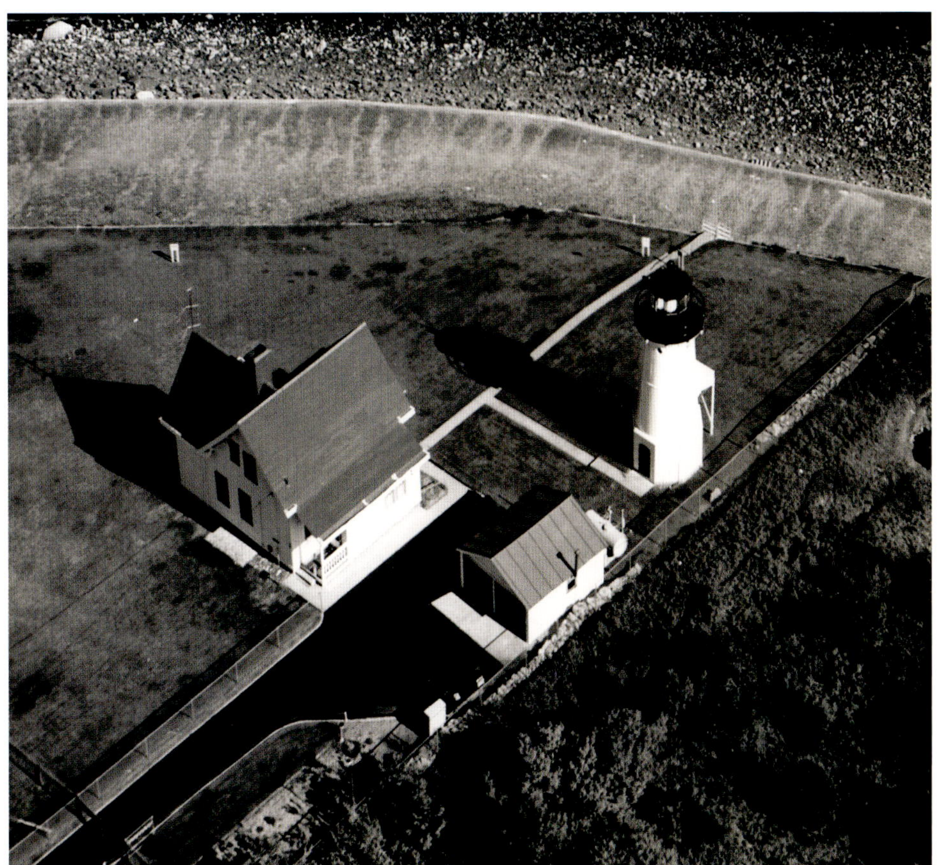

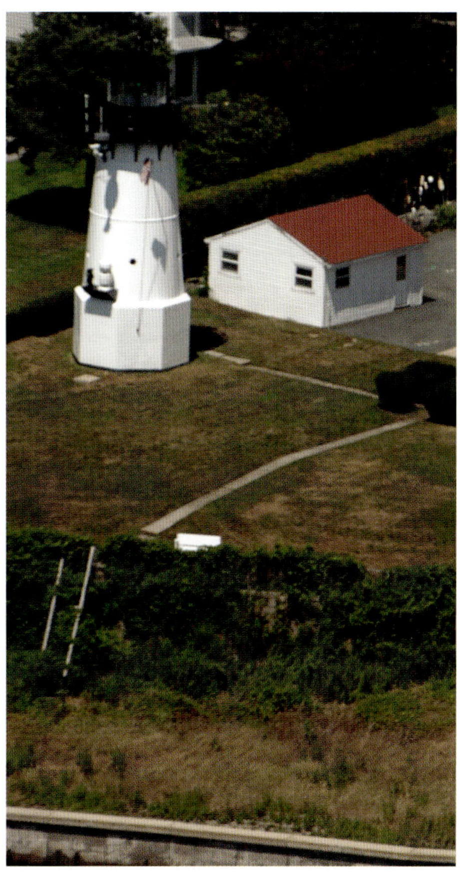

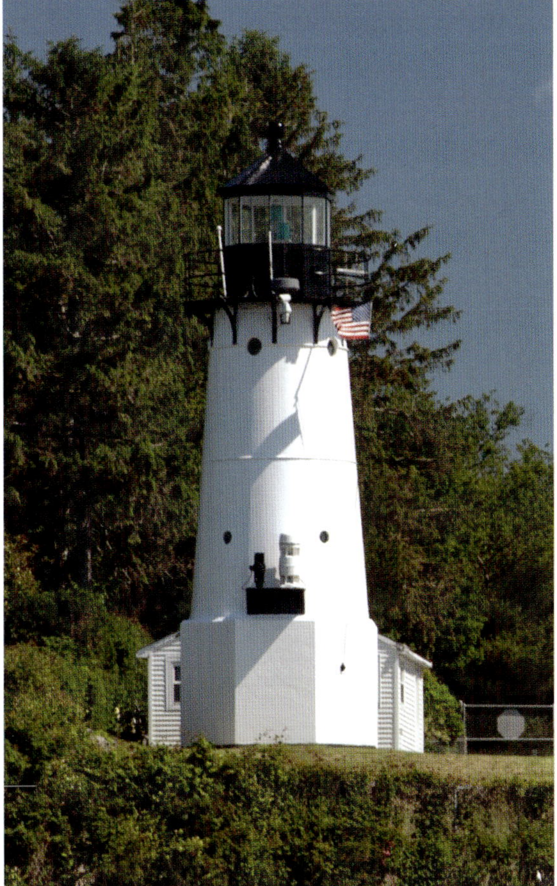

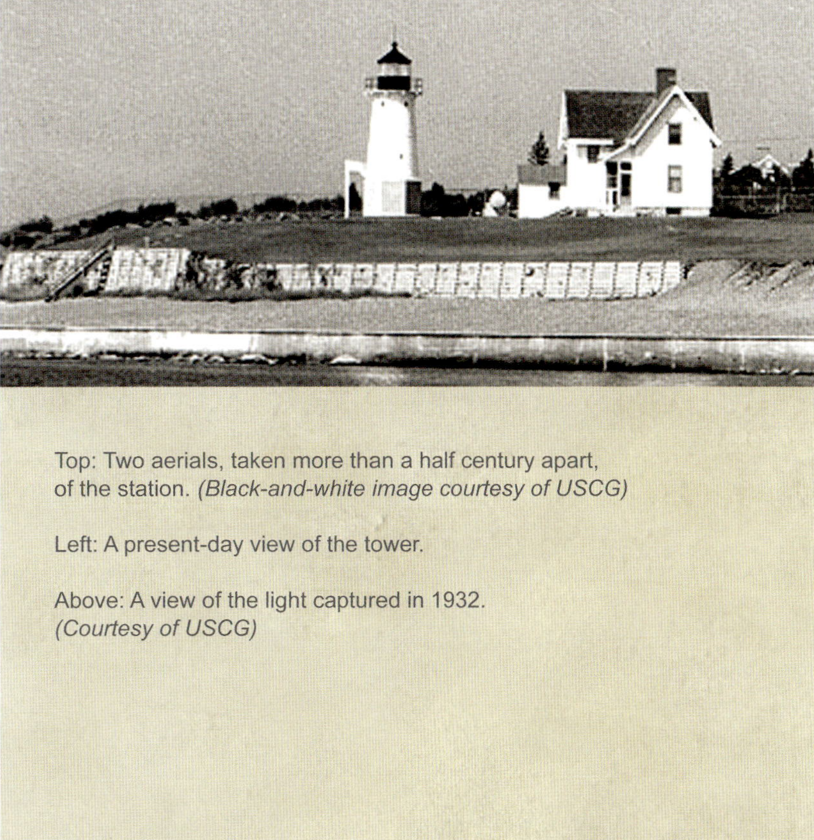

Top: Two aerials, taken more than a half century apart, of the station. *(Black-and-white image courtesy of USCG)*

Left: A present-day view of the tower.

Above: A view of the light captured in 1932. *(Courtesy of USCG)*

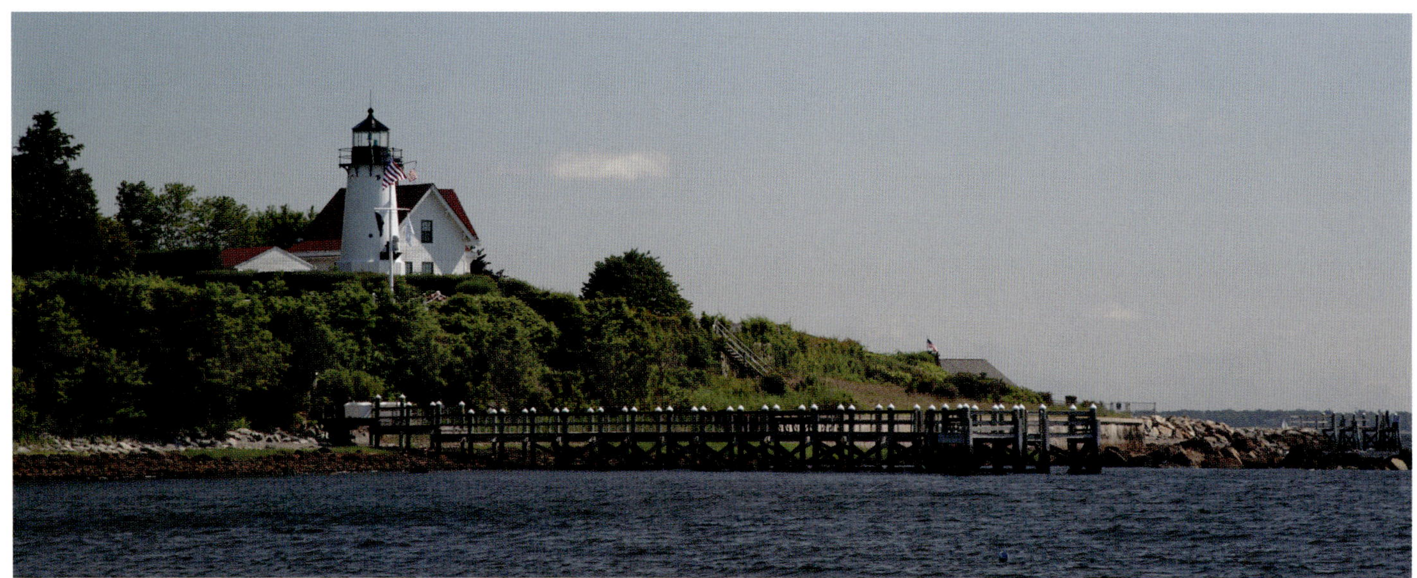

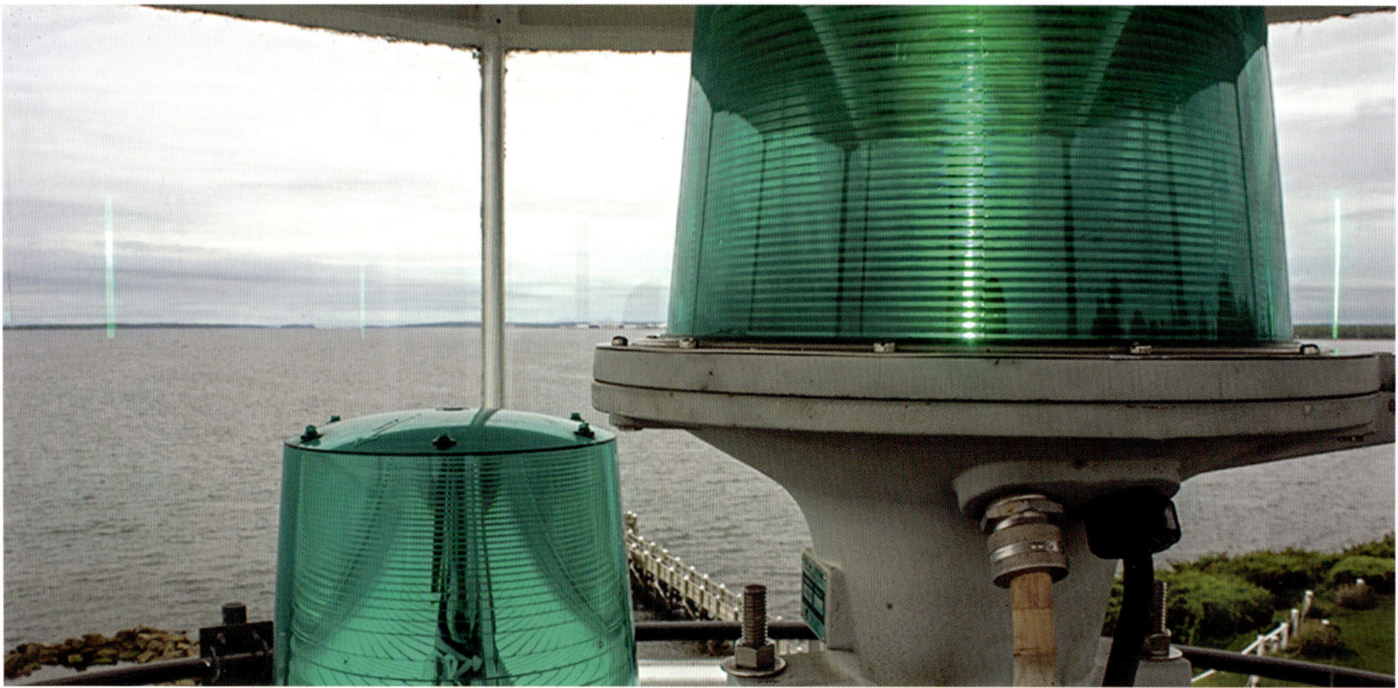

Top: Warwick Light from the water.

Bottom: The distinctive green lamp with its replacement.

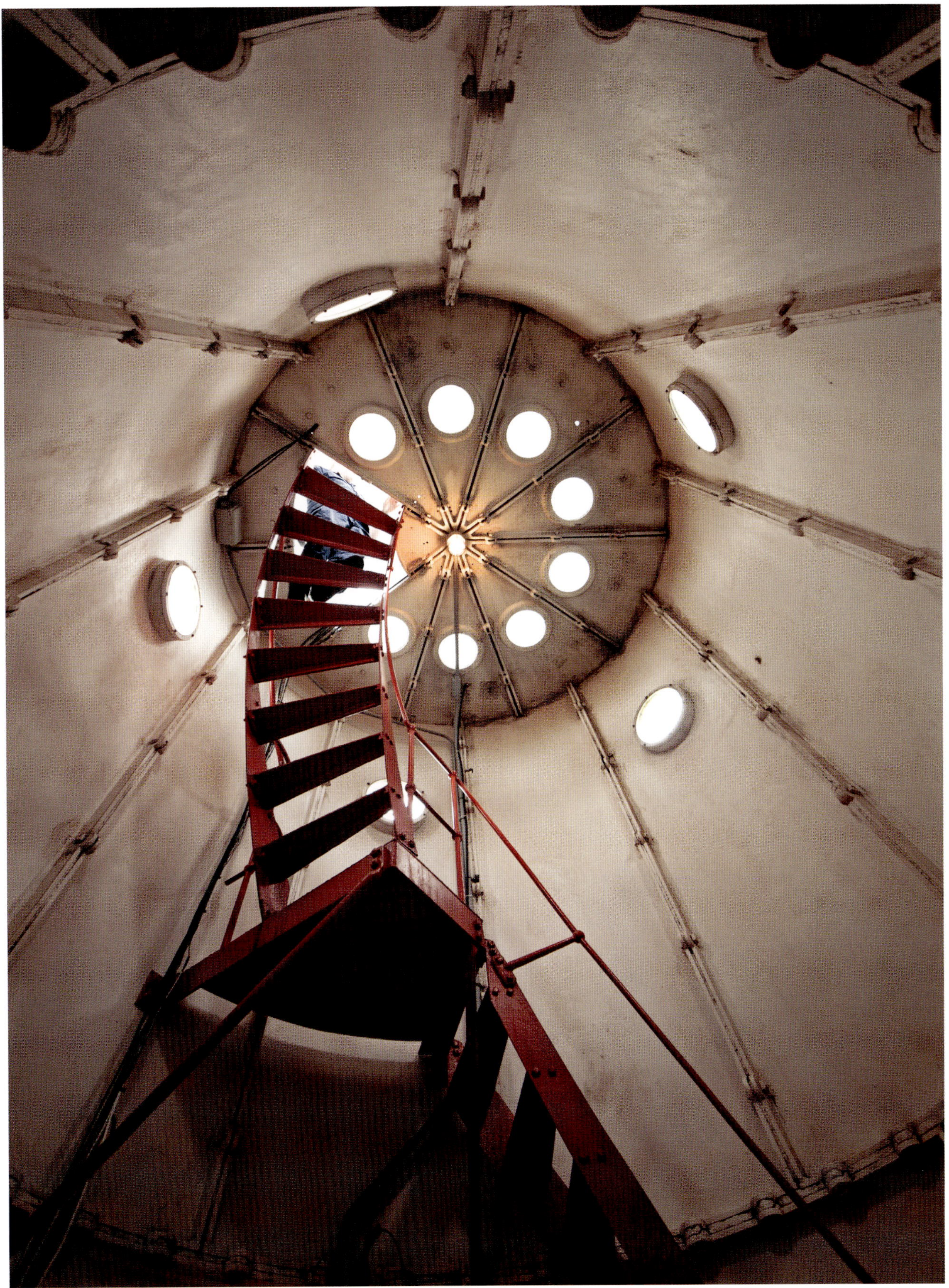

A flight of circular stairs leads to the lantern room.

EAST PASSAGE

Ships sailing this waterway leading to Providence would use the off-shore Brenton Reef Lightship as their first aid in charting a course. Then transiting between Beavertail Light to the west and Castle Hill Light to the north and east, they would first encounter the safe and busy harbor of Newport—for many, their final destination. Other ships might sail on to Mount Hope Bay, Massachusetts (Fall River), the harbors at Bristol and Warren, or maybe their final destination of Providence. Whatever their destination, distinct and well lit aids were required to sail these relatively narrow and course-changing channels.

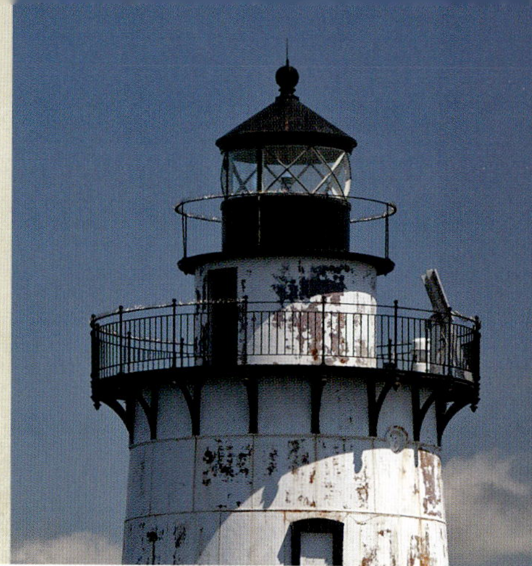

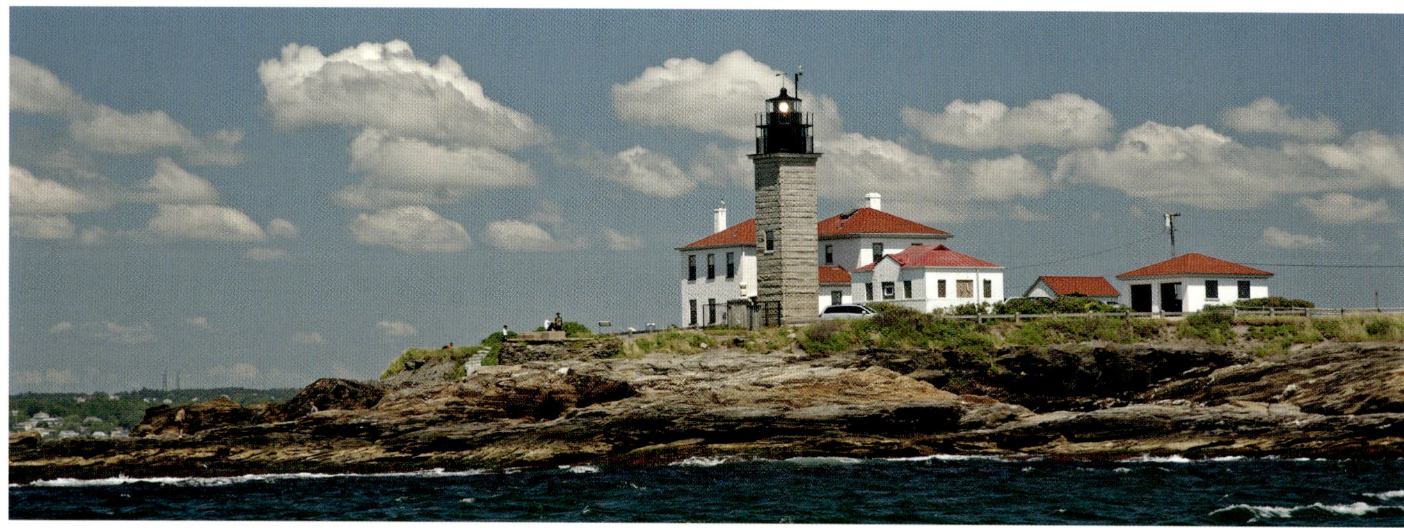

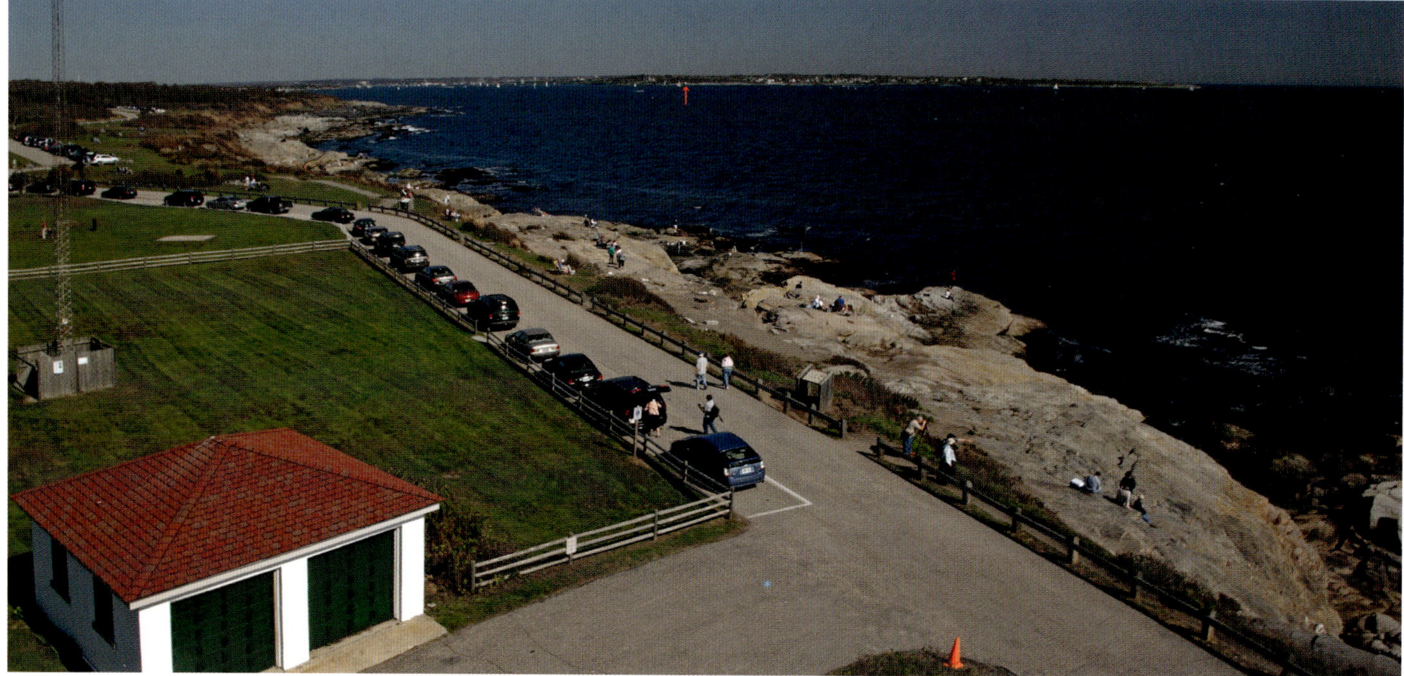

Center: From the water, looking at the east side of Beavertail Light; this would be the view that mariners saw, and see today, if heading to Newport and beyond.

Bottom: Seen from the lantern room of Beavertail Light is the East Passage waterway. In the distance on the far shore is Castle Hill Light. The red arrow points to its location.

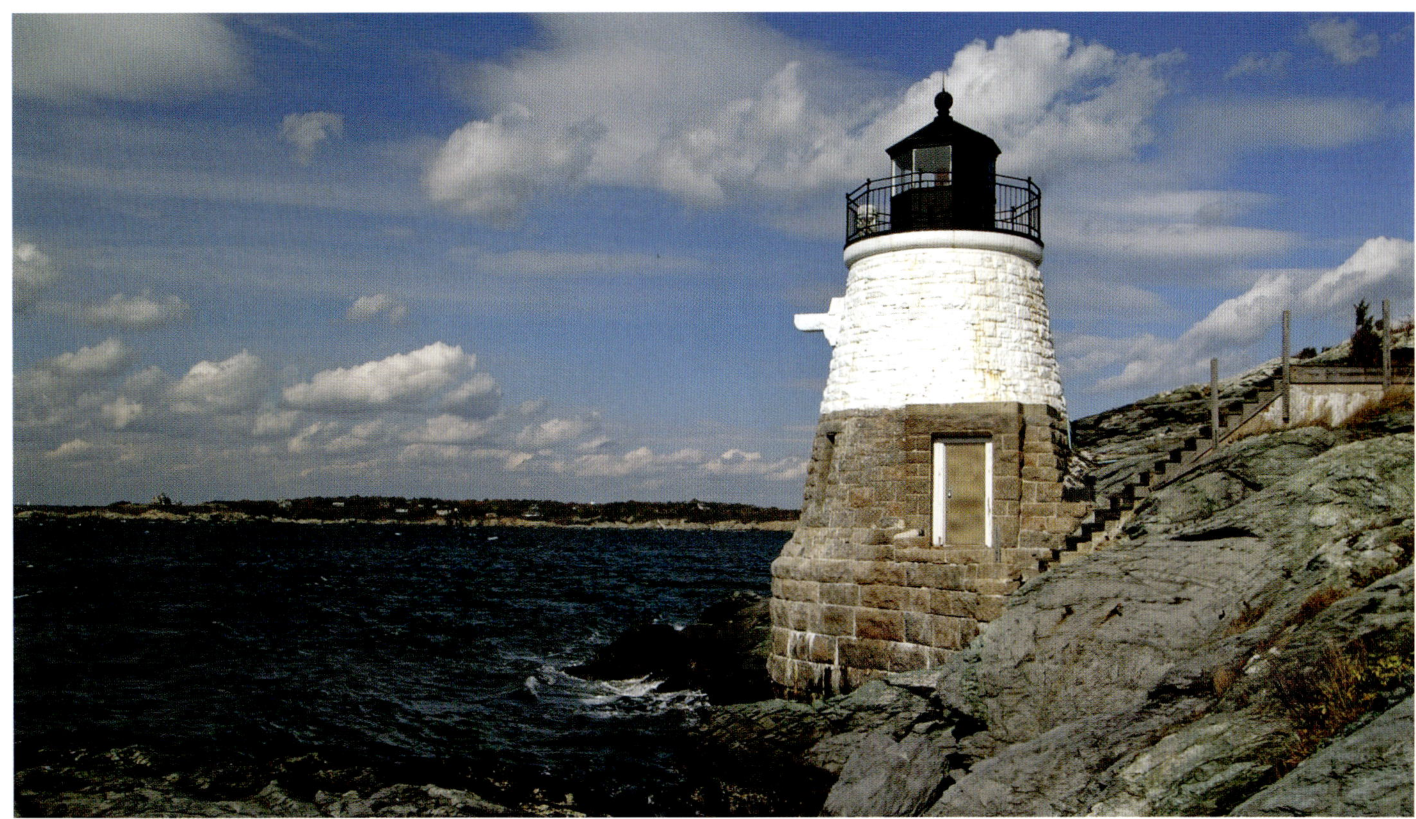

CASTLE HILL

Location: The Neck, Newport, N41°27′44″, W71°21′47″
Appropriation: $2,500 in March 1823; $13,000 in March 1842; $6,000 in July 1864 (keeper's house)
Established: May 1890
Automated: 1957 and lens replaced
Tower: White, conical, granite, 34 feet, black lantern room, natural granite base
Other Structures: Keeper's house about a quarter mile inland
Restored: 2012
Original Lens: 5th order Fresnel lens, focal plane 40 feet, 1890, flashing red every 10 seconds; 1907 flashing red every 30 seconds; 1939, red flash 9 seconds with eclipse 21 seconds
Present Lens: 300 mm plastic
Light Characteristics: 6 seconds red, 6 seconds dark (Iso R 6s)
Range: 12 nm
Fog Signal: One second blast every 10 seconds
Status: Active U.S. Coast Guard aid to navigation
Access: Grounds open year-round, tower closed.
Comments: Nearby keeper's house a private residence; original keeper's house near tower destroyed by hurricane in 1938; Castle Hill Light visible from Rose Island Light; beautiful spot for a picnic; listed in NRHP.

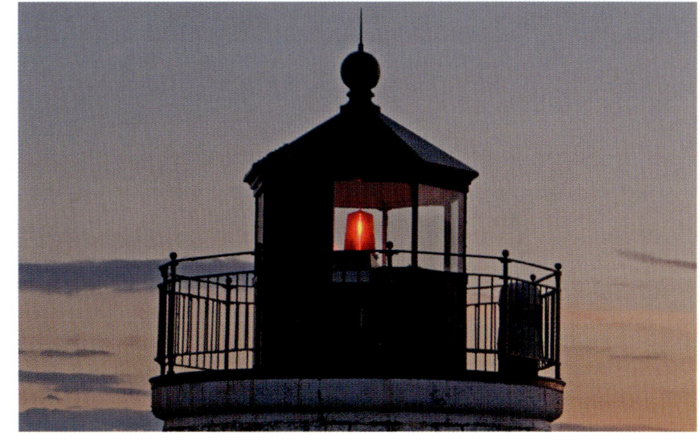

Top: A present-day view of the tower.

Bottom: At sunset, the red navigational light is distinctive.

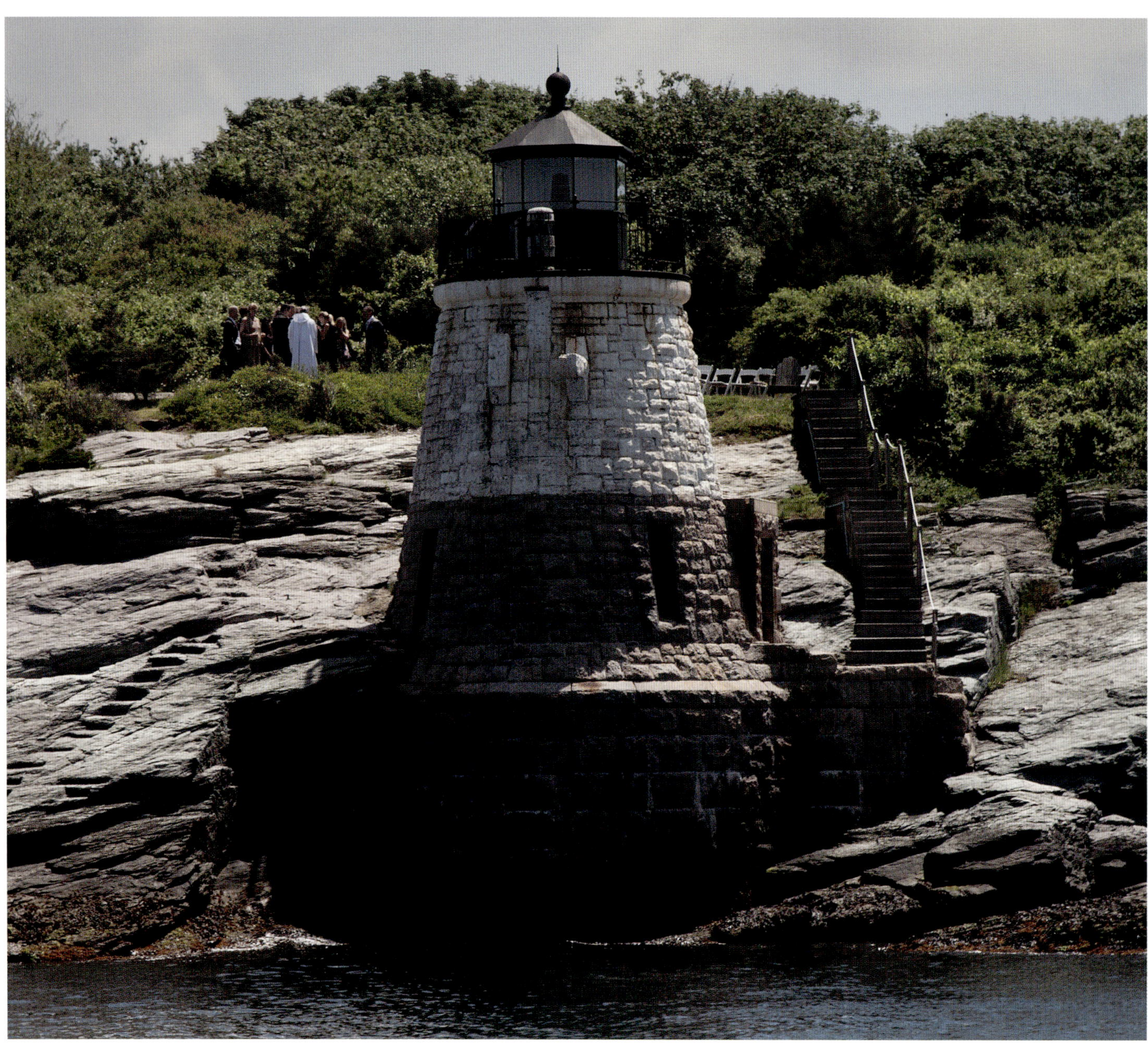

The site is popular with visitors; here, a wedding is held on the scenic grounds.

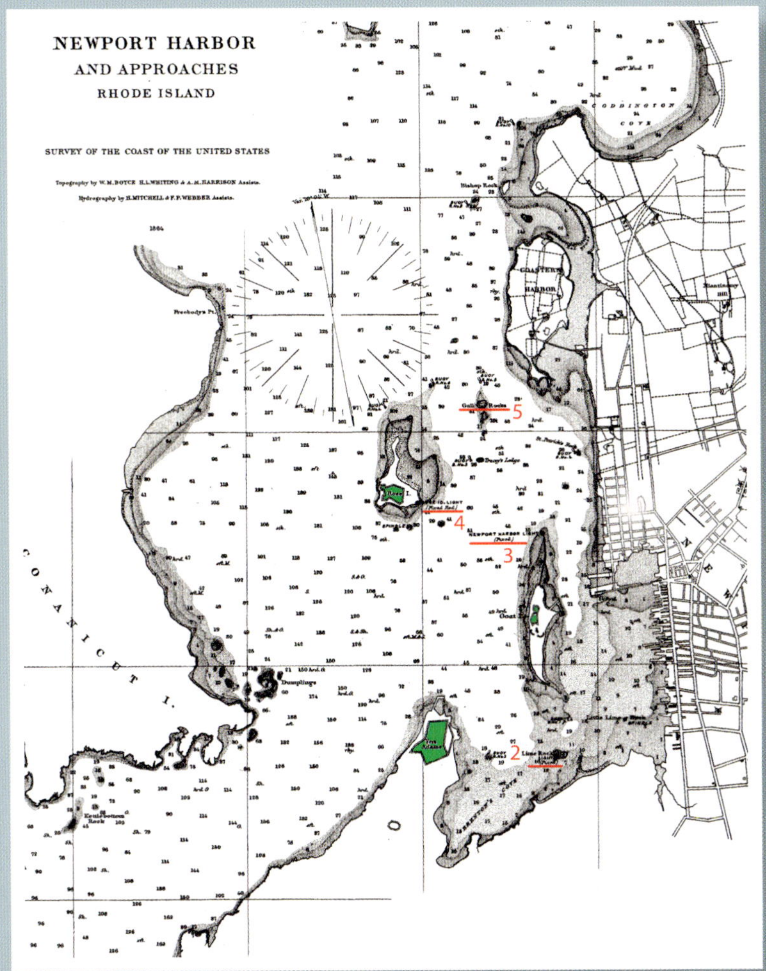

Left: This 1864 chart illustrates the southern boundary of the East Passage; the lighthouses are numbered and identified in red and the forts are highlighted in green. Castle Hill, 1 (where a tower would be erected in 1890), would be the first light mariners would encounter; Fort Adams protected Newport Harbor. Lime Rock, 2, on the southern edge and Newport Harbor, 3, at the north end of Goat Island marked the inner harbor. Rose Island, 4, also had a fort on the island. Gull Rocks, 5, at the northern edge of the harbor, indicated a dangerous, rocky ledge.

Below: This archival image, probably taken shortly after the tower was built in 1890, shows Castle Hill Light in the foreground and provides information on the perspective taken by the photographer. The house to the left is now a popular inn. *(Courtesy of NA)*

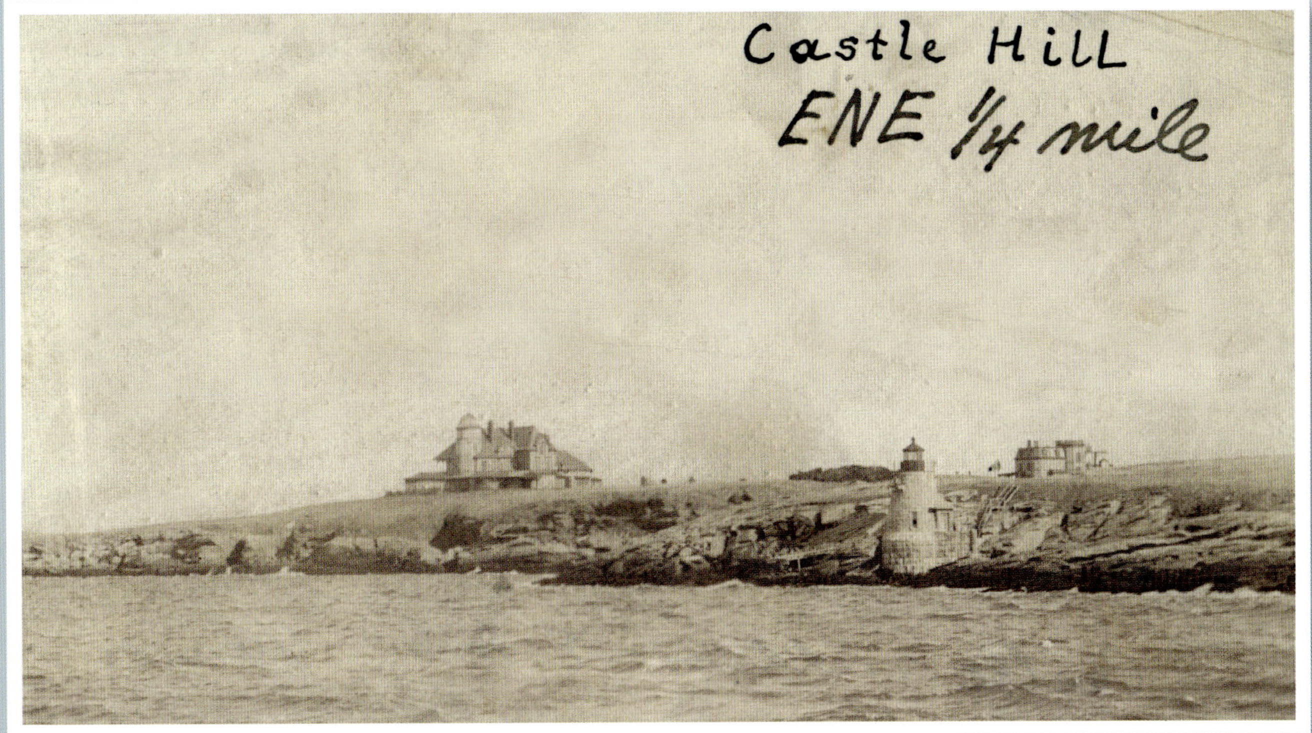

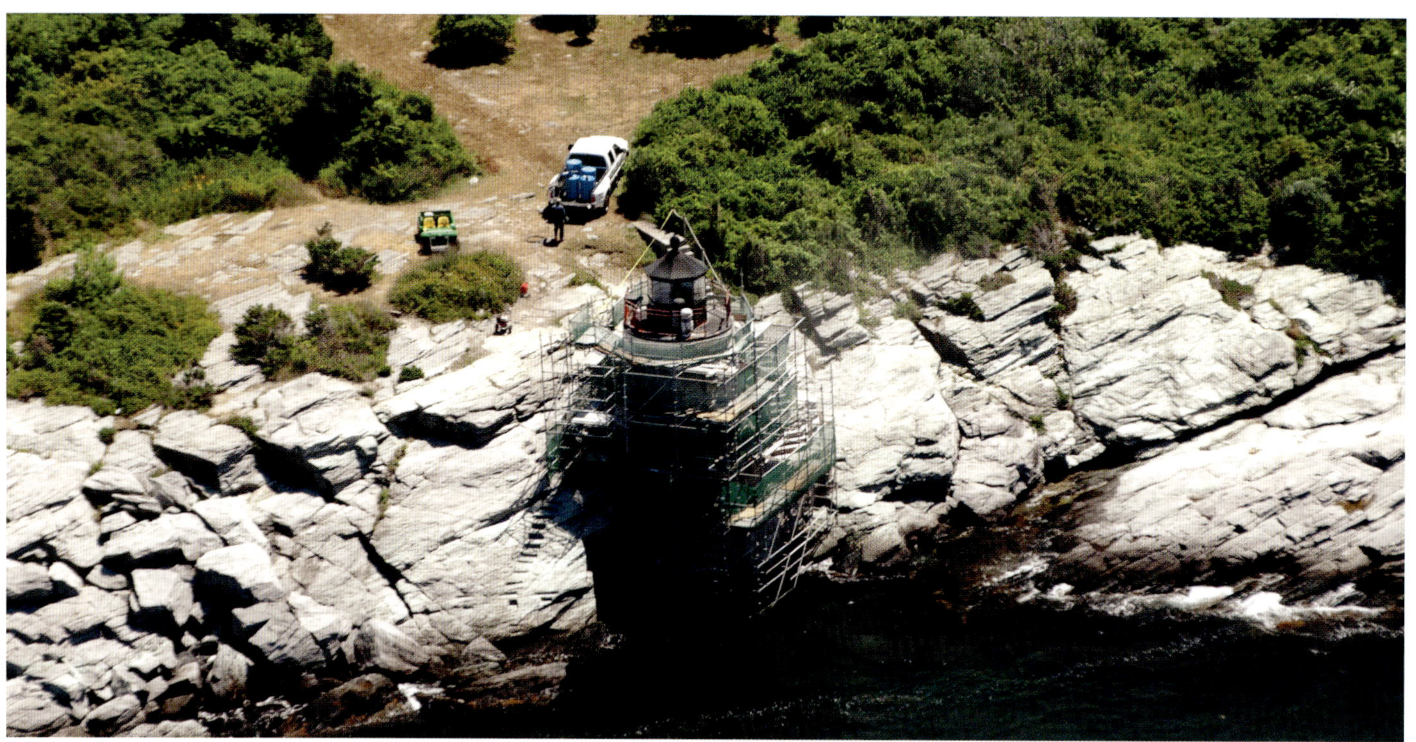

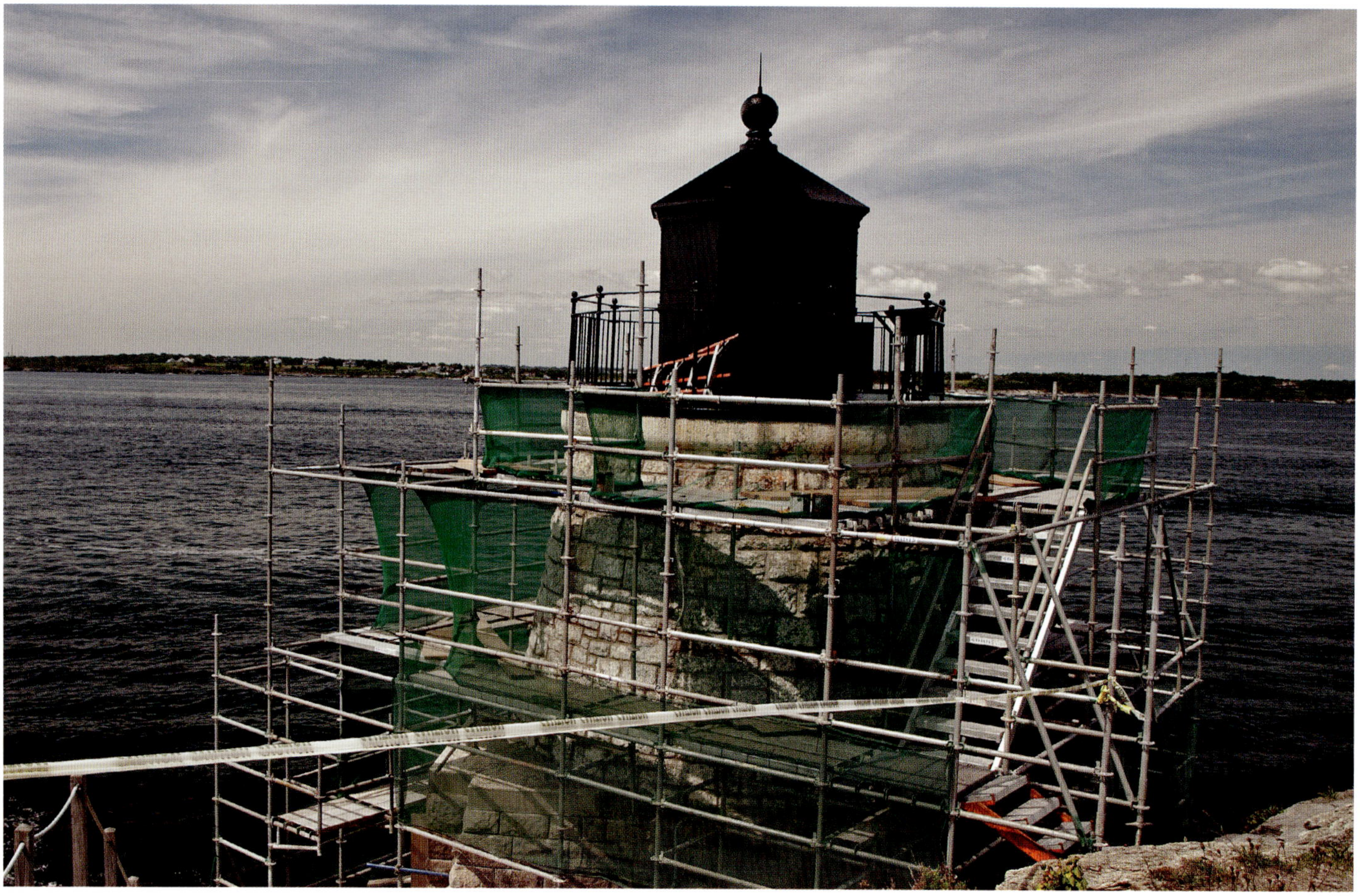

Top: An aerial view of the tower on the rocky promontory.

Bottom: Constant exposure to harsh conditions makes the tower's maintenance important; in 2012 Castle Hill was totally restored.

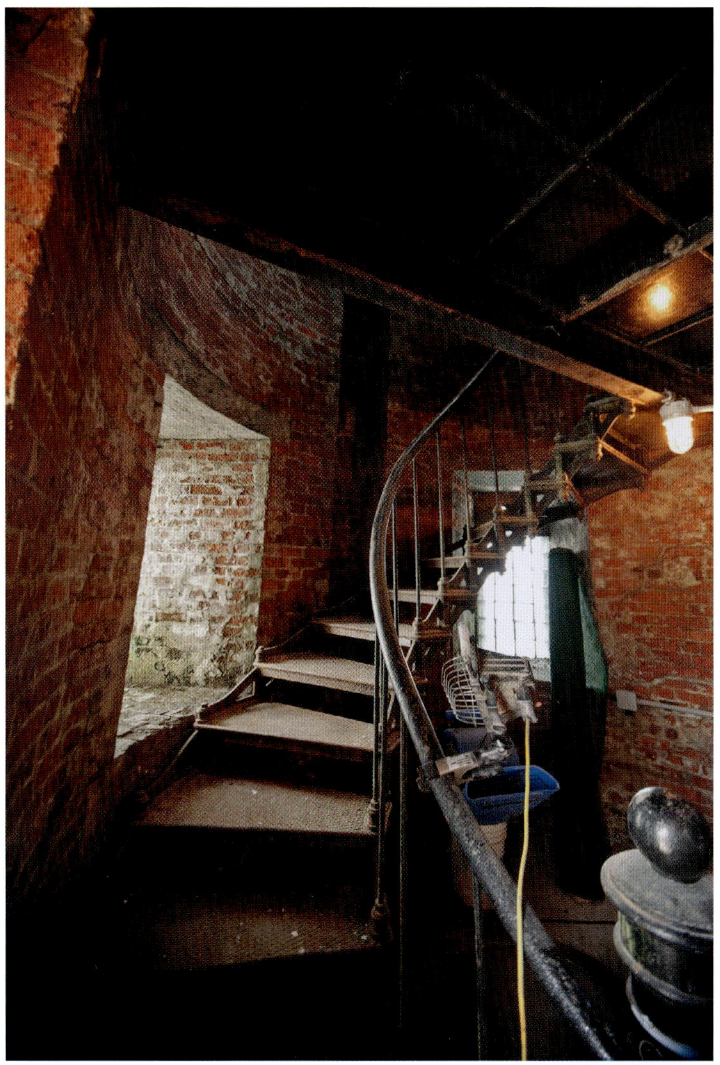

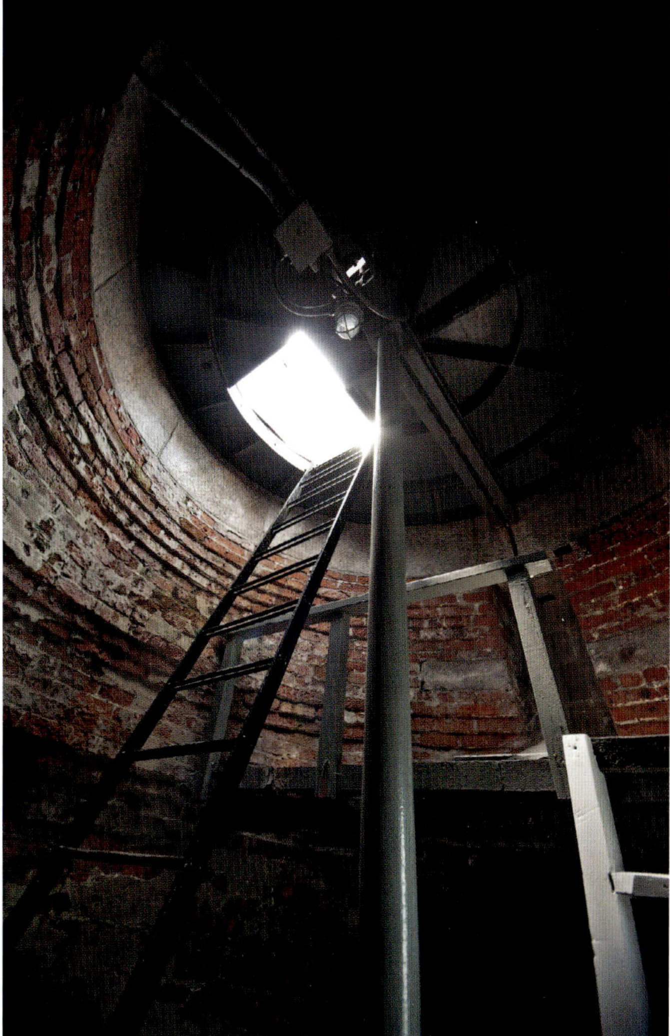

Top: In the relatively short tower, circular stairs lead to a floor where a ladder heads to the lantern room.

Right: Looking north, this is the view towards Newport; note the house in the distance, now an inn, that was also in the previous archival image. In addition, several panels at the rear of the lantern room are blocked off.

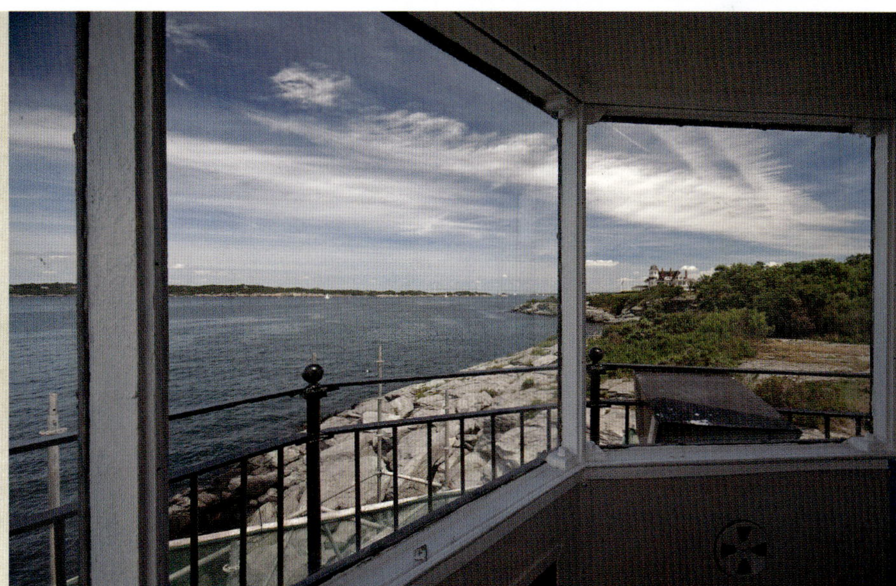

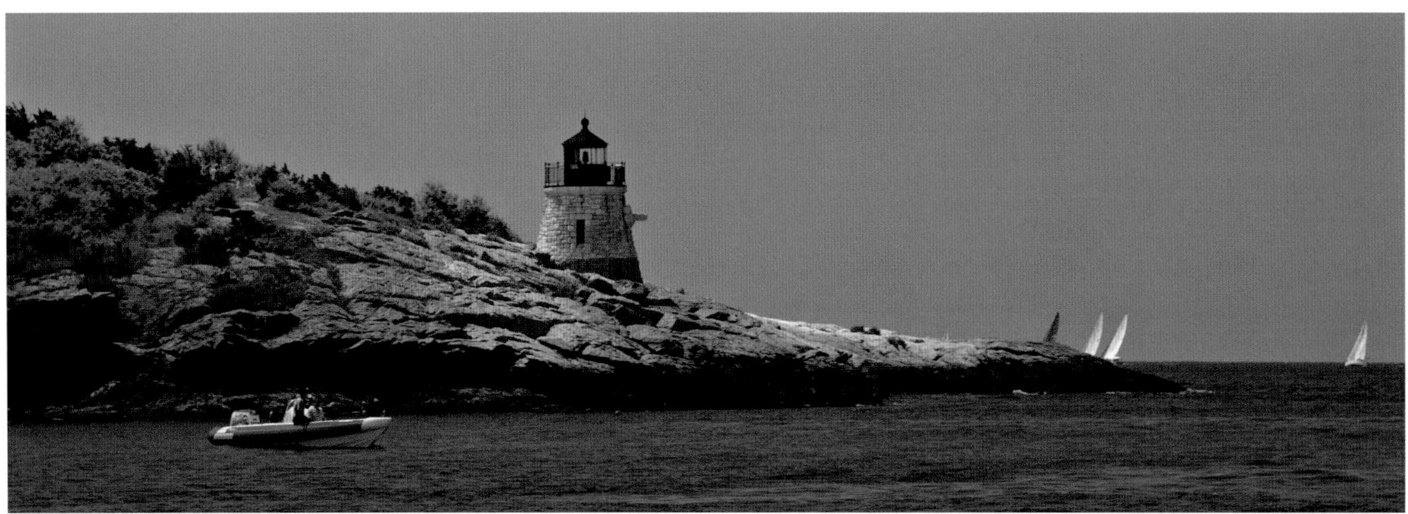

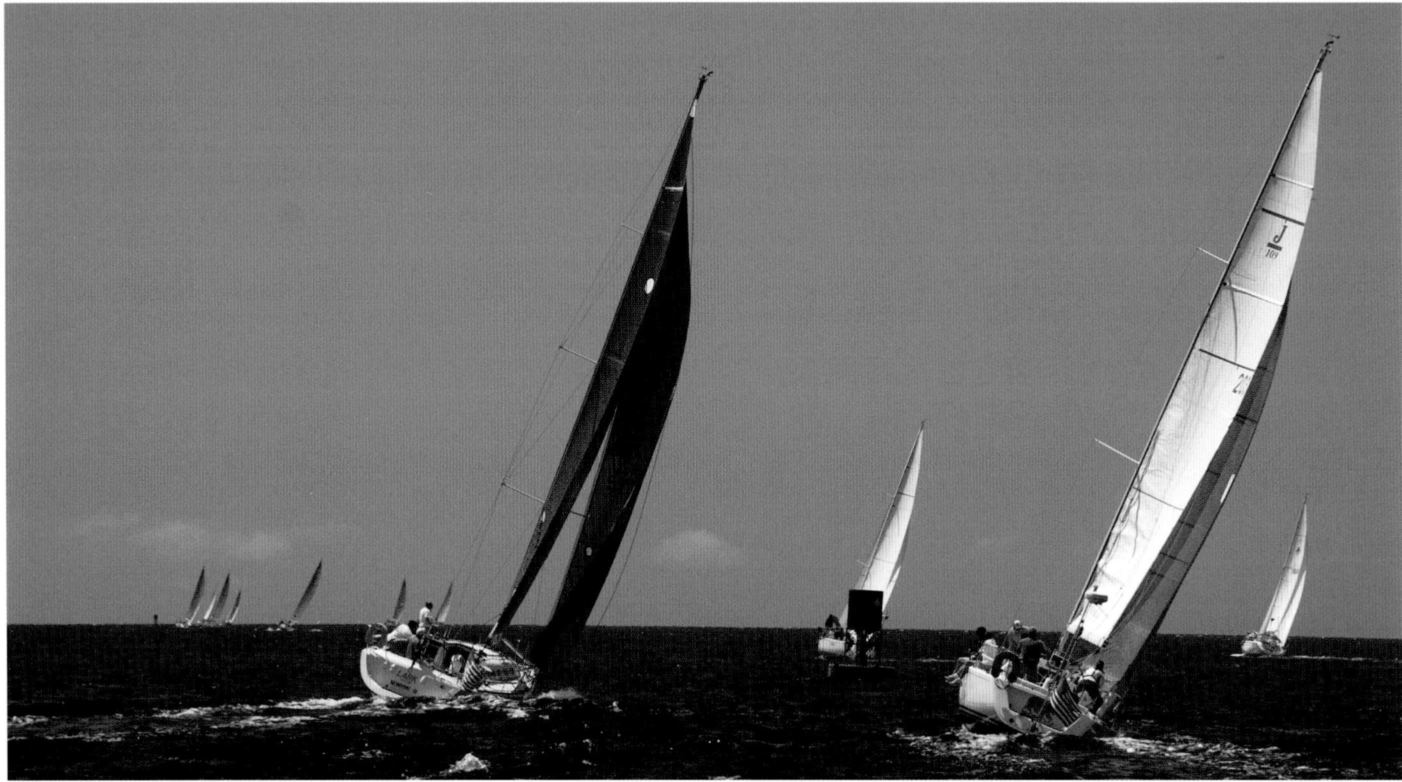

Looking south towards the Atlantic Ocean; Castle Hill, with its red signal, guides present-day sailors. Newport, at one time the home of the America's Cup Races, is home to numerous sailboats that ply these waters.

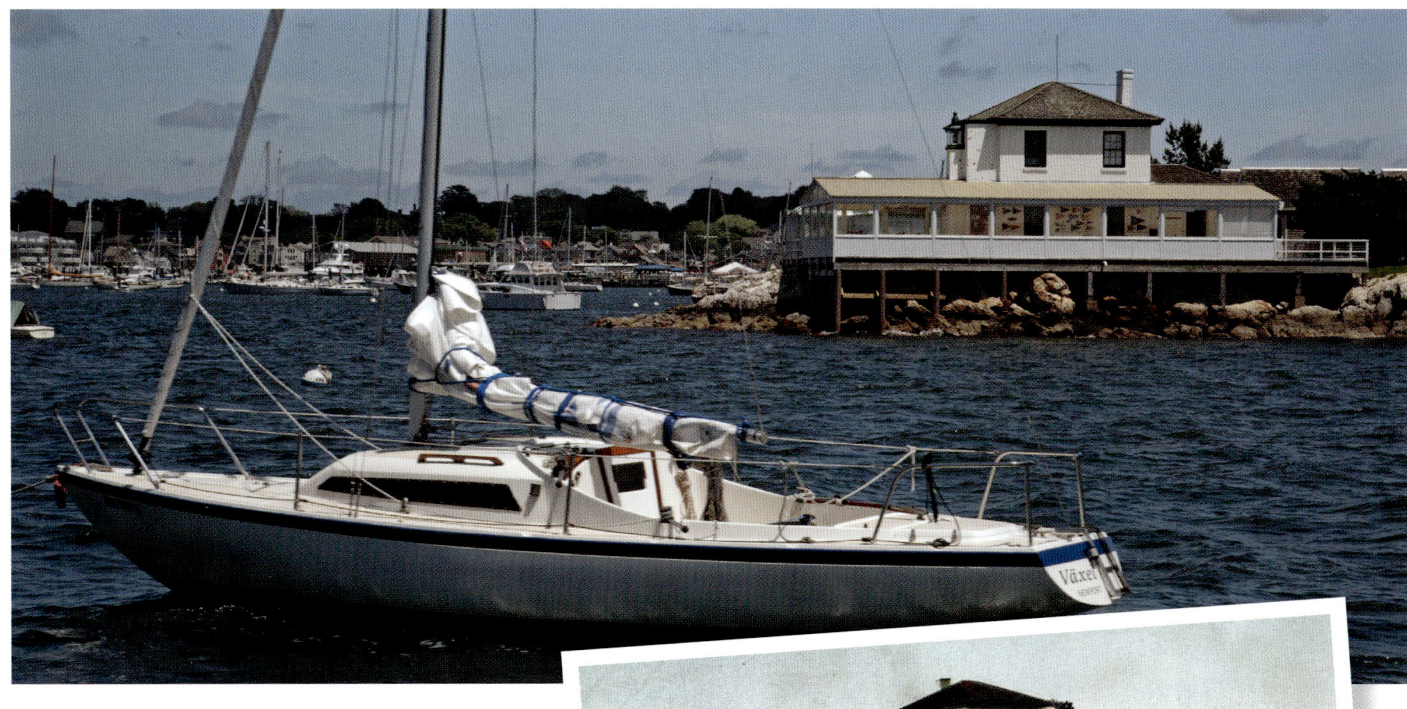

IDA LEWIS (Lime Rock)

Location: Newport Harbor, N41°28′39″, W71°19′34″

Appropriation: $1,000 in March 1853; $1,500 in August 1858 (dwelling)

Established: 1854

Disestablished: July 1927

Replacement: 1927–1963, skeleton tower, 30 feet, flashing white every 3 seconds (F1 W 3s)

Tower: Brick, white, 13 feet, integral part of keeper's house, black lantern room

Other Structures: Keeper's house (1856)

Original Lens: 6th order Fresnel lens, fixed white, focal plane 30 feet

Present Lens: Plastic

Light Characteristics: Fixed red (FR)

Range: 7 nm

Fog Signal: None

Status: Private aid to navigation, owned and maintained by Ida Lewis Yacht Club since 1928, operational mid-May to mid-October

Access: None; tower/light best seen by boat; keeper's house can be seen from nearby streets.

Comments: Keeper Ida Lewis famous for her rescues; listed in NRHP; original lens on display inside yacht club; in 1924 Rhode Island voted to change name to Ida Lewis Rock Light.

Top: Sailboats moored in Newport Harbor; Ida Lewis Yacht Club and the light are in the background.

Above: Almost a century old, this postcard captures the Lime Rock Lighthouse.

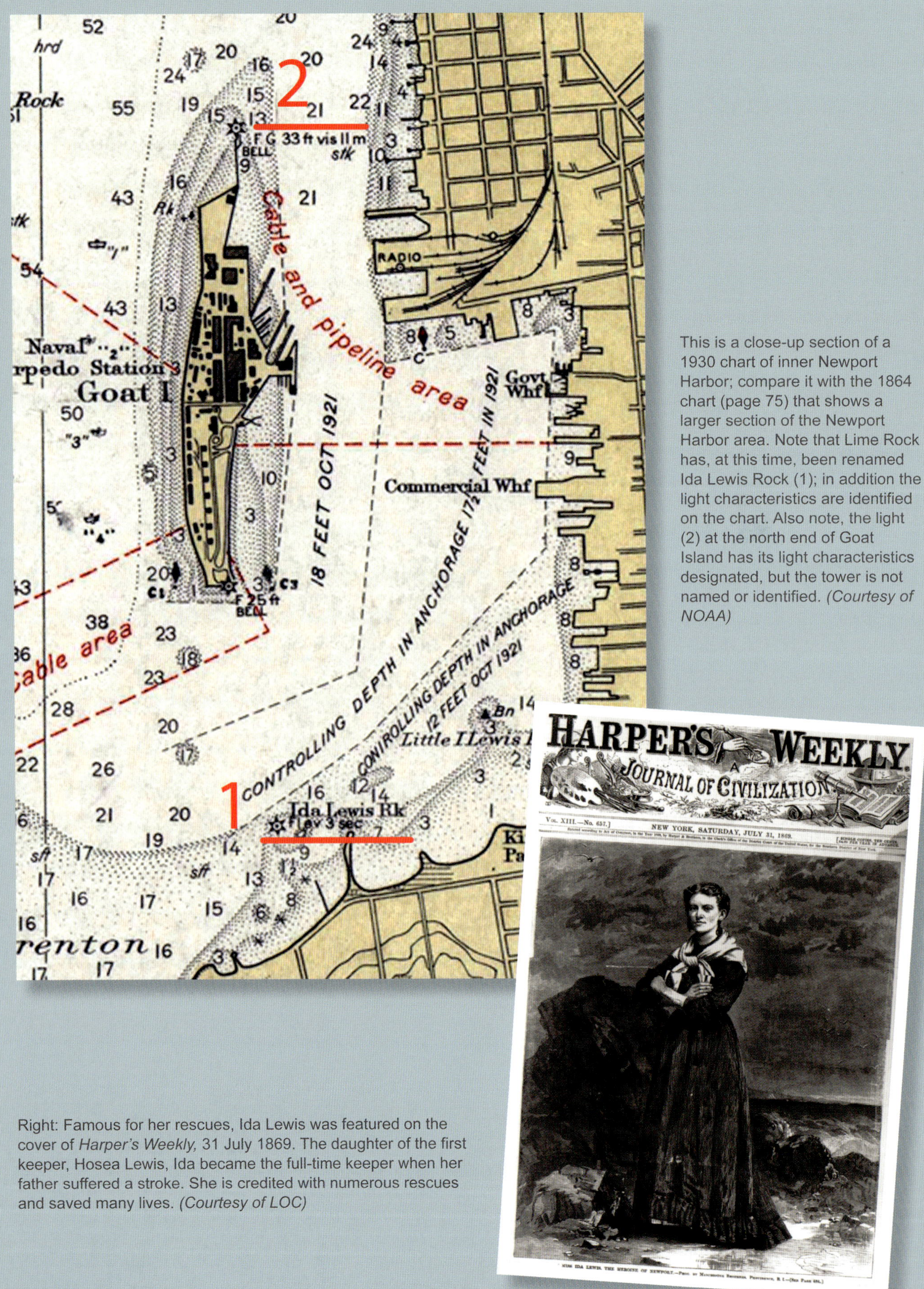

This is a close-up section of a 1930 chart of inner Newport Harbor; compare it with the 1864 chart (page 75) that shows a larger section of the Newport Harbor area. Note that Lime Rock has, at this time, been renamed Ida Lewis Rock (1); in addition the light characteristics are identified on the chart. Also note, the light (2) at the north end of Goat Island has its light characteristics designated, but the tower is not named or identified. *(Courtesy of NOAA)*

Right: Famous for her rescues, Ida Lewis was featured on the cover of *Harper's Weekly,* 31 July 1869. The daughter of the first keeper, Hosea Lewis, Ida became the full-time keeper when her father suffered a stroke. She is credited with numerous rescues and saved many lives. *(Courtesy of LOC)*

Right: Compare these two pictures of the light; the black-and-white (1936) image includes the skeleton tower (1927) that flashed white every three seconds; the present-day color image, top, shows the station that is now a private aid to navigation and maintained by the Ida Lewis Yacht club. The light is fixed red. *(Black-and-white image courtesy of USCG)*

Bottom: Undated, but identified, this archival image shows the hip-roofed brick keeper's house that was built in 1857. Closer examination of the right side of the house reveals the small attached lantern. *(Courtesy of USCG)*

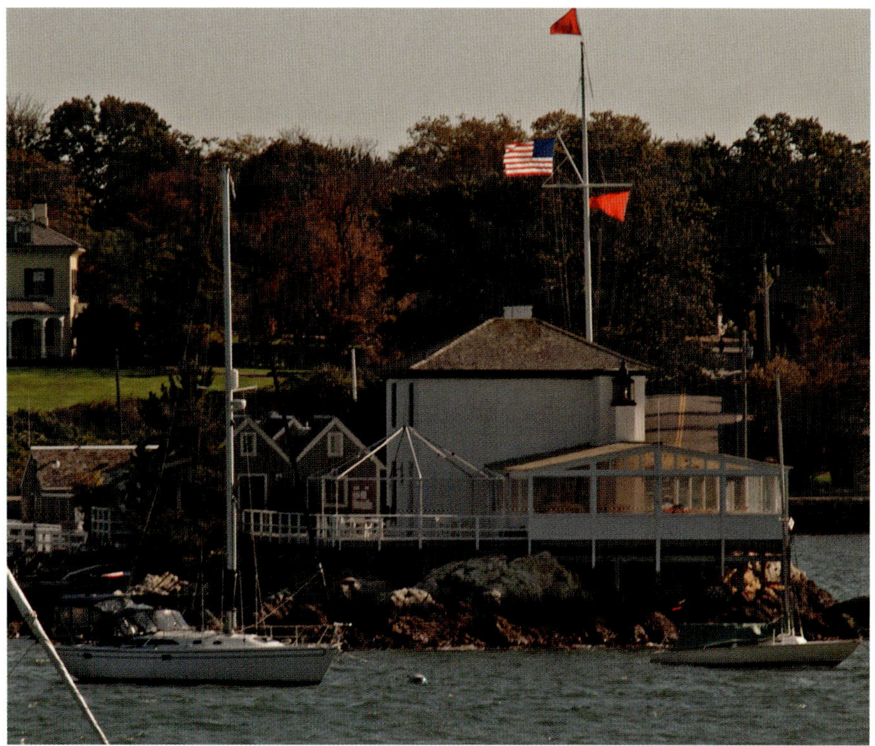

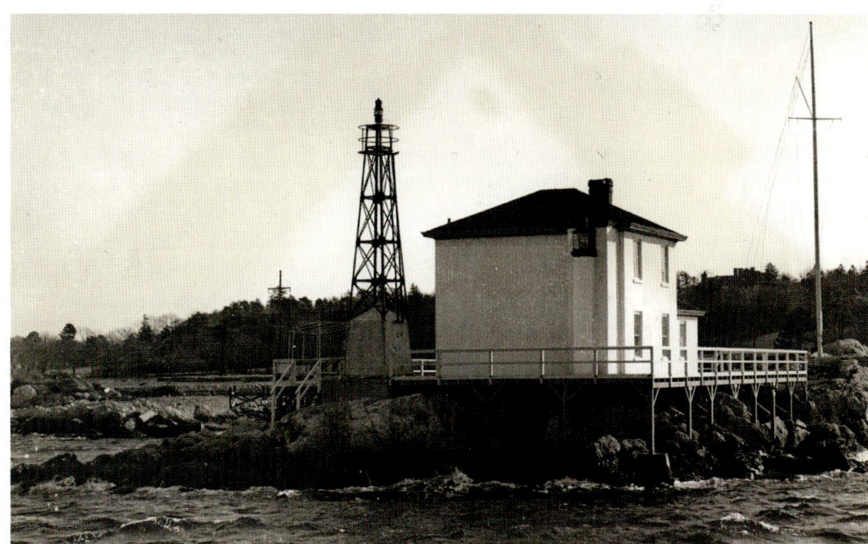

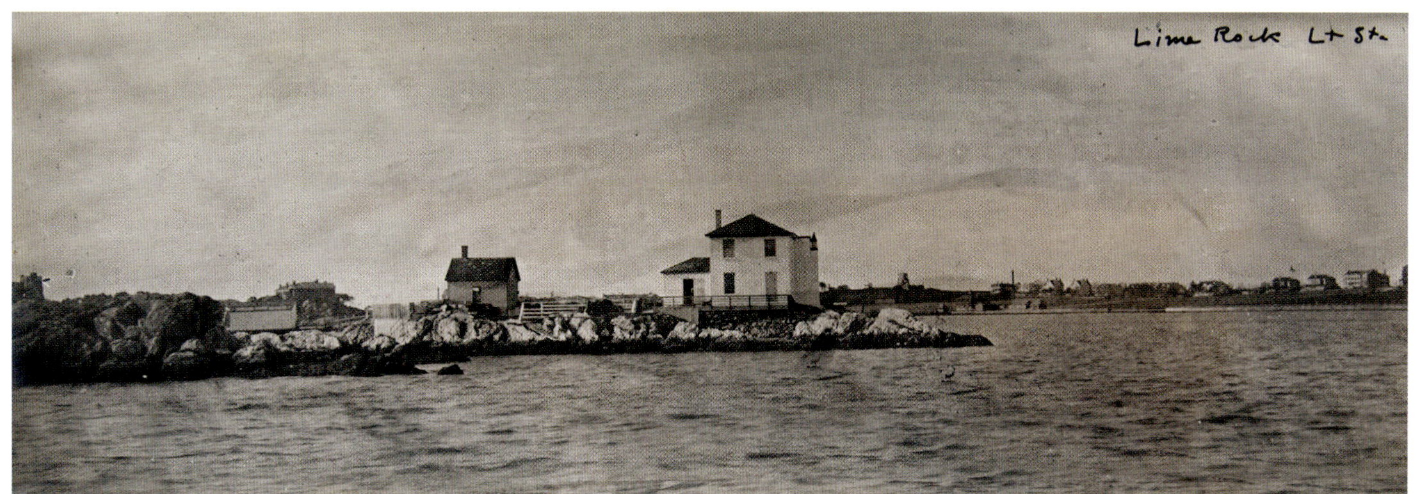

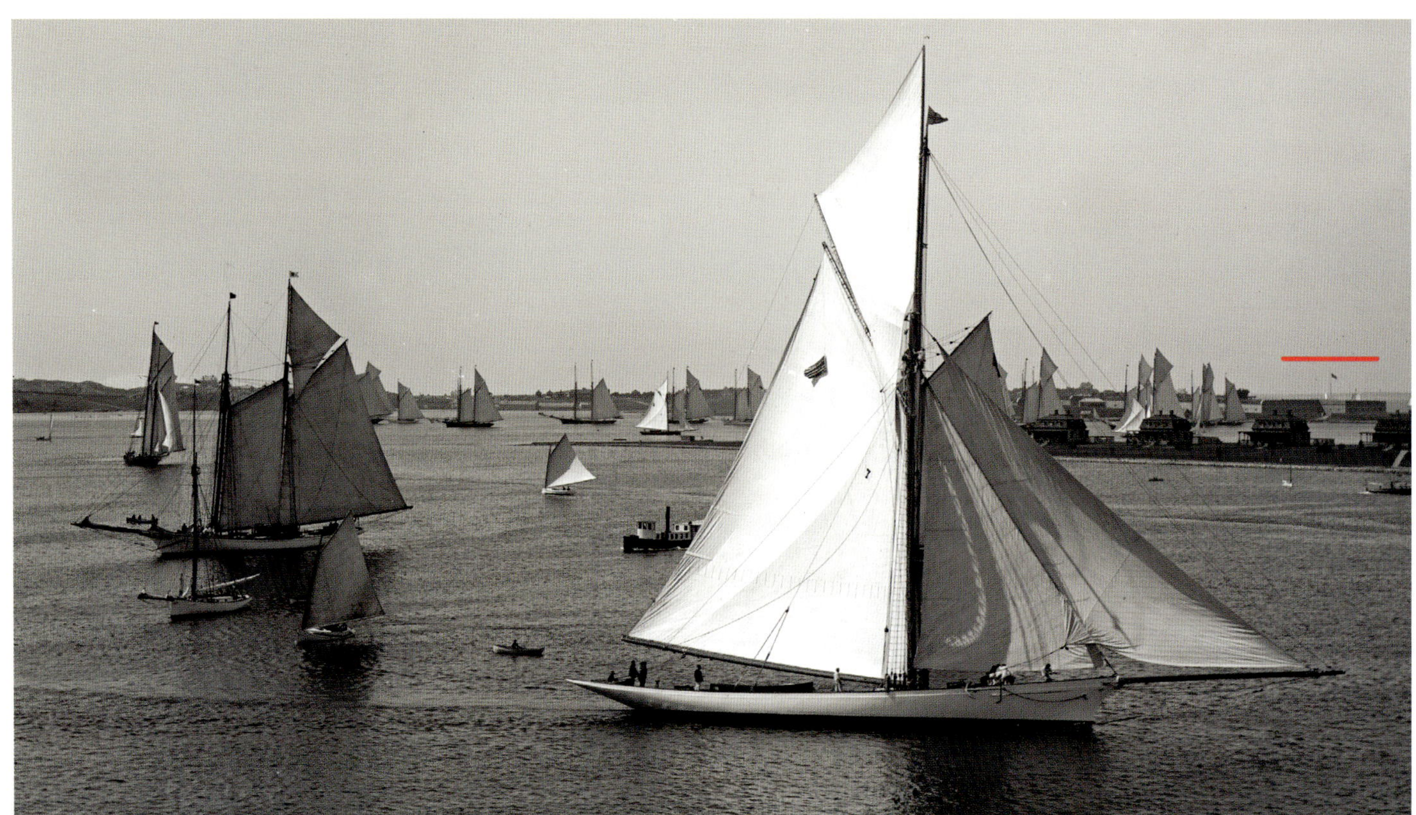

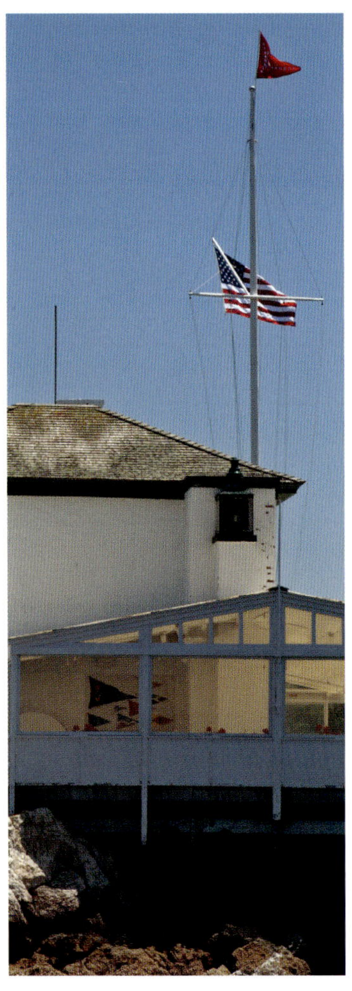

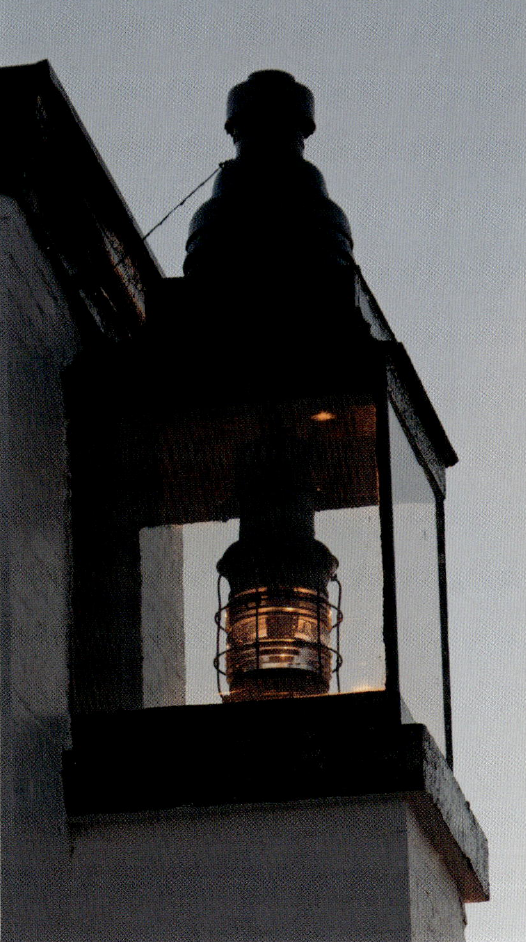

Top: Famous for the offshore America's Cup Races, the waters around Newport and Narragansett Bay are excellent for sailing. This image from the late 1880s shows some of these boats in the harbor. Use the preceding chart as a point of reference; the red line indicates Fort Adams. *(Courtesy of LOC)*

Left: Two views of the lantern on the side of the keeper's house.

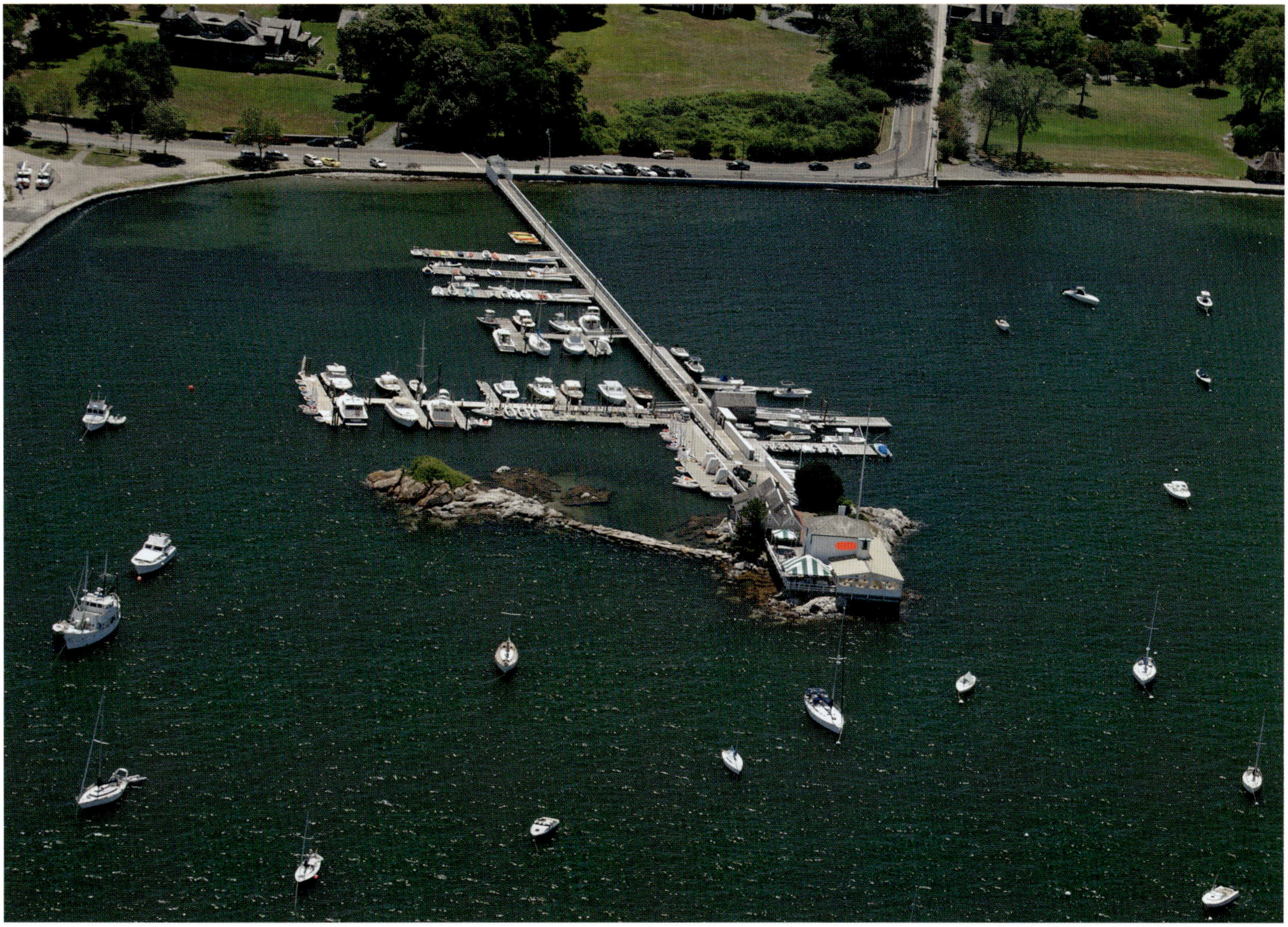

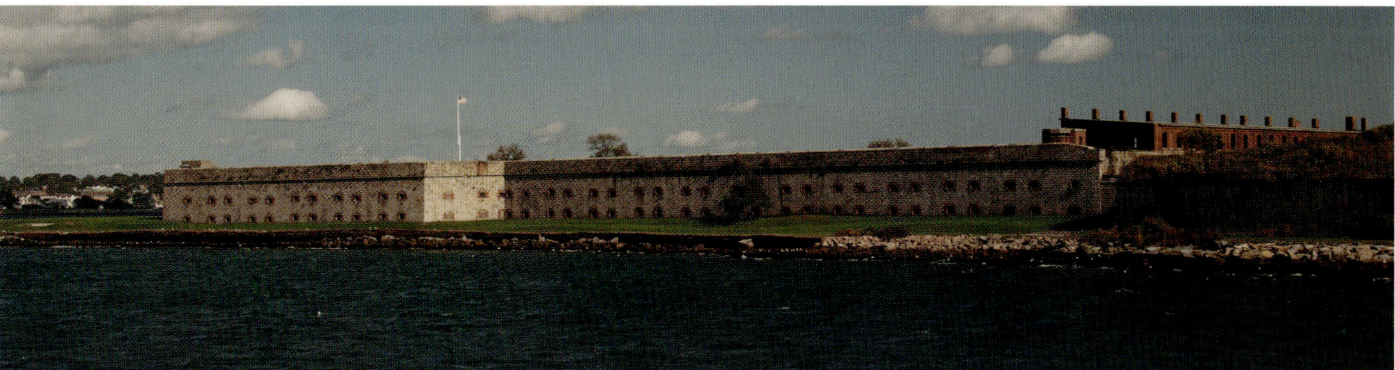

Top: An aerial view of the yacht club; just to the right of the red line is the lantern.

Bottom: A view of part of Fort Adams; Newport Harbor is to the left.

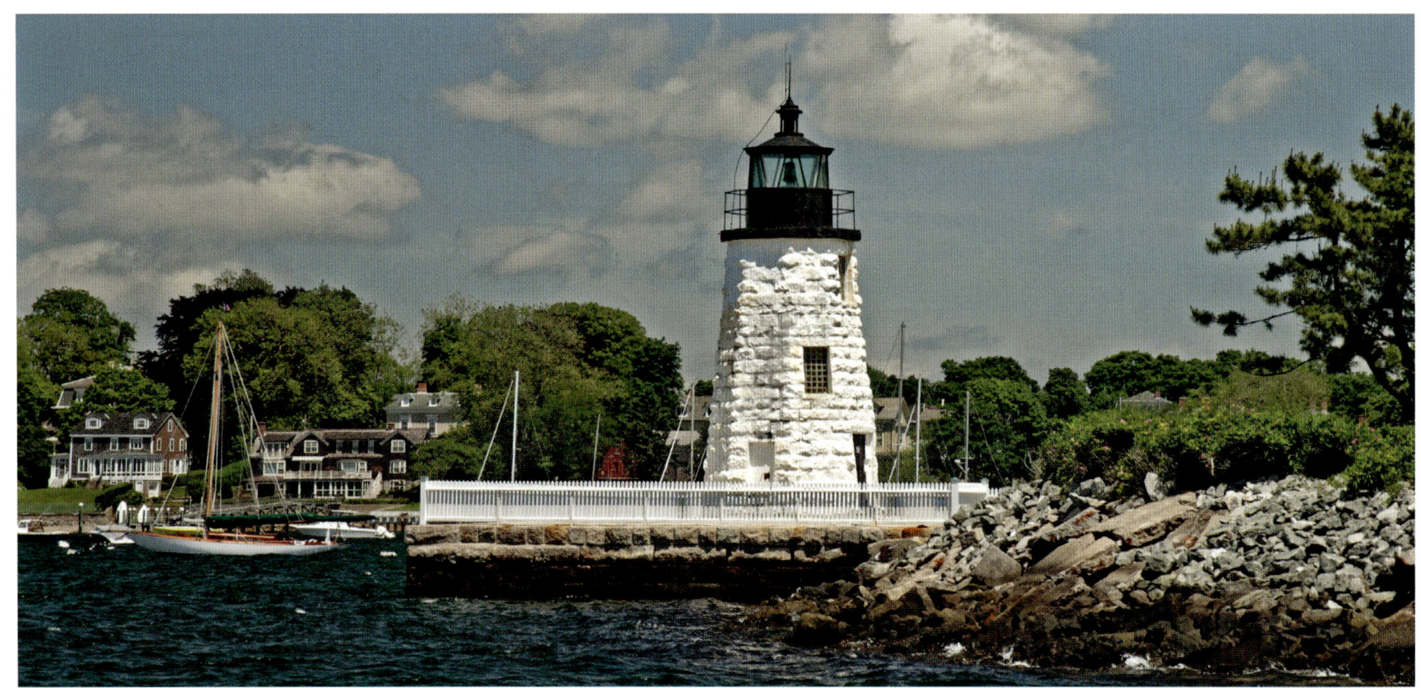

NEWPORT HARBOR
(Goat Island)

Location: North end of Goat Island, Newport Harbor, N41°29′36″, W71°19′38″

Established: 1823

Rebuilt: 1842 with 6 room keeper's house

Automated: 1963

Tower: Granite blocks, octagonal, white, 35 feet high, black lantern room

Other Structures: None remain

Original Optics: 1838, 8 lamps with 9 inch reflectors, fixed white (FW); 1842 15 lamps with reflectors

Original Lens: 1857, 4th order Fresnel lens (FW); 1924 fixed green; 1939 5th order Fresnel lens fixed green (FG)

Present Lens: 250 mm, focal plane 33 feet

Light Characteristics: Fixed green (FG)

Range: 11 nm

Fog Signal: 1873, machine-struck bell once every 15 seconds; at present, none

Status: Active U. S. Coast Guard aid to navigation

Access: Grounds open year-round, tower closed.

Comments: Original (1823) tower moved to Prudence Island (Sandy Point) in 1842; U.S. Navy used island to make torpedoes; electrified in 1922; managed by American Lighthouse Foundation; listed in NRHP.

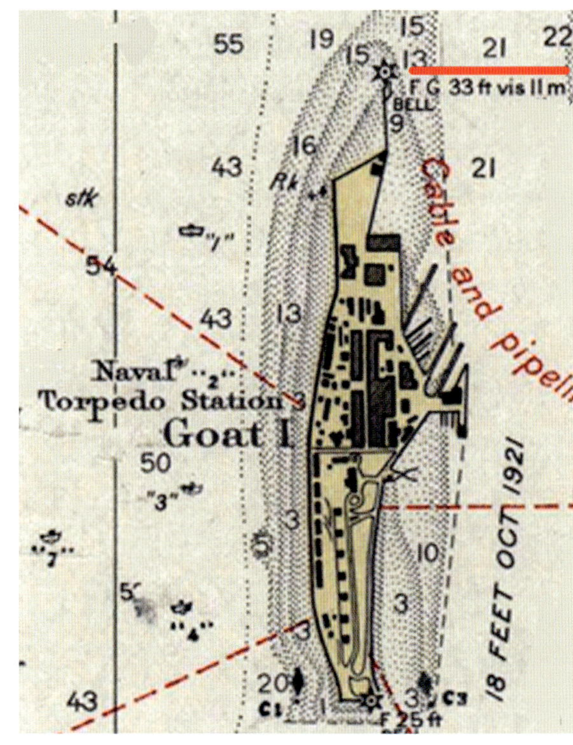

Top: Goat Island Light from the water.

Above: This 1930 chart identifies the lighthouse, located at the northern end of Goat Island, as displaying a fixed green light at 33 feet, and visible for 11 miles. Once the site of a Naval Torpedo Station (first built in 1869), the island now has a luxury hotel and exclusive marinas.

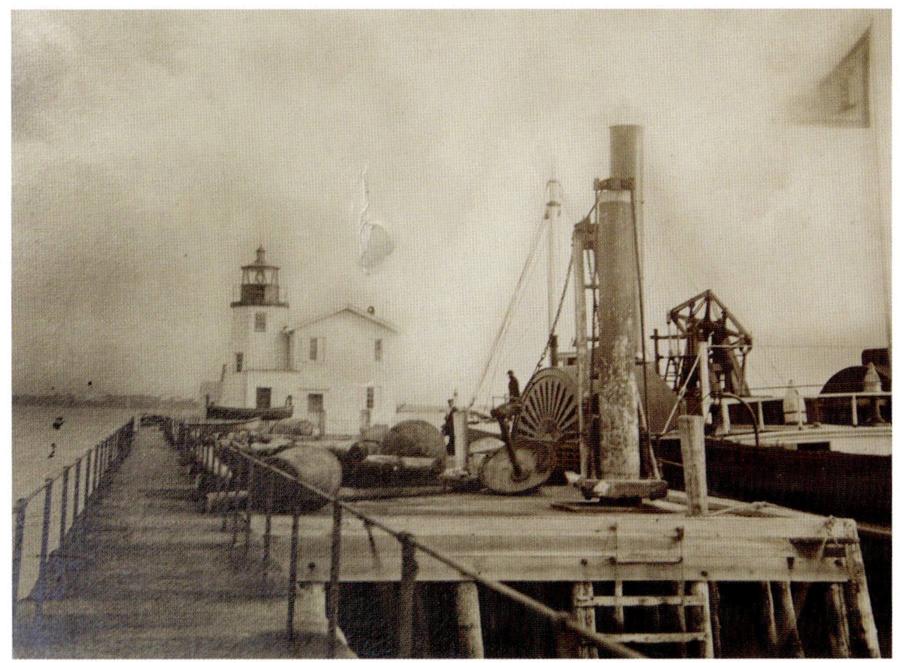

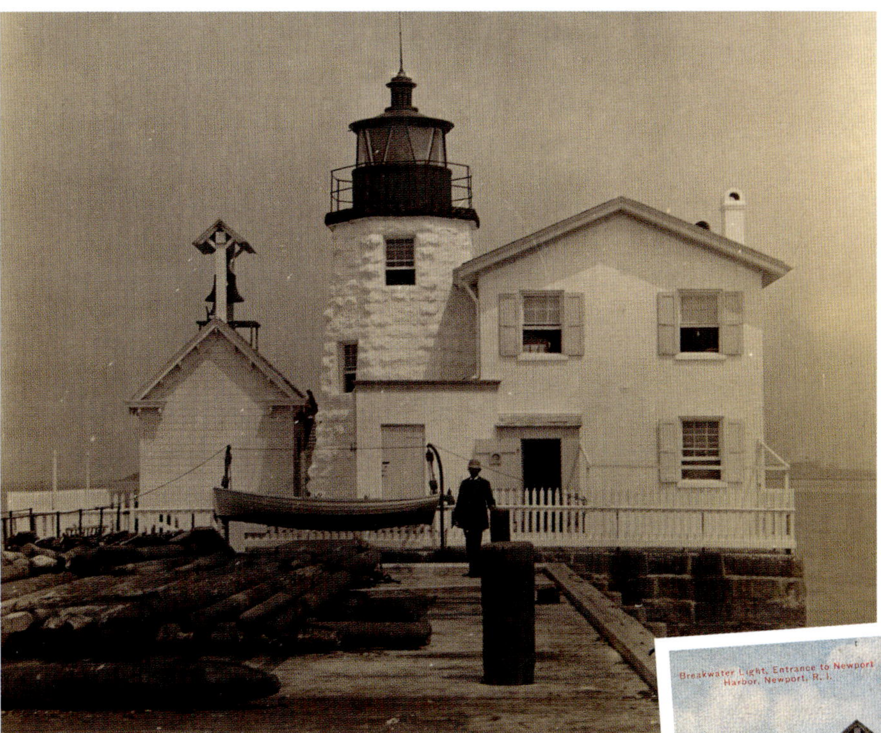

Top: This archival image shows a side-wheeler ship in the foreground with buoys and mushroom anchors to the left; in the background is the Newport Light with the keeper's house attached. *(Courtesy of NA)*

Left: Showing the keeper standing to the left of the door, this photograph is the Goat Island Light Station as it looked in 1884. Compare this with the postcard below; the building with the bell has now been painted red. Also the station has been identified as the Breakwater Light. *(Black-and-white image courtesy of NA)*

Right: This image was taken in September 1938 after the hurricane. Rammed by a submarine in 1922, the keeper's house sustained damage and was removed shortly thereafter. The tower, after the storm, had received minimal damage. Note the bell in the foreground, which would strike once every fifteen seconds. *(Courtesy of USCG)*

Below: The tower with its distinctive green signal light.

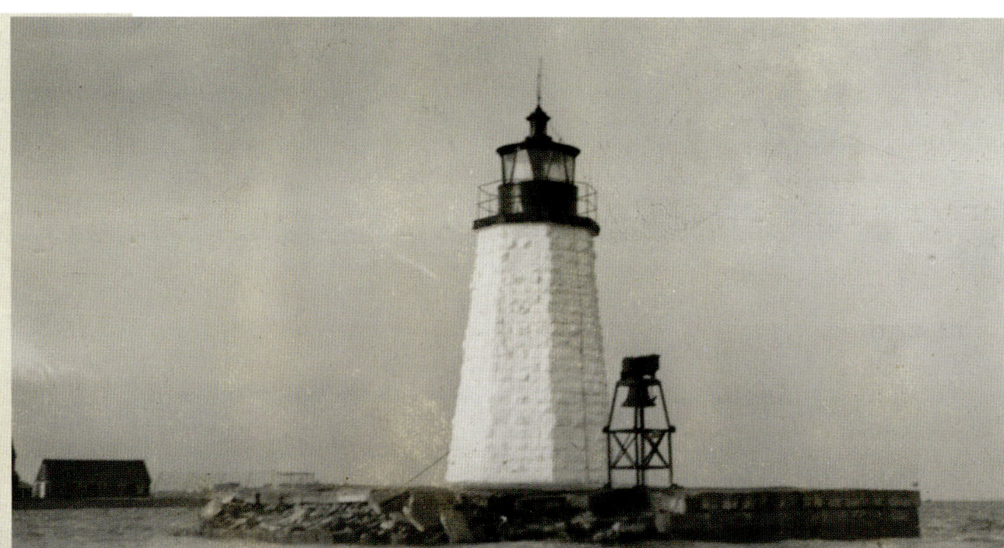

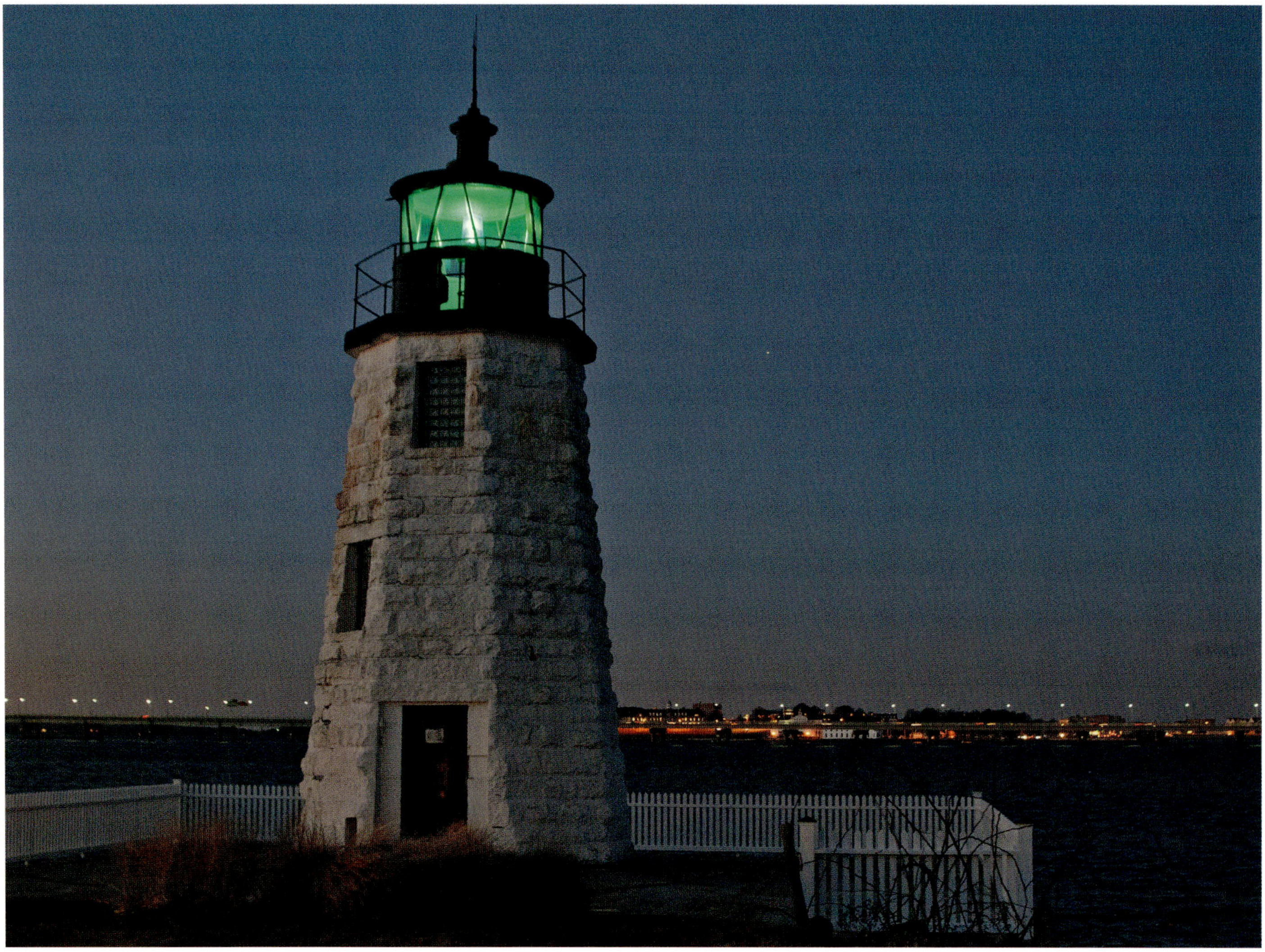

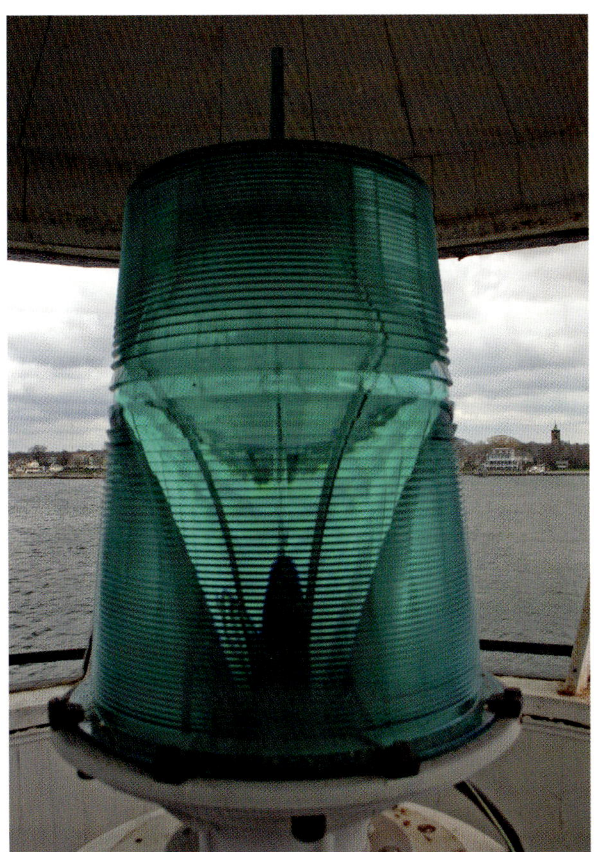

Left: The modern plastic beacon in the lantern room; electrified in 1922, the light was automated in 1963. *(Courtesy of J. D'Entremont)*

Center: Looking down the granite stairs in the tower. *(Courtesy of J. D'Entremont)*

Bottom: Once the home of the America's Cup races, Newport still boasts many of the competition's 12-meter sailboats. These two are sailing past the lighthouse; US 6 is the *Onawa*, the oldest 12 meter (built in 1928) still active. US 11 *Gleam* was built nine years later.

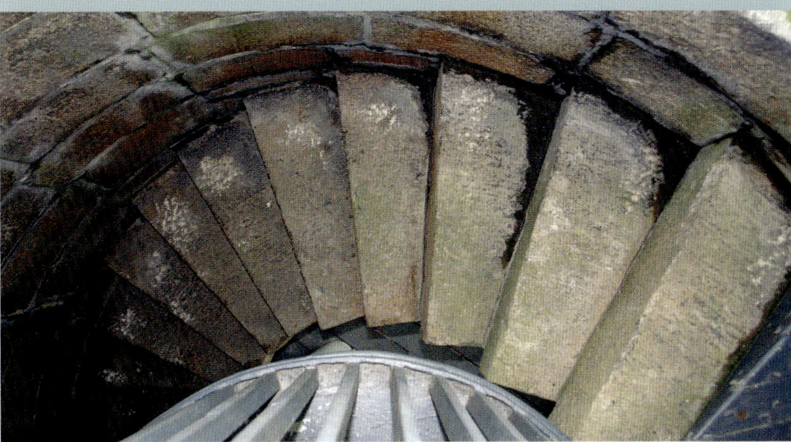

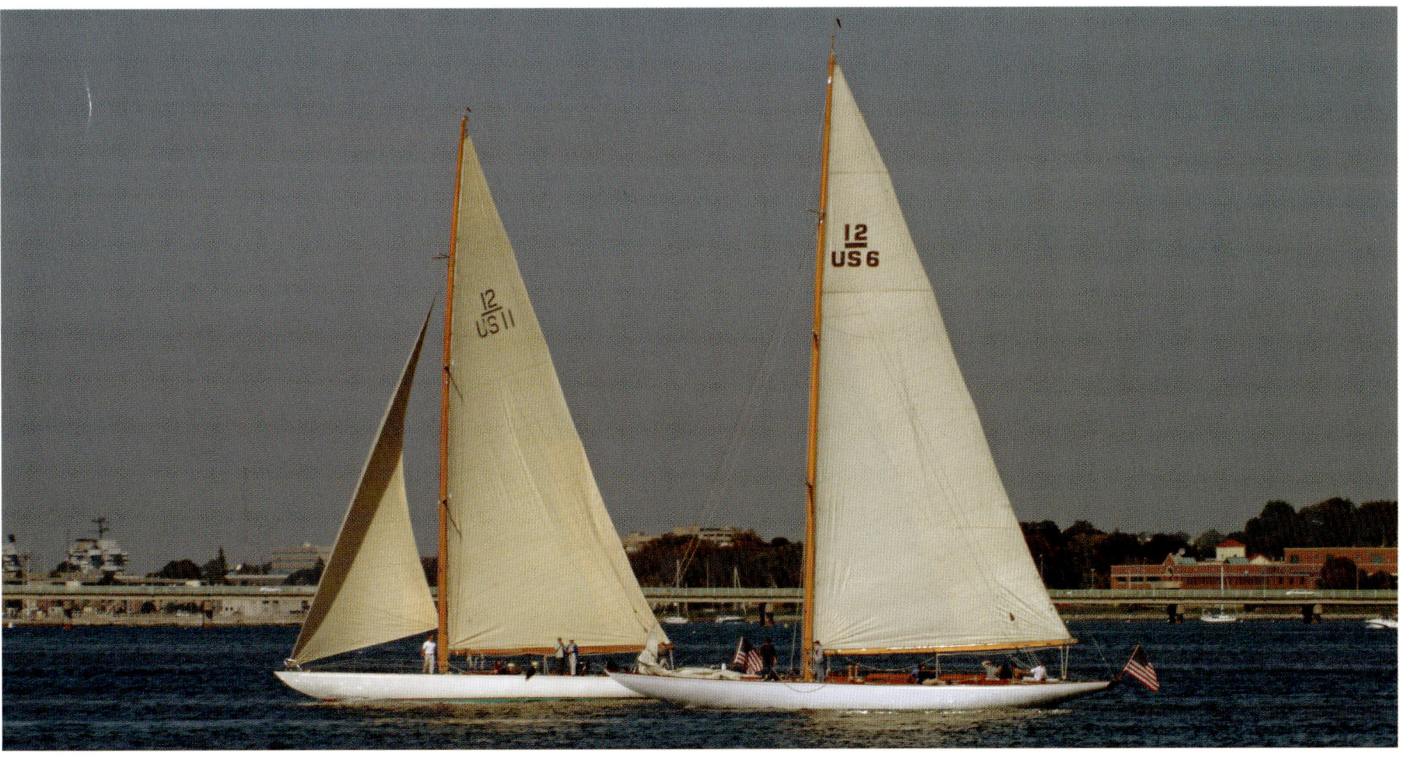

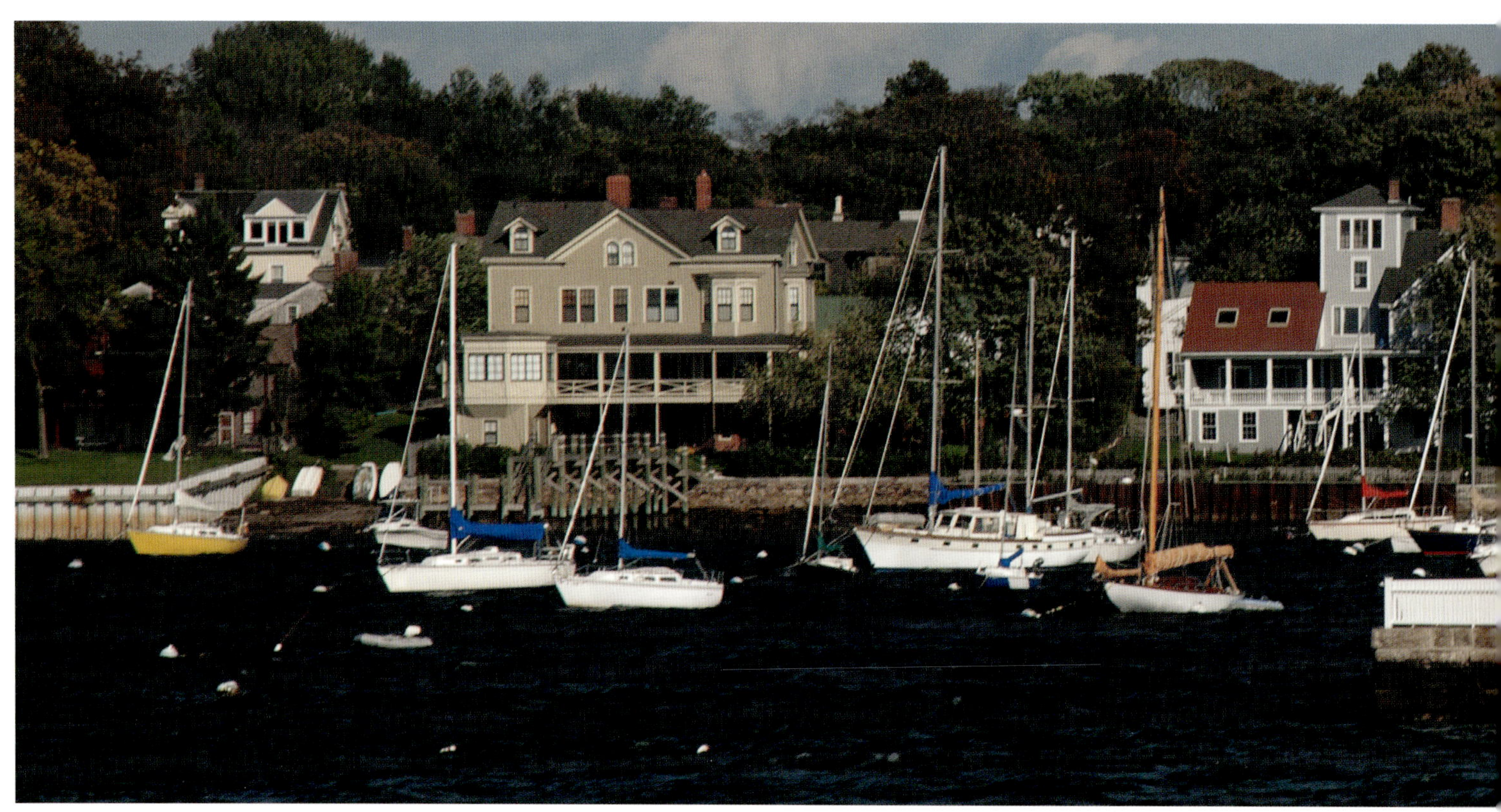

Compare this panorama taken from a boat (above) with the aerial vista at right, and identify several of the same boats.

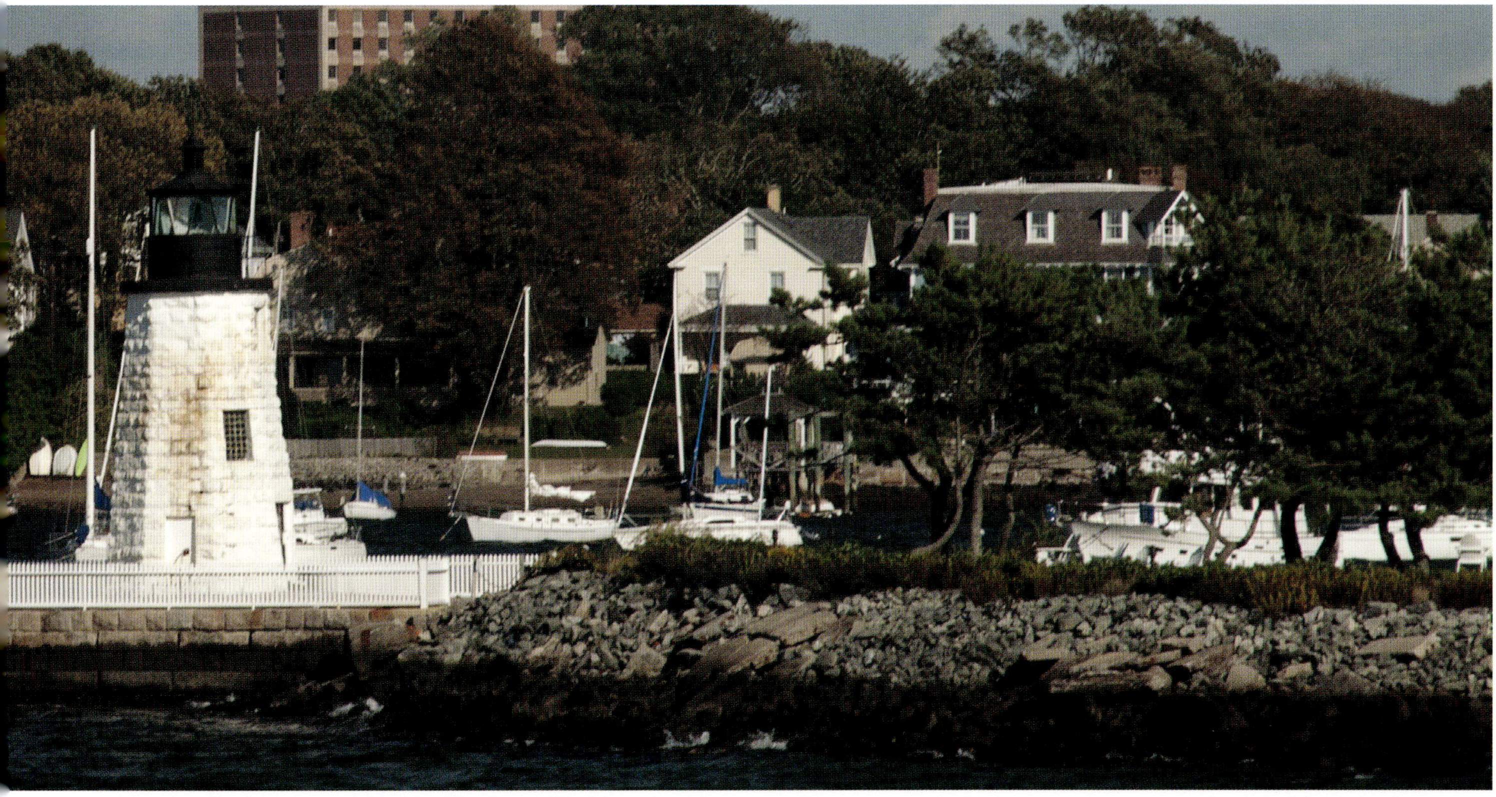

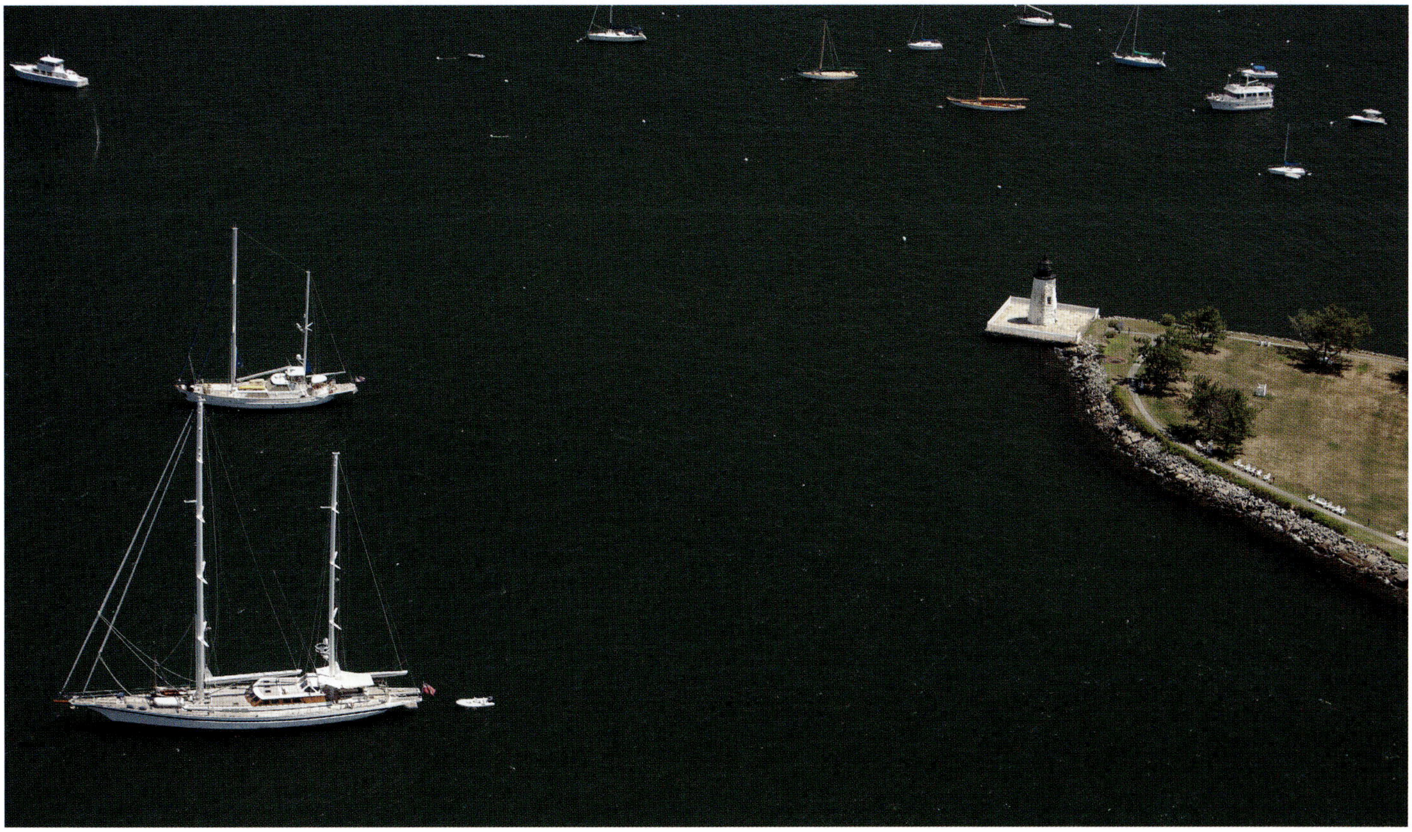

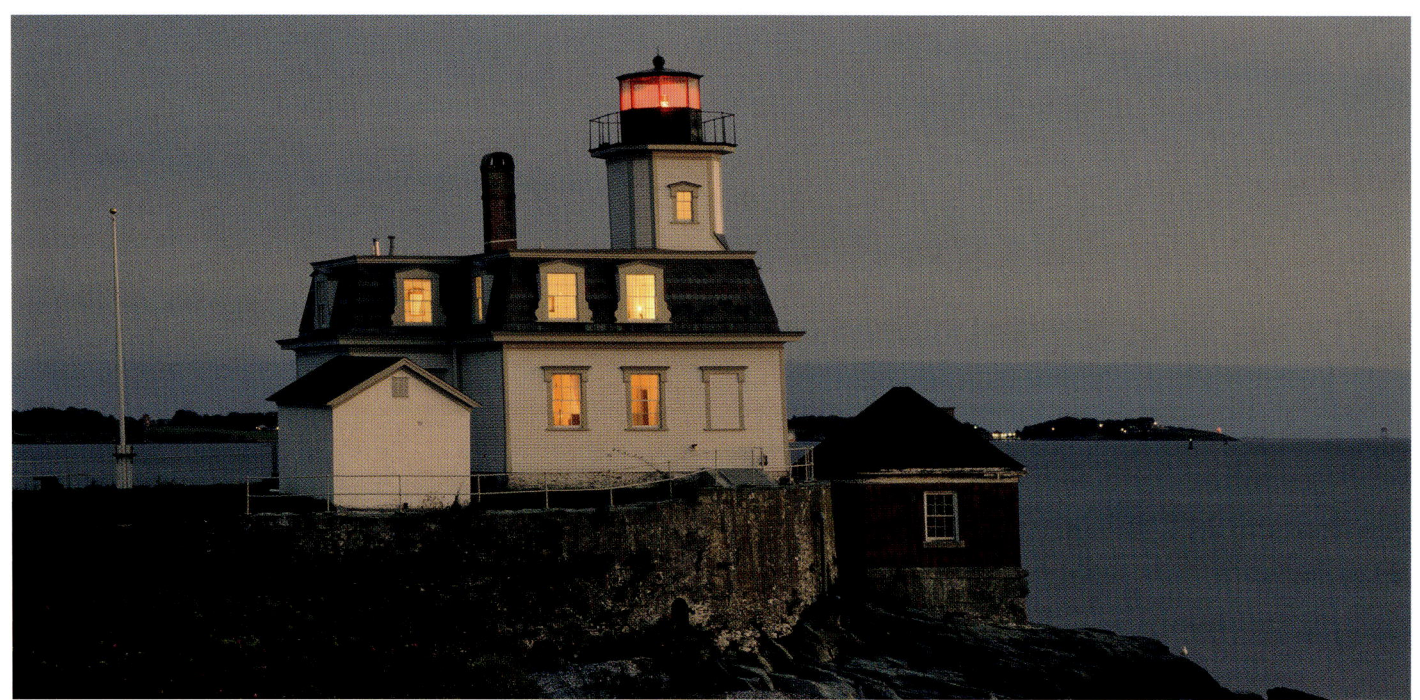

ROSE ISLAND

Location: North end of Newport Harbor, N41°29′44″ W71°20′4″
Appropriation: $7,500 in July 1868
Established: January 1870
Deactivated: 1971–1993
Reactivated: August 1993 and automated
Tower: Integral with French Second Empire Revival style 8-room keeper's house, white, wood, octagonal, black lantern room, 35 feet
Other Structures: Oil house (1912), fog-signaling house, U.S. Navy, Fort Hamilton, buildings for torpedoes and mines (off-limits)
Original Lens: 1873, 6th order Fresnel lens, fixed red (FR)
Present Lens: Plastic
Light Characteristics: Flashing white every 6 seconds (FLW 6s), focal plane 48 feet
Range: 5 nm
Fog Signal: Original, none; 1885 fog bell; present, none
Status: Made obsolete by Newport-Pell Bridge lights in 1970; now a private aid to navigation
Access: Grounds open to the public; ferry service and lighthouse tours during summer; house available for rental; owned by the City of Newport; preserved and maintained by the Rose Island Lighthouse Foundation; most of island off-limits due to previous storage of military explosives.
Comments: Sister lighthouse to Pomham Rocks; listed in NHRP.

(Note: Nearby Pomham Rocks, page 128, is the same design as Rose Island. It has not been restored to the extent that Rose Island has; observe the interior images of Rose Island to presume what the interior of Pomham Rocks would look like.)

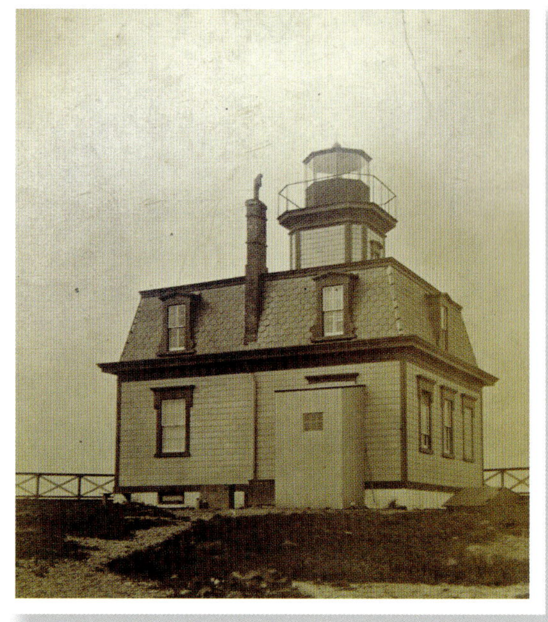

Top: Captured in the early evening and looking south; barely visible, the light on the right side of the tip of land is Castle Hill Light. *(Courtesy of LOC)*

Bottom: Undated, this is an image of the rear side of Rose Island Light. *(Courtesy of NA)*

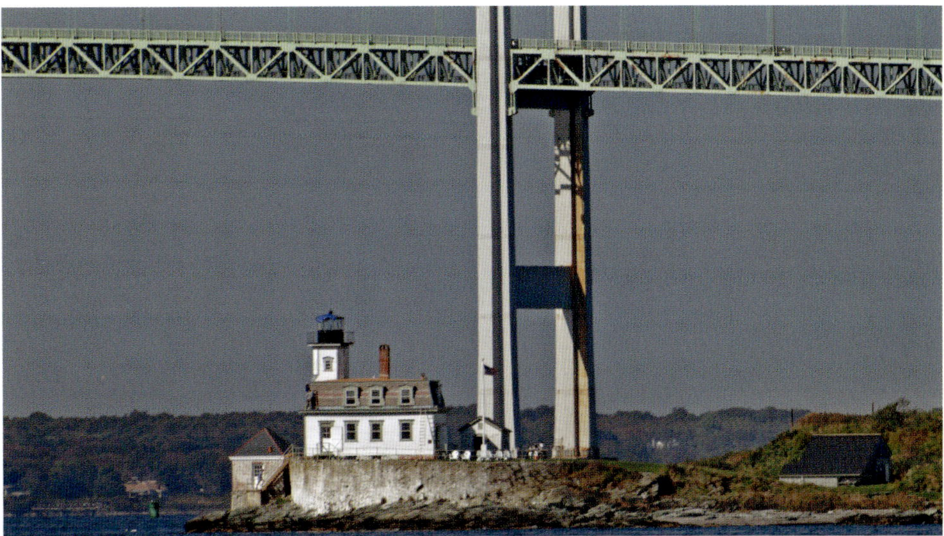

Top: Looking north with the Jamestown-Verrazano Bridge in the background; restored Rose Island now provides accommodations for visitors.

Center: Looking east with Newport in the background, this is the channel side of the light. Closer examination reveals Goat Island Light just to the left of the red lightship. The white boat shown brings visitors to the island, and the red Nantucket lightship, the LV 612, was the last lightship on active duty and retired in 1983.

Below: A view of the entire island, once a U.S. Navy facility. Most of the island is off limits.

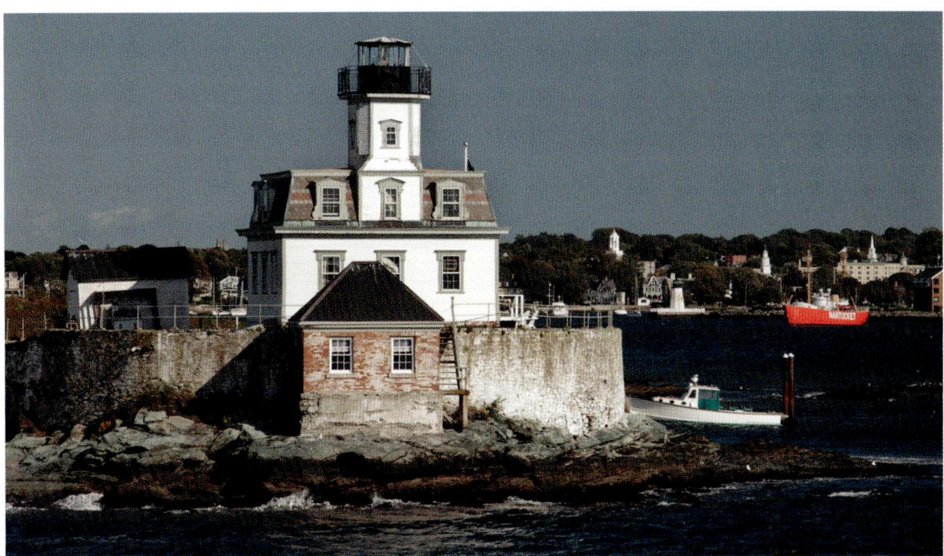

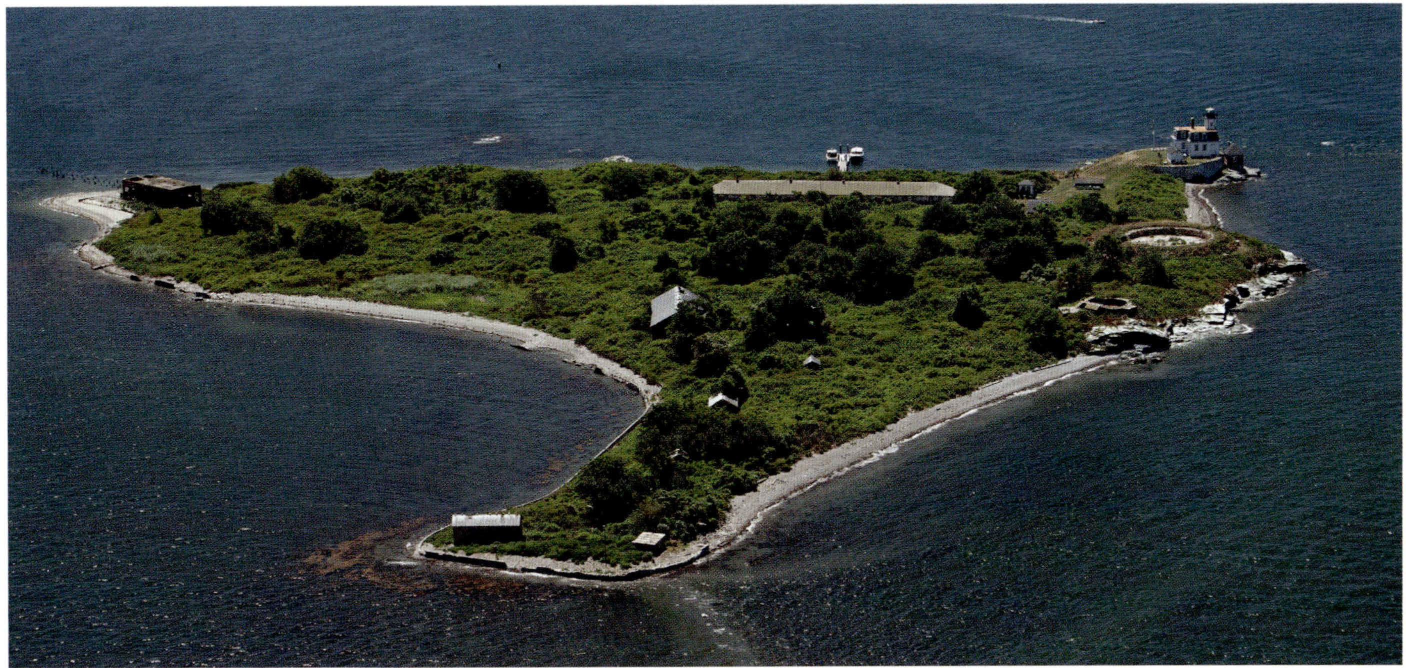

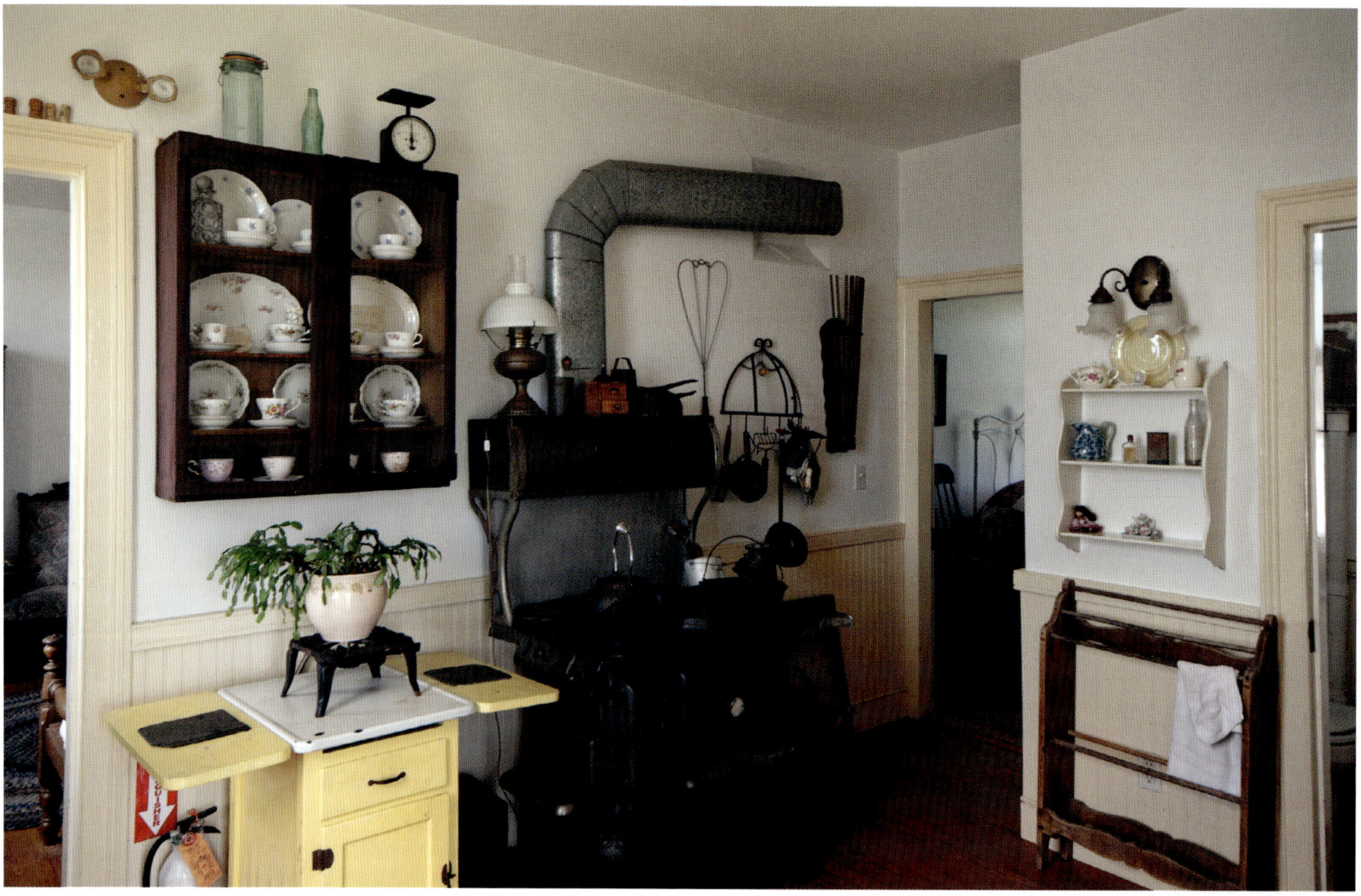

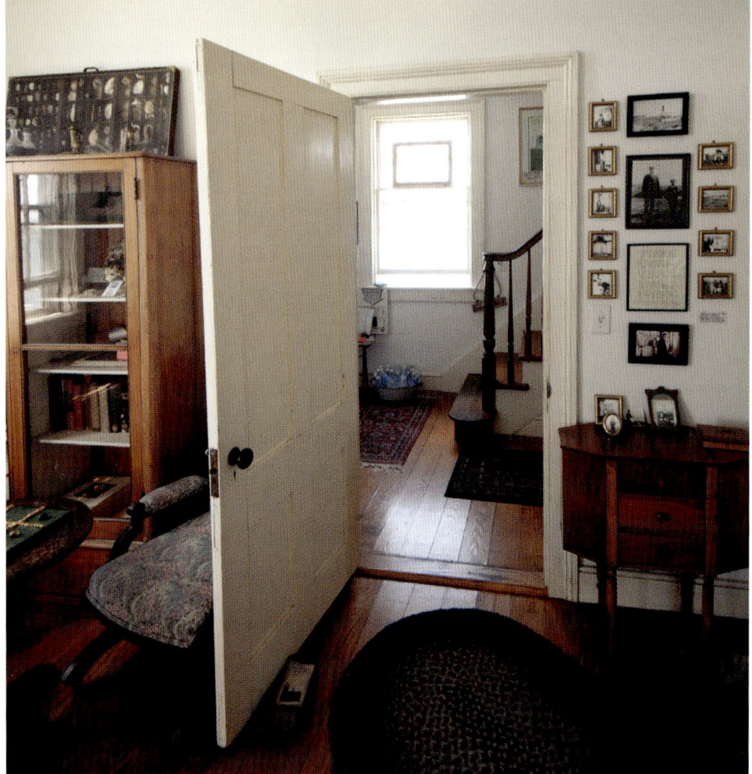

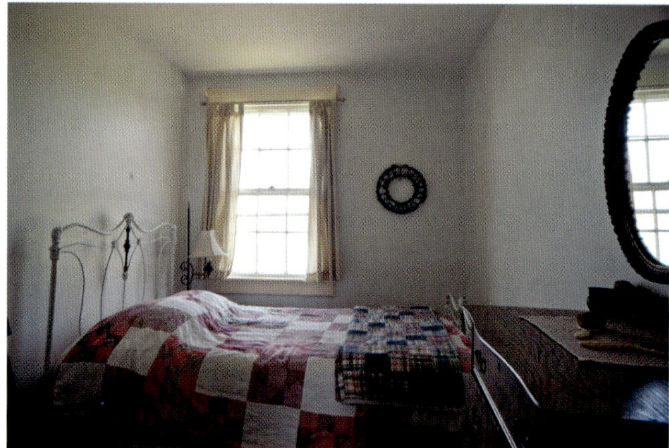

Top: The kitchen is restored and now functional for guests.

Left: Historic images of the light hang on the wall; the stairs in the background lead to the second floor.

Above: One of the bedrooms available for guests.

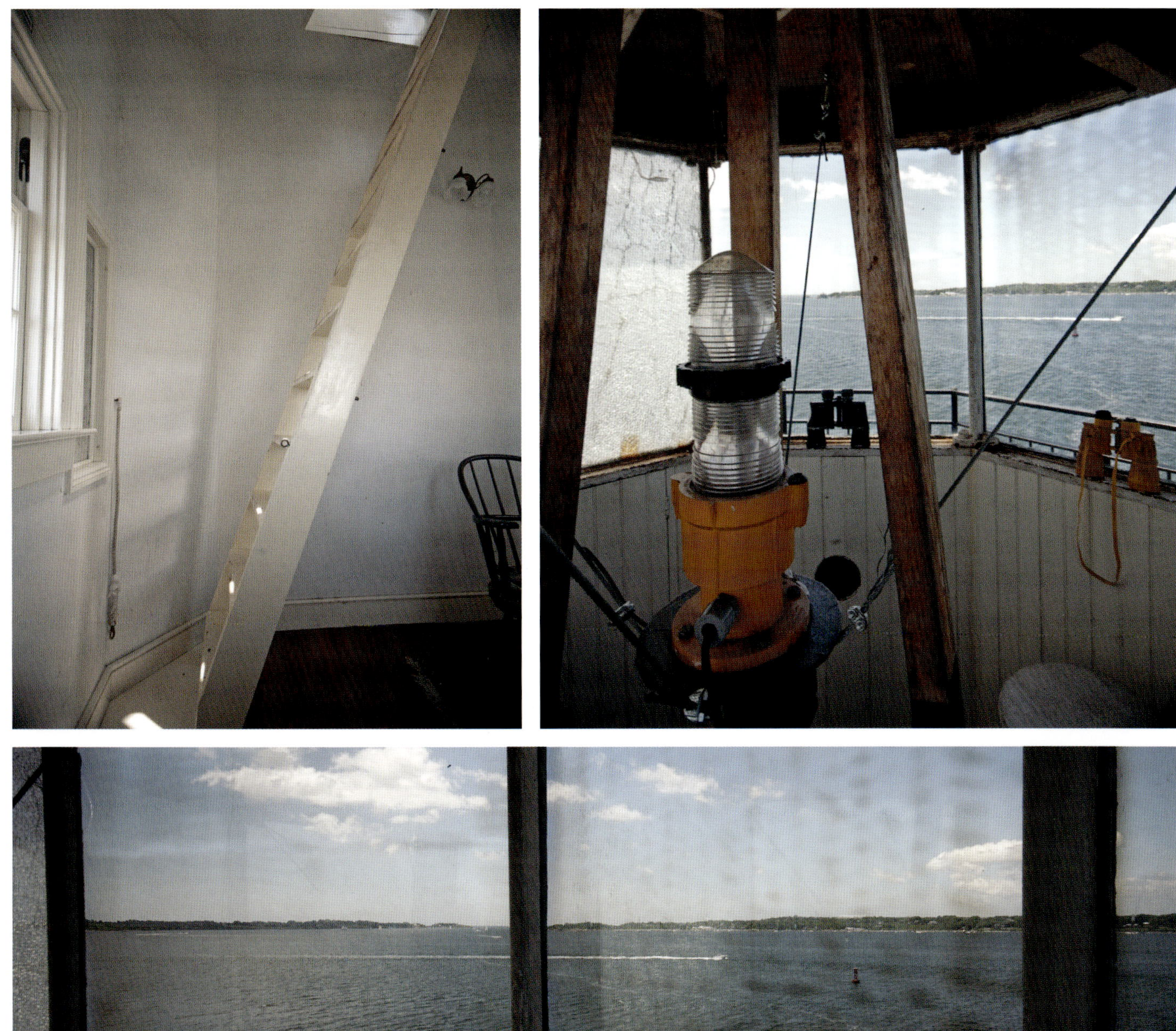

Top left: A final flight of wooden stairs leads to the lantern room.

Top right: A modern plastic beacon provides the light; Conanicut Island is in the distance.

Bottom: There are outstanding views in the lantern room; binoculars are provided for guests. Looking south, Castle Hill Light is visible just to the left of the center support.

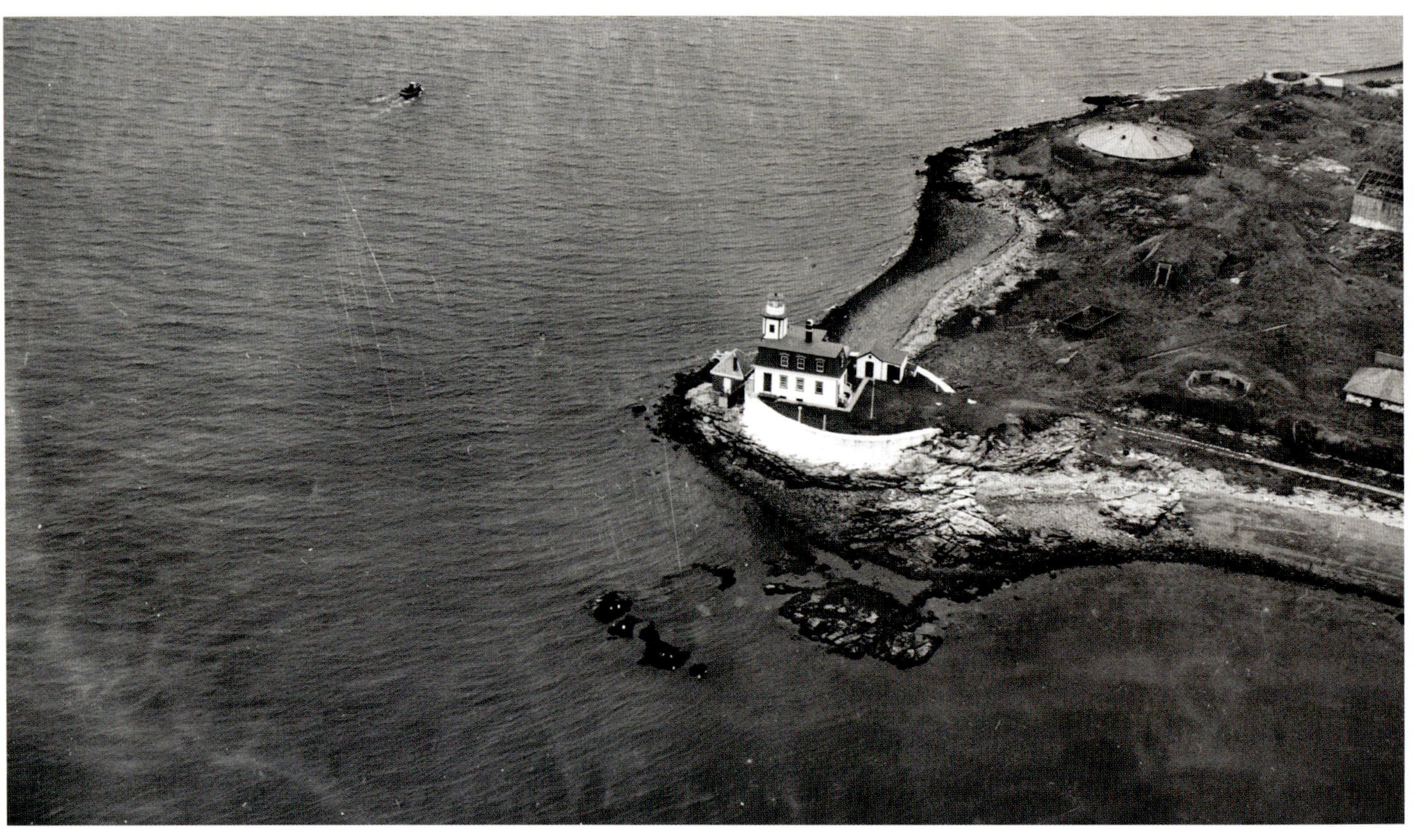

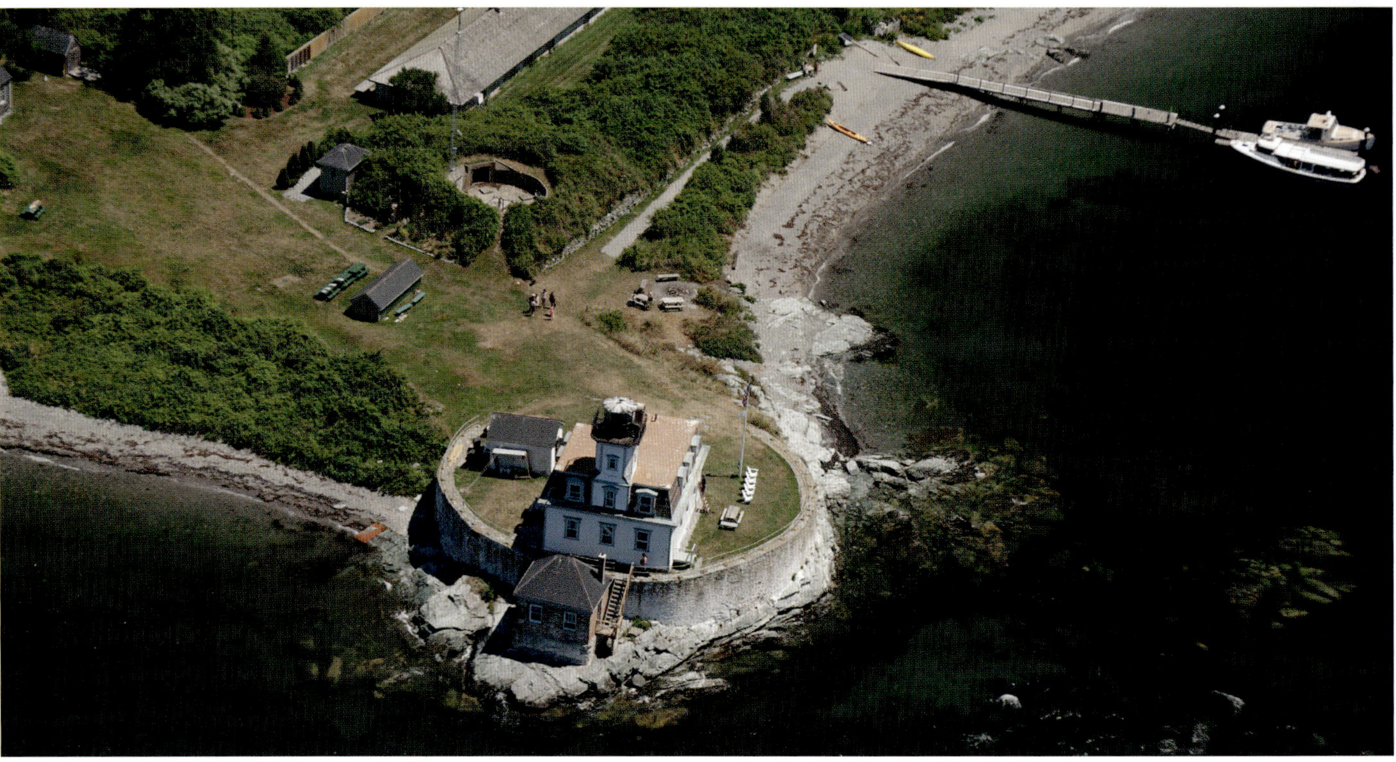

Two aerial views of the light taken more than sixty years apart. *(Black-and-white image courtesy of USCG)*

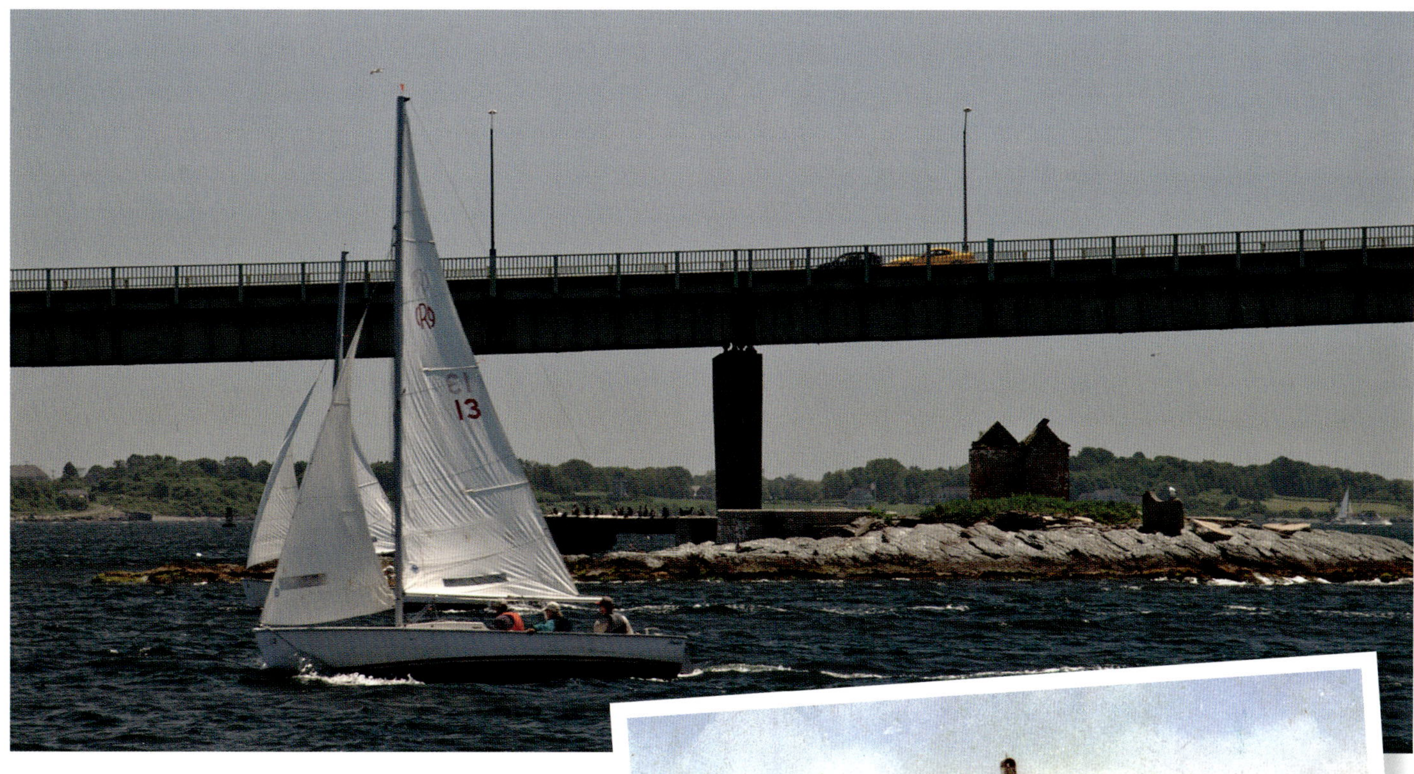

GULL ROCKS

Location: Newport Harbor, north entrance, N41° 30′78″, W71°19′84″, station no longer exists
Appropriation: Unknown, August 1886
Established: September 1887
Disestablished: 1928
Tower: Wood, A-frame house, 44 feet, two lanterns, one at each end of roof
Other Structures: Roofless brick oil house
Original Optics: 1891 tubular lanterns, focal plane 44 feet
Light Characteristics: East light, fixed red (FR), west light, fixed white (FW)
Range: 12 nm
Fog Signal: Machine-struck bell every 5 seconds
Status: Station no longer exists, razed in mid-1960s
Access: None.
Comments: Original lights replaced by skeleton tower (1928); removed in 1970; made obsolete by Newport-Pell Bridge lights.

Top: The bridge in the background that made the light redundant; all that remains on the island is the frame of the oil house.

Bottom: Unusual in its design, Gull Rocks Lighthouse was an A-frame building with a light at each end of the peak of the roof. The east lantern showed fixed white while the west lantern was fixed red. *(Courtesy of R. Holmes)*

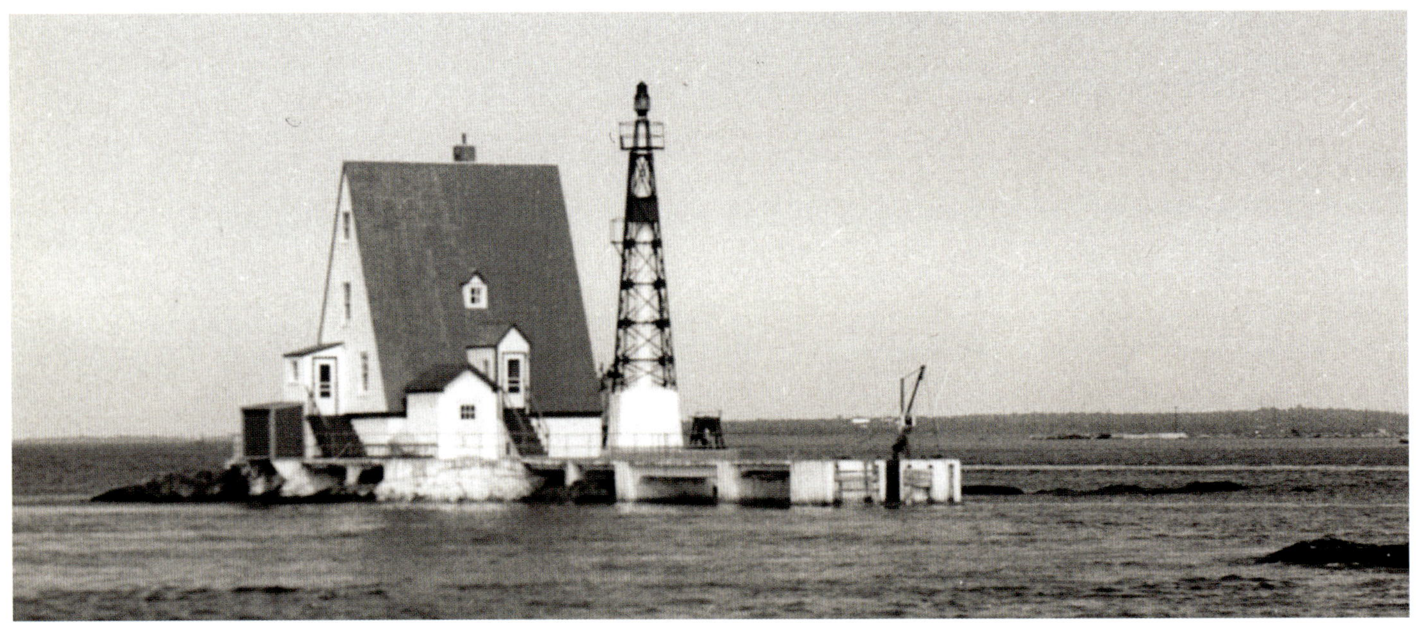

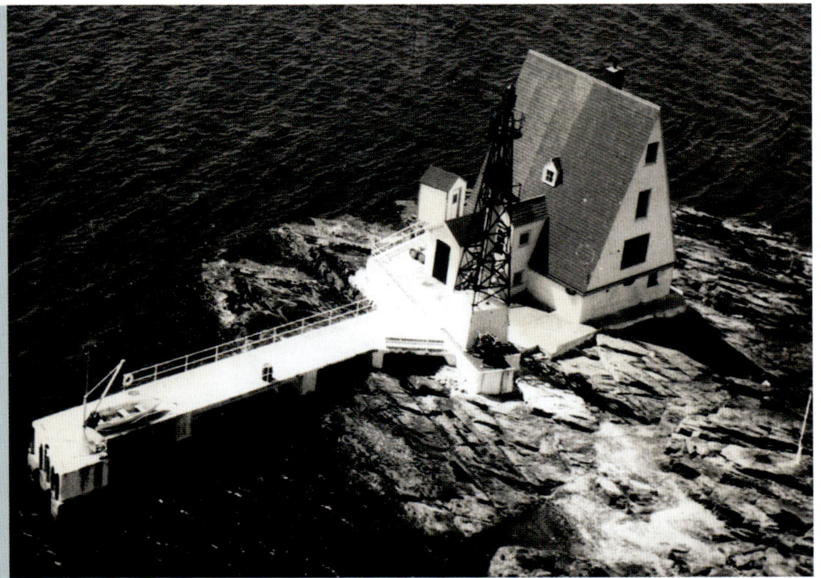

Above: Erected in 1928, this skeleton tower replaced the twin lights on the roof. During the hurricane of 1938, the station lost its boat and some stairs, and the cistern was contaminated with salt water. The station was manned until 1960; the house was torn down shortly after. With the building of the nearby Newport Bridge, the tower was discontinued and eventually removed. *(Courtesy of USCG)*

Right and bottom: Taken from opposite sides, these two aerials show Gull Rocks Light Station while it was still manned, and today with birds being the only visitors. It is possible to identify where the buildings and structures stood. *(Black-and-white image courtesy of USCG)*

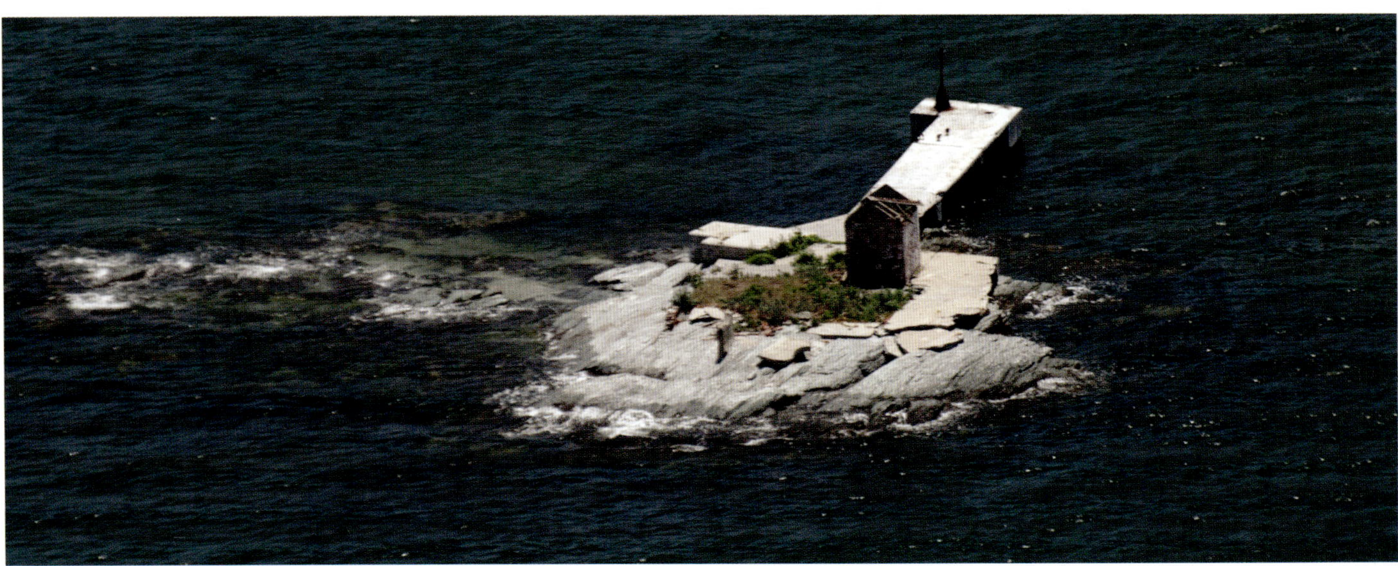

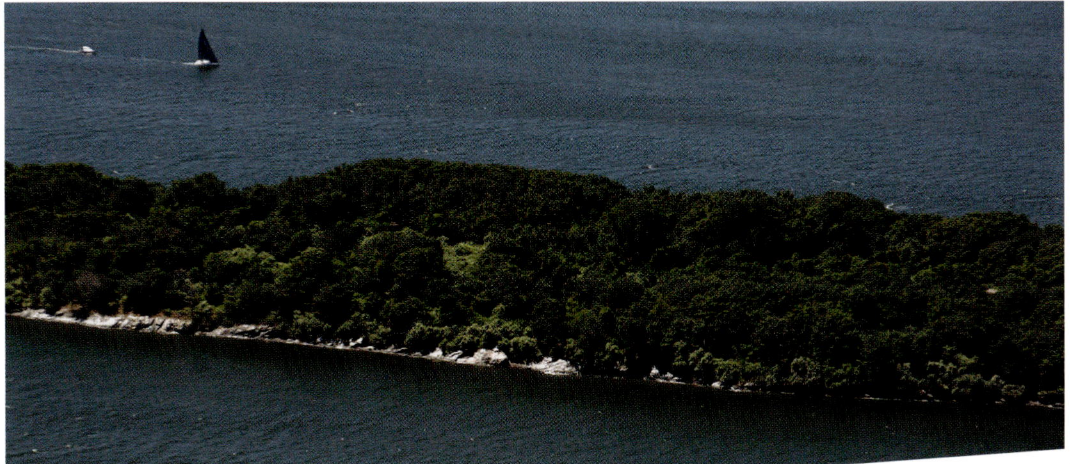

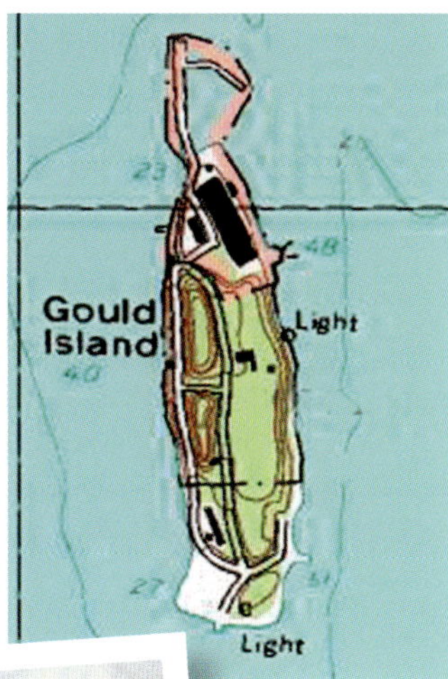

GOULD ISLAND

Location: Between Conanicut Island and Newport, N41°32′2″, W71°20′45″, station no longer exists

Appropriation: $10,000 in March 1887

Established: June 1889

Disestablished: 1947, replaced by skeleton tower

Tower: White, brick, conical, 30 feet, black lantern room

Other Structures: None remain, all demolished 1960

Original Lens: 5th order Fresnel lens, focal plane 52 feet

Light Characteristics: Flashing white every 10 seconds (FW 10s)

Fog Signal: Bell struck by machine every 15 seconds

Status: Station no longer exists, torn down in 1960; skeleton tower (1932) crumbled in 1988

Access: Island restricted; former U.S. Navy torpedo test facility.

Comments: Originally a private beacon, limited in visibility when trees grew up and blocked light; skeleton tower erected at southern tip of island.

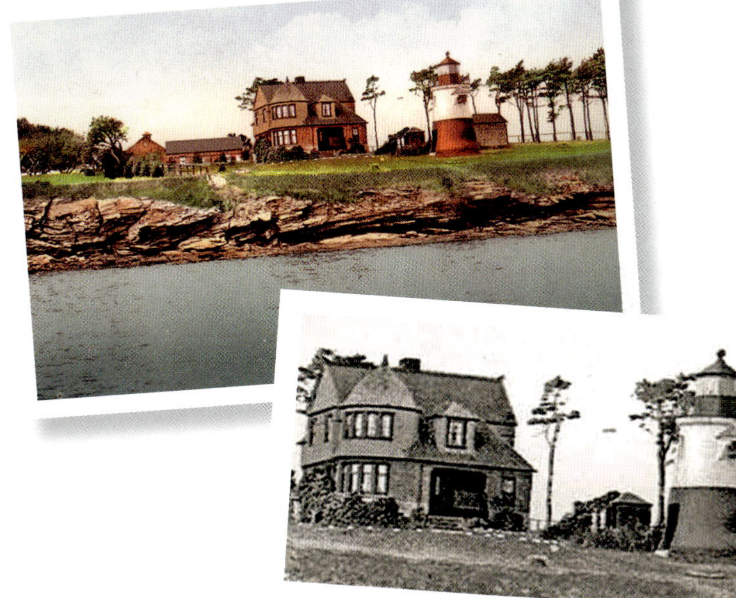

Top: Two views, one from the water and the other from the air, of Gould Island. Nothing remains to indicate a lighthouse was ever there.

Top right: Not to be used for navigation (no light characteristics, etc.), this archival topographic map shows Gould Island and indicates the location of the two lights. The light in the following images was found in the middle of the island. *(Courtesy of USCG)*

Bottom: A postcard and a close-up photo of the Gould Island Light. When the trees grew to obscure the light, a skeleton tower was erected at the southern tip of the island.

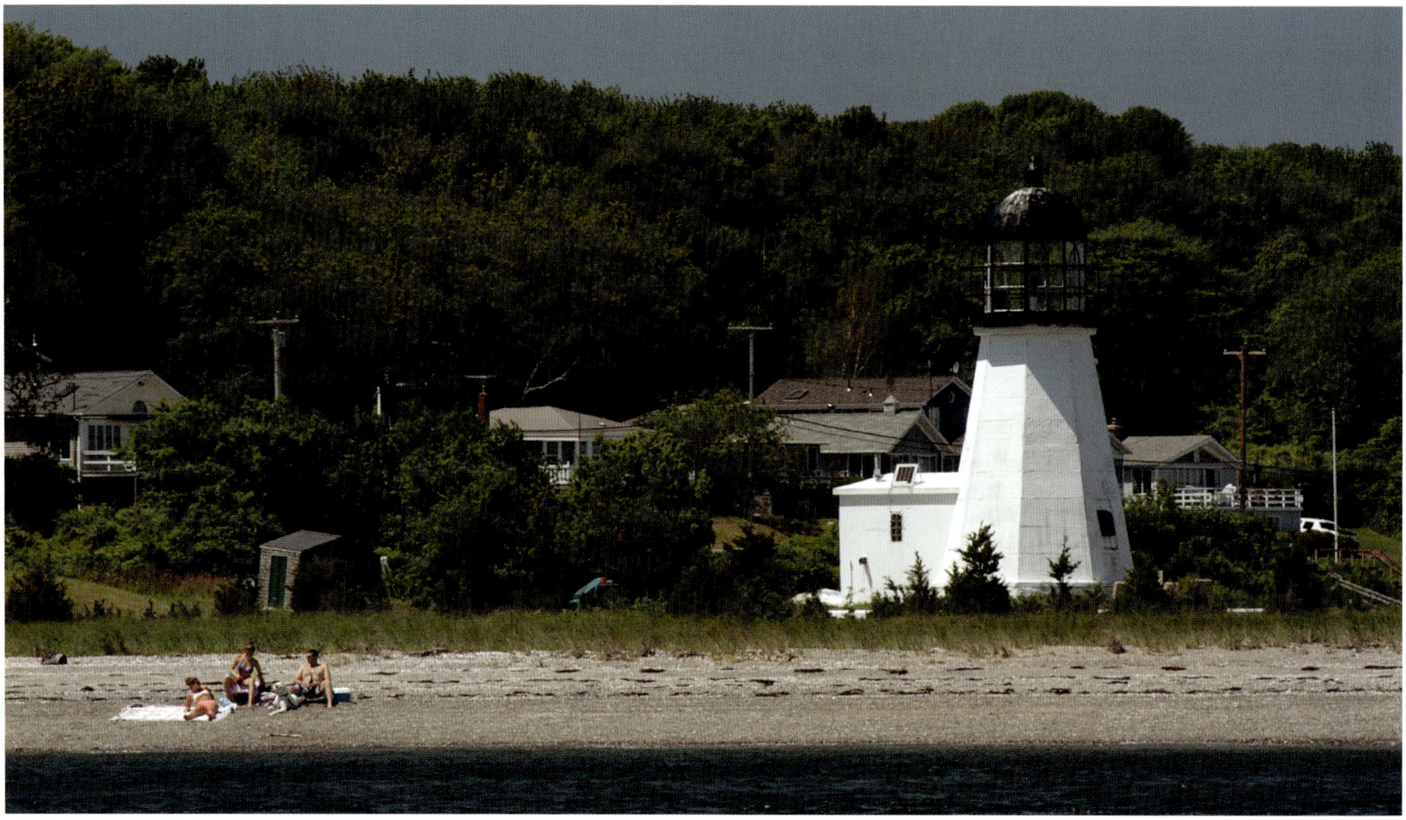

PRUDENCE ISLAND / SANDY POINT

Location: Prudence Island, eastern shore, N41°36′21″, W71°18′13″

Appropriation: $3,500 in 1850

Established: 1852

Automated: 1961

Tower: White, granite, octagonal, pyramidal, 25 feet, black lantern room, moved from Goat Island, Newport

Other Structures: None; keeper's house destroyed by 1938 hurricane

Original Optics: Oil lamps and reflectors

Original Lens: 1857 5th order Fresnel lens, fixed white (FW)

Present Lens: 250 mm

Light Characteristics: Flashing green every 6 seconds (Fl G 6s), focal plane 28 feet

Range: 6 nm

Fog Signal: 1891 machine-struck bell every 15 seconds; present, none

Status: Active U.S. Coast Guard aid to navigation

Access: Grounds open year-round, tower closed.

Comments: Tower originally located on Goat Island, Newport Harbor; licensed to the Prudence Island Conservancy; rare "bird cage" style lantern room; listed in NRHP.

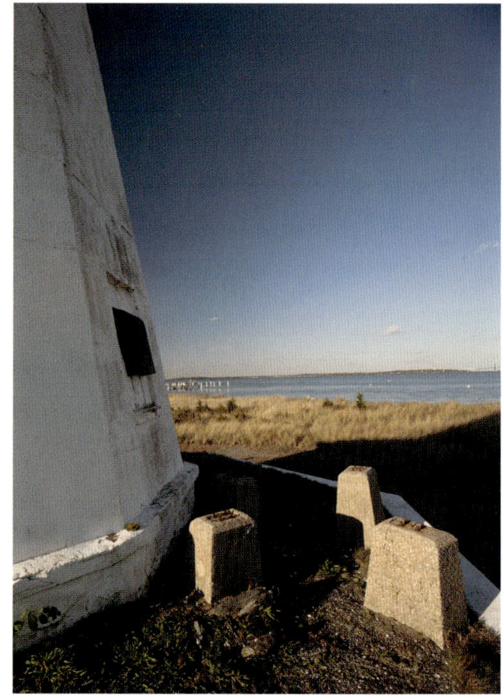

Top: Compare this current view of the tower with the archival images.

Bottom: A present-day view of where the foghorn used to stand in front of the tower.

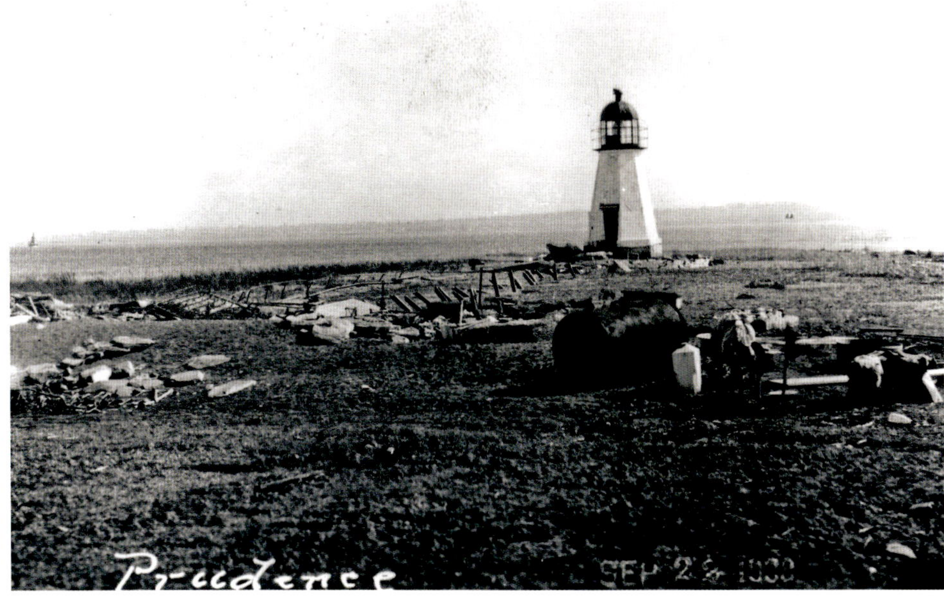

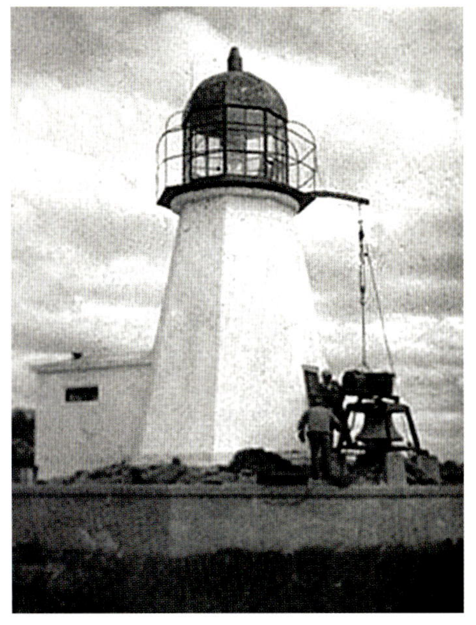

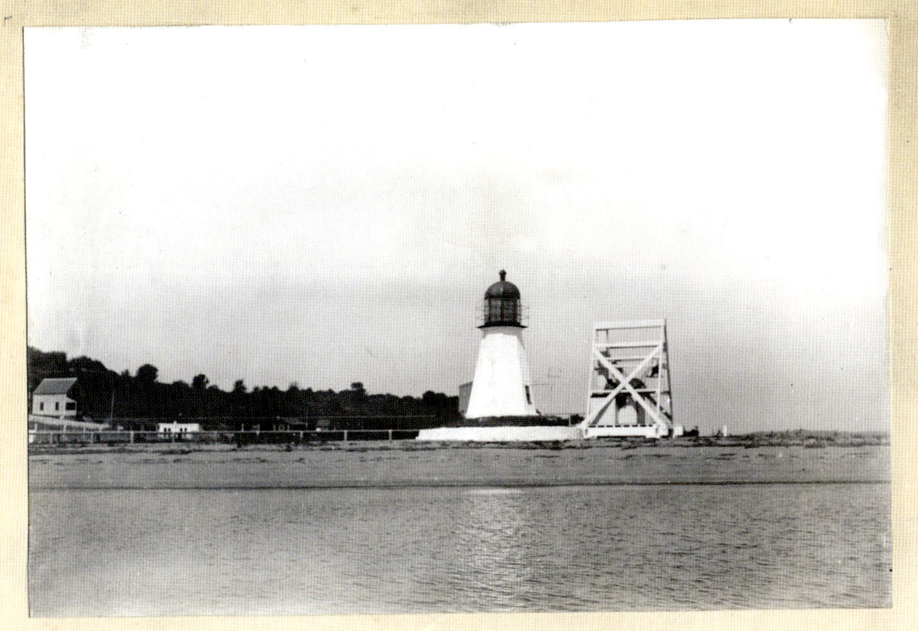

Top left: Dated 22 September 1938, this Coast Guard image shows the destruction to the site caused by the hurricane. Five people, including the keeper's wife, were killed by the storm. *(Courtesy of USCG)*

Top right: Coast Guard personnel can be seen in this image working on the fog signaling device. *(Courtesy of USCG)*

Left: This photograph, captured in 1917, identifies the location of the photographer. *(Courtesy of USCG)*

Below: This vintage postcard shows the same perspective.

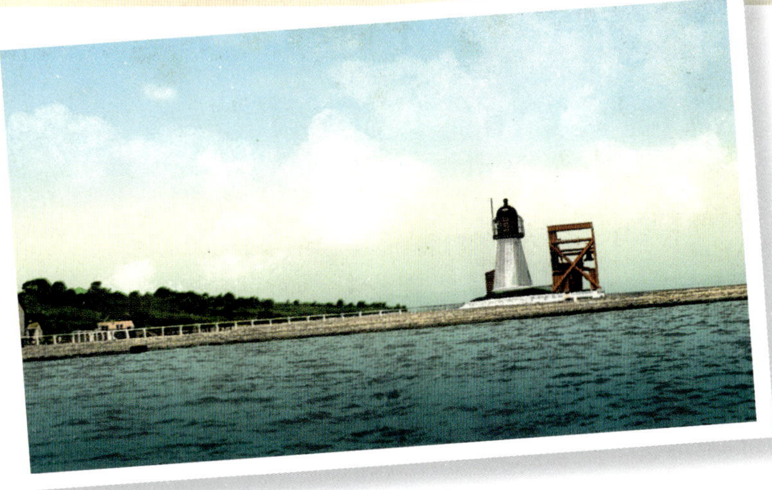

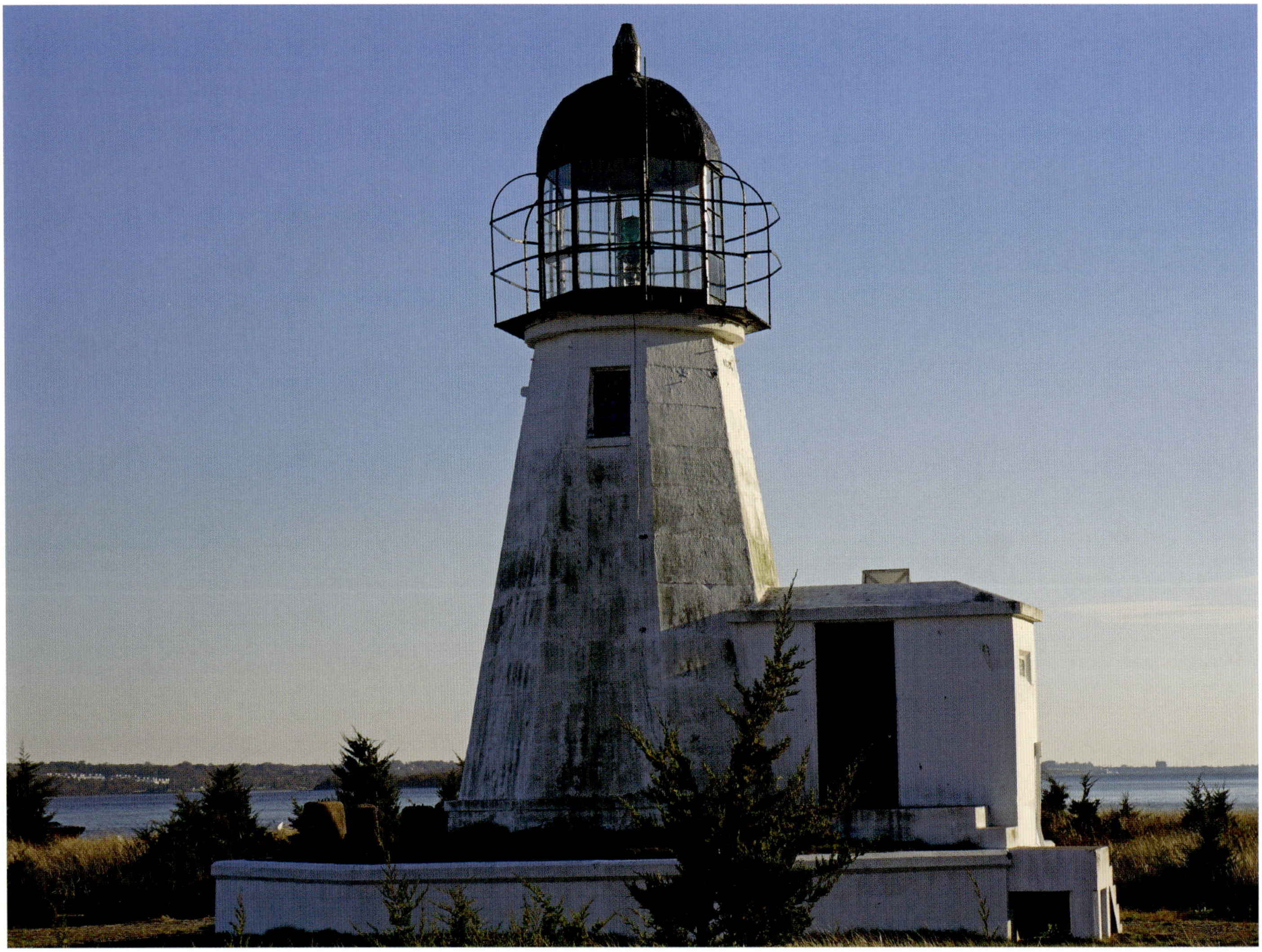

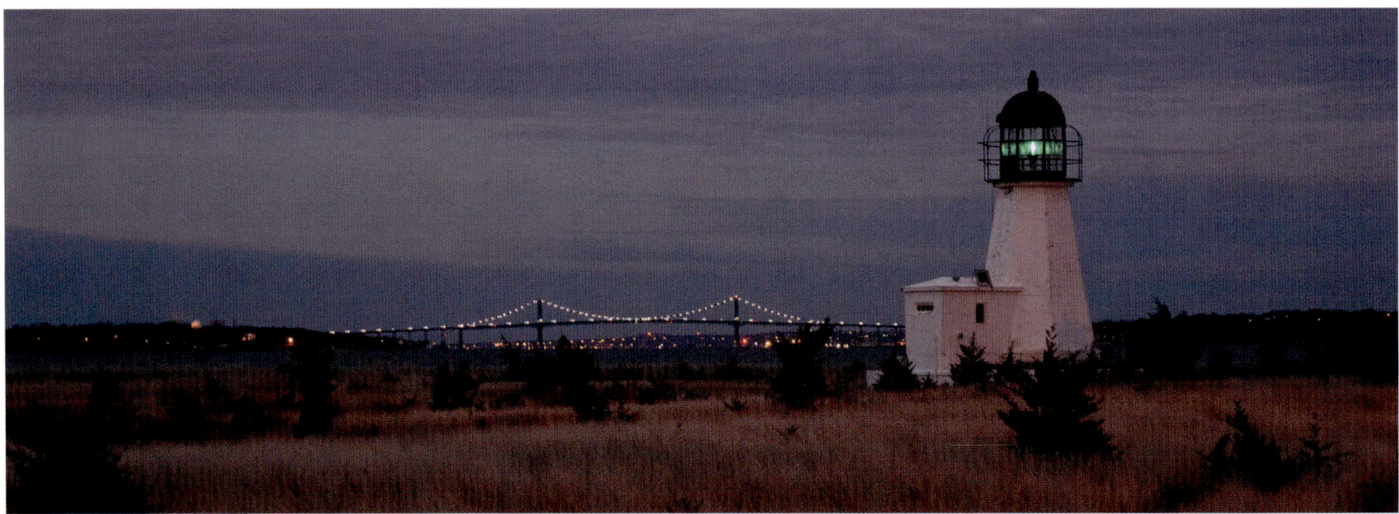

Top: With Narragansett Bay in the background, present-day Prudence Island Light.

Bottom: In the distance and lit up at night is the Mount Hope Bridge; the green light in the tower marks for navigators the east side of Prudence Island.

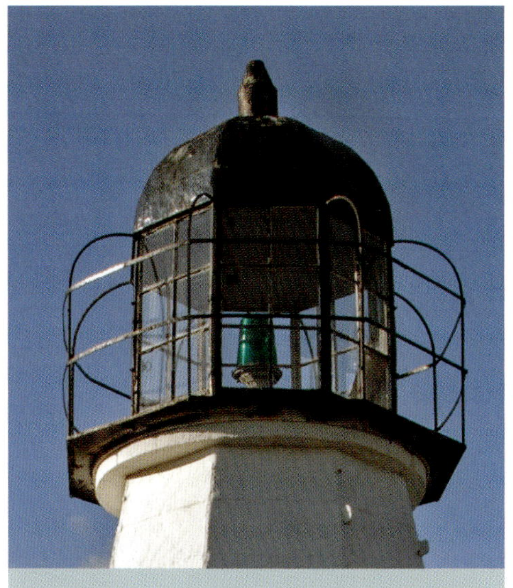

Top and right: Day and night images of the distinctive bird-cage around the lantern room.

Bottom: Looking out the lantern room in the late afternoon with the characteristic green lamp lit.

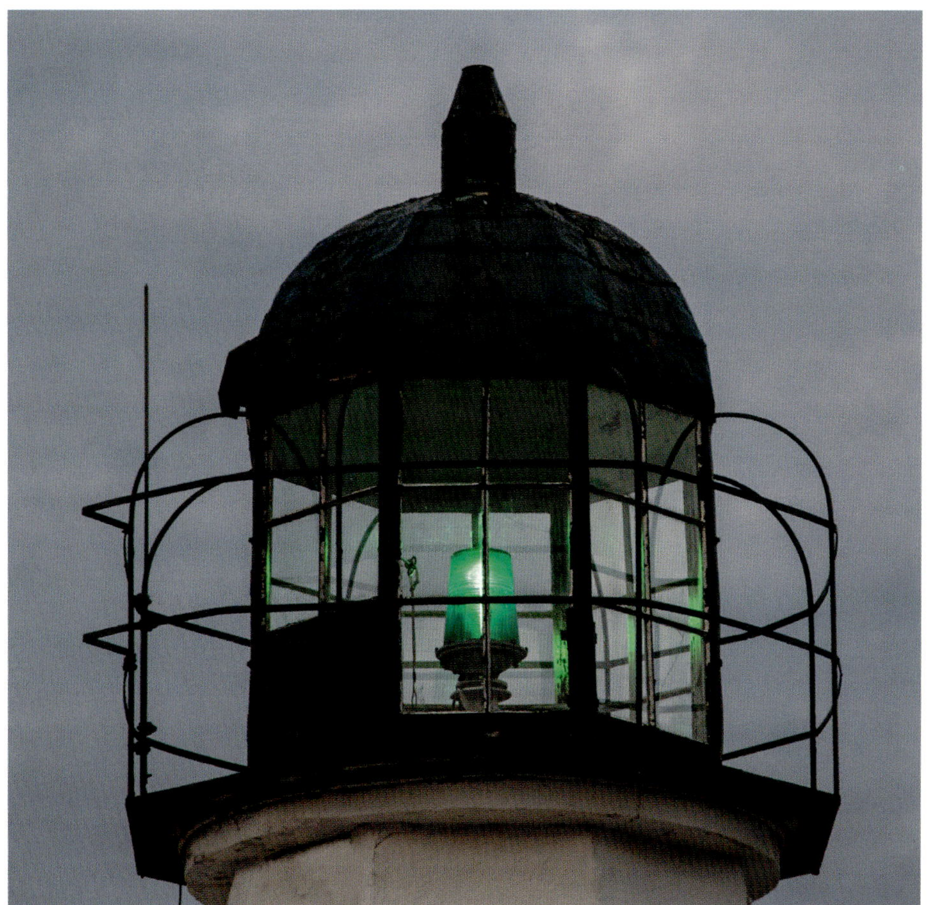

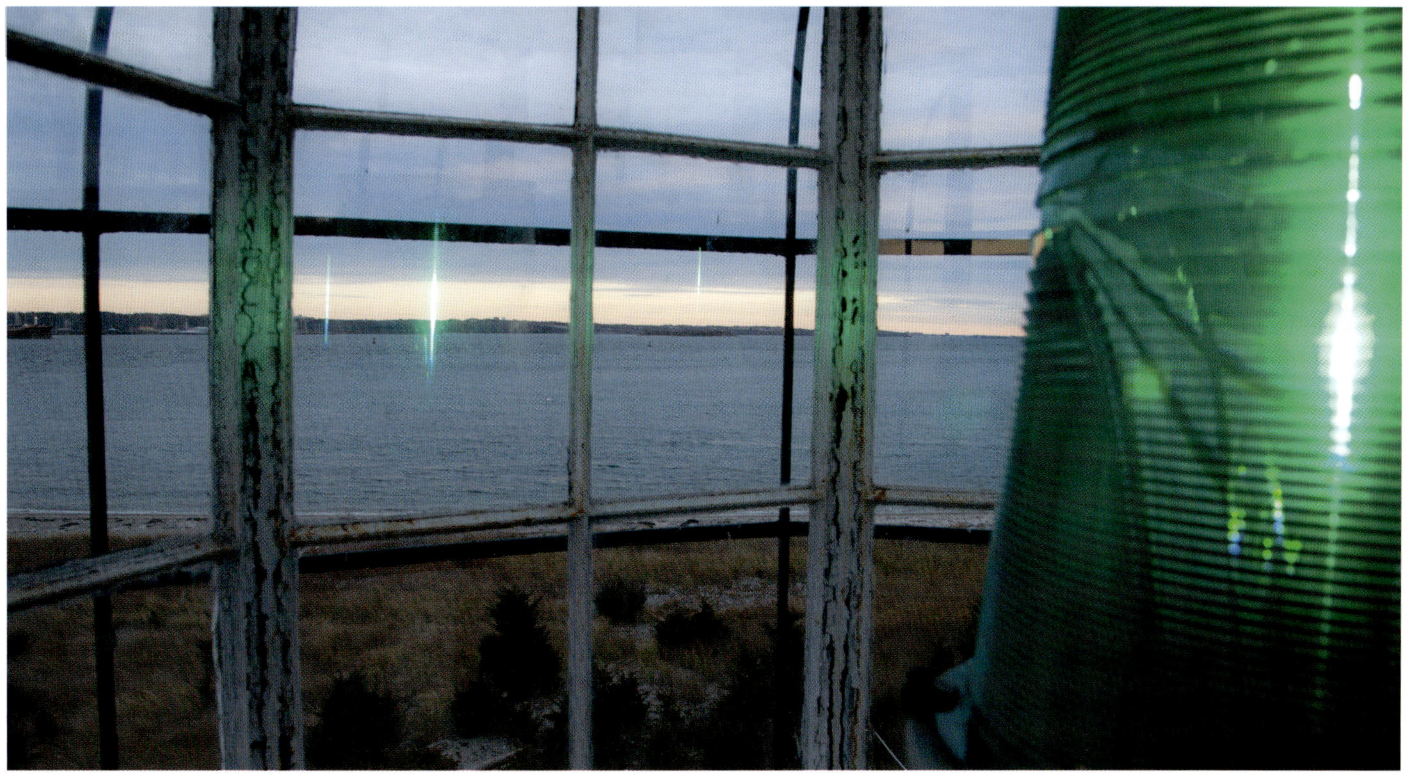

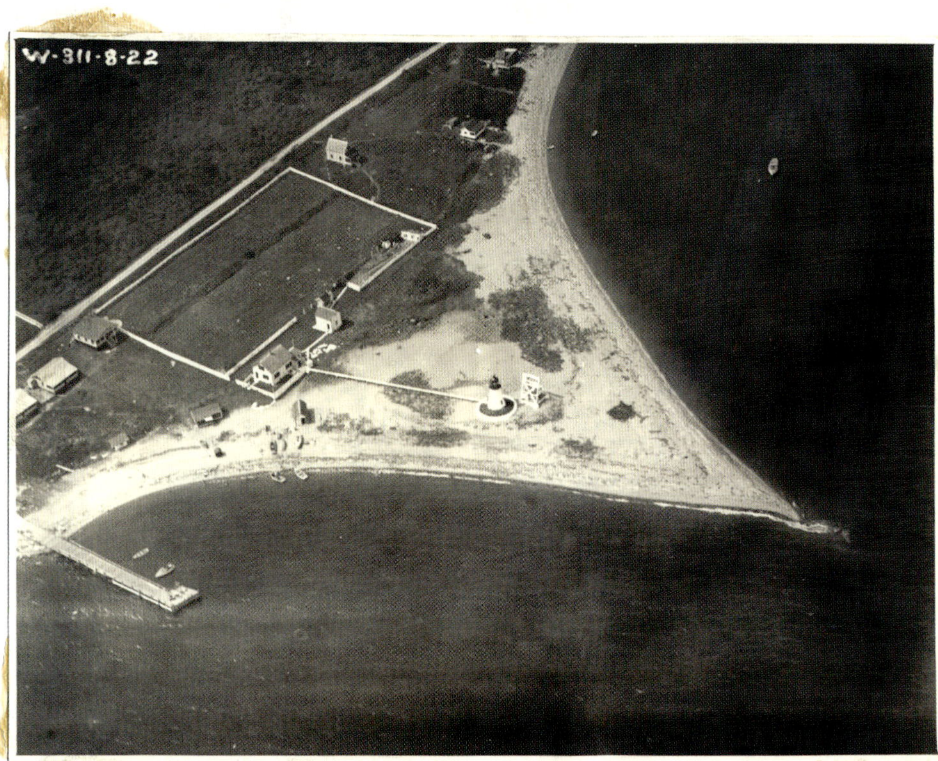

Note the differences in these aerial images of Prudence Island Light. *(Black-and-white image courtesy of USCG)*

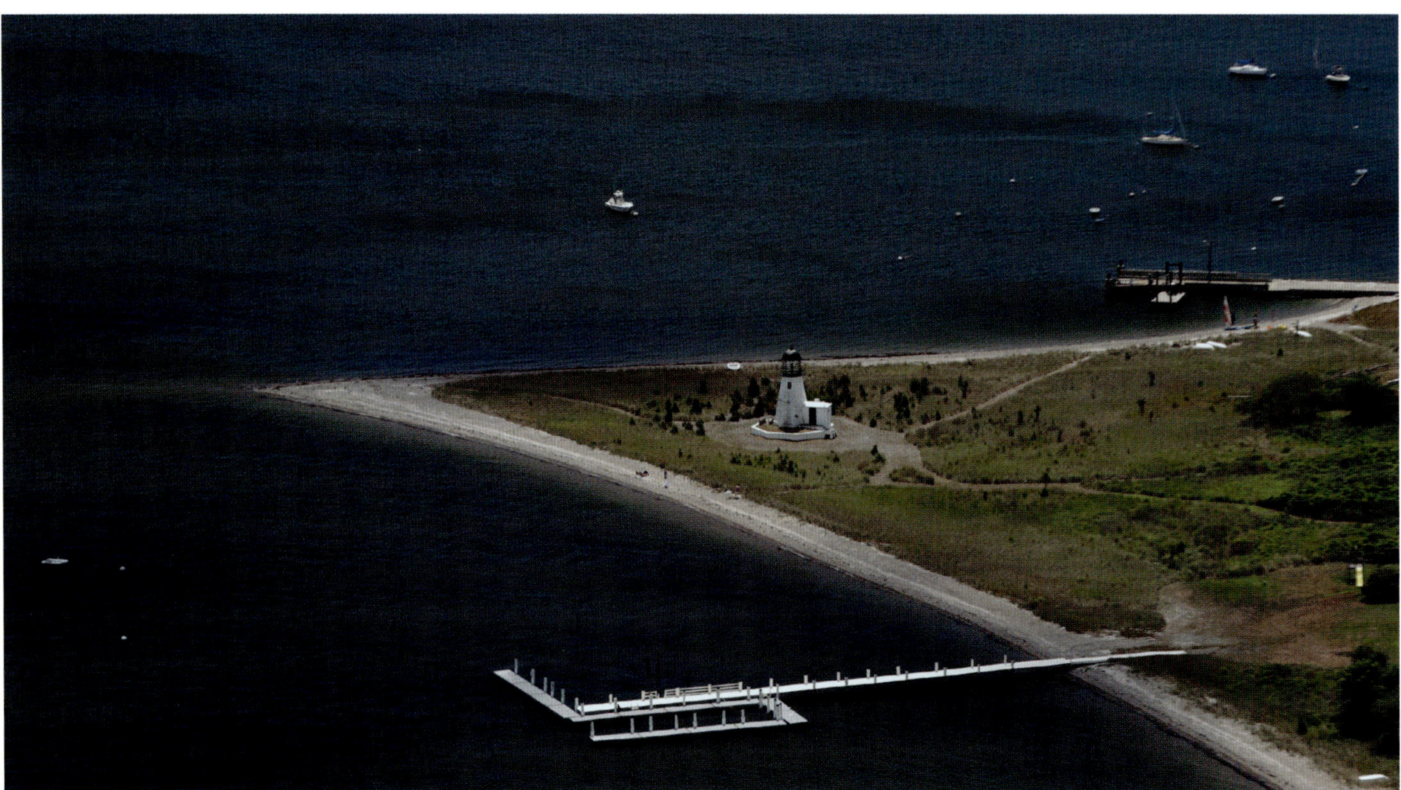

The following three navigational aids, Hog Island Shoal, which had originally been a lightship station, Musselbed Shoals, and Bristol Ferry, provided signals for ships transiting to and from Mount Hope Bay and the city of Fall River, to the east.

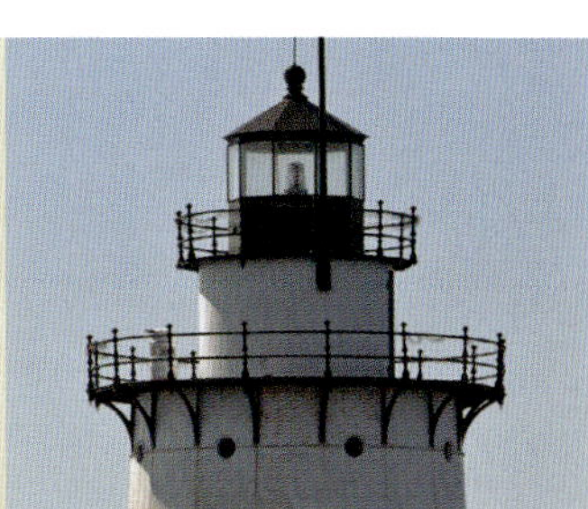

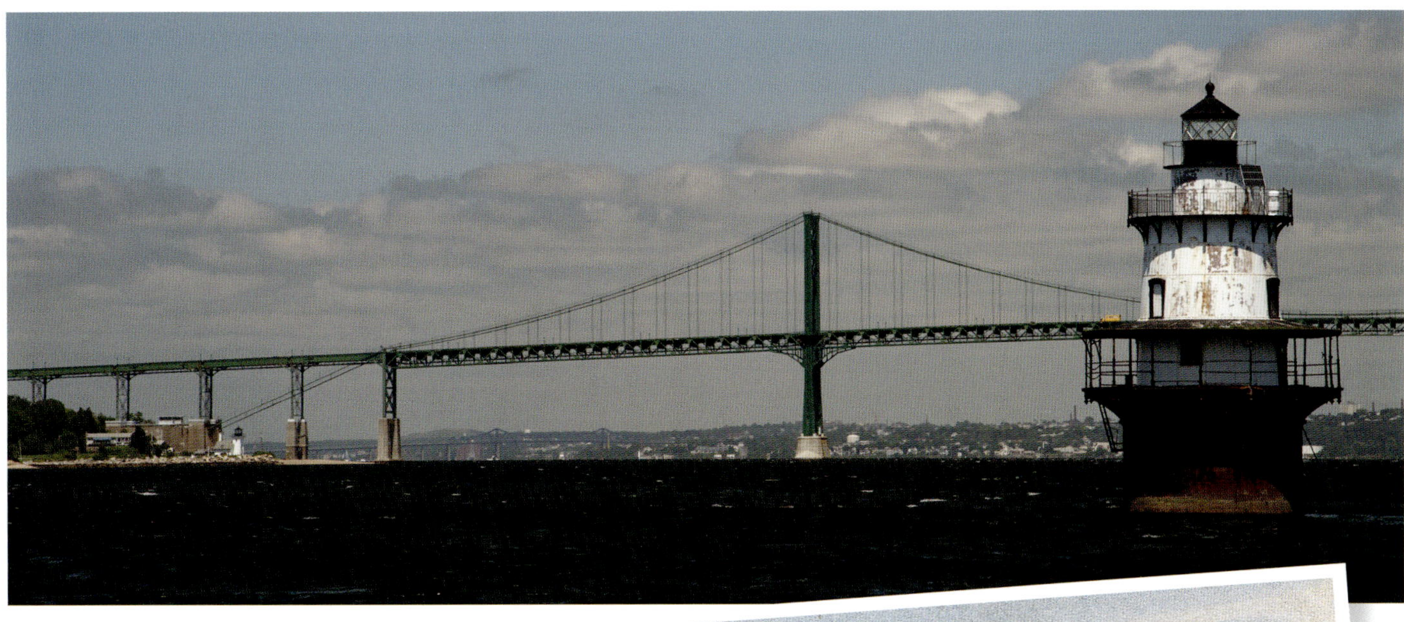

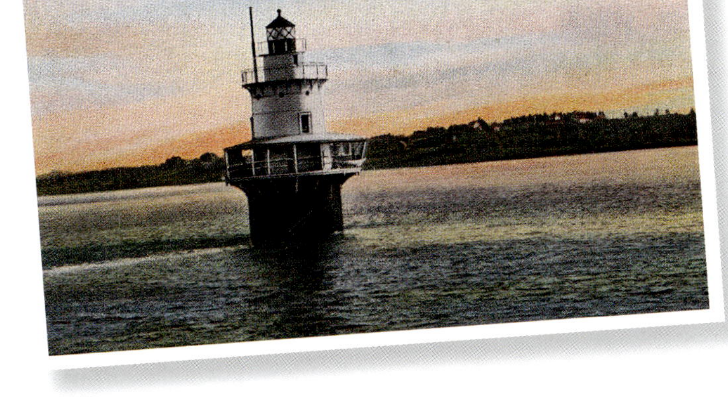

HOG ISLAND SHOAL

Location: South of Hog Island, N41°37′56″, W71°16′24″, original station was a lightship
Appropriation: $35,000 in 1899
Established: August 1886
Rebuilt: 1901 to replace lightship
Automated: 1964
Tower: 1901, white, cast-iron, spark plug design, black base, black lantern room, 60 feet
Original Lens: 5th order Fresnel lens, flashing white, (Fl W), focal plane 54 feet
1903: 4th order Fresnel lens, fixed white (FW)
Present Lens: 250 mm plastic
Light Characteristics: Isophase white 6 seconds (Iso W 6s)
Range: 12 nm
Fog Signal: 1902 siren
Status: Active U.S. Coast Guard aid to navigation, privately owned
Access: None.
Comments: 1959 converted to electrical power; major repairs by Coast Guard in 1995; built by the same company that built Plum Beach; listed in NRHP.

Top: Looking east toward the Mount Hope Bridge with Hog Island Shoal on the right. Bristol Ferry can be seen on the tip of land to the left. Compare this water view with the archival chart on page 105 to locate these aids.

Bottom: An antique postcard of Hog Island Shoal Lighthouse; compare this image to the Plum Beach and Conimicut towers.

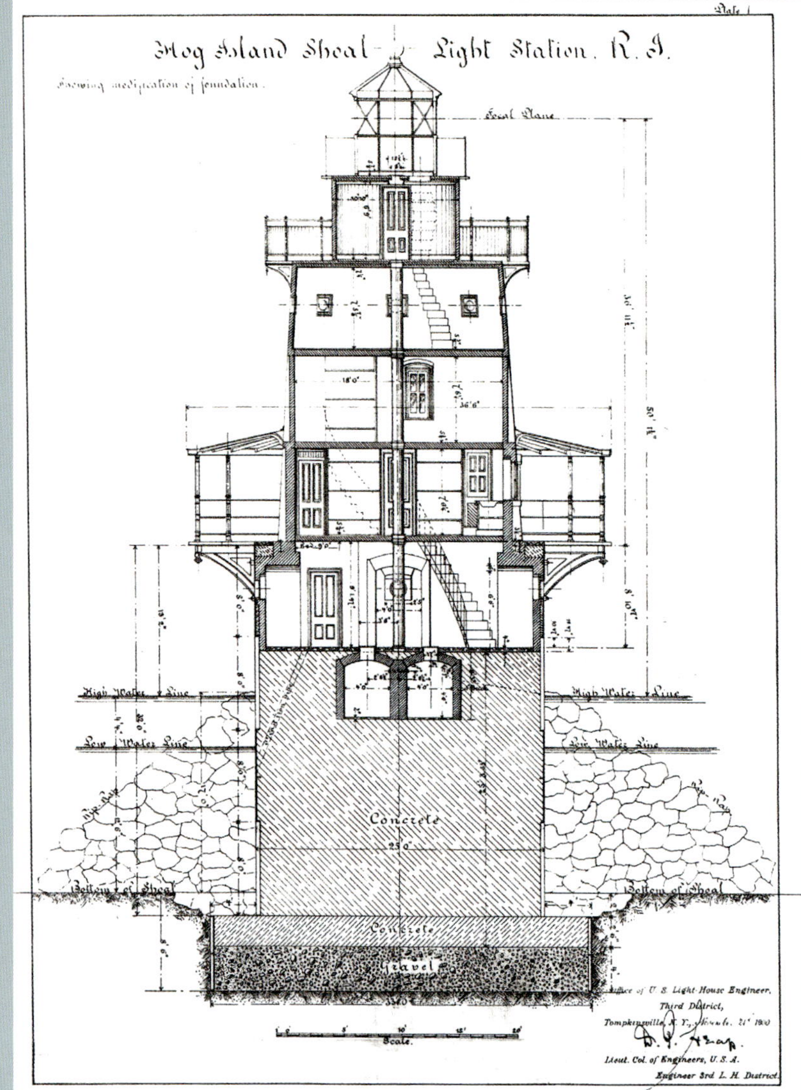

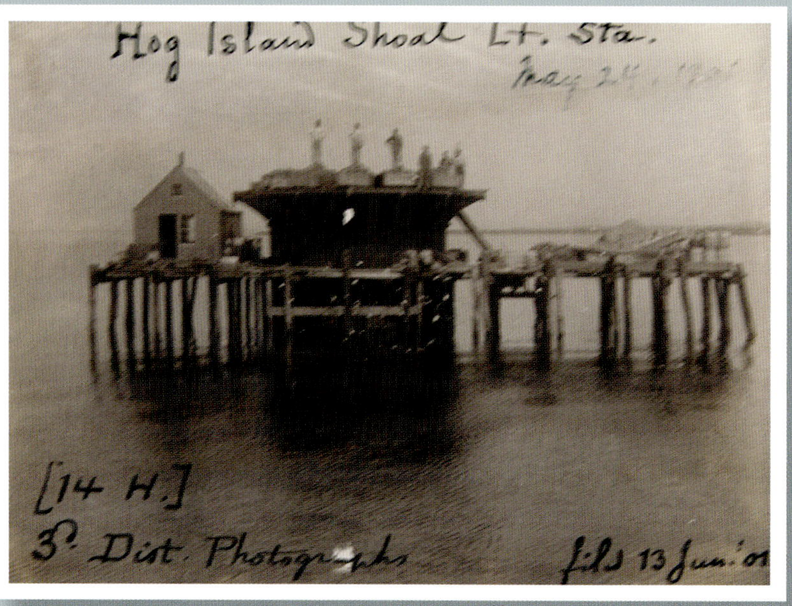

Top: Dated 1900, this plan for Hog Island Shoal was also basically used for Plum Beach and Conimicut. *(Courtesy of J. D'Entremont)*

Left: Captured 24 May 1901, this photograph shows the construction of the tower. *(Courtesy of NA)*

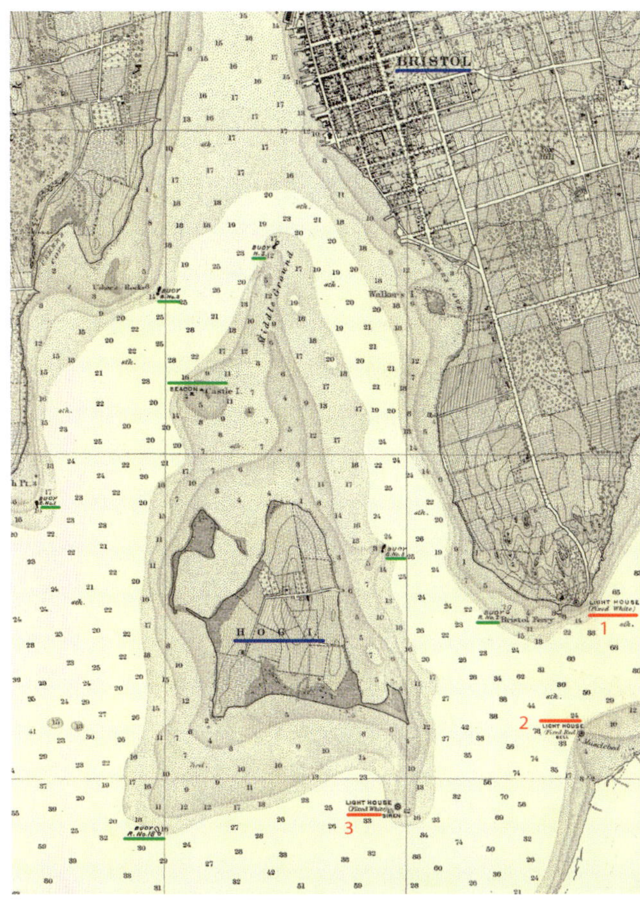

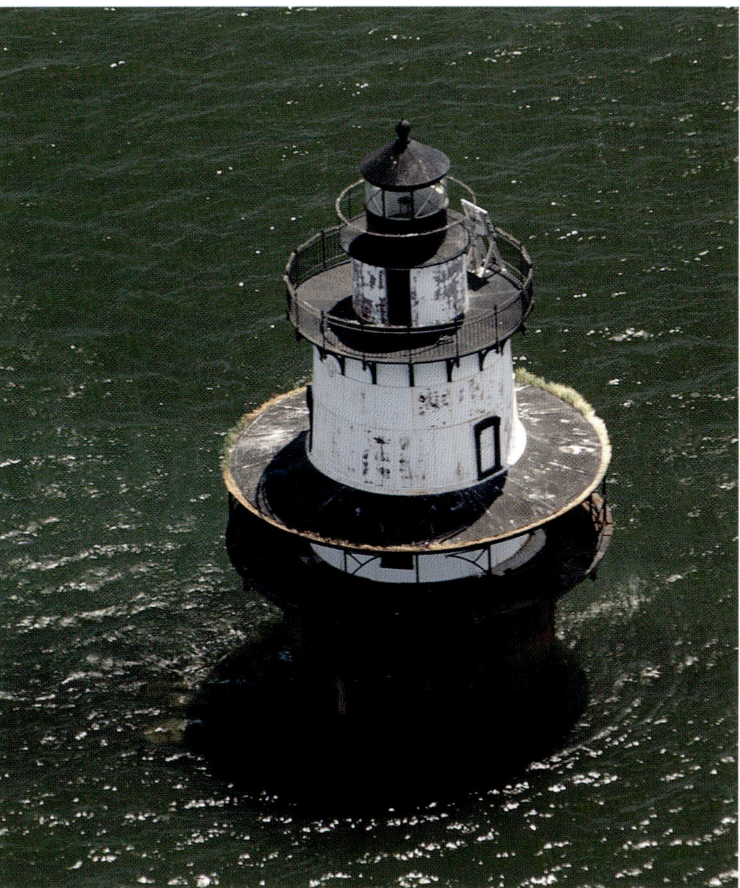

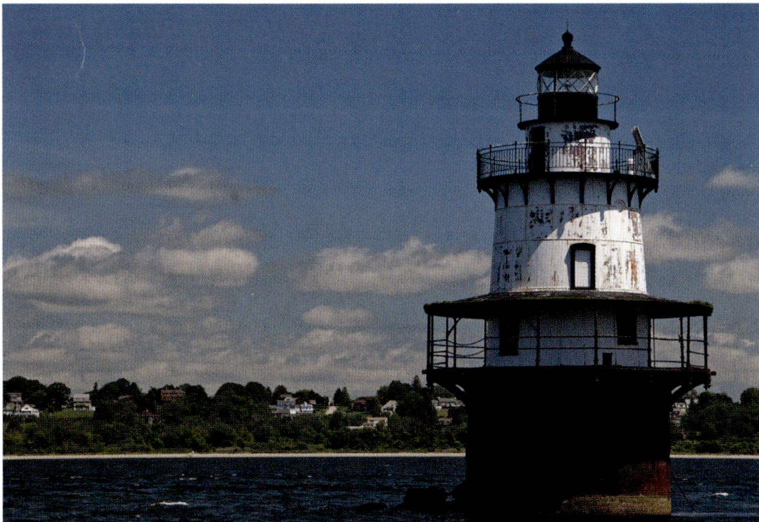

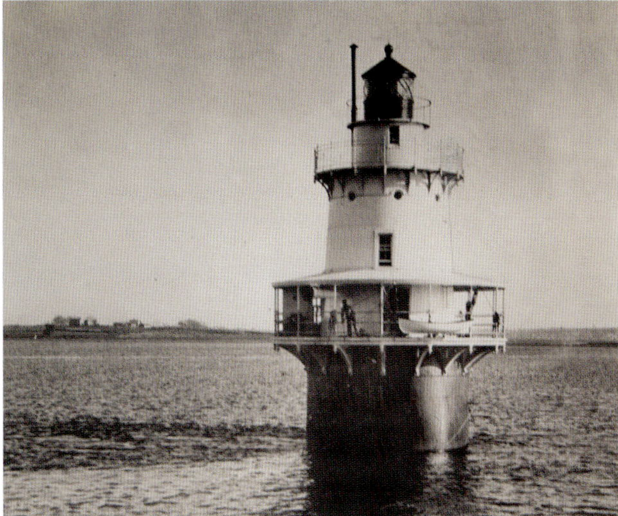

Top left: This archival chart of the eastern side of Narragansett Bay identifies the aids to navigation near Hog Island (underlined in blue). Underlined in red, number 1 is Bristol Ferry, number 2 is Musselbed Shoals and number 3 is Hog Island Shoal. The green lines are the locations of buoys in the channels. *(Courtesy of NOAA)*

Top right: Still an active aid to navigation, Hog Island Shoal, like many of these towers, is in need of constant maintenance.

Bottom: Two images of the tower taken as much as seventy years apart. *(Black-and-white image courtesy of NA)*

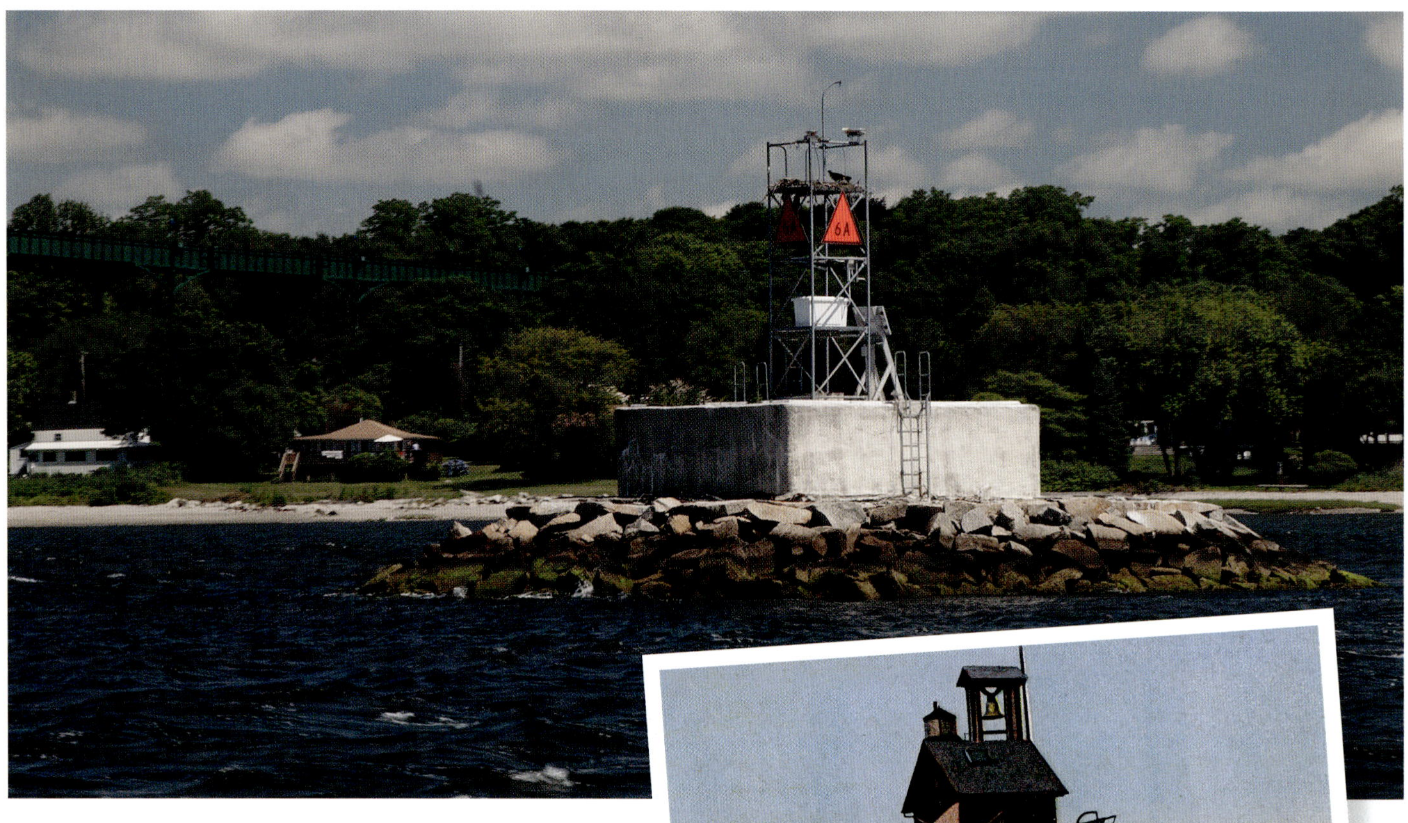

MUSSELBED SHOALS / MUSSEL SHOALS

Location: Channel leading into Mount Hope Bay, N41°38′10″, W71°15′35″, original station no longer exists

Appropriation: $3,000 in 1873; $6,000 in 1877

Established: 1873

Tower: White, hexagonal, tower mounted on roof, black lantern room, bell also mounted on roof

Rebuilt: 1877

Demolished: 1939, replaced by skeleton tower

Original Lens: 6th order Fresnel lens, fixed red (FR), focal plane 35 feet

Present Aid: Skeleton tower, identification TR on original base

Light Characteristics: Flashing red every 6 seconds (Fl R 6s), focal plane 26 feet

Range: 6 nm

Fog Signal: 1873 bell every 20 seconds

Status: Active U.S. Coast Guard aid to navigation

Access: None; skeleton tower on original base can be seen from boat.

Comments: Decommissioned in August 1938 (leaky roof, ceiling caved in); more damage by hurricane in September 1938; subsequently demolished.

Top: From the water, all that remains from the original station is the rip-rap; a skeleton tower with a solar-powered light and a red triangle with 6A are navigational characteristics of this aid. The Mount Hope Bridge in the background is barely visible.

Center: A postcard of 1910s vintage; the outhouse can be seen on the left side.

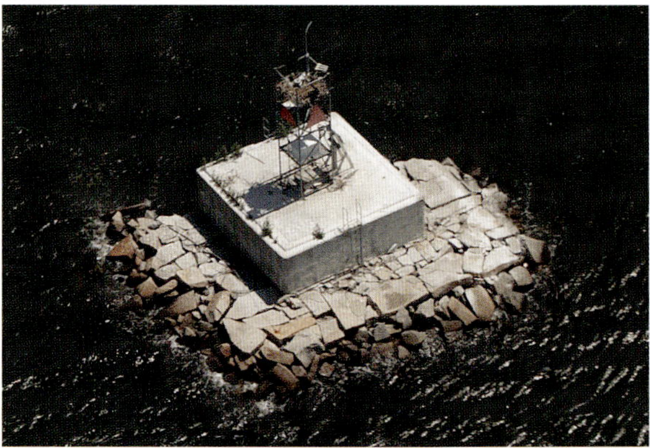

Above: An aerial view of the aid; observe the osprey nesting on the top of the tower.

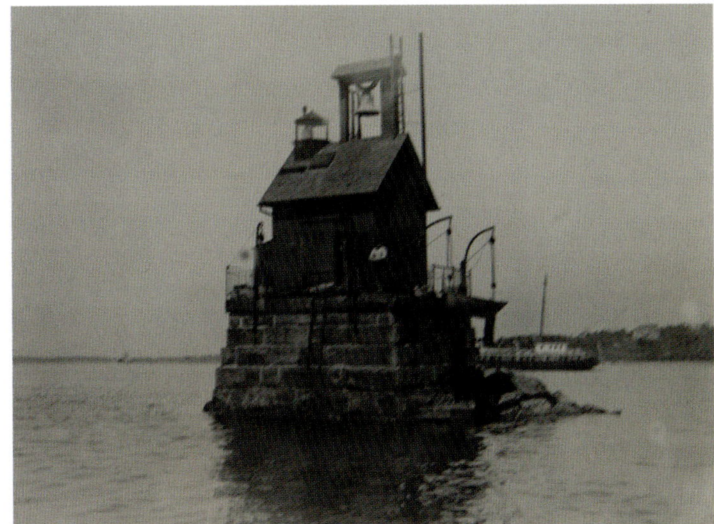

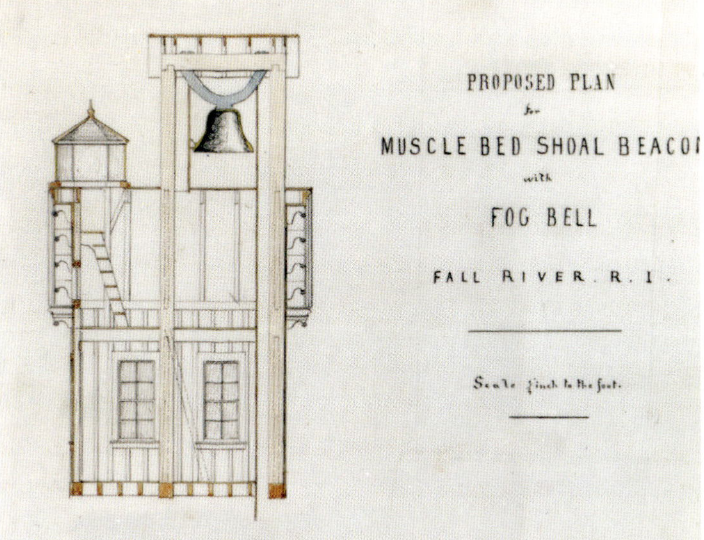

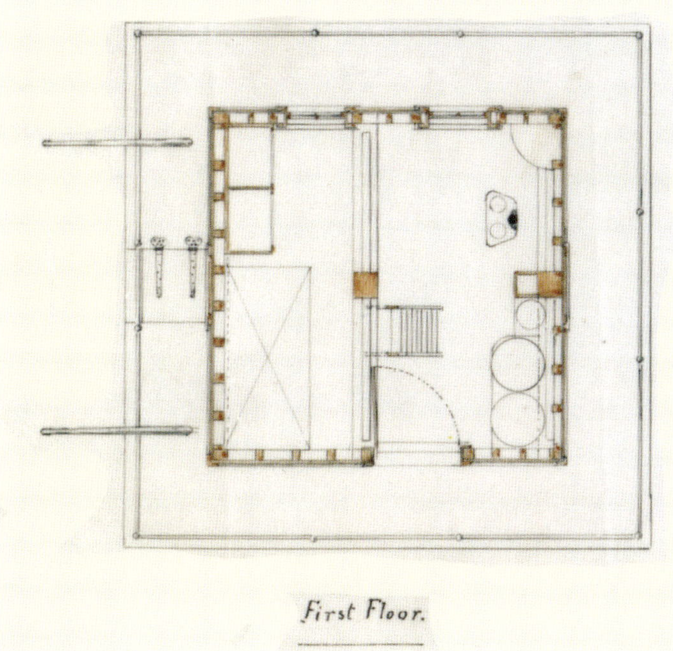

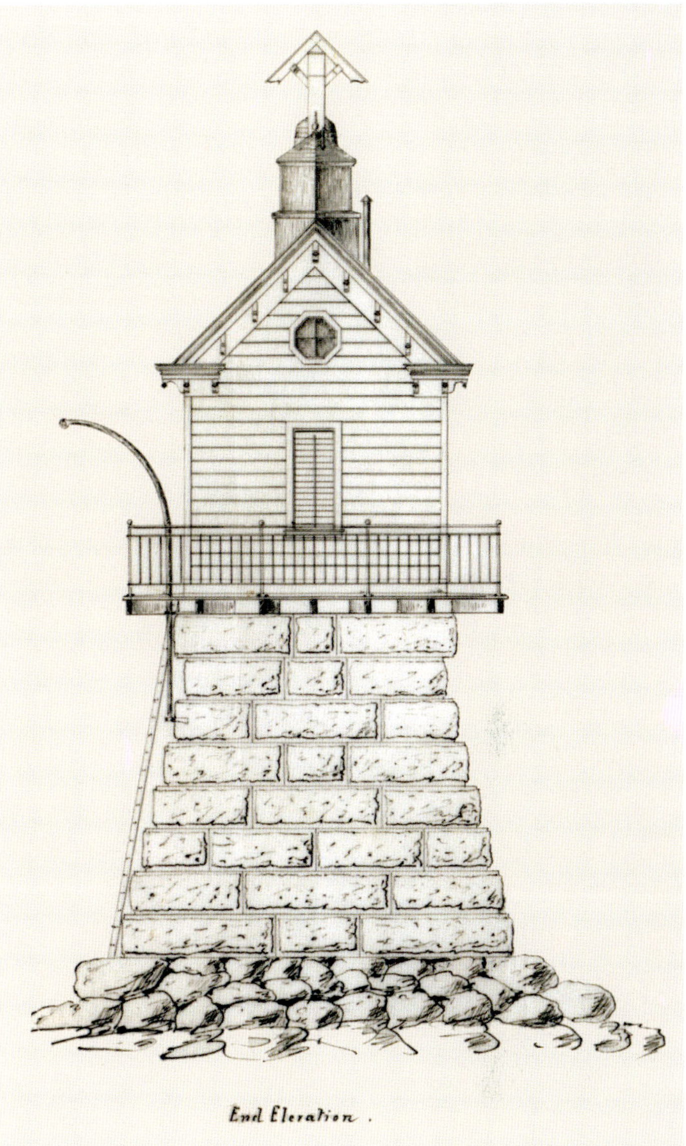

Top left: Information on the back of this photograph of Musselbed Shoals indicated that this image was taken in June 1917 by N. A. Yates. Note the keeper on the walkway and the ship partially hidden in the background. *(Courtesy of NA)*

Center left: A plan of 1879 for the lighthouse; note the spelling and location. *(Courtesy of NA)*

Left and above: Two more pages of the plan show the first-floor plan and the end elevation. *(Courtesy of NA)*

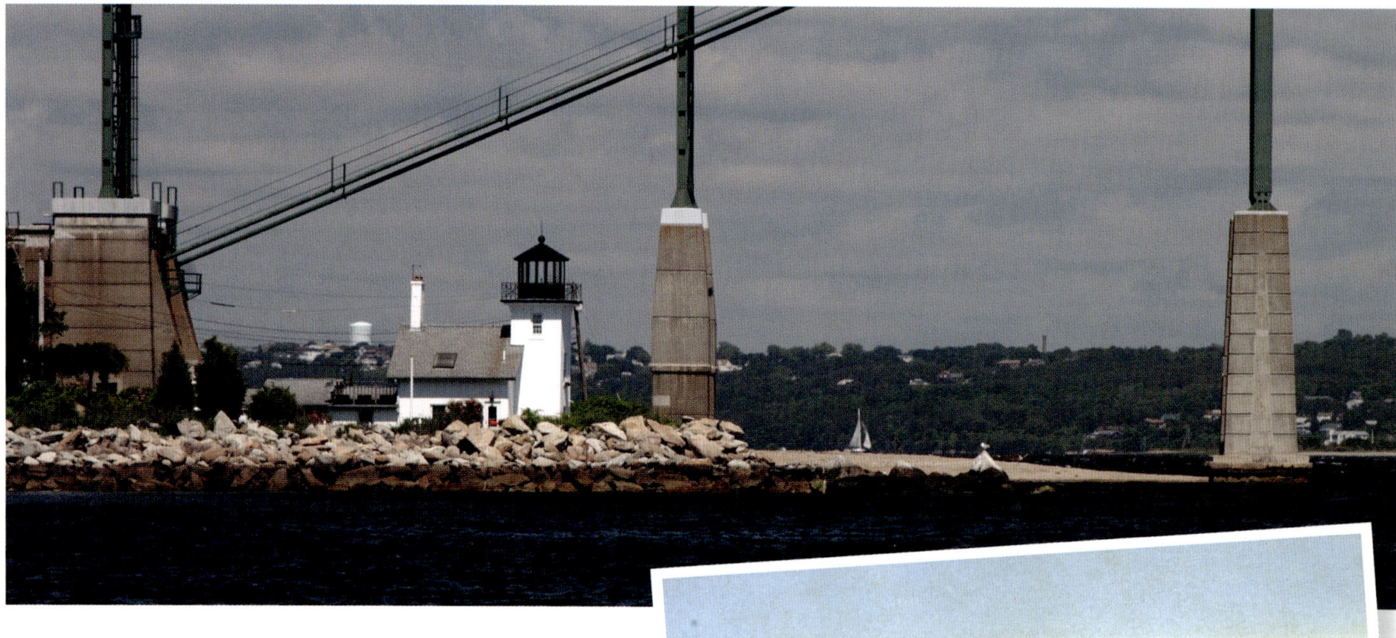

View of the station and the nearby bridge.

BRISTOL FERRY

Location: Bristol, southern tip, N41°38′34″, W71°15′37″

Appropriation: $5,000 in 1837; $1,500 in 1854

Established: 1855

Disestablished: 1927, replaced by skeleton tower with acetylene powered lamp

Tower: White, brick, square, black lantern room, 6 feet added to tower in 1916

Original Lens: 1863 6th order Fresnel lens, fixed white (FW), focal plane 35 feet

1902: refitted with 5th order Fresnel lens and electric lamp

Automated: 1927

Present Lens: None

Light Characteristics: N/A

Range: N/A

Fog Signal: None

Status: Private residence, not an aid

Access: Restricted; private residence.

Comments: Became obsolete when Mount Hope Bridge was completed in 1929; replica lantern room added in 1996; listed in NRHP.

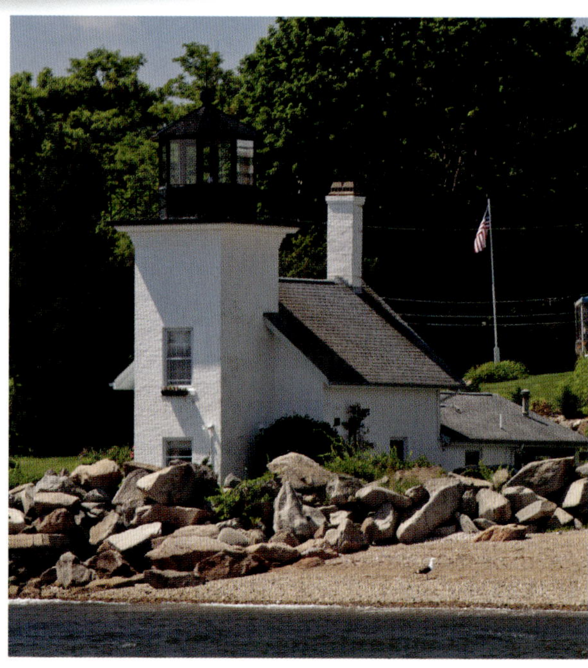

Center: Compare this old postcard with the present-day images.

Above: Lighthouse cruises pass close by the tower and the house, which is now a private residence.

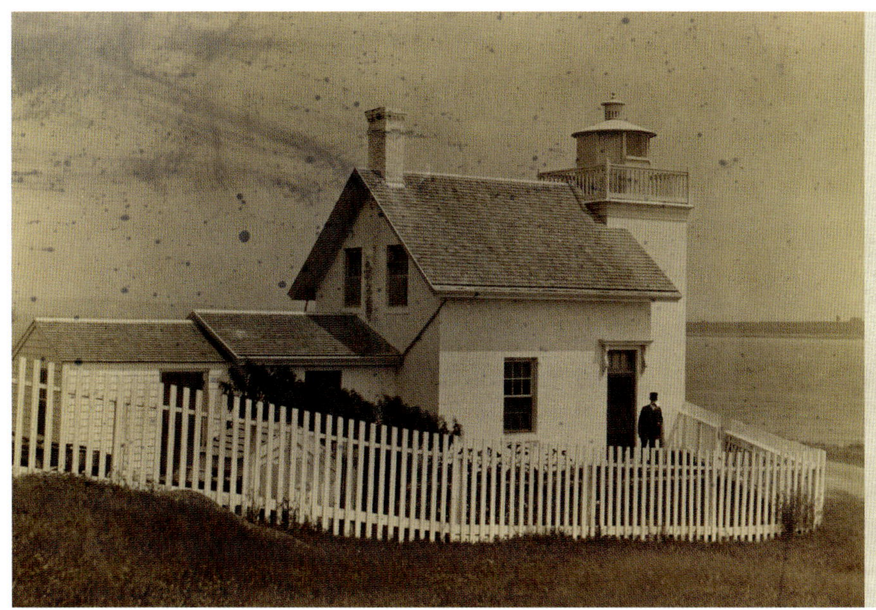

Left: The keeper is standing by the door of this 1894 image of Bristol Ferry light. *(Courtesy of NA)*

Below: Captured in the early 1900s, the Bristol Ferry station. Flooding was a problem so a rip-rap was built in front of the tower.

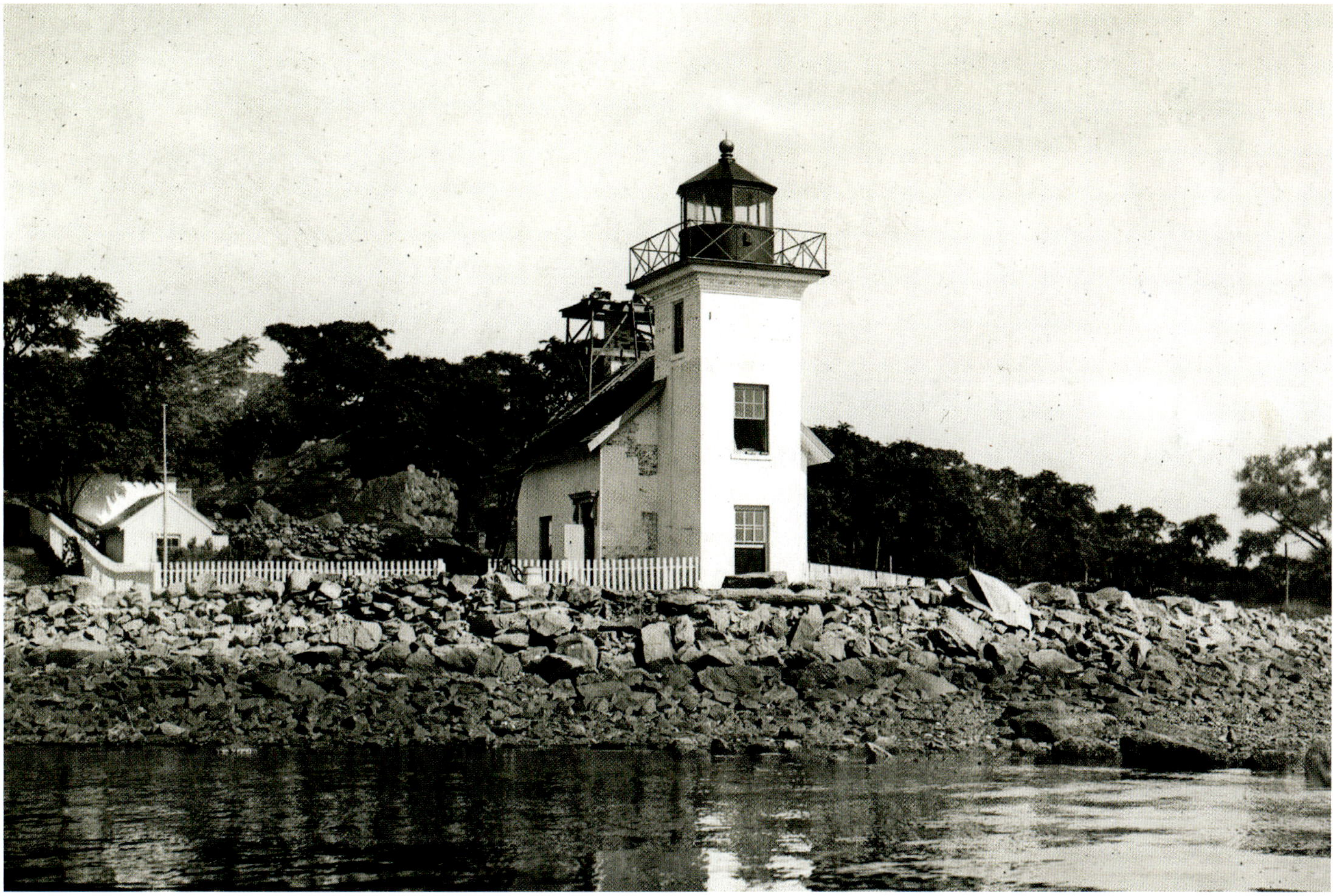

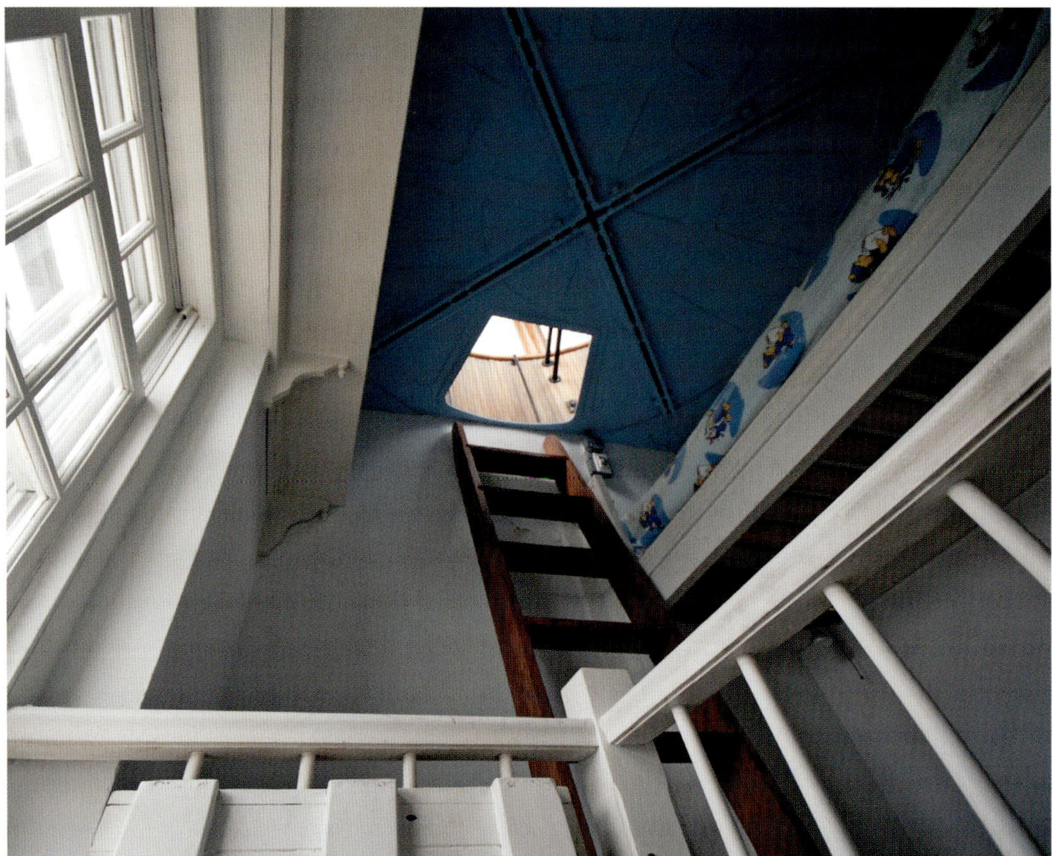

Top: A short flight of stairs leads to the lantern room. The window to the left is the one in the front of the tower.

Below: A view of the lantern room from the stairs.

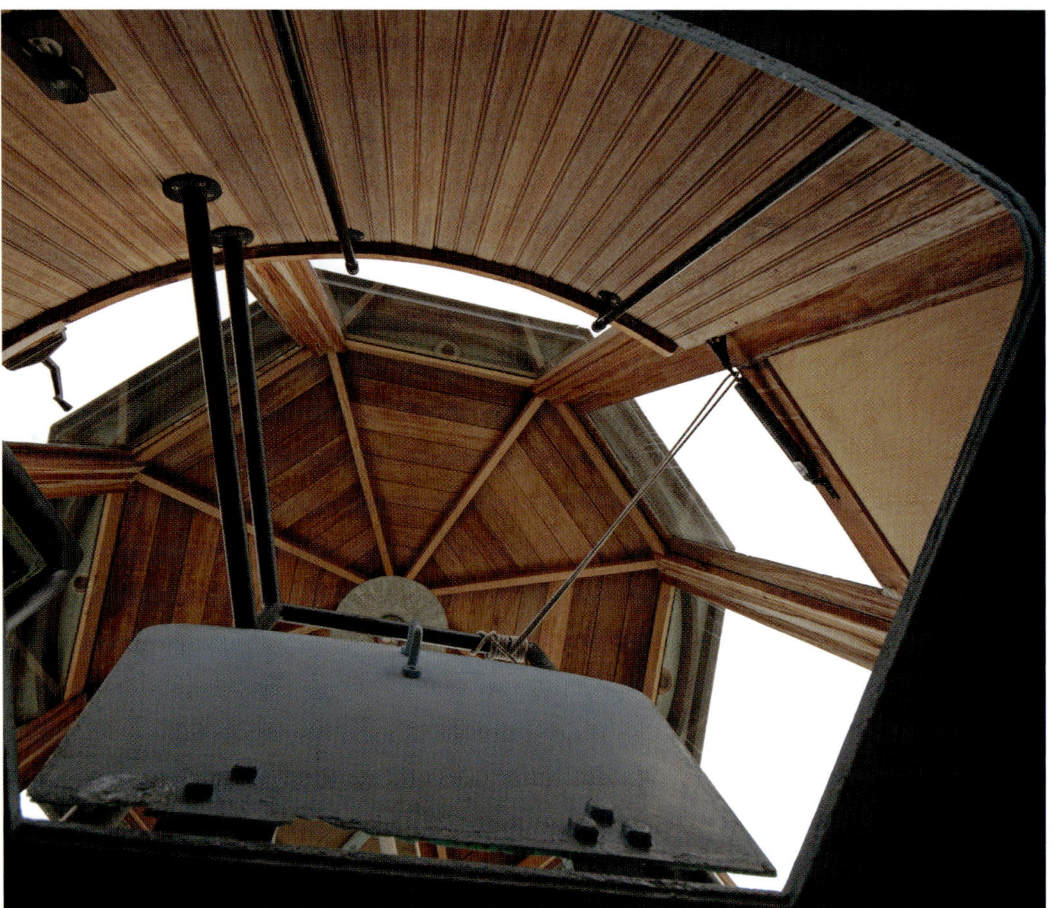

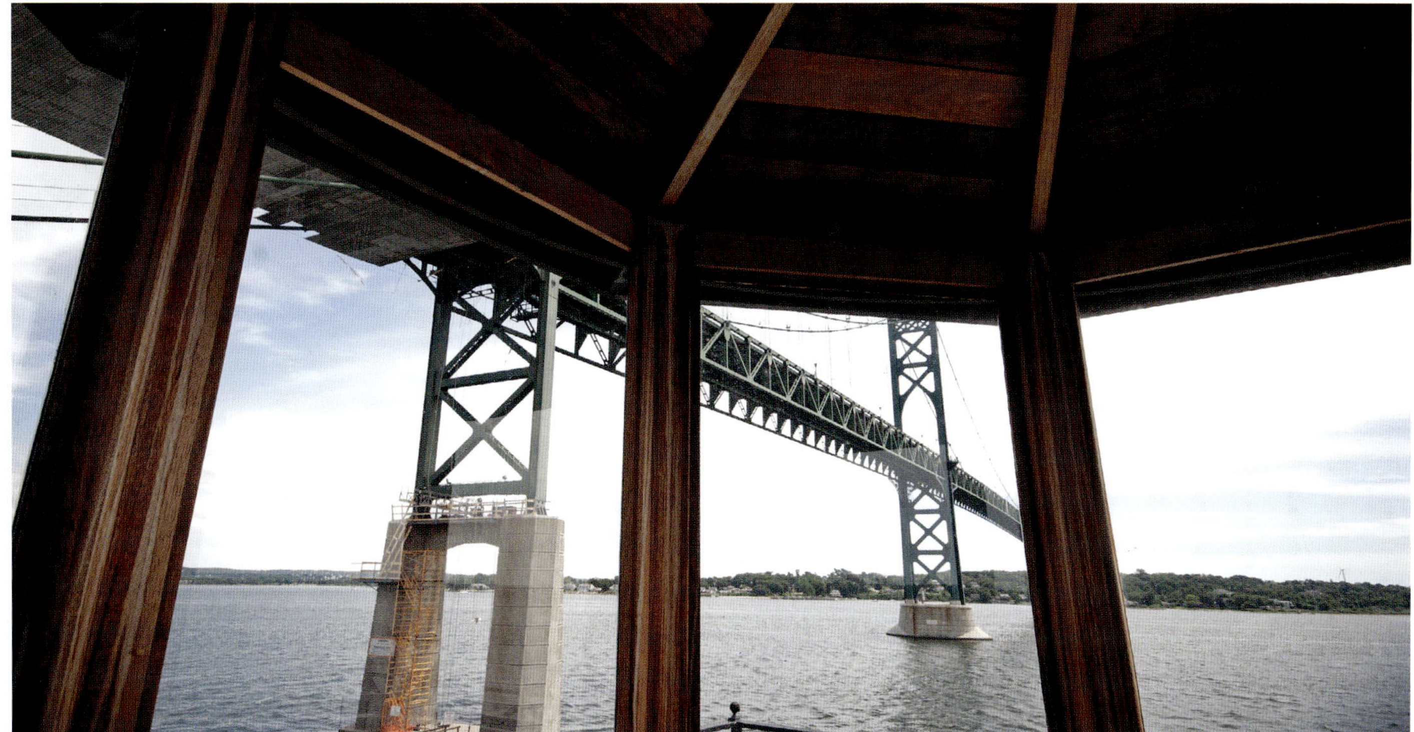

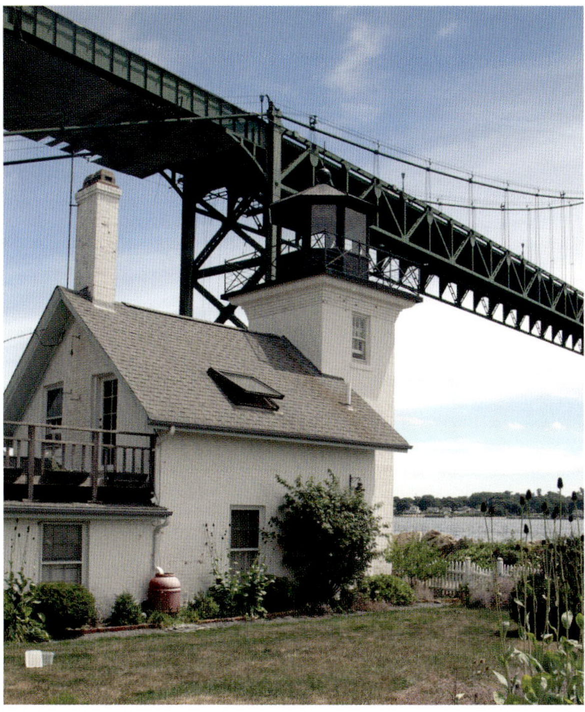

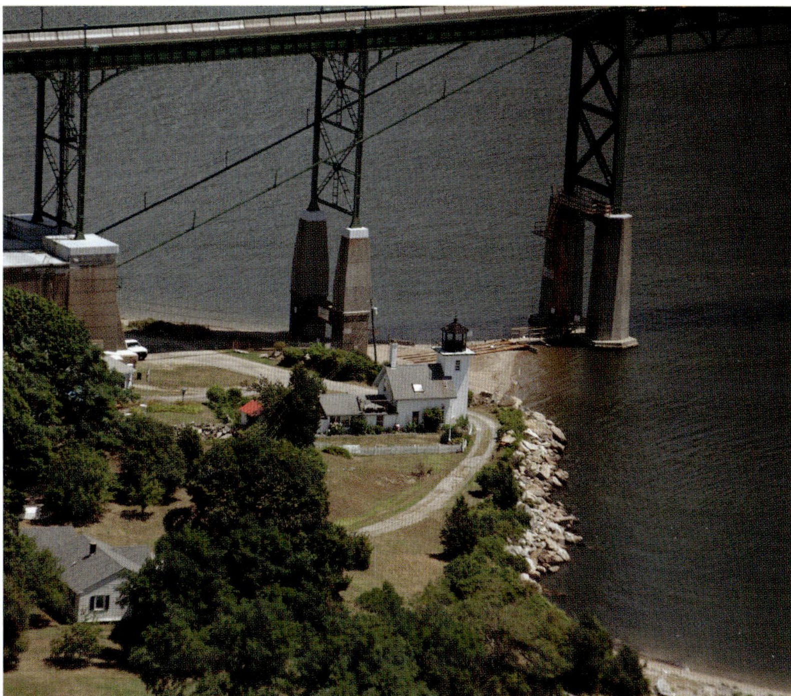

Top: No optic is present in the lantern room; the Mount Hope Bridge made the tower obsolete.

Bottom left: A view of the station and the nearby bridge.

Bottom right: An aerial view of the station.

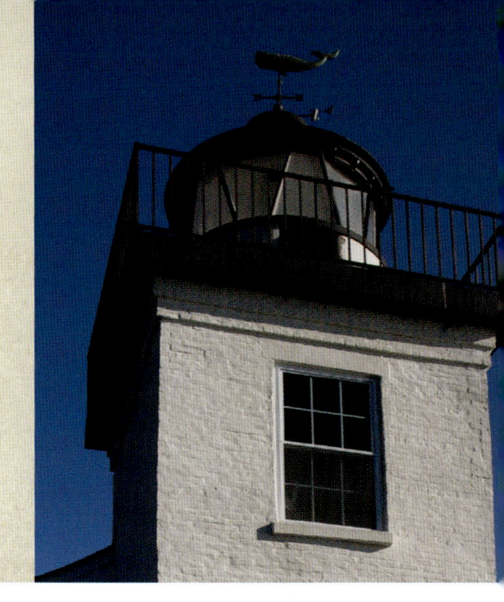

PROVIDENCE RIVER

For the nearly eight miles to the Port of Providence, mariners more than a century ago had six significant and distinctive aids to facilitate their passage. Today, four no longer exist, having been replaced by towers and buoys. Only one, Conimicut, is still an active aid to navigation. In the mid-1800s, and due to the increased maritime traffic to the Port of Providence, a concerted effort was made to improve and upgrade the navigational aids in the Providence River. A sharp bend in the river at its mouth necessitated a better and more precise set of aids to guide the mariner. Many of the original navigational aids were simply day marks with no lights, no tower and no keepers. Examine the charts, note the dates in the tables, and surmise the process of building the following navigational aids that made this shipping channel safer.

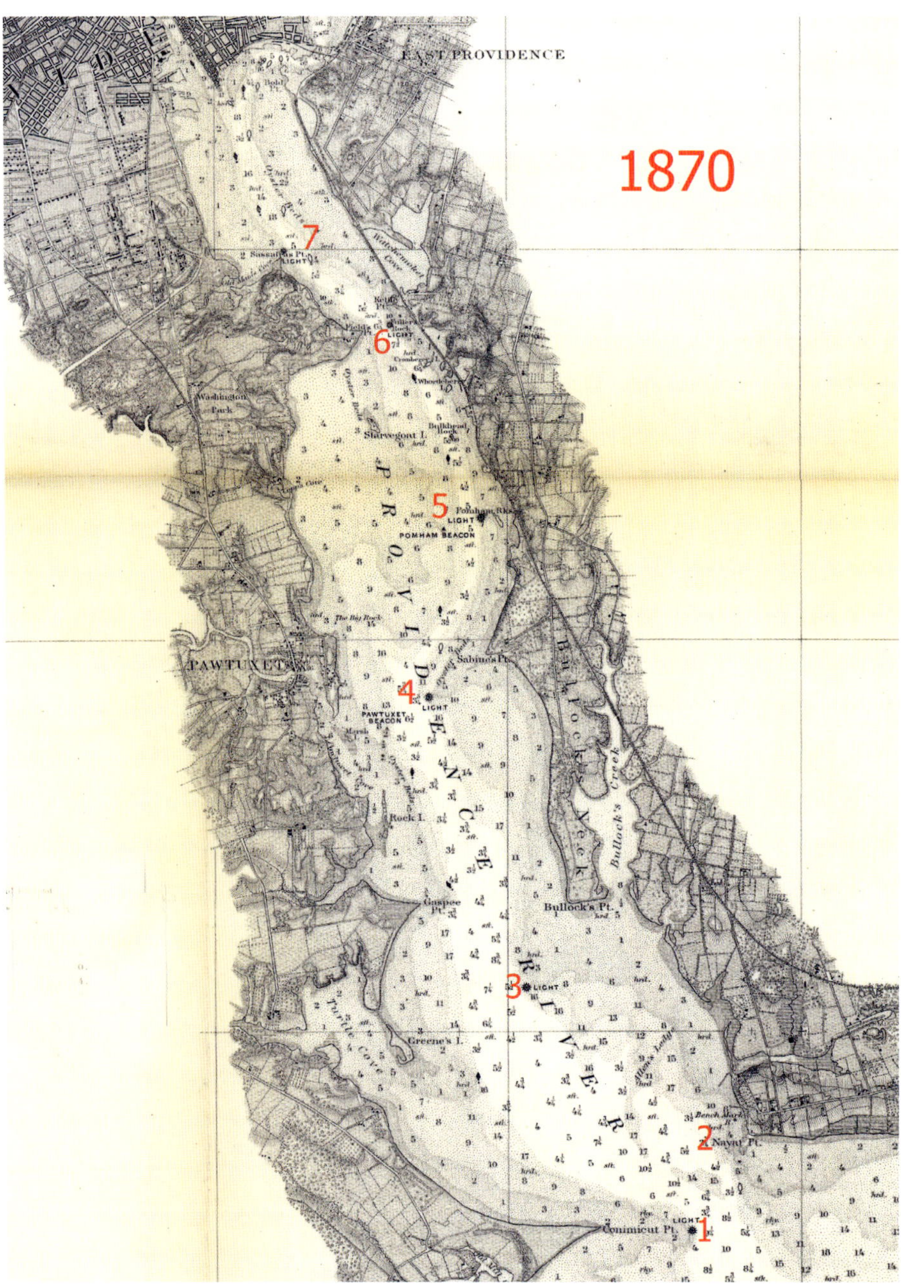

Compare these three charts (1870, 1924, and 2004) and note the progression in the aids to navigation. The first chart shows the lighthouses that were built to aid navigators in this waterway. The third chart (2004) identifies the modern aids that were built to replace destroyed or no longer functional towers.

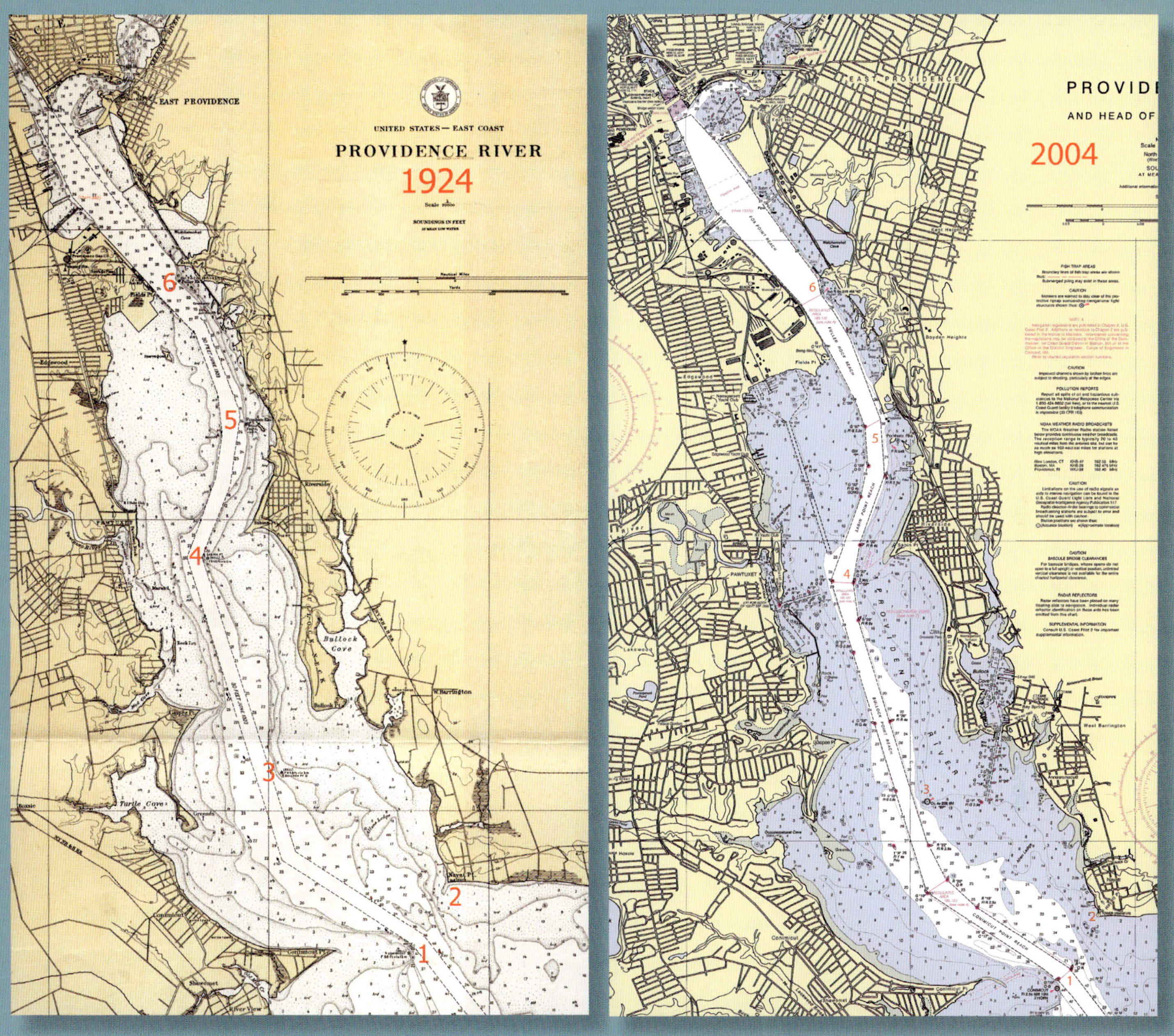

A sharp bend in the river at its mouth necessitated a better and more precise set of aids to guide the mariner.

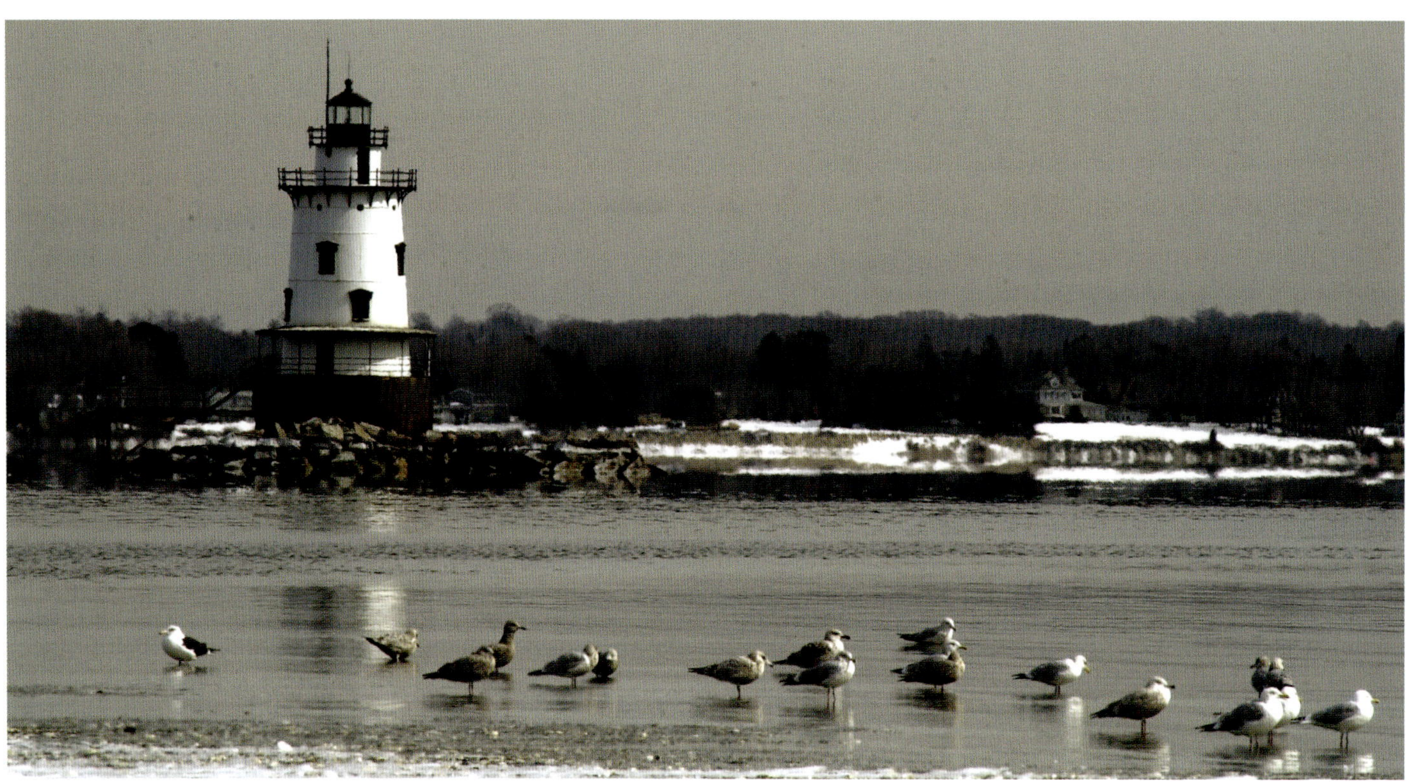

CONIMICUT SHOAL

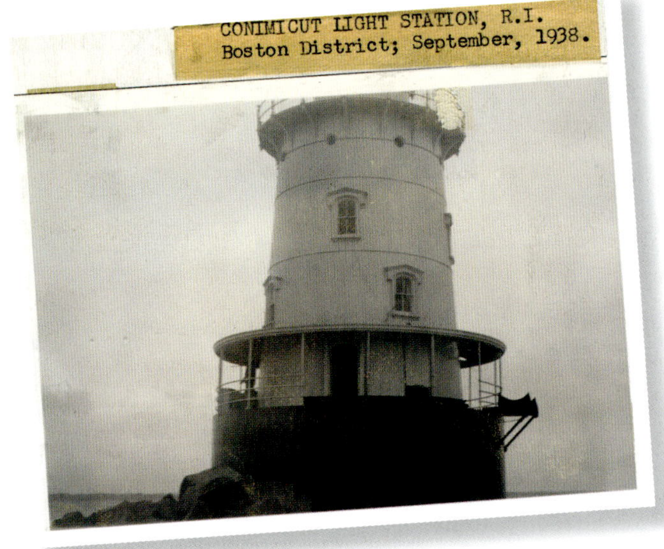
CONIMICUT LIGHT STATION, R.I.
Boston District; September, 1938.

Location: Providence River, between Barrington and Warwick, N41°43′01″, W71°20′42″

Appropriation: $15,000 in March 1867; $5,000 in March1877

Established: November 1868

Tower, original: Round, granite, 5-room keeper's house (destroyed by ice March 1875), first used as daymark

Rebuilt: 1883

Tower: White, conical, cast-iron, spark plug design, 58 feet, black lantern room

Original Lens: 4th order Fresnel lens, (moved from Nayatt Point) 1868, fixed white (FW), 1939 red sector added

Present Lens: 250 mm

Automated: 1963

Light Characteristics: Flashing white every 2.5 seconds with red sector (Fl W 2.5s R sector), red sector 322° to 349°

Range: White 15 nm, red 13 nm

Fog Signal: 2 blasts every 30 seconds

Status: Active U.S. Coast Guard aid to navigation

Access: None, best seen from boat.

Comments: Made Nayatt Point obsolete; built by same company as Plum Beach; 1960 converted to electrical power (was kerosene); owned by Conimicut Lighthouse Foundation; tours possible in future; listed in NRHP.

Top: A winter view of the tower. *(Courtesy of D. Zapatka)*

Bottom: Captured after the hurricane of 21 September 1938, this image shows the tower that survived the storm. *(Courtesy of USCG)*

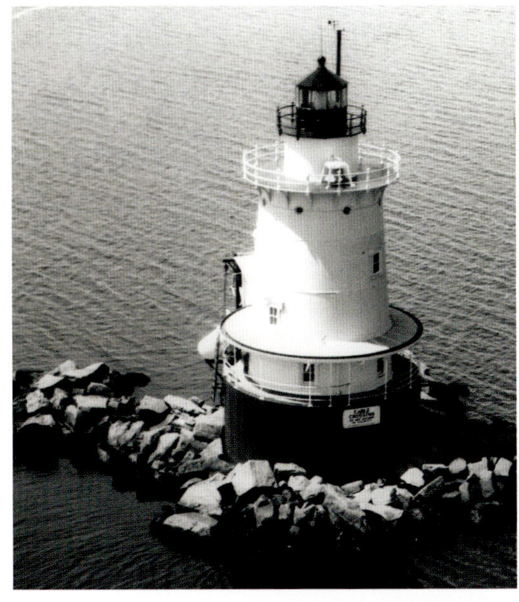

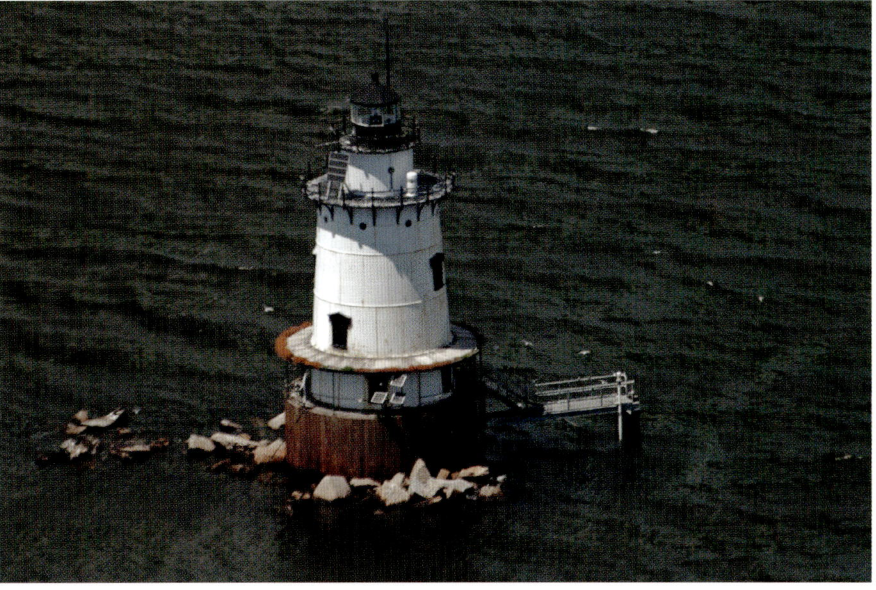

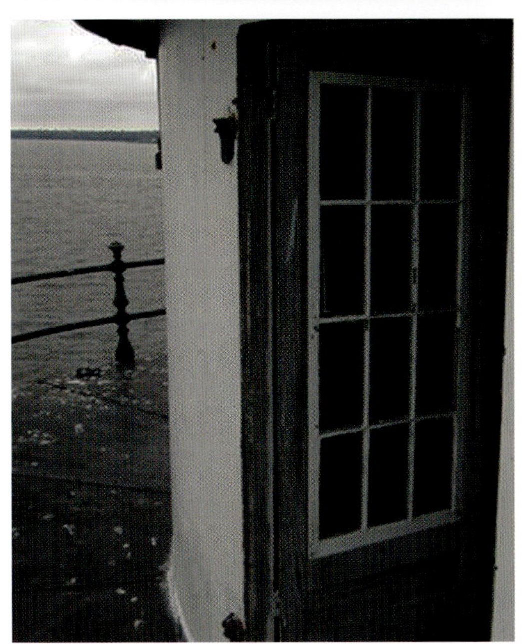

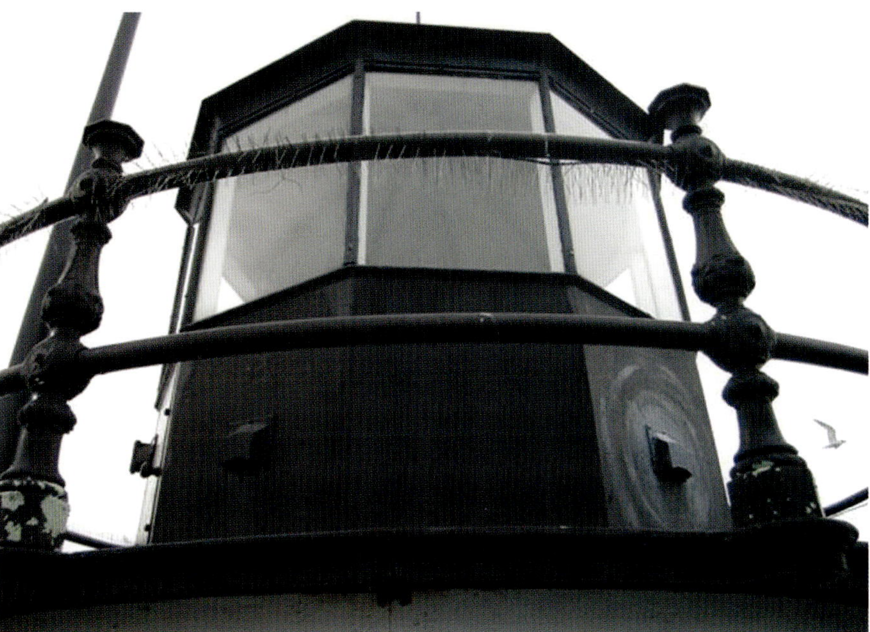

Top: Two aerial images of the tower taken more than a half century apart. *(Black-and-white image courtesy of USCG)*

Bottom left: The door leading into the tower. *(Courtesy of R. Crenna)*

Bottom right: A view of the lantern room. *(Courtesy of R. Crenna)*

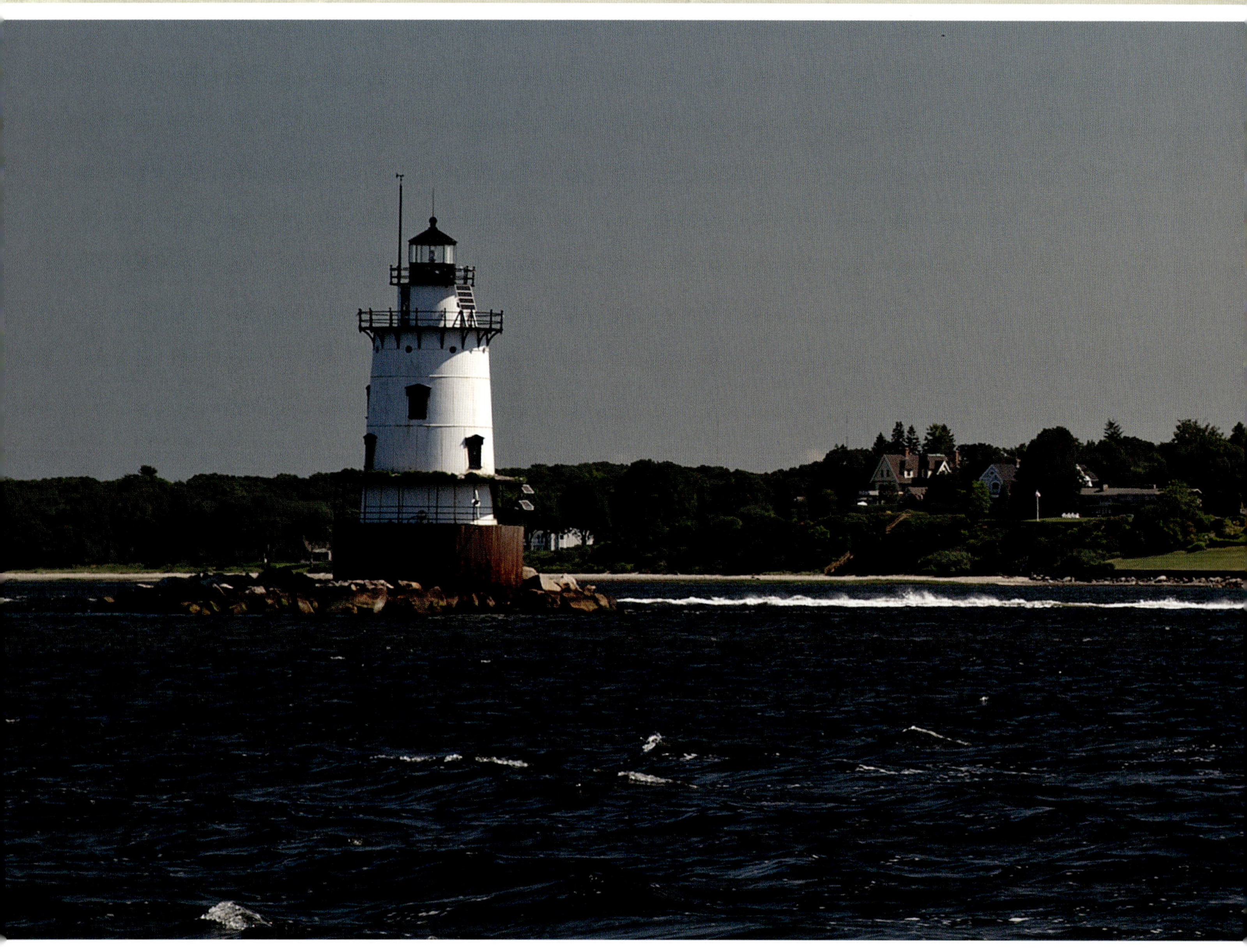

Top: Looking northeast with the Conimicut tower on the left. In the distance, underlined in red, is the Nayatt Point tower.

Right: The Conimicut station was first established in 1868; this cast-iron tower was erected in 1883 and is the subject of this early 20th-century postcard.

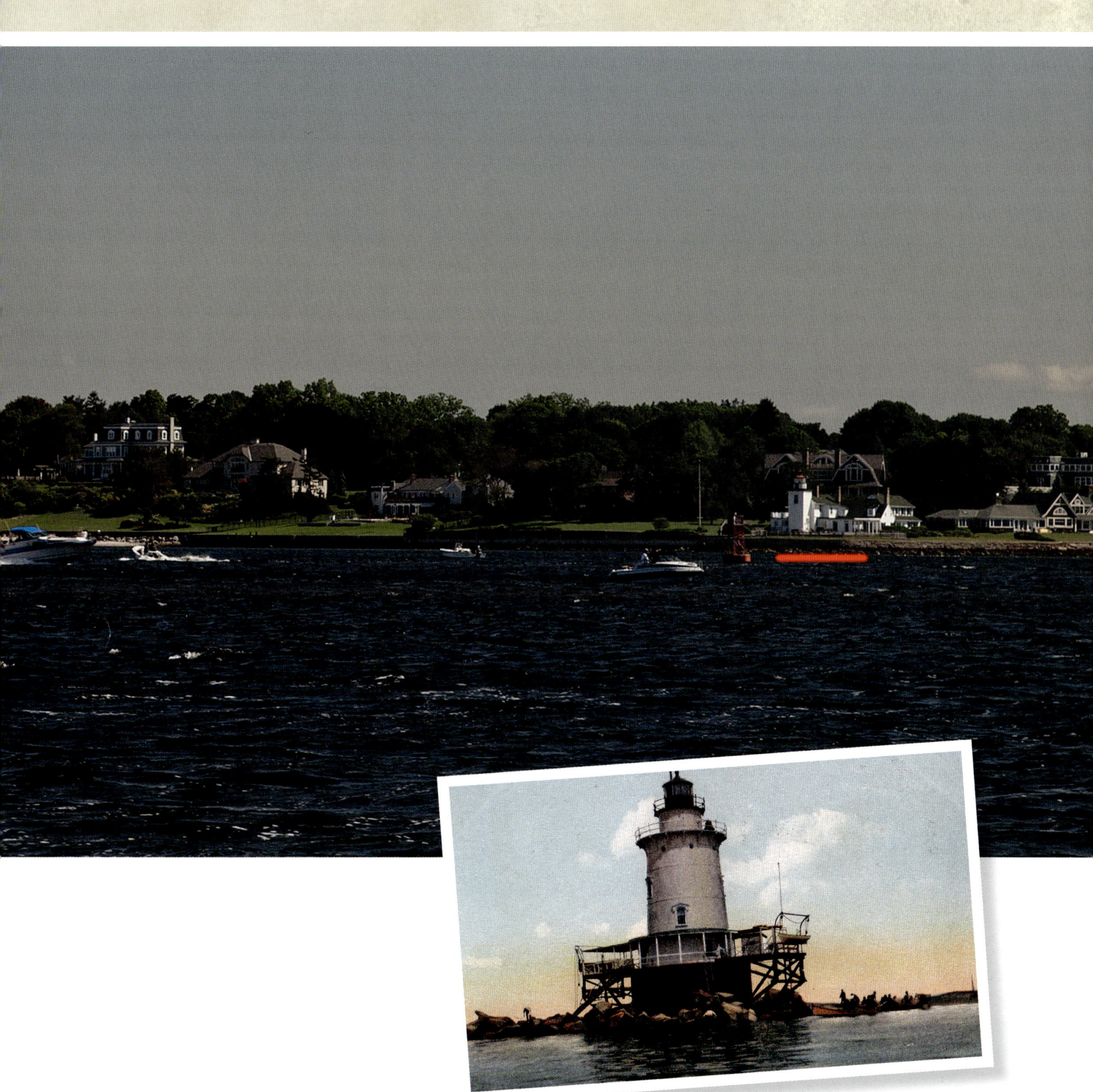

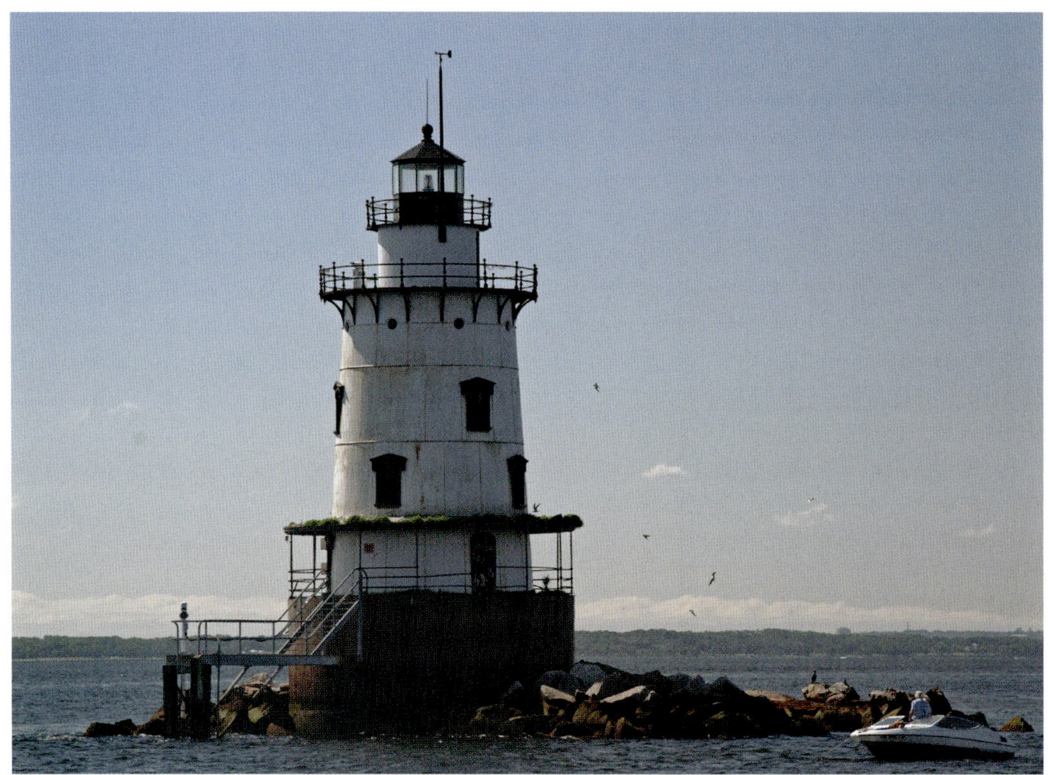

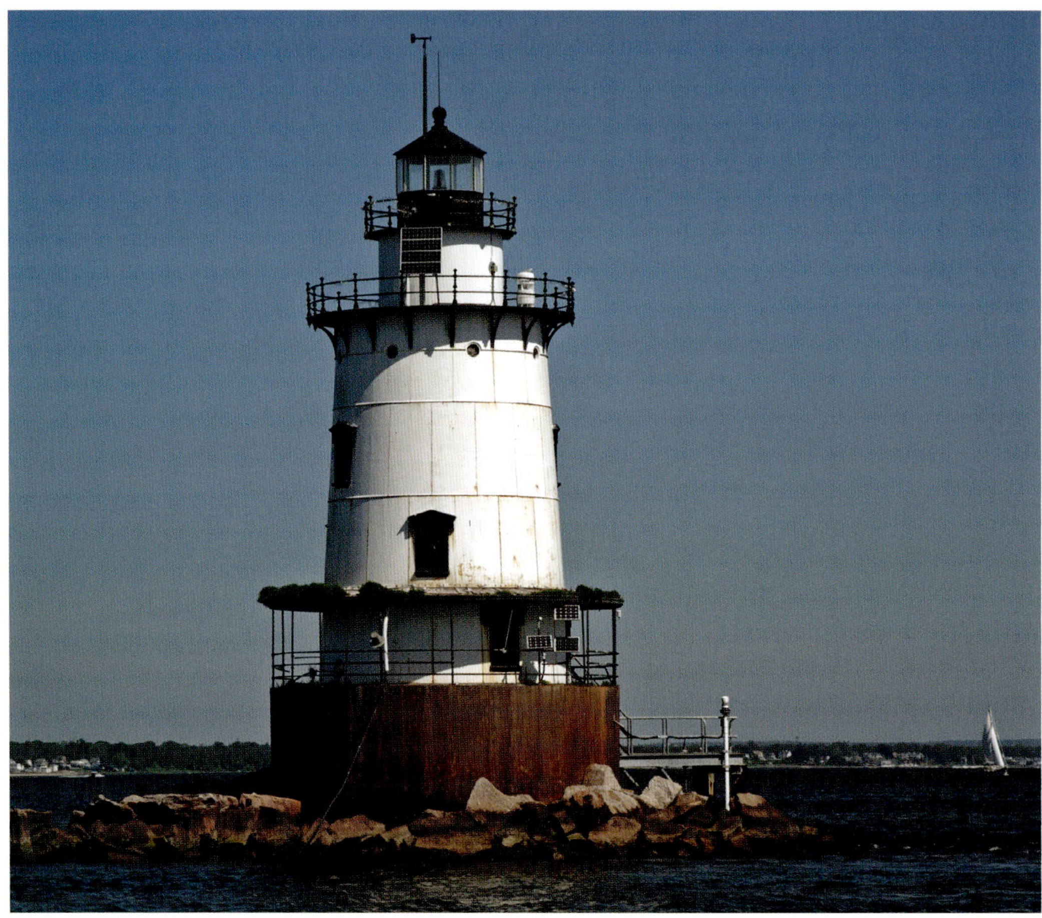

Two present-day images of Conimicut Light Tower taken from opposite sides.

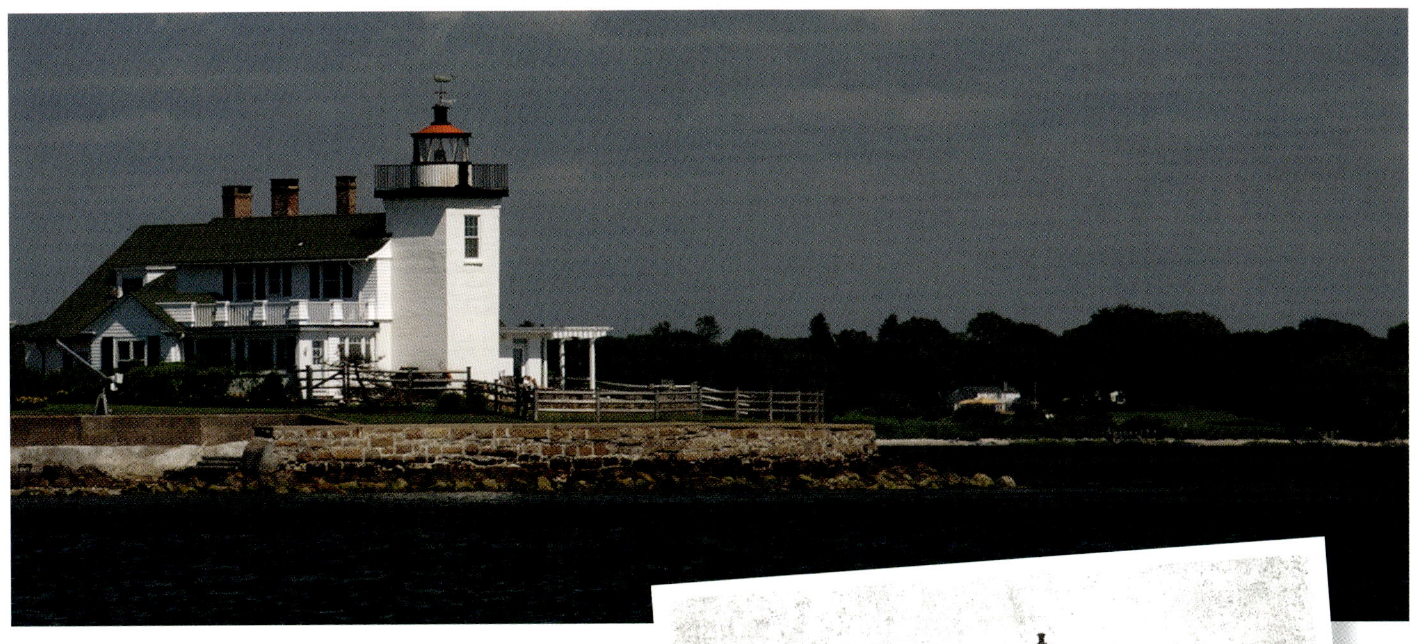

NAYATT POINT

Location: Barrington, mouth of Providence River, N41°43′30″, W71°20′20″

Appropriation: $3,500 in 1828; $6,500 in 1856; $6,500 in 1866

Established: May 1828

Rebuilt: 1856

Tower, original: Brick, white, wooden stairs, 23 feet, may have been attached to 5-room keeper's house

Disestablished: 1868

Tower: White, brick, square, 25 feet, black lantern room

Original Optics: 1842, 6 lamps with 9-inch reflectors, fixed white (FW); 1850 6 lamps with 14-inch reflectors, FW

Original Lens: 4th order Fresnel lens, fixed white, focal plane (1863) 31 feet

Present Lens: Not operational, Fresnel lens from lightship (1890)

Light Characteristics: N/A

Range: N/A

Fog Signal: None

Status: Private residence, not an aid to navigation

Access: None.

Comments: Privately owned since 1890; became obsolete when Conimicut was built; 4th order Fresnel lens moved to Conimicut in 1868; listed in NRHP.

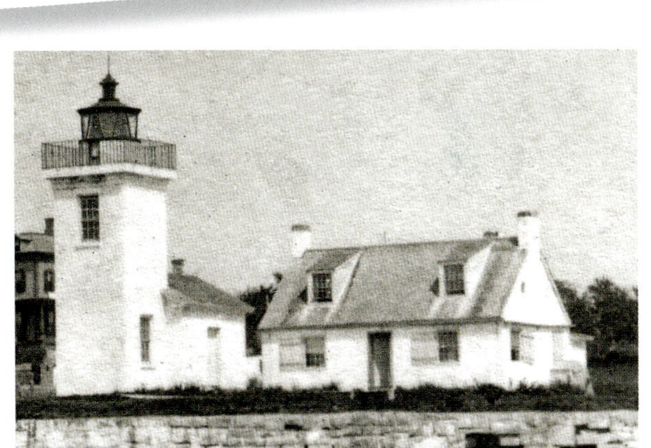

Top: A view of the former Nayatt Point Light Station from the Providence River/Narragansett Bay, captured during a lighthouse cruise.

Center and bottom: Nayatt Point was disestablished in 1868, and these two archival photographs were taken sometime after 1883. In the view from the back of the tower, it is possible to see the cast-iron Conimicut tower that was built in 1883. *(Courtesy of R. Holmes)*

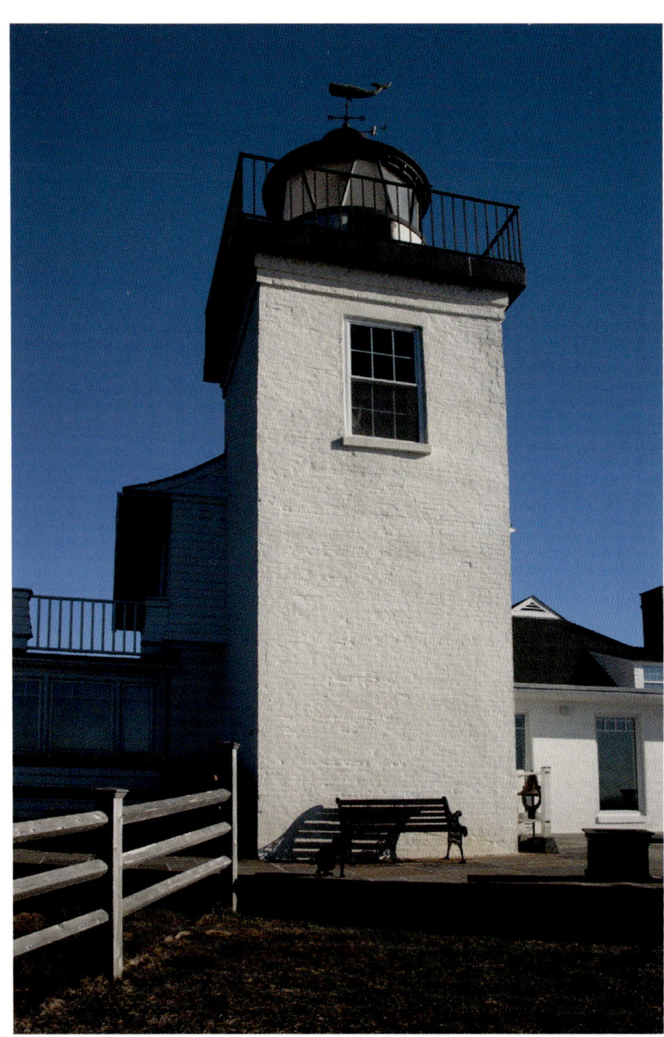

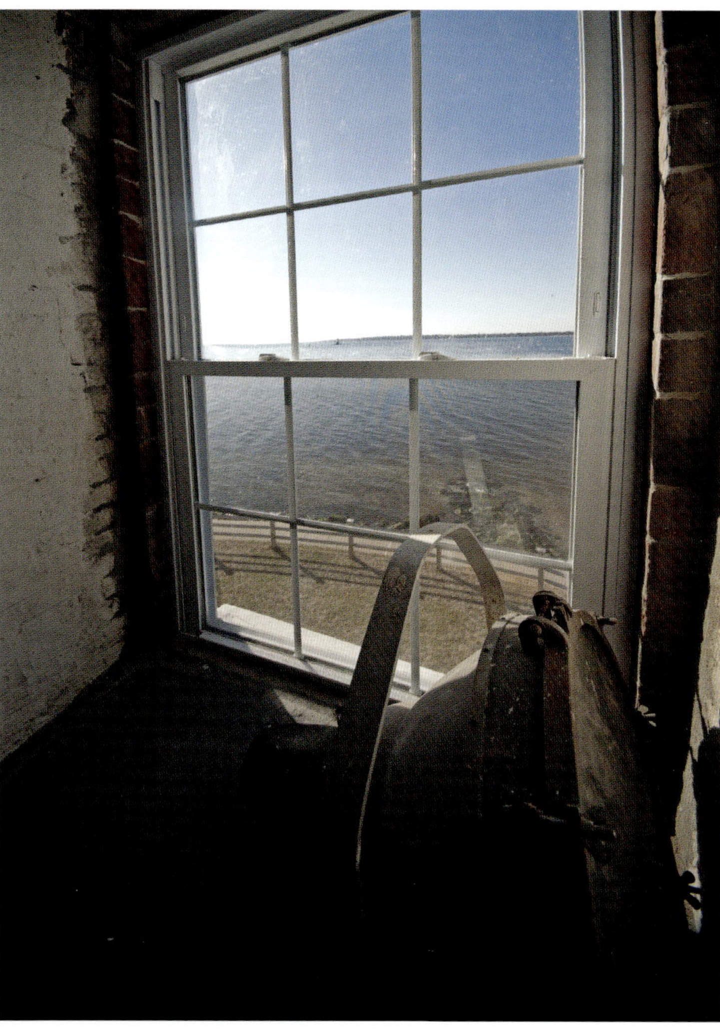

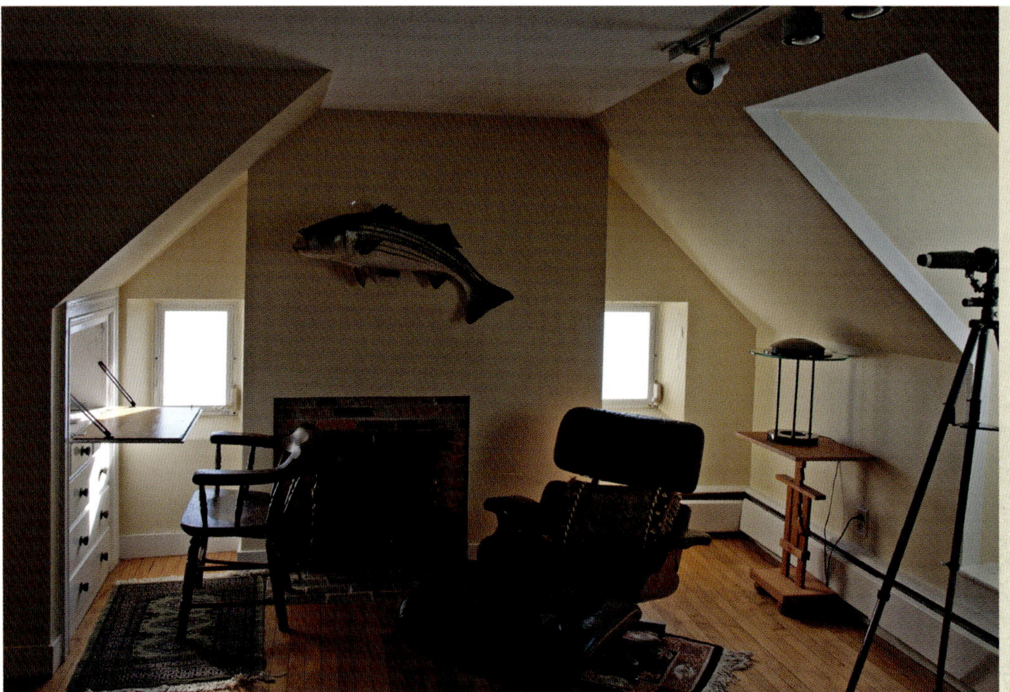

Top left: A present-day view of the 1856 tower.

Top right: A view out the tower window; barely visible in the center pane is the Conimicut tower.

Bottom: Now updated and modernized, this room was the keeper's office; his desk is on the left wall.

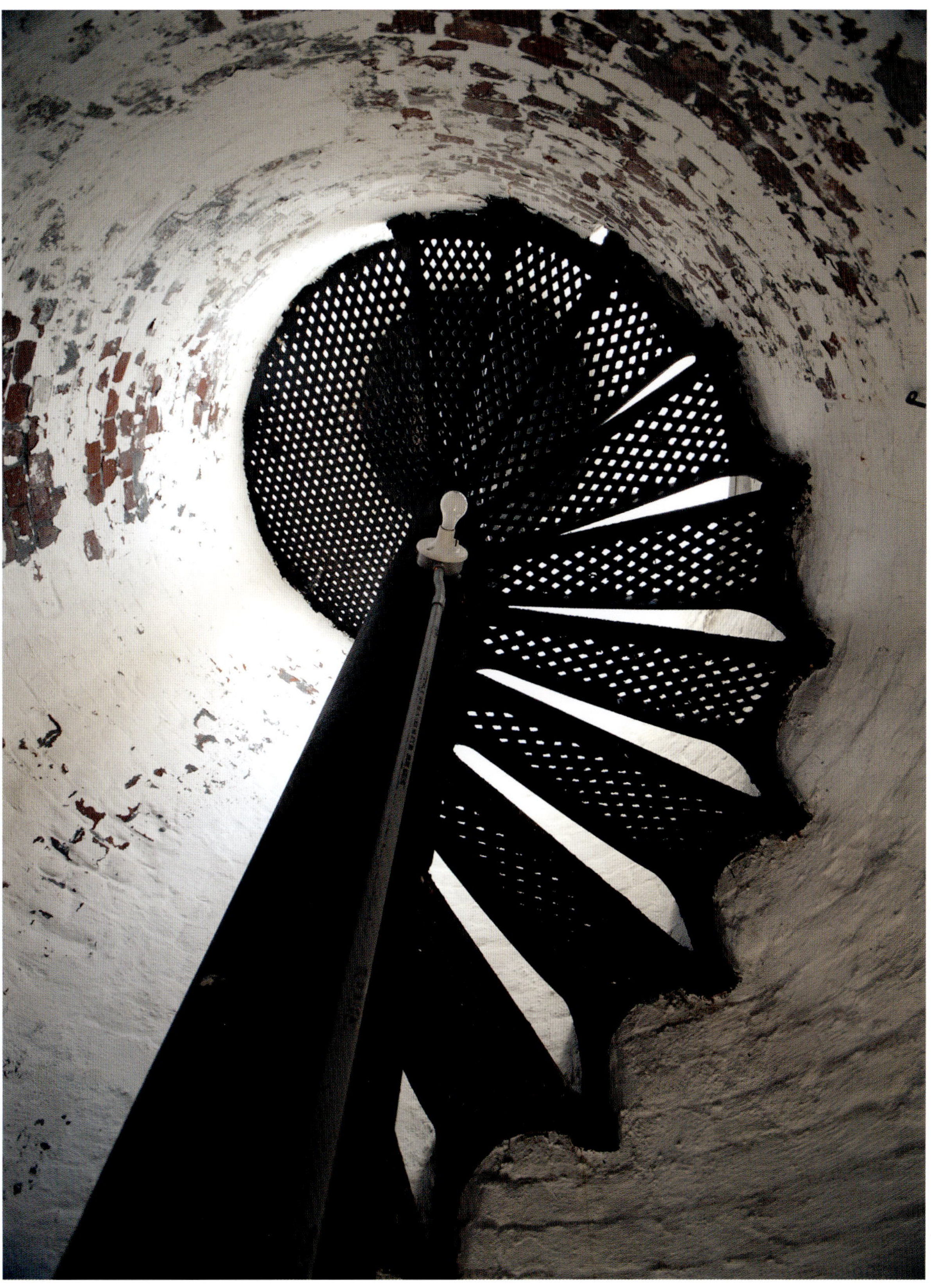

A flight of cast-iron stairs leads to the lantern room.

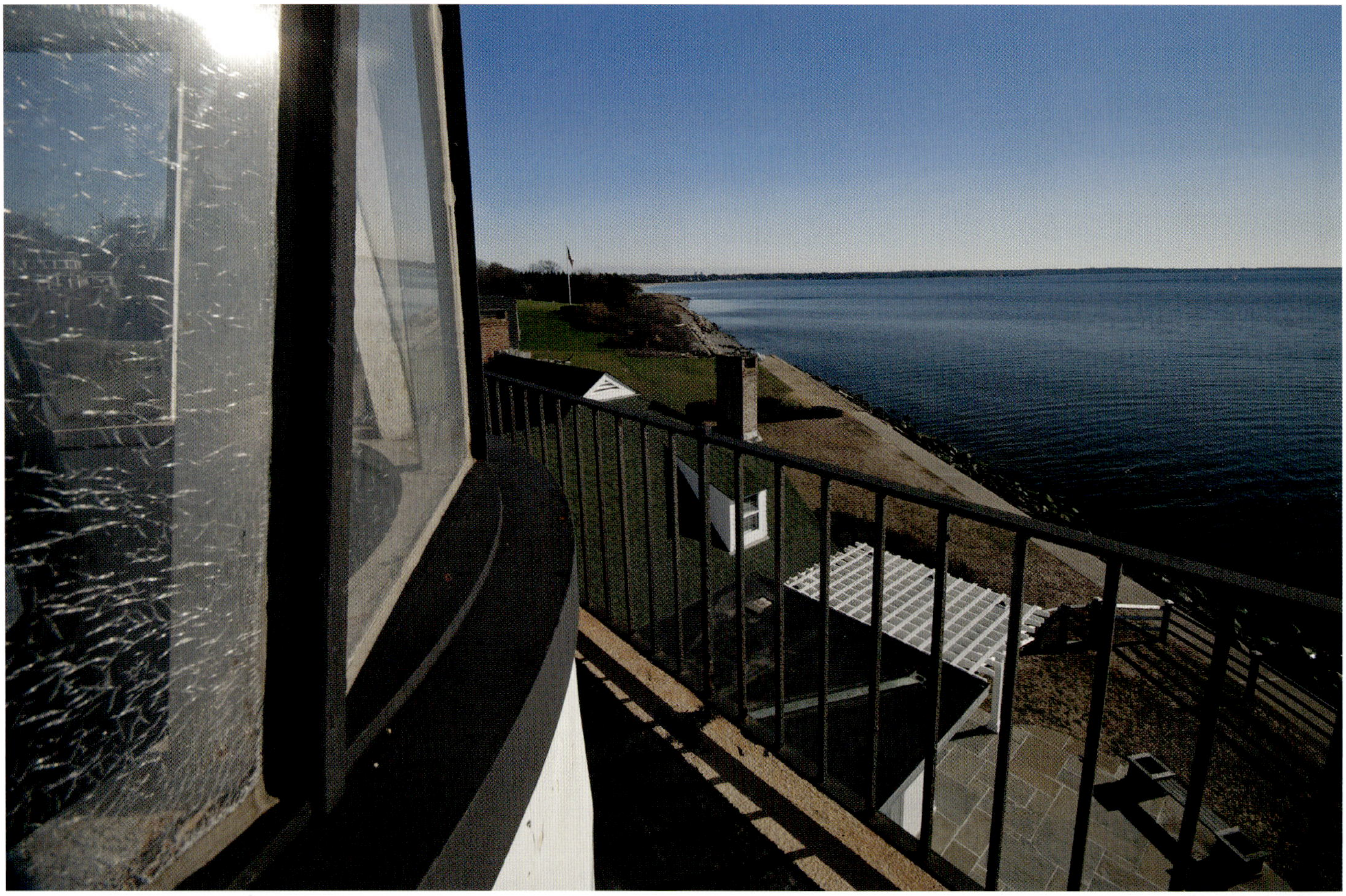

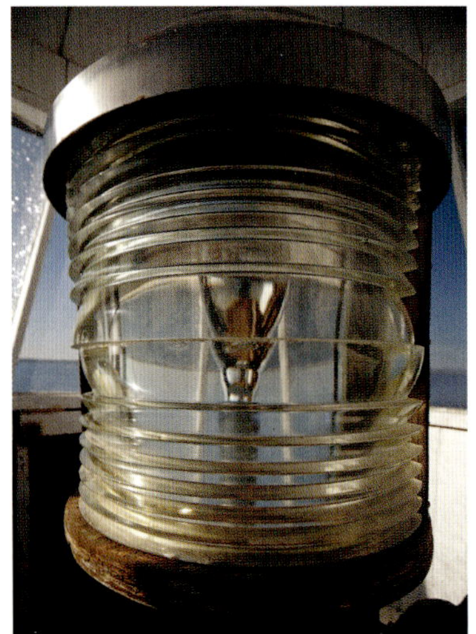

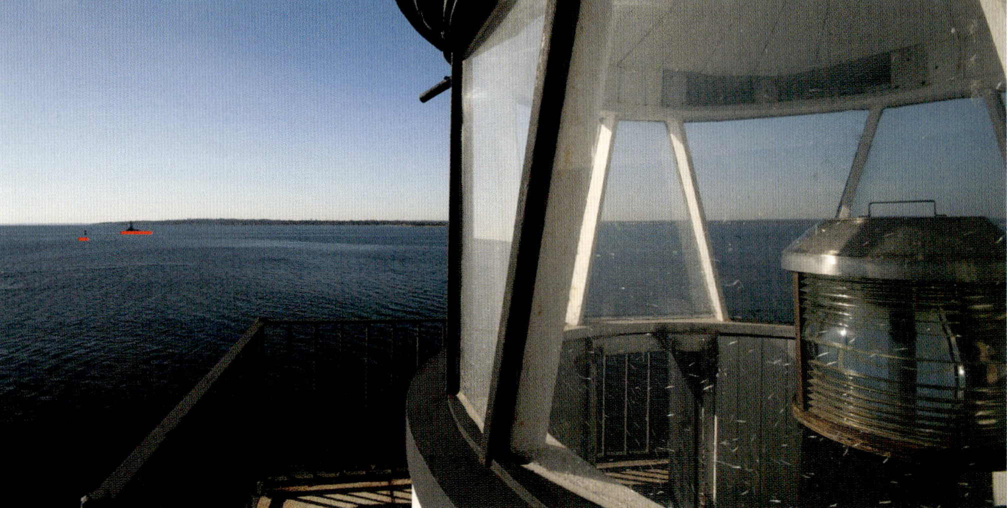

Top: Looking east from the lantern room walkway.

Bottom left: Once the lamp on a lightship, this lens was purchased by a previous owner.

Bottom right: Looking southeast from the walkway around the lantern room. The still active Conimicut tower (indicated in red) can be seen in the distance.

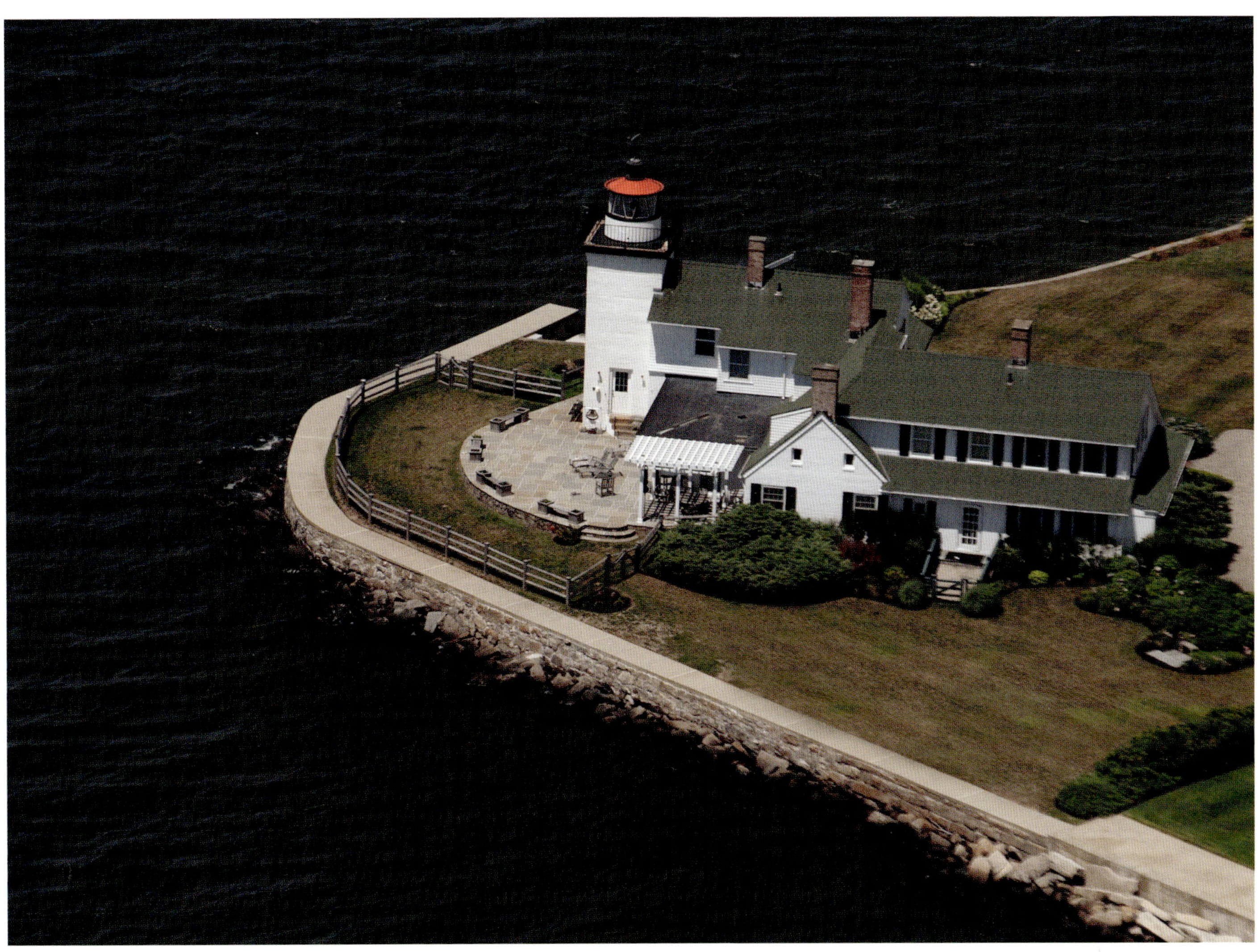

Nayatt Point Light from the air. Its distance from the channel and obstructions closer to the navigational channel led to its demise as an active aid to navigation.

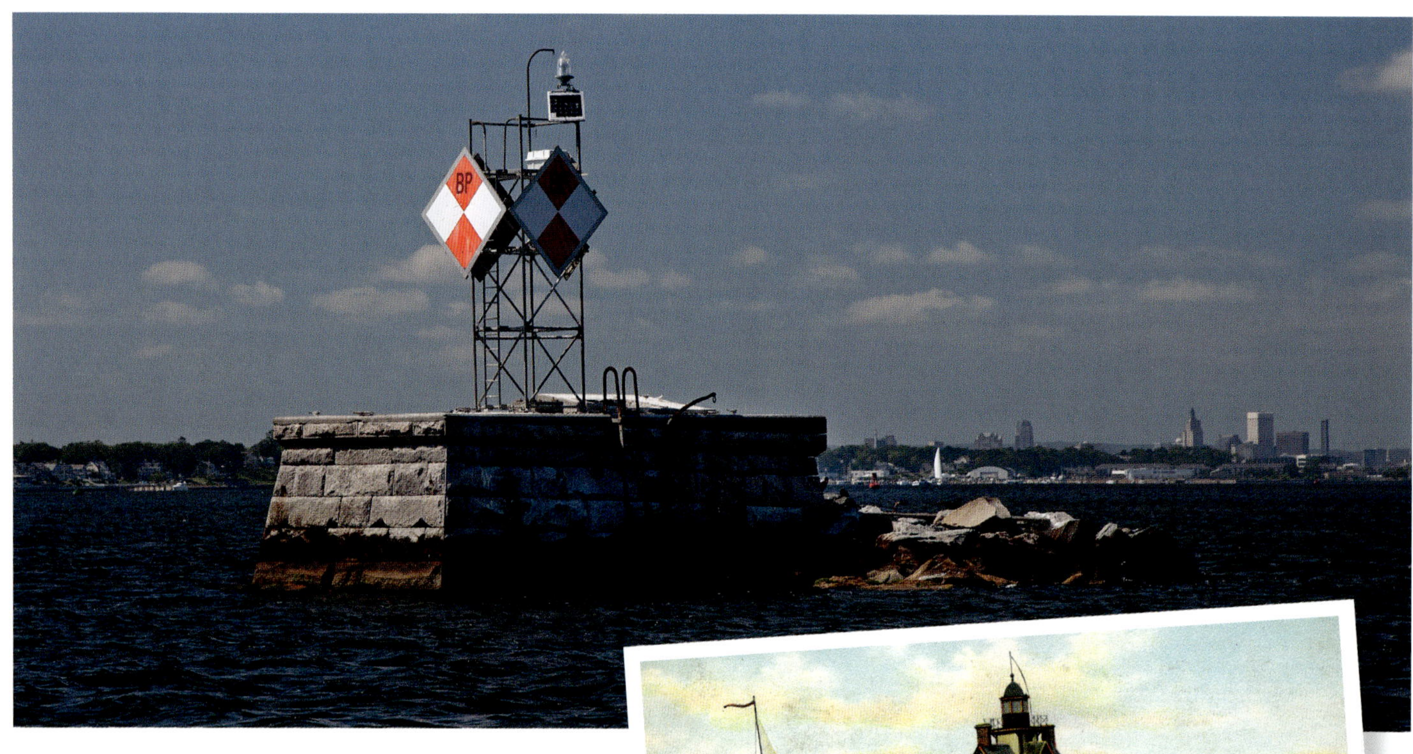

BULLOCK'S POINT

Location: Providence River, N41°44′12″, W71°21′54″, original station no longer exists

Established: October 1872

Appropriation: $3,000 in 1860; $1,000 in 1872; $15,000 in 1874

Station built: 1876

Disestablished: 1938, demolished after severe damage from hurricane

Tower: White, square, on roof of Victorian house

Original Lens: 6th order Fresnel lens, fixed red (FR), range 7.5 nm

Present station: Identification NR on skeleton tower

Present Lens: Plastic lens, automated, solar-powered, focal plane 29 feet

Light Characteristics: Occulting white light every 4 seconds (Oc W 4s)

Range: 6 nm

Fog Signal, original: 1924, bell twice every 15 seconds; present, none

Status: Active aid to navigation, skeleton tower on original foundation

Access: None, can be seen from boat.

Comments: When built in 1876, house was most expensive station ever built; damaged by hurricane of 1938; dismantled shortly after.

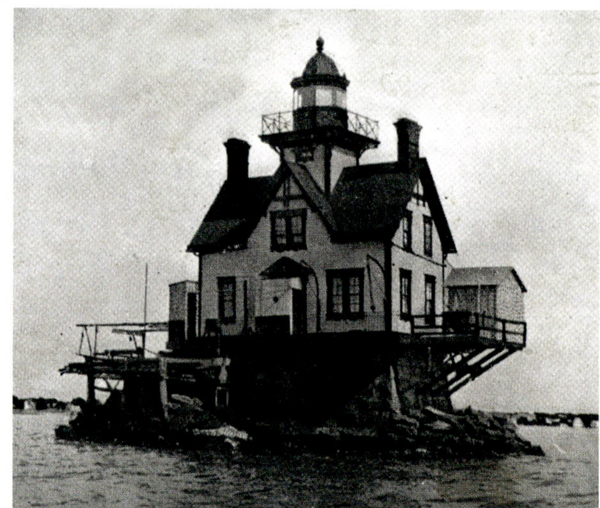

Top: A present-day view of the skeleton tower on the original base. Barely visible is the BP identification on the red section of the diamond-shaped sign. In the distance is the skyline of Providence.

Center: A postcard of the lighthouse on a calm summer day, early in the last century.

Bottom: Built in 1876, Bullock's Point Light Station marked the beginning of the channel that would lead to Providence. *(Courtesy of NA)*

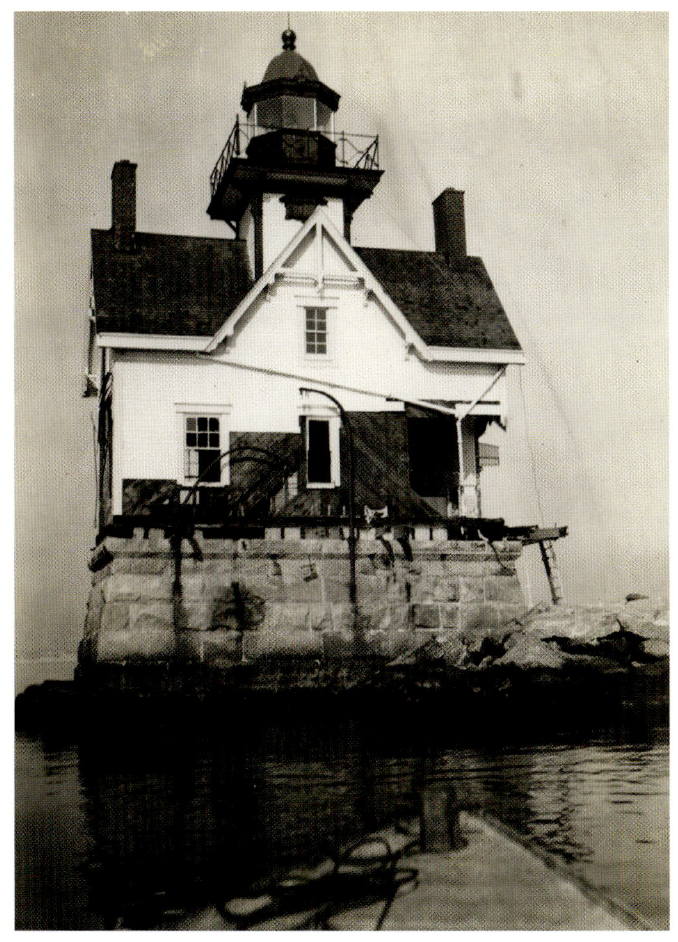

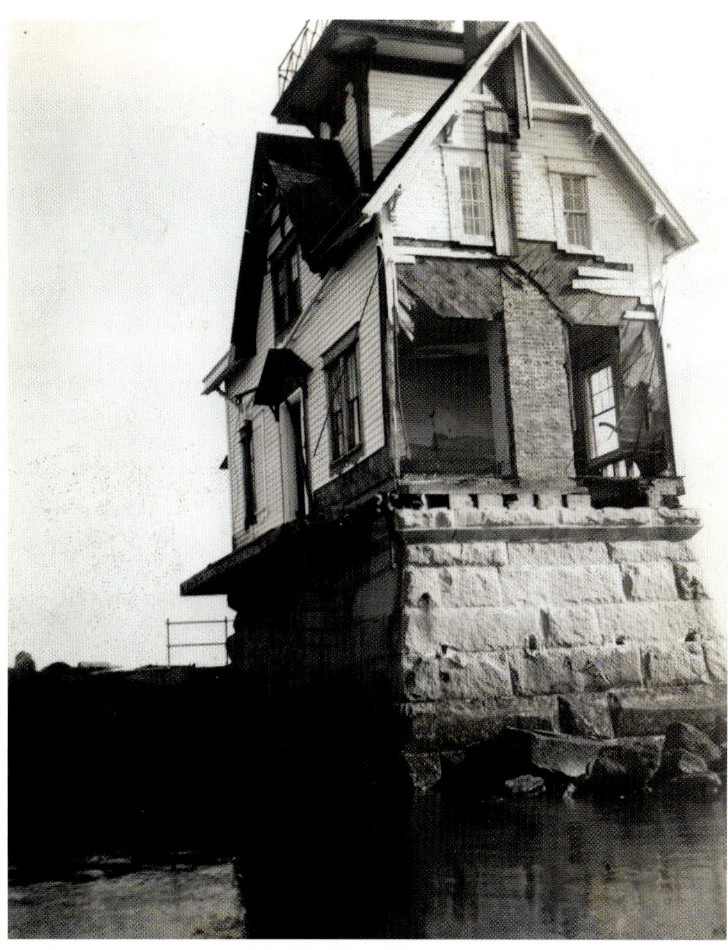

Top: The hurricane that struck Rhode Island on 21 September 1938 so brutally destroyed the coast that several lighthouses ceased to exist. Bullock's Point, while still standing, received substantial damage; a short time later it was demolished and only the base remains from the original station. *(Courtesy of NA)*

Right: Compare this current aerial image of the original base and the present-day skeleton tower with the archival images to determine the location of the building.

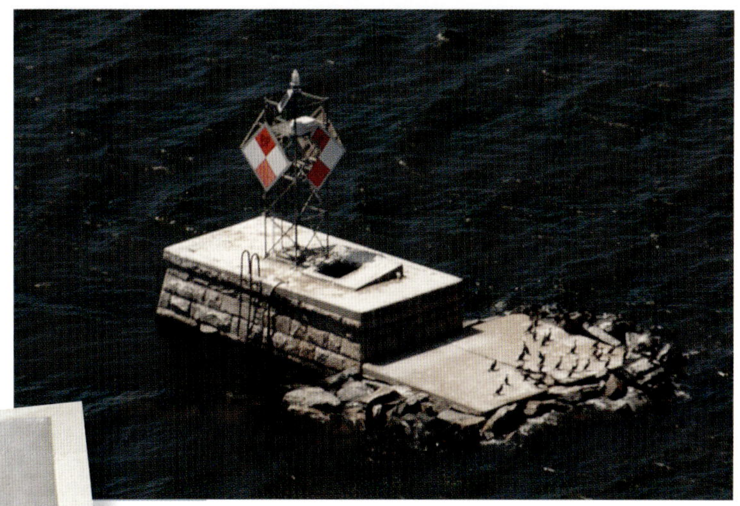

Enlargement of small picture sent by keeper showing ice condition

Left: Unlikely as it seems nowadays, waterways would freeze and snow would accumulate; several lighthouses along these channels were severely damaged by ice. In this case, however, Bullock's Point seems none the worse for the winter conditions. *(Courtesy of NA)*

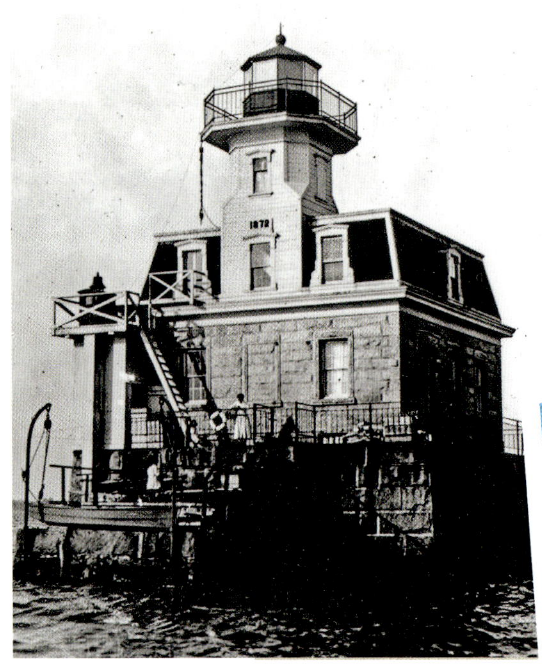

Left and below: These two pictures of Sabin Point are probably about a century old. In the close-up image, note that there are at least three people near the boat. Is that the keeper's wife hanging over the railing? *(Black-and-white images courtesy of USCG)*

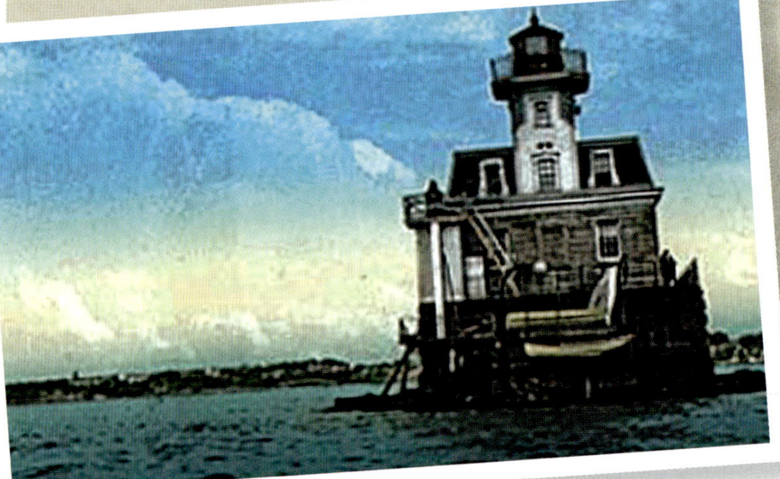

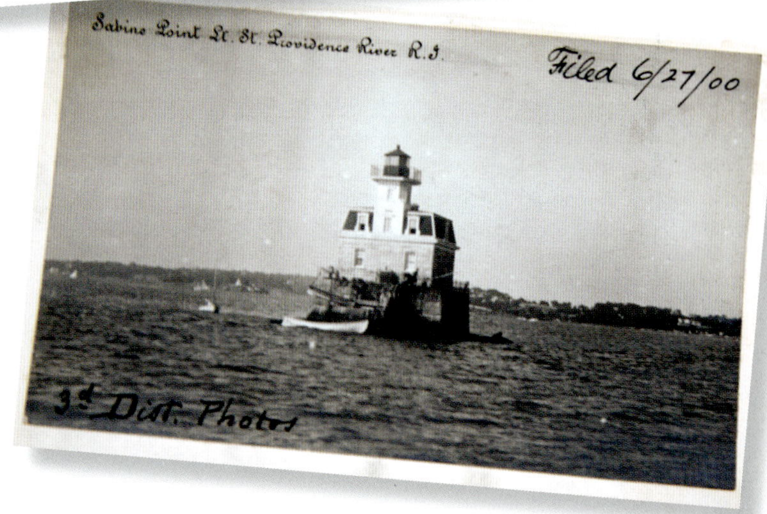

Above: Taken sometime before 27 June 1900, this image not only identifies the lighthouse and its location but also the district that was responsible for maintaining it. *(Courtesy of USCG)*

SABIN POINT

Location: Providence River, east side, N41°45′42″, W71°22′30″, original station no longer exists

Appropriation: $42,000 in 1871

Established: November 1872

Demolished: 1968, burned and razed when channel was widened and deepened

Tower: Integral with French Second Empire revival style keeper's house, octagonal, white, black lantern room

Original Lens: 6th order Fresnel lens, focal plane 49 feet 1939, 4th order Fresnel lens, fixed red (FR)

Present Lens: None

Light Characteristics: 1906 Fixed red (FR)

Range: N/A

Fog Signal: Fog bell, once every 9 seconds

Status: Station no longer exists, replaced by skeleton tower, active aid to navigation

Access: Present aid can be seen from boat.

Comments: Similar to Rose Island light; severely damaged by 1938 hurricane.

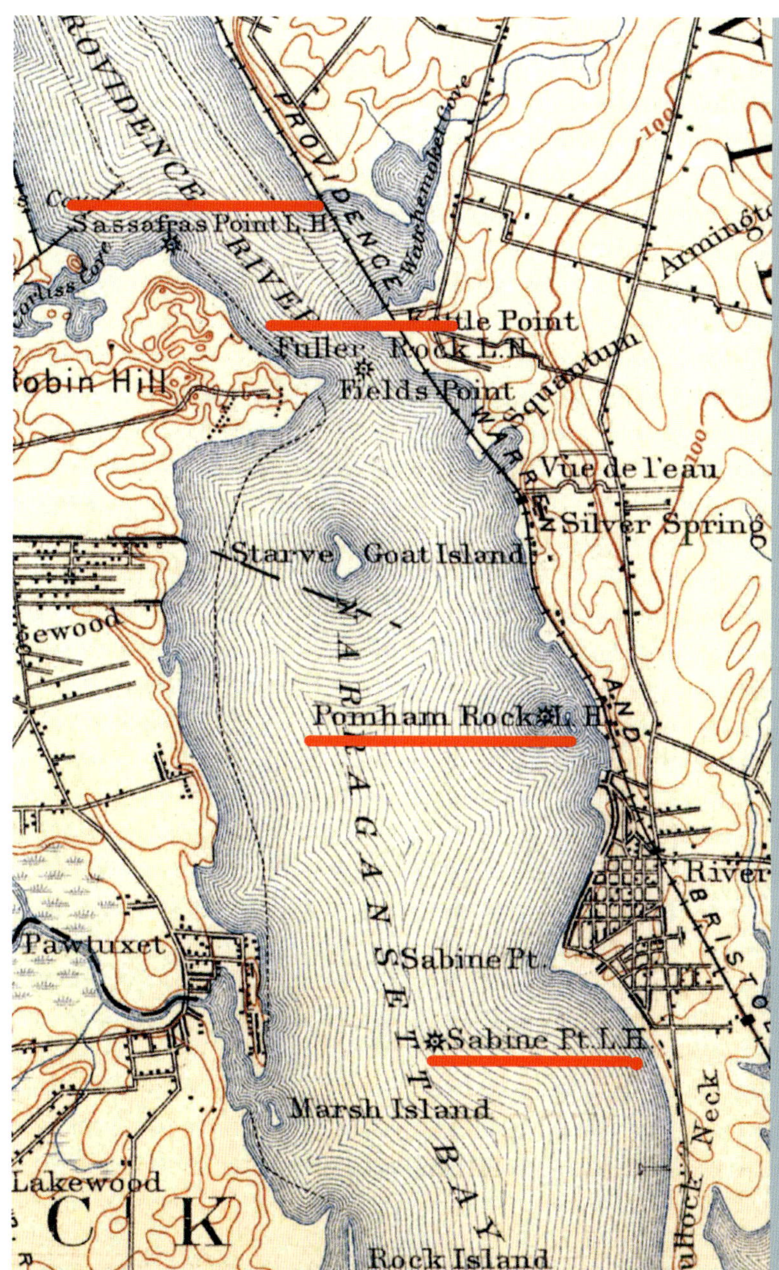

Left: This 1894 topographical map shows the location of the final four lighthouses in the Providence River/Narragansett Bay area. From bottom to top, as ships would come upon these aids, they are Sabin Point, Pomham Rocks, Sassafras Point, and Fuller Rocks. Pomham is the only original lighthouse still remaining. Notice on this map primarily used for land (not for navigation) that no characteristics are identified with each lighthouse. *(Courtesy of USCG)*

Below: Two present-day views of the aid that replaced Sabin Point, which was demolished in 1968. The *SP* on the diamond-shaped red and white sign is for Sabin Point. Compare the background in the wider view with the older images to determine a point of reference on the map.

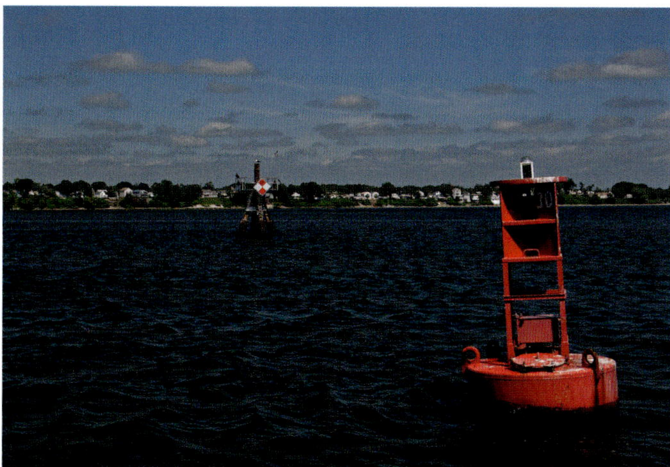

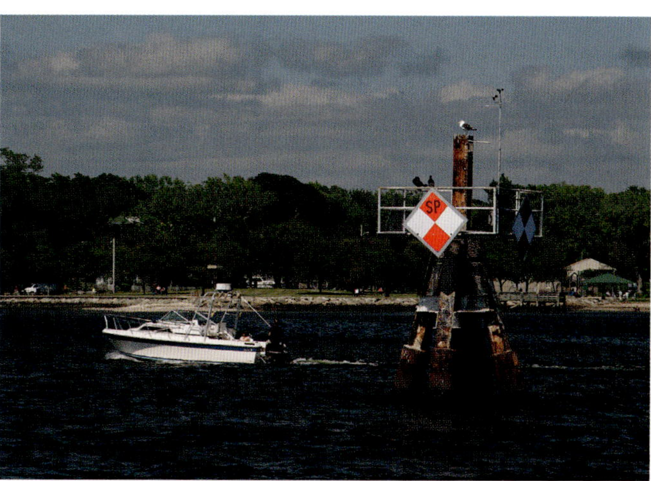

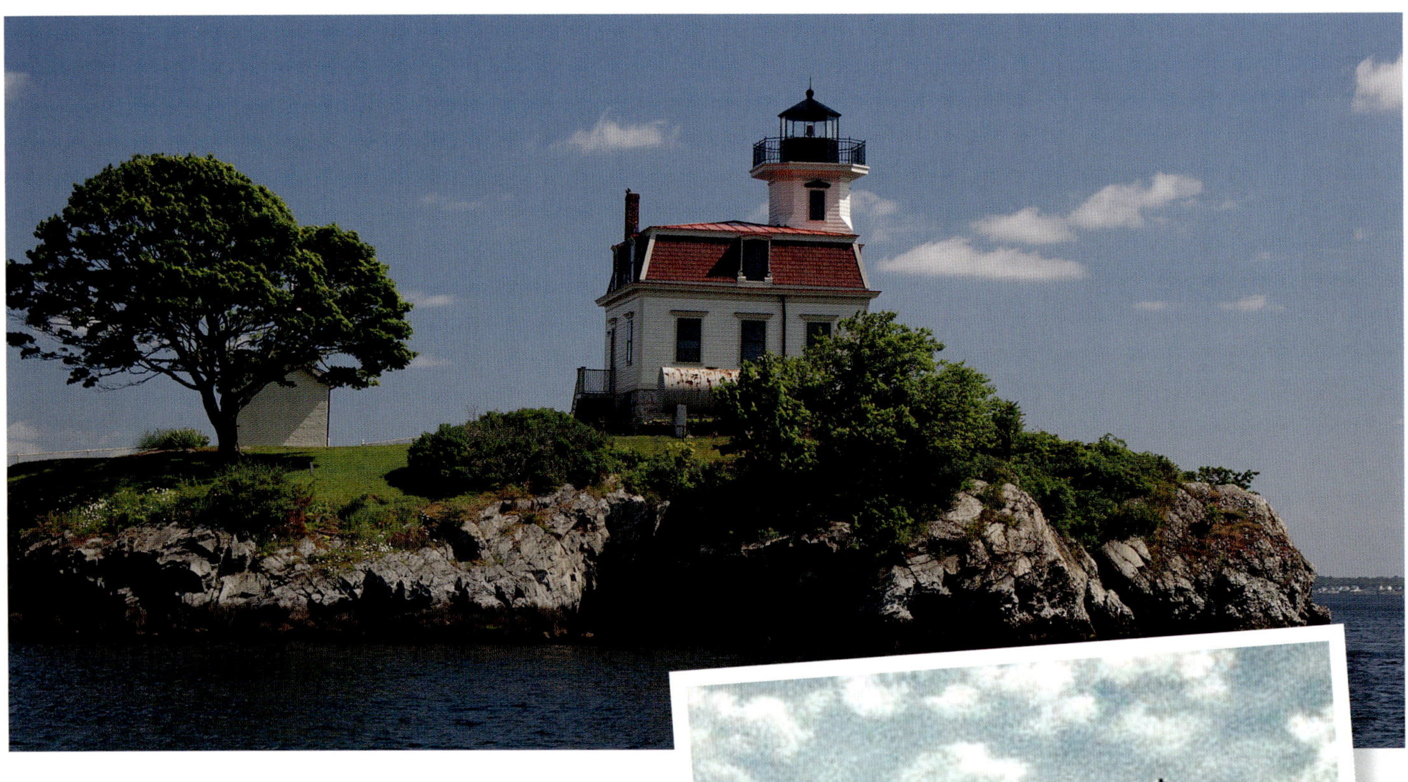

POMHAM (Pumham) ROCKS

Location: East side of Providence River, N41°46′36″, W71°22′12″

Appropriation: $20,000 in July 1870 (also included Sassafras Point and Fuller Rocks)

Established: December 1871

Deactivated: 1974–2006

Relit: July 2006

Tower: White, octagonal, 42 feet, black lantern room, integral with French, Second Empire style, 8-room keeper's house

Other buildings: Oil house

Original Lens: 1873, 6th order Fresnel lens, focal plane 67 feet, fixed red (FR)

Present Lens: Skeleton tower, 250 mm solar-powered and automated, 40 feet, focal plane 54 feet

Light Characteristics: Fixed red (FR)

Range: 6 nm

Fog Signal: 1902 none; 1924, bell 2 strokes every 20 seconds

Status: Active U.S. Coast Guard aid to navigation

Access: None, best seen from boat; also nearby bike path.

Comments: Station designed by Albert R. Dow; sister to Rose Island Light and Colchester Light, VT; owned by the American Lighthouse Foundation; maintained by Friends of Pomham Rocks Lighthouse; restoration in progress; listed in NRHP.

Top and opposite top: Two views of the island with the lighthouse station.

Above: A century-old postcard of Pomham Lighthouse, which is located on this rocky ledge on the east side of the Providence River.

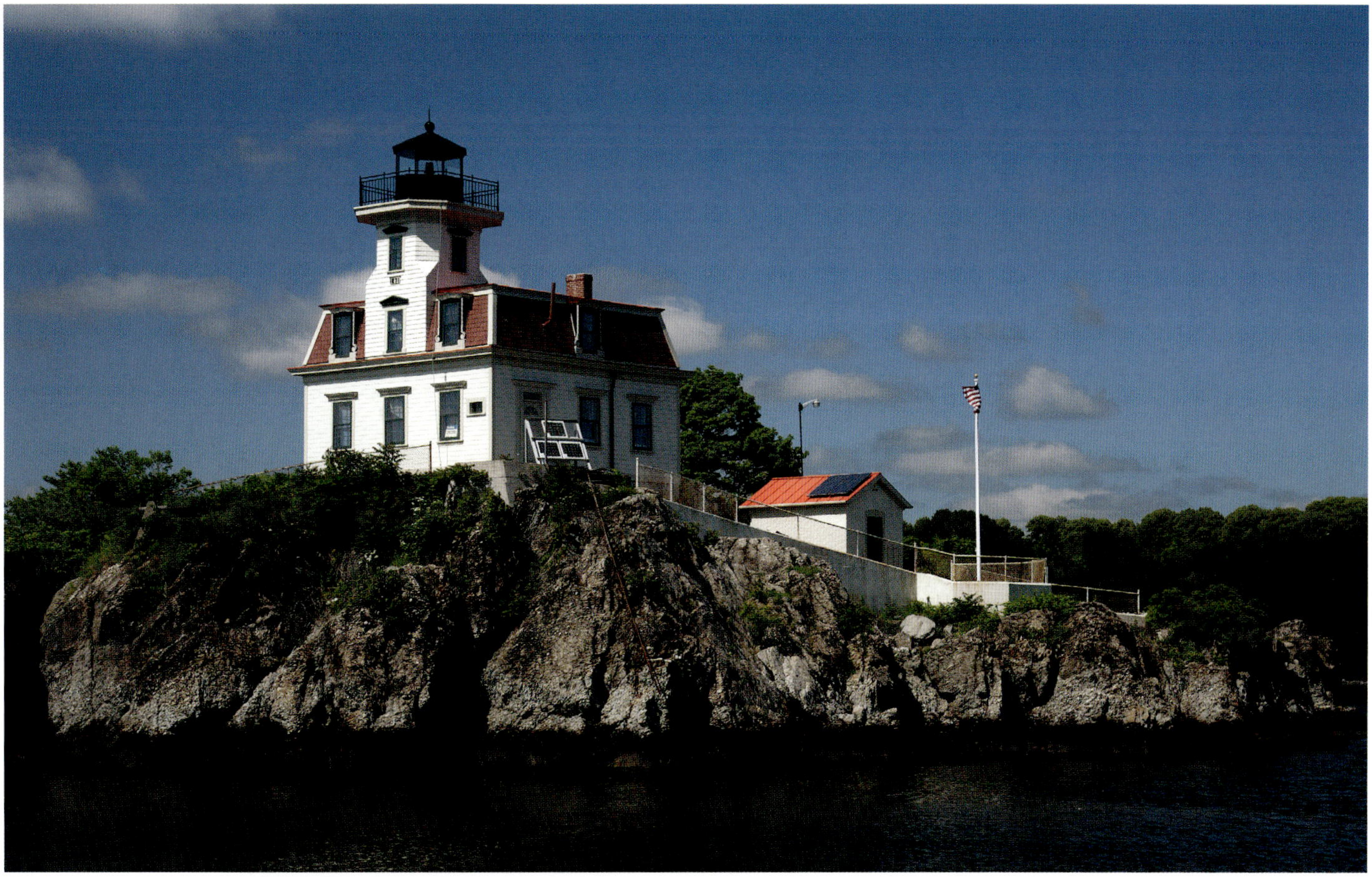

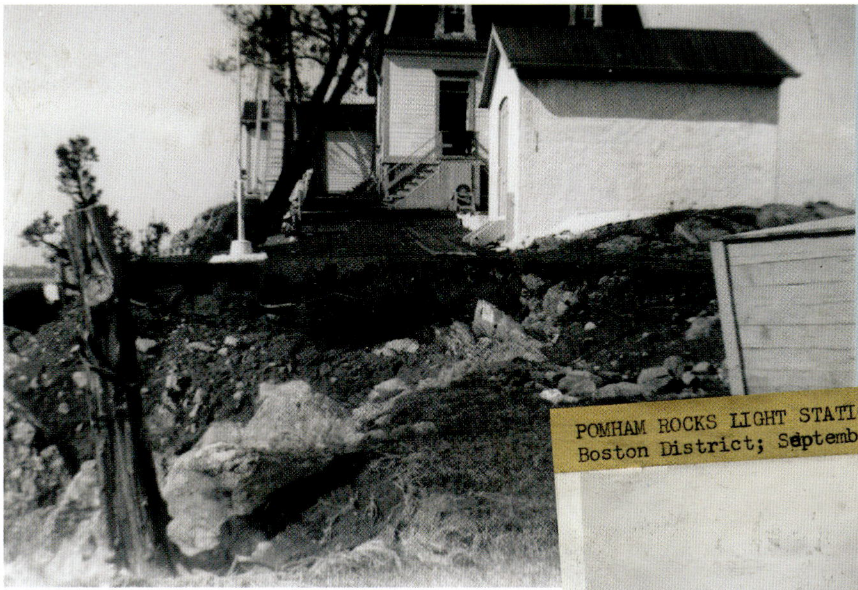

Left and bottom: The hurricane of September 1938 destroyed some and damaged many of the lighthouses along the Rhode Island coast. These two photographs, captured by a Coast Guard survey team, show the damage at Pomham Rocks. *(Courtesy of USCG)*

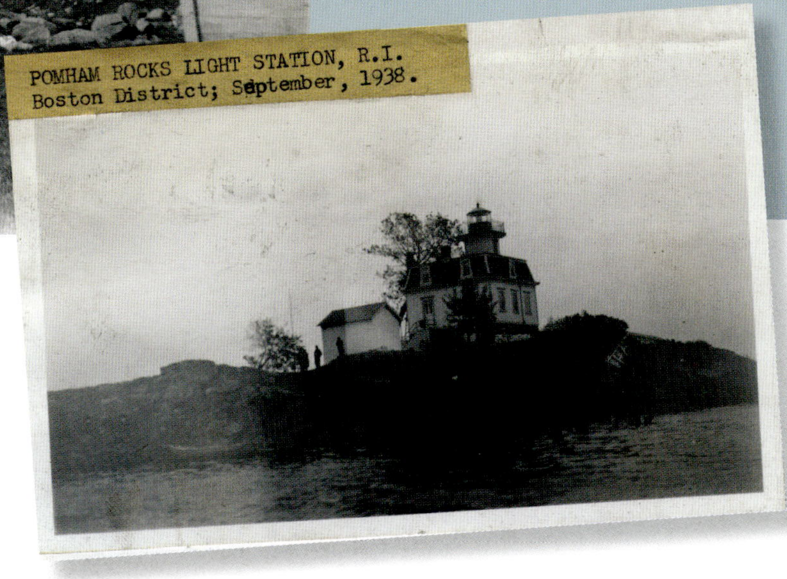

POMHAM ROCKS LIGHT STATION, R.I.
Boston District; September, 1938.

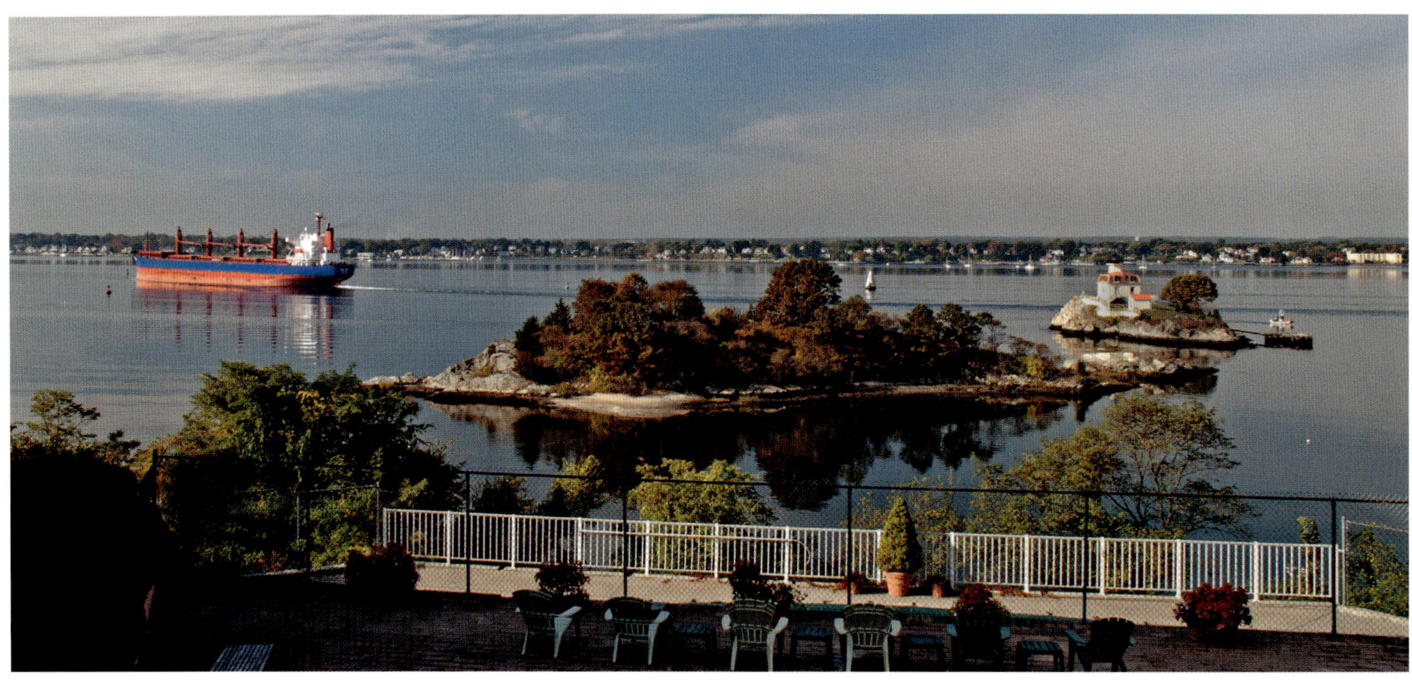

Top: From a nearby apartment complex, the Providence River with the lighthouse station to the right.

Right: Typical wooden stairs lead to the lantern room.

Far right: On the right side of the channel, Pomham Rocks's light characteristic is fixed red with this modern plastic beacon.

Bottom: In the lantern room, distant southward views of the Providence River.

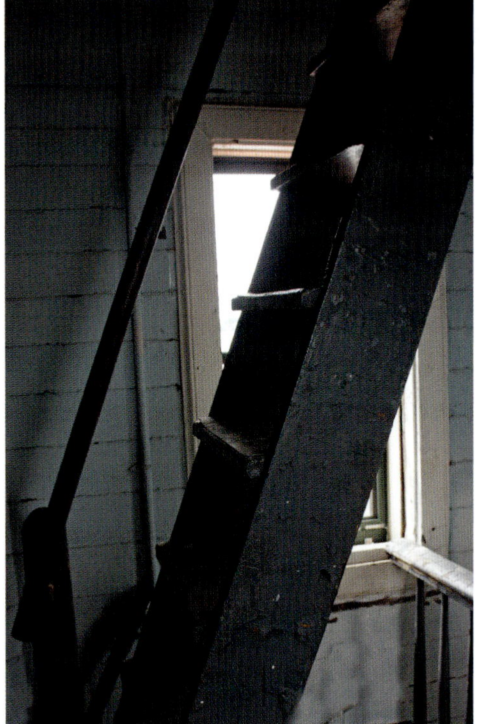

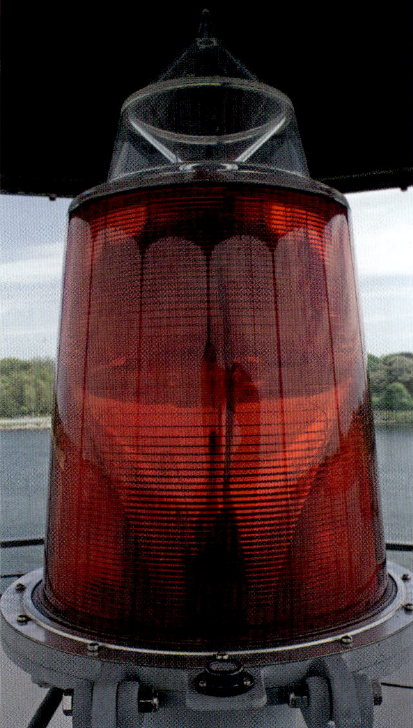

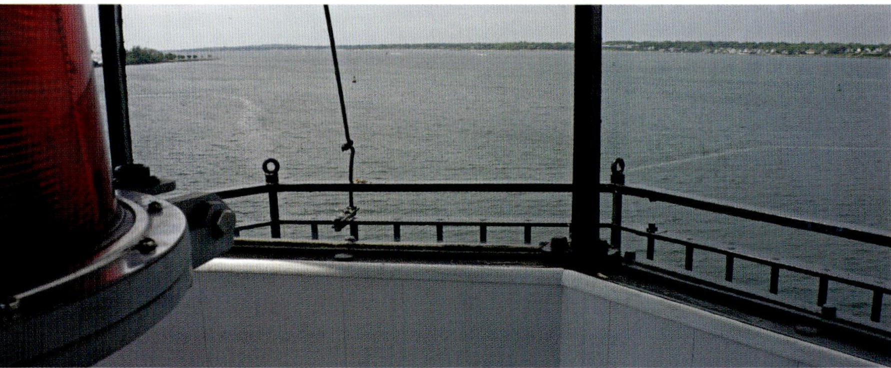

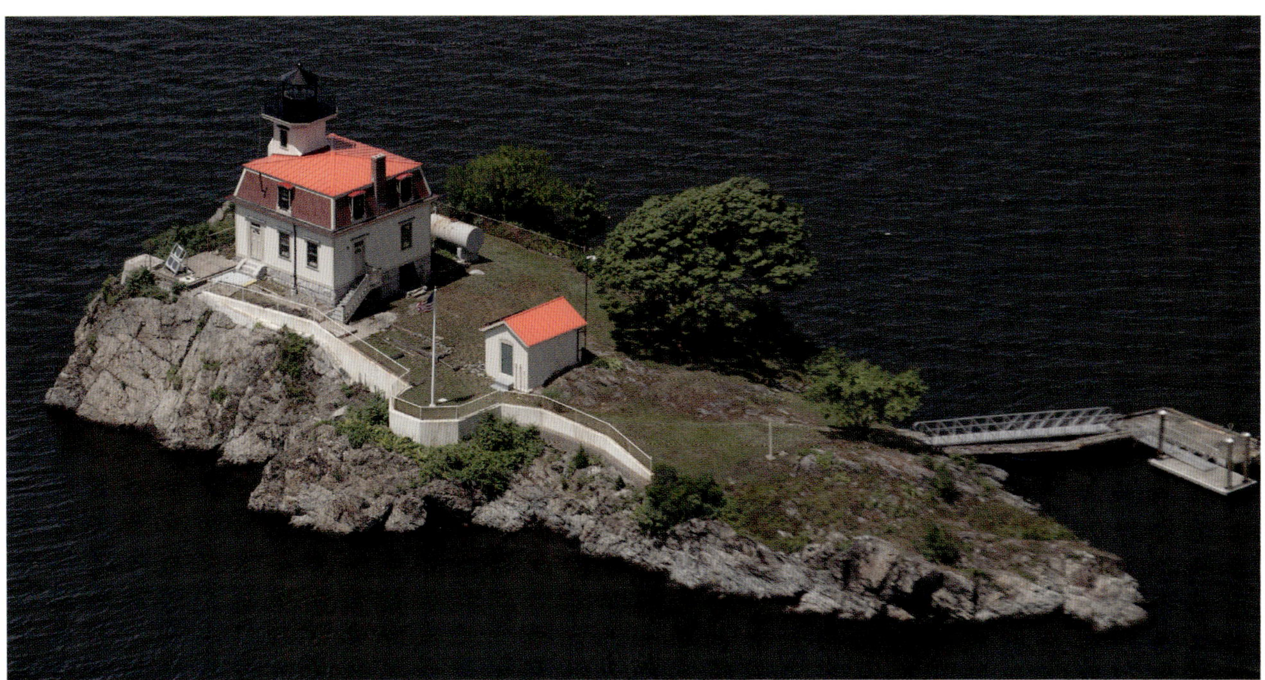

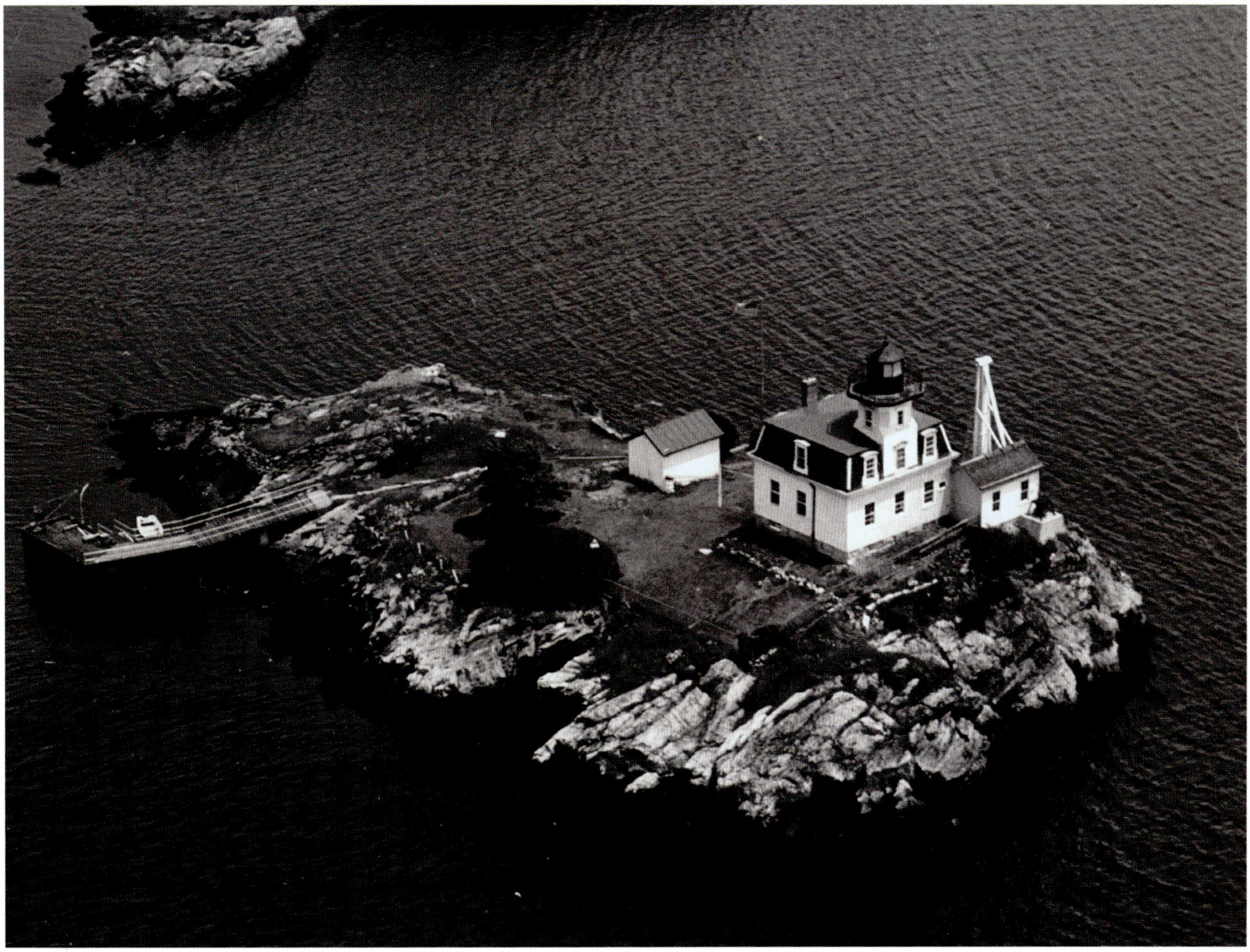

Two aerial images of the Pomham Rocks Lighthouse Station taken about fifty years apart.
(Black-and-white image courtesy of USCG)

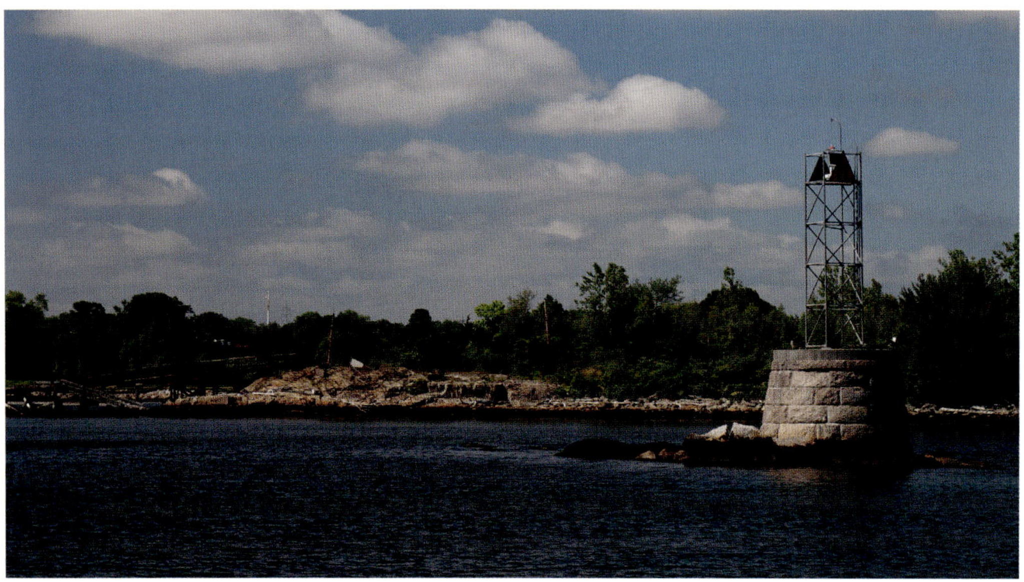

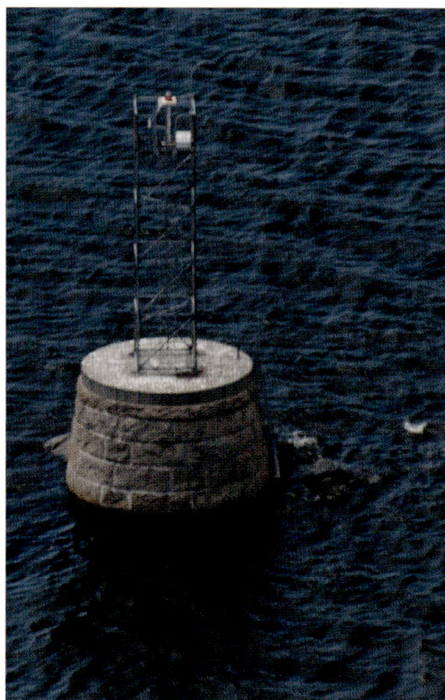

Above: Two present-day images of the aid. The solar-powered light on the skeleton tower is also identified with a red triangle and the number 42.

FULLER ROCKS

Location: headwaters of Providence River, N41°47′38″, W71°22′48″, station no longer exists

Appropriation: $20,000 in July 1870 (also included Sassafras Point and Pomham Rocks)

Established: 1872

Destroyed: February 1923, acetylene tank explosion

Tower: Wood, white, hexagonal, black lantern room, 17 feet, built on a granite pier, replaced by skeleton tower

Original Lens: 6th order Fresnel lens used as portable beacons

Present Lens: Plastic lens 250 mm, automated

Light Characteristics: 1873, fixed white (FW), 1912 flashing red every 3 seconds (FL R 3s)

1906: Fixed white (FW)

2005: Isophase red 6 seconds (Iso R 6s), focal plane 31 feet

Range: 1872, 7.5 nm; 2005, 4 nm

Fog Signal: None

Status: Original station no longer exists, replaced by skeleton tower that is U.S. Coast Guard active aid to navigation

Access: None, present aid can be seen from boat.

Comments: Built in conjunction with sister tower at Sassafras Point; keeper was responsible for both lights.

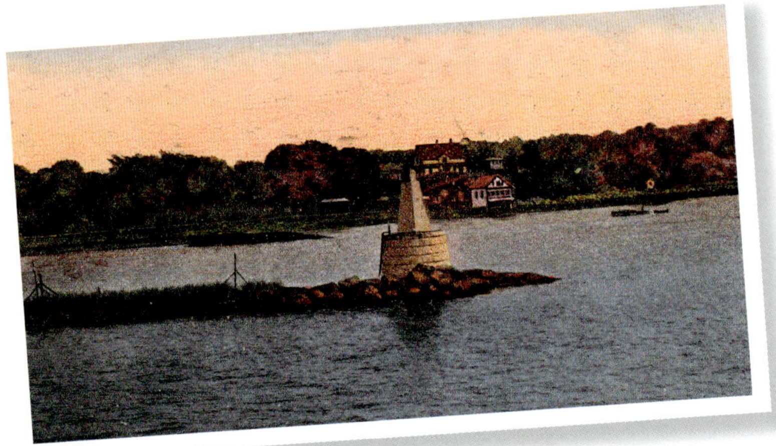

Above: An old postcard of Fuller Rocks; all that remains of the original is the granite base.

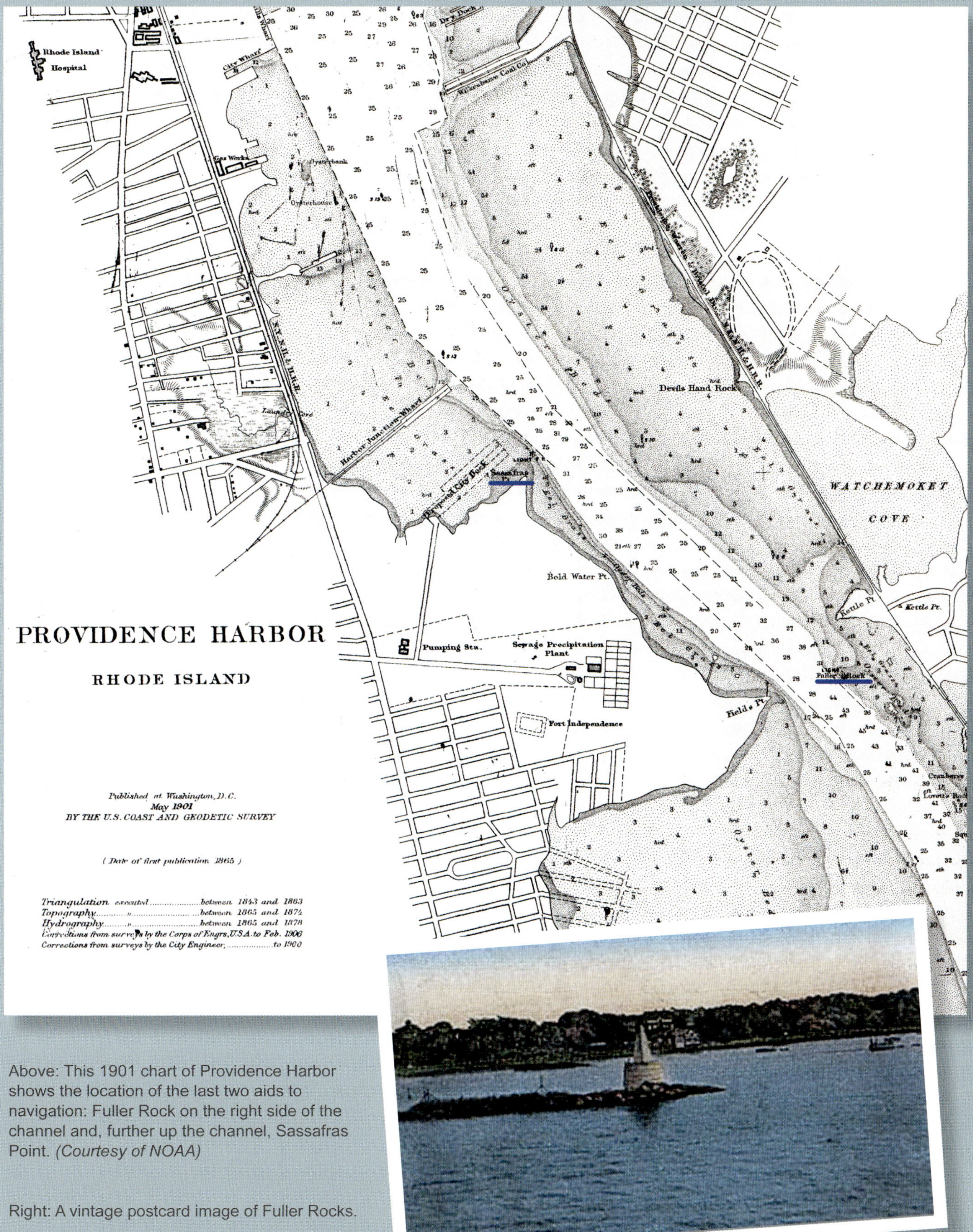

Above: This 1901 chart of Providence Harbor shows the location of the last two aids to navigation: Fuller Rock on the right side of the channel and, further up the channel, Sassafras Point. *(Courtesy of NOAA)*

Right: A vintage postcard image of Fuller Rocks.

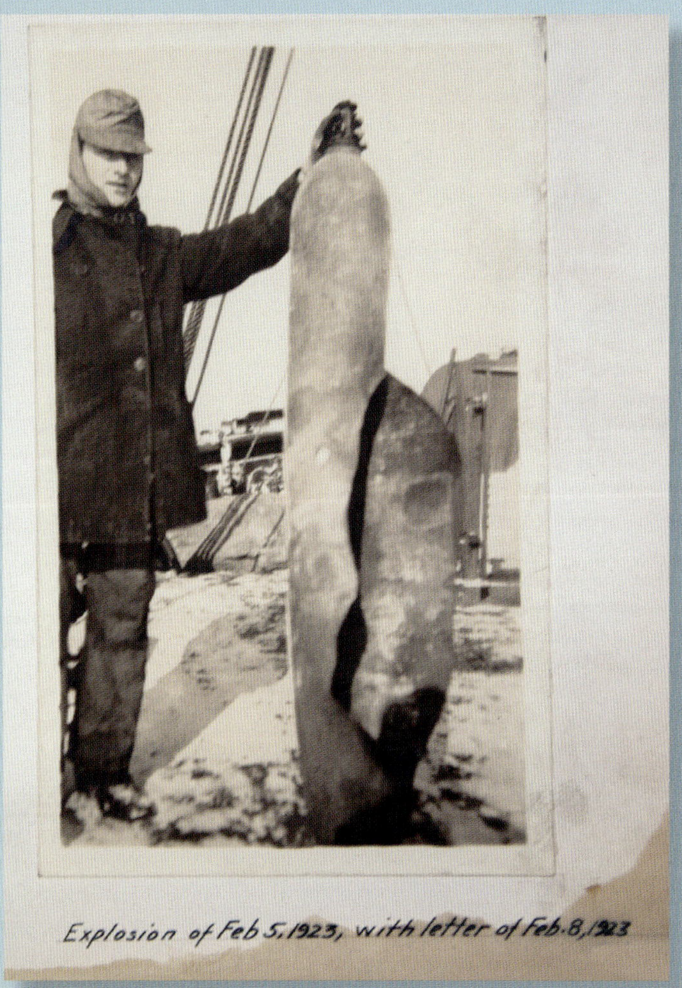

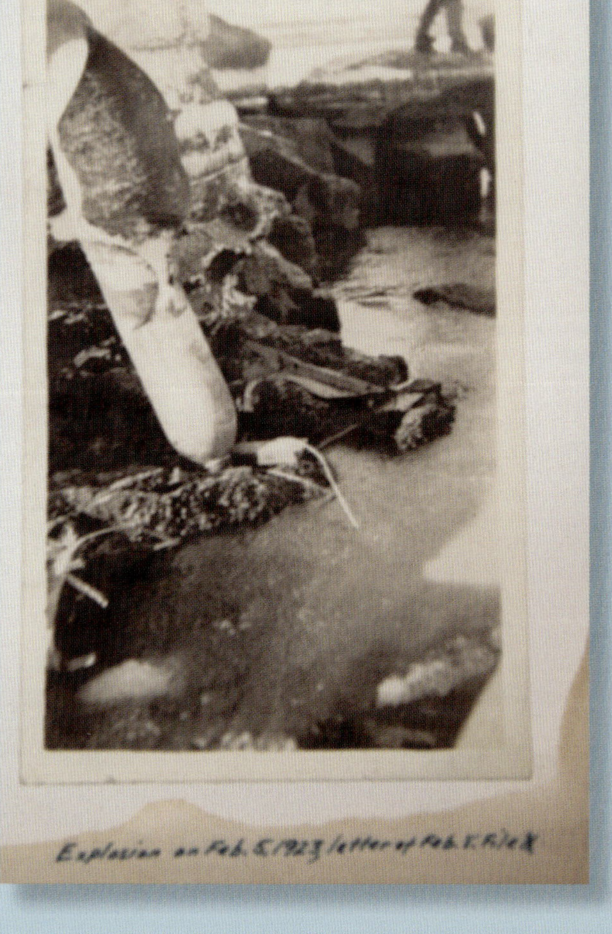

On 5 February 1923, during replacement of the acetylene tanks, there was an explosion that destroyed the tower. Fortunately, nobody died. These images were shot by the Coast Guard after the accident. *(Courtesy of USCG)*

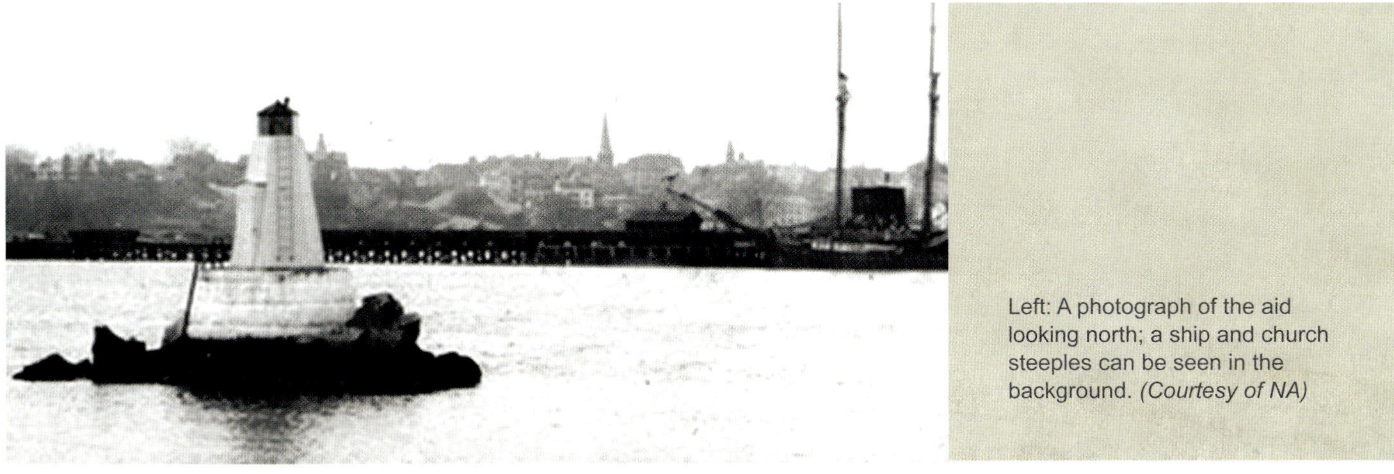

Left: A photograph of the aid looking north; a ship and church steeples can be seen in the background. *(Courtesy of NA)*

SASSAFRAS POINT

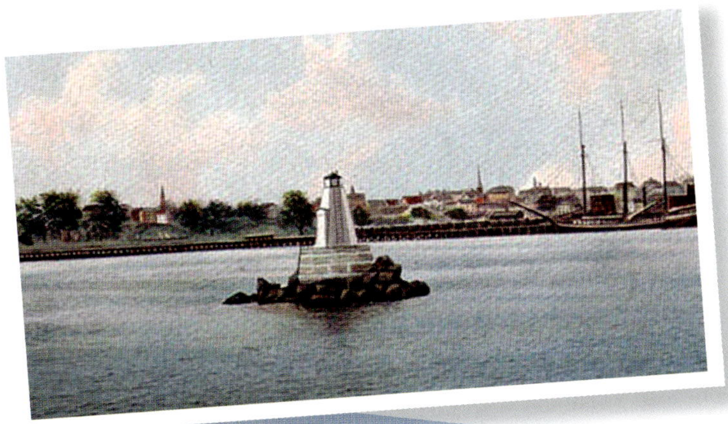

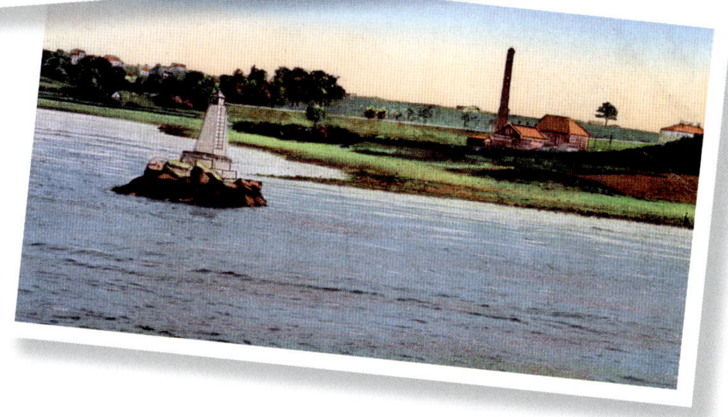

Location: Headwaters of Providence River, west side, N41°48′1″, W71°23.5′; station no longer exists, nothing remains

Appropriation: $20,000 in 1872 (also included Fuller Rock)

Established: 1872

Tower: Wood, white, hexagonal, 14 feet on granite pier, black lantern room

Disestablished: July 1912, dismantled and shoal dredged and removed

Original Lens: 6th order Fresnel lens as portable beacons

Present Lens: N/A

Light Characteristic: 1873 Fixed red (FR), focal plane 25 feet

Range: 7.5 nm

Fog Signal: None

Status: Station no longer exists, site demolished and shoal dredged

Access: N/A

Comments: Built in conjunction with Fuller Rocks; maintained by the same keeper.

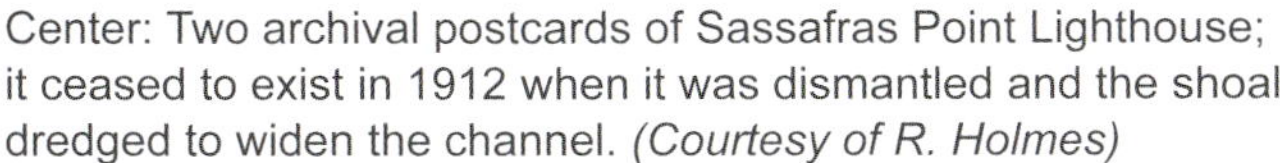

Center: Two archival postcards of Sassafras Point Lighthouse; it ceased to exist in 1912 when it was dismantled and the shoal dredged to widen the channel. *(Courtesy of R. Holmes)*

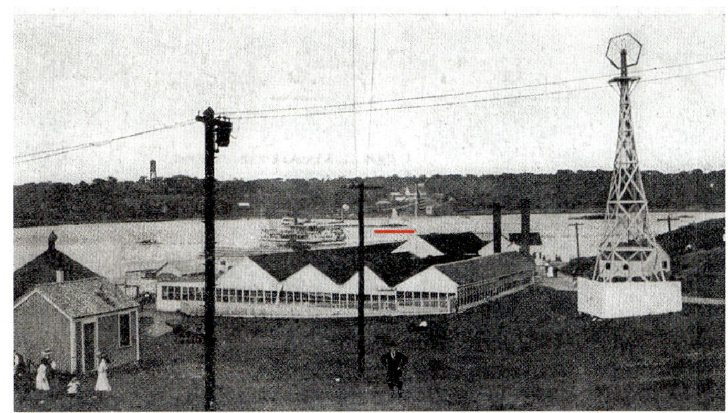

Bottom: A postcard of Field's Point with Sassafras Point Light in the background, underlined in red. *(Courtesy of R. Holmes)*

LIGHTSHIPS

Brenton Reef Lightship Station

While Hog Island Shoal Lightship could have been considered an "inshore" station, Brenton Reef was an "offshore" station more than three miles southeast of Beavertail Light. Established in 1853, four lightships were assigned to this station until 1962, when the ship was replaced by a Texas Tower. The four lightships and their years of service were the *LV 14* (1853–1856), the *LV 11* (1856–1897), the *LV 39* (1897–1935), and the *LV 102/WAL-525*.

After an appropriation of $15,000 in 1851, the *LV 14* was built in nearby Newport as a sloop rigged vessel. Constructed of white oak and yellow pine, the two masted (foremast higher) vessel was 91′ long with a beam of 22′, a draft of 9′, and almost 160 gross tons. Previous to the start of assigning lightships numbers, she was possibly named *Ledyard* when she was launched. Her signaling apparatus consisted of a single lantern with eight lamps and a bell and horn that were hand operated. On station in 1853, it was only three years later when an inspection determined that she would be more suitable at an "inside station." For the next sixteen years, the *LV 14* was assigned to Cornfield Point, Connecticut. While on station in 1866, she was rammed by a steamer from New London and received considerable damage. By 1872, she was retired from duty and sold at auction for $615.

The second lightship assigned to Brenton Reef, *LV 11*, encountered several historically significant events. Built the same year as the *LV 14* and only slightly larger, her major difference was her tonnage, 320 gross. With her two masts and day marks at the masthead, she had two lanterns with eight oil lamps for lighting apparatus; a hand-operated bell as well as a horn and gong provided fog signals. She was equipped with a radio in 1919. Her first station, as the first lightship assigned there, was Nantucket New South Shoal, 1854–1855.

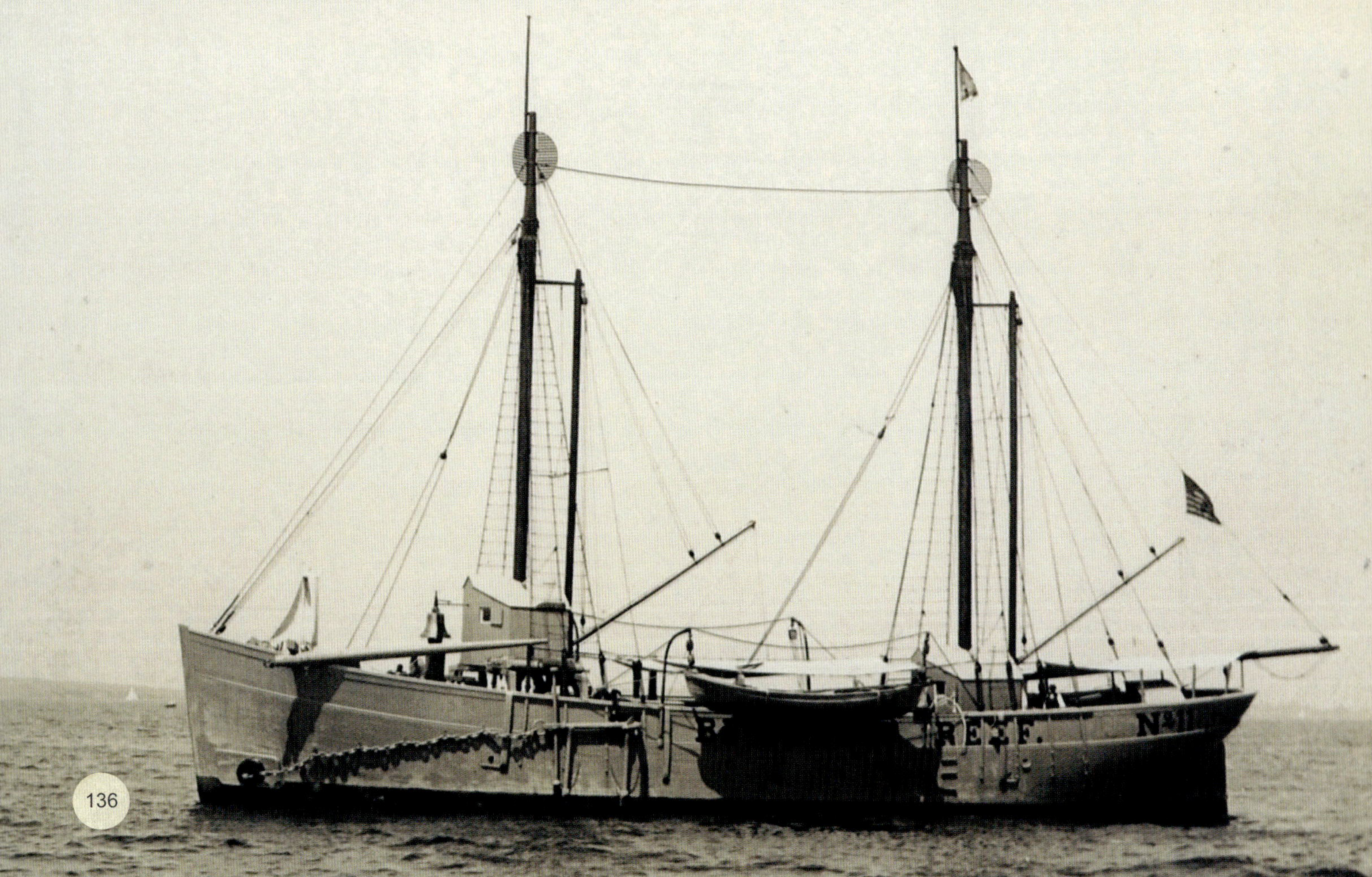

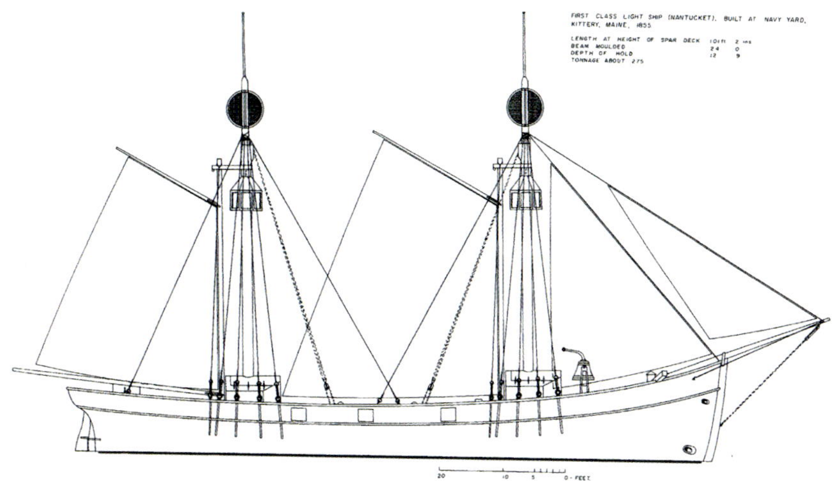

Placed on station in June, the following February (1855) she was blown off her location and drifted ashore at Montauk, New York. She was salvaged, repaired, and then assigned to Brenton Reef (1856). Her time on station was not without incident; in October 1865, she was blown off station and badly damaged on the rocks and in November 1890, the British steamer *Curlew* collided with her. She was replaced by the *LV 39* in 1897. Subsequent duties included assignments as Relief vessel and station Scotland, New Jersey. A Relief lightship would replace a lightship that would be assigned to a specific station that required maintenance and updating of equipment. This could take up to several months and an aid to navigation would be necessary at that location. When the *LV 11* was retired from duty in 1925, she was the oldest vessel in the Lighthouse Service (72 years).

The third lightship assigned to the station, the *LV 39*, like the previous two, was a schooner rigged wood sailboat with no sister vessels. These ships were built with a contract at a determined price and usually with a specific station in mind. Built in 1875 for $42,200, she was larger than her predecessors: about 120′ long, 27′ beam, almost 13′ draft, and 387 gross tonnage. The *LV 39* was also equipped with two auxiliary steam boilers that included a steam pump and a steam fog-signaling apparatus. Her illuminating apparatus included two lanterns with eight oil lamps. She was the first vessel to be built with a steam whistle (12″) as well as a hand-operated bell. Lightships were constantly modified and modernized; in 1909 a six-inch fog whistle was added, in 1911 a submarine bell was installed, and a radio was equipped in 1919 but discontinued in 1923. The most significant structural change was made in 1921 when the lanterns and foremast were removed and replaced with a skeleton tower that had an acetylene lamp. Previous to Brenton Reef, the *LV 39* was assigned to Vineyard Sound, Massachusetts (1875–1876), Five Fathom Bank, New Jersey (1876–1877), Relief MA (1877–1897), and Relief NY (1897). She was assigned to the Brenton Reef Station from November 1897 to 1935, when she was replaced by the *LV 102/WAL-525*. After retirement in 1935, the *LV 39* was a floating restaurant and a CG Auxiliary clubhouse; she sank off Beverly, Massachusetts, in 1975 while being towed to a shipyard.

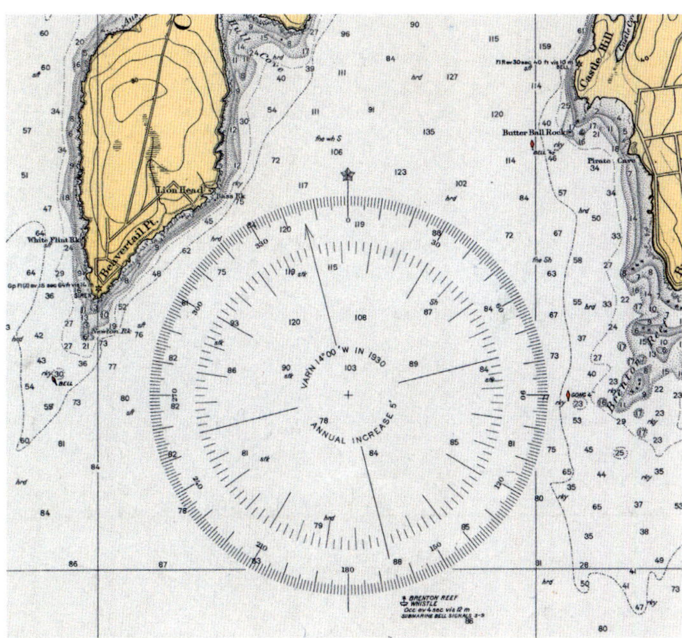

Above: A 1931 chart identifies the location of the Brenton Reef lightship station. The characteristic signals at that time were a white light occluded every 4 seconds that was visible for 12 miles, a whistle, and a submarine bell code of 3-9. *(Courtesy of NOAA)*

Top: This is a plan for the *LV 1* and, although not a sister ship of the *LV 14*, is a similar design to the first ship assigned to the Brenton Reef station. *(Courtesy of NA)*

Opposite: The *LV 11*, from 1856 to 1897, was the second lightship assigned to this station. Note the name of the station under the lifeboat and the vessel designation on the stern. *(Courtesy of NA)*

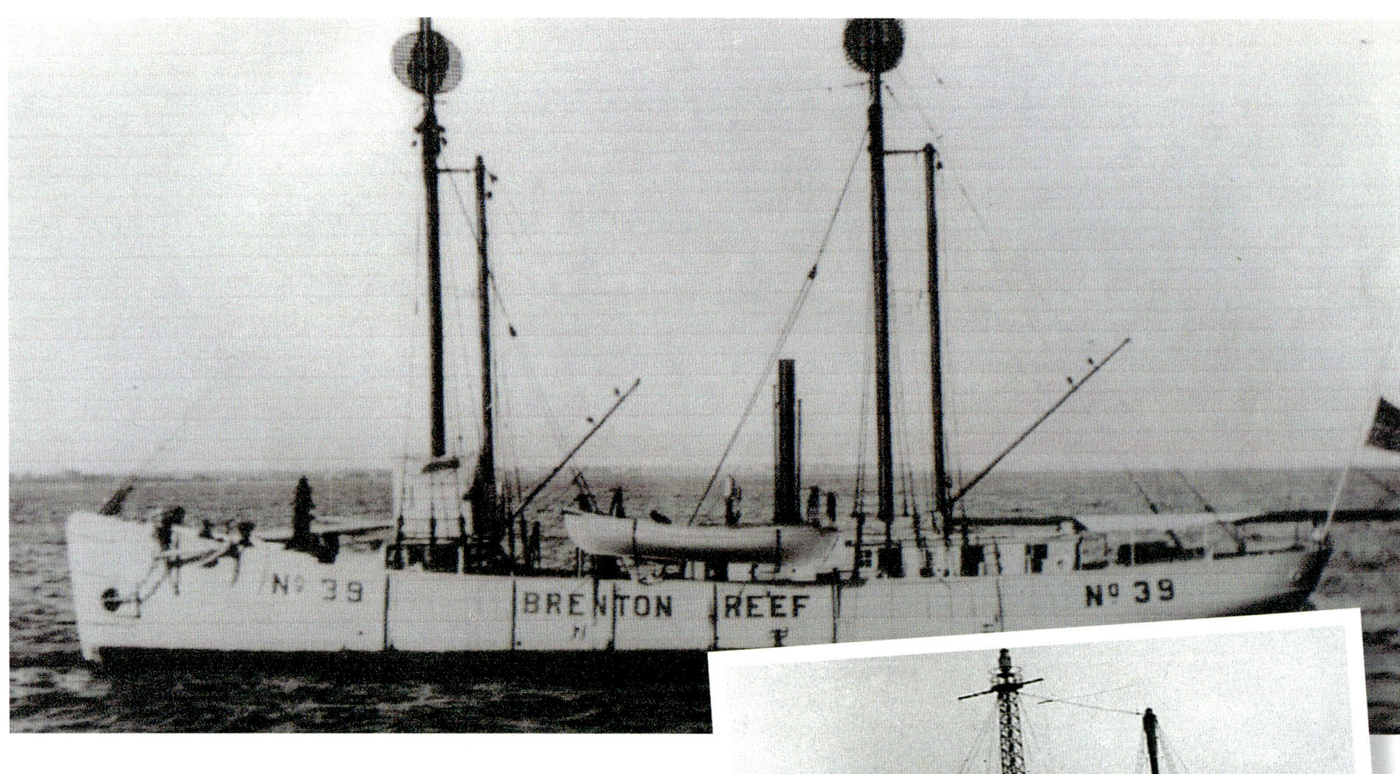

BRENTON REEF LIGHTSHIP STATION

Location: Entrance to East Passage of Narragansett Bay, approximate location N41°25′, W71°22′

(Note, since lightships were not fixed, they would be moved within a certain area.)

Established: 1853

Lightships assigned: *LV 14* (1853–1856), *LV 11* (1856–1897), *LV 39* (1897–1935), and the *LV 102/ WAL-525* (1935–1962)

Tower: 1962, replaced lightship *LV-102*

Deactivated: 1989, tower torn down, sunk nearby to make artificial reef

Status: Buoy marks the reef at the present time.

Access: N/A

Comments: Lightships assigned to this station were involved with America's Cup races.

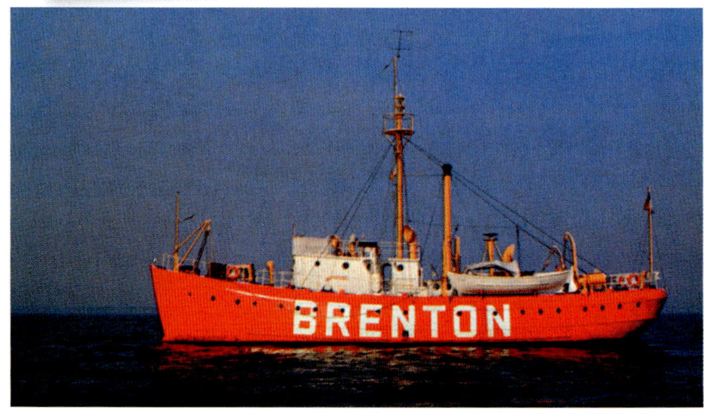

Top: The next lightship assigned to Brenton Reef was the *LV 39* from 1897 to 1935. This image was taken before 1921. The ship was kept on a regular maintenance schedule, and the ship repairs were mostly undetectable; examine the post-1921 image. *(Courtesy of USCG)*

Center: Post 1921, the *LV 39* had the lanterns and lantern house removed with the foremast replaced with a skeleton tower light structure. An acetylene lamp was the signal lamp. *(Courtesy of USCG)*

Bottom: The *LV 102* on station.

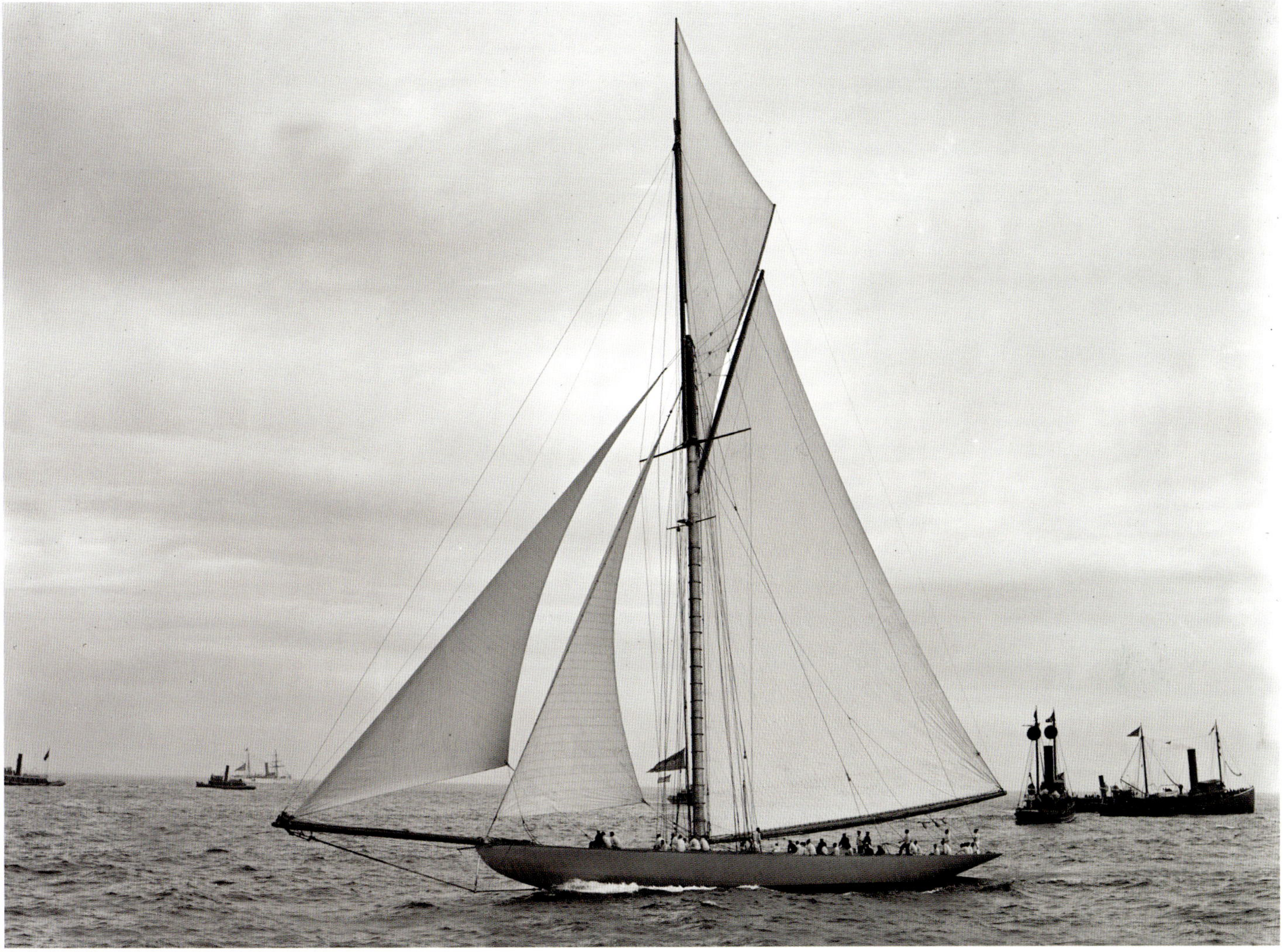

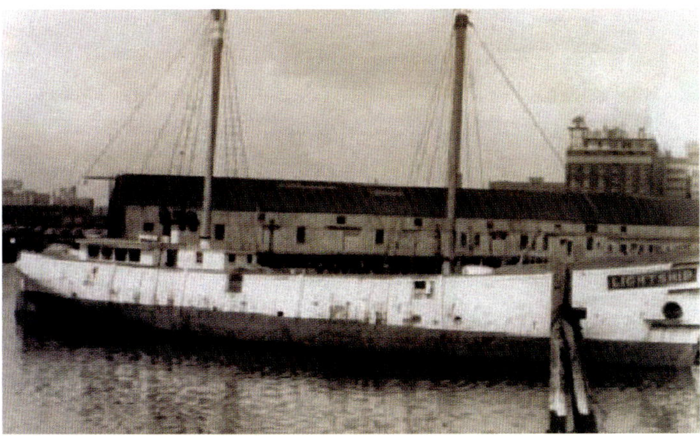

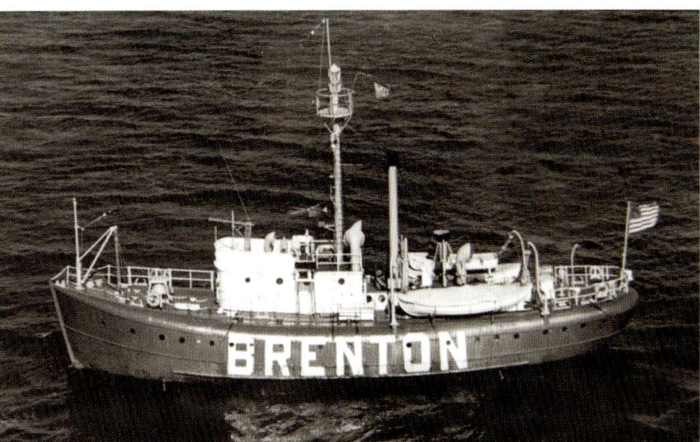

Top: The *Shamrock* sails off Newport in 1899; in the background is the *LV 39*. *(Courtesy of LOC)*

Left: Retired from duty in 1935, the *LV 39* served as a restaurant and a Coast Guard auxiliary clubhouse; she sank off Beverly, Massachusetts, in 1975. *(Courtesy of USCG)*

Right: This an aerial image of the last lightship assigned to Brenton Reef; she was the *LV 102/WAL-525* and on station from 1935 to 1962. *(Courtesy of USCG)*

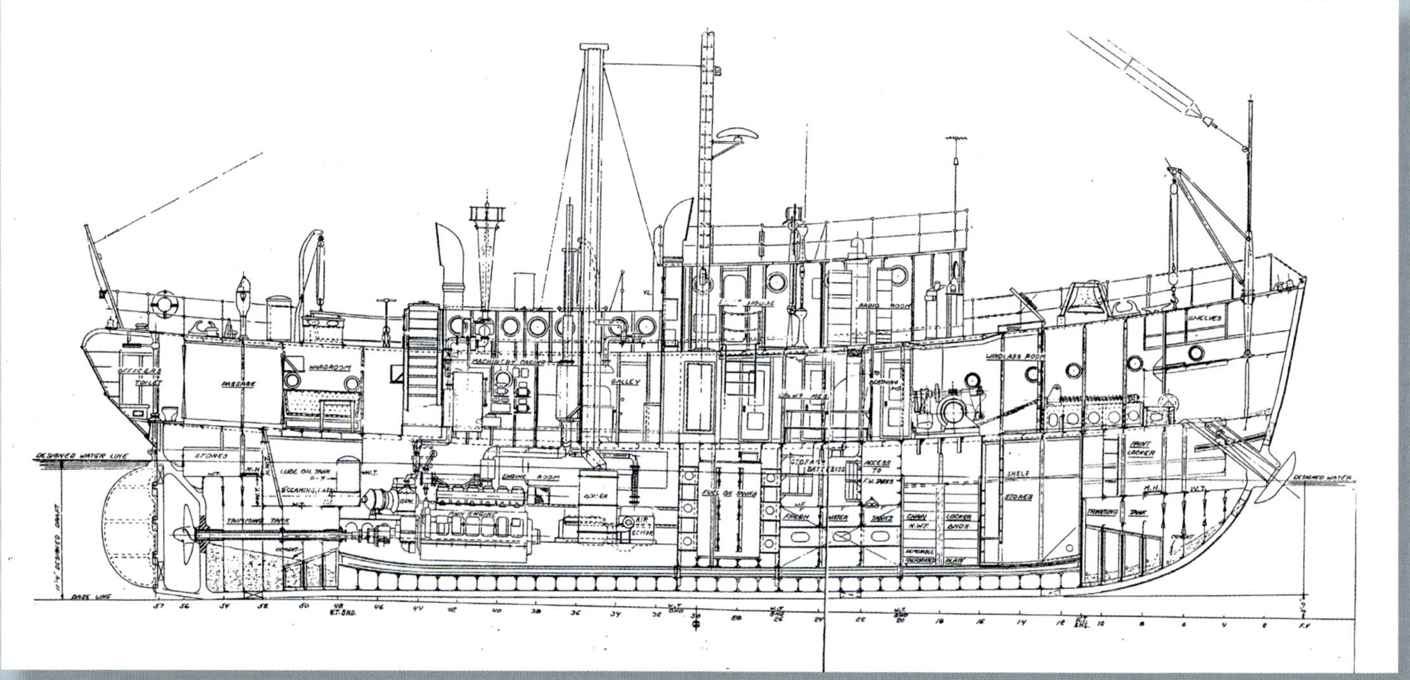

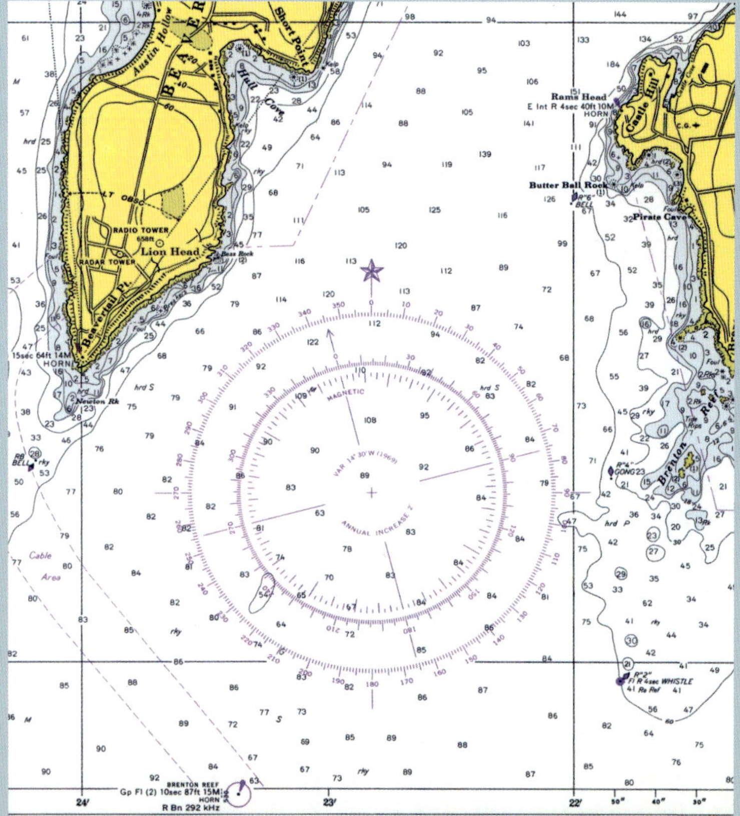

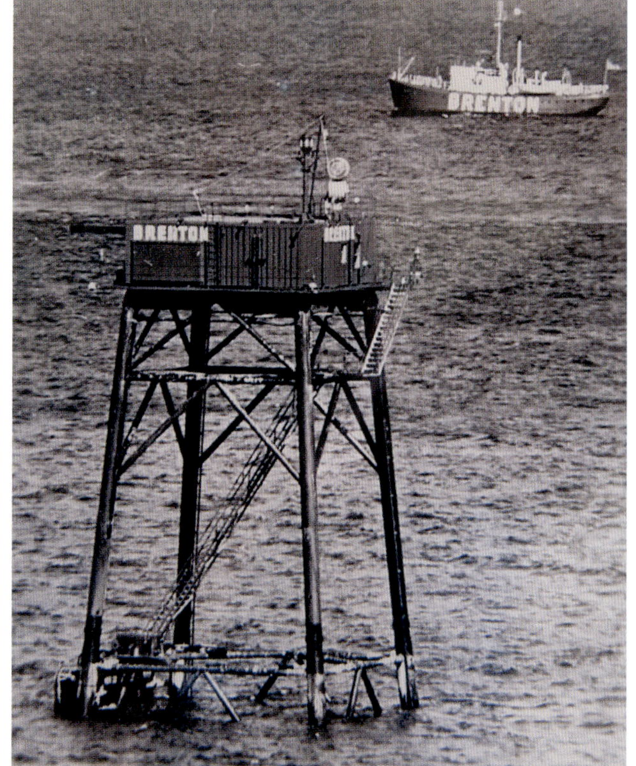

Top: Cross-section plans for the *LV 102*. *(Courtesy of R. Holmes)*

Above: This 1971 chart indicates the Brenton Reef aid along the bottom edge.

Above: The two aids: the *LV 102* in the background and the "Texas Tower" that replaced the lightship. *(Courtesy of USCG)*

Hog Island Shoal Lightship

As was the case with many of the early lighthouses in Rhode Island where the original stations were privately maintained by companies transporting passengers along the coast, the same was true with the Hog Island lightship. First marked as a buoy as early as 1838, a floating light at this location was maintained by the Old Colony Steamboat Company from 1866 to 1885. At that time, the U.S. government established a lightship station. Only one vessel, the *LV 12*, from 1885 to 1901, was assigned to this location. In 1901, it in turn was replaced by a permanent caisson style lighthouse.

HOG ISLAND SHOAL LIGHTSHIP

Location: N41°37′48″, W71°16′18″

Established: Private aid as early as 1838, U.S. Government 1885

Ship: *LV 12,* two masted sail schooner rigged, built 1846

Dimensions: 72′ beam, 20′6″ beam, 9′7″draft, 159 gross tonnage

Original Optics: Single lantern on foremast, eight lamps

Light Characteristics: Fixed white (FW)

Range: 4 nm

Fog Signal: Hand-operated bell

Status: Replaced 1901 by spark plug design lighthouse

Access: N/A; ship no longer exists, sold at auction in 1903.

Comments: Originally numbered *LV 22,* renumbered in 1871 to *LV 12;* previous stations include York Spit (Virginia), Eel Grass Shoal (Connecticut), Cornfield Point (Connecticut), and as a Relief vessel.

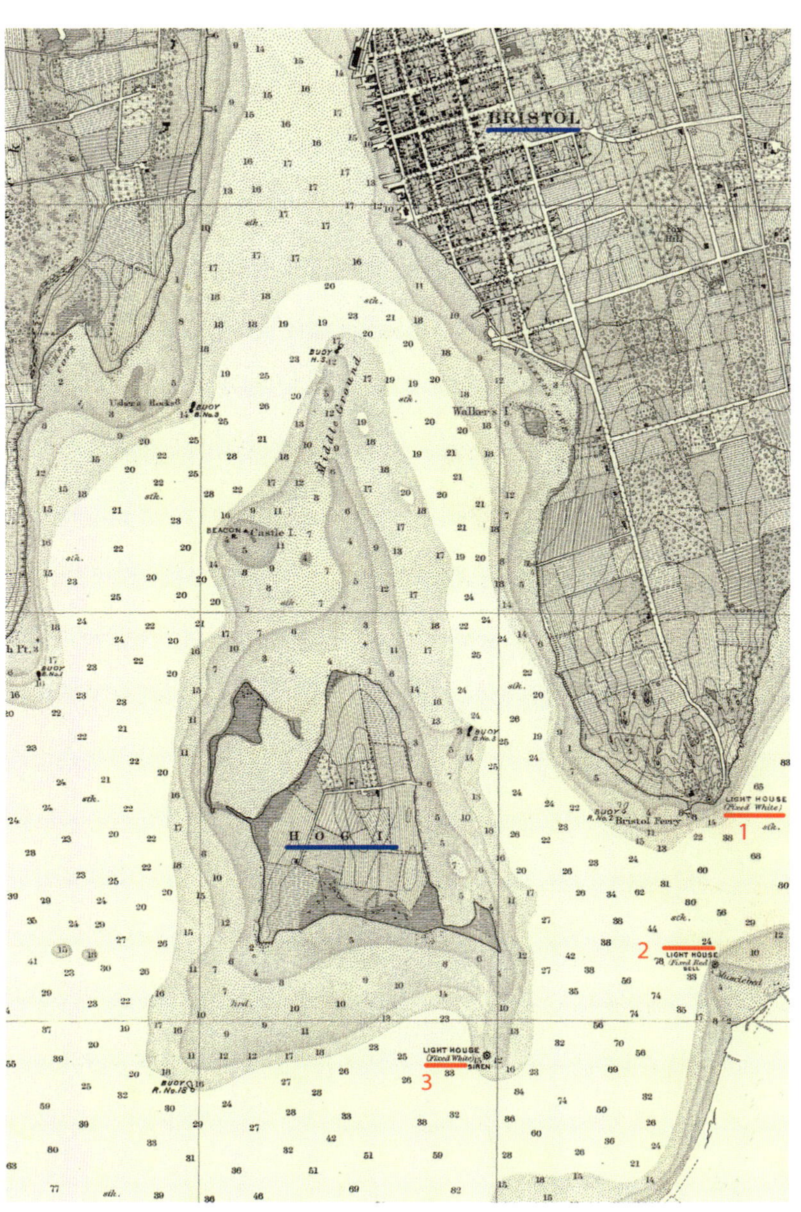

A chart published in 1864 is interesting in that it shows a lighthouse at #3. At that time, the station was privately maintained. *(Courtesy of NOAA)*

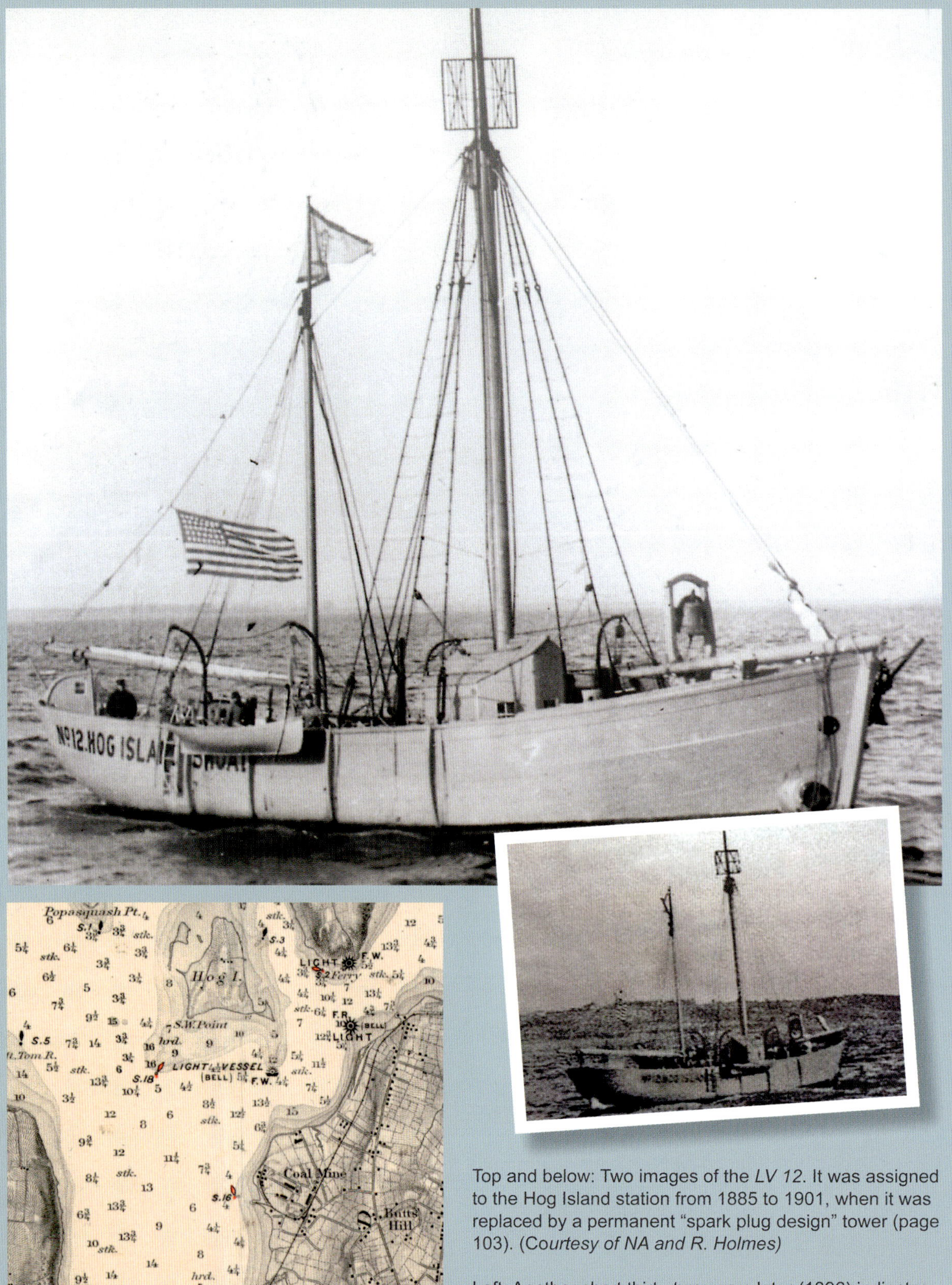

Top and below: Two images of the *LV 12*. It was assigned to the Hog Island station from 1885 to 1901, when it was replaced by a permanent "spark plug design" tower (page 103). (*Courtesy of NA and R. Holmes)*

Left: Another chart thirty-two years later (1896) indicates the aid as a light vessel with a FW (fixed white) light and a bell. Note Sand Point on Prudence Island with a fixed white light; now it is flashing green every six seconds. *(Courtesy of NOAA)*

CONCLUSION

Originally there were thirty, and now in the twenty-first century twenty-one lighthouses remain standing in Rhode Island. Nine of those have the surrounding grounds open to visit; three have the towers open for tours during an active summer season schedule. Six towers are along the waterways and can only be closely seen by boat. For the lighthouse enthusiast, several cruises sail Narragansett Bay and pass by several former towers as well as still-active aids to navigation, both on land and in the water. Whatever the season, the lighthouses of Rhode Island offer the photographer and the maritime aficionado a wealth of opportunities to visit these aids to navigation. Hopefully this guide, past and present, will be a welcome resource for the lighthouse admirer.

ACKNOWLEDGMENTS

This pictorial guide would not have been possible without the contributions of numerous individuals. Jeremy D'Entremont, first and foremost, the outstanding guru of lighthouses, provided images and information. To all those who allowed me to visit lighthouses that are now residences and no longer active; Neil and Christine Feins, Ras and Helene Lischio, Russell and Carol Shippee, Todd and Paula Butlin; thank you for opening your home to me and for your congeniality. In addition, David Kelleher, Rob Gilpin, Lisa Nolan, Charles Hall, Scott Brown, Scott Chapin, Craig Amerigian, David Zapatka, David McGurdy, Harry Sterling, and Beth Correira; thank you for the private guided tours. To all the "Coasties," Chief Chase and Chief Baruzzi, thank you. To all those guides and docents at the maritime historical museums, thank you. The errors are mine. As I have visited numerous places, finding inconsistencies and a lack of data in the records, I have tried to present to the reader what is most likely the correct information.

Like many other maritime enthusiasts, I have been intrigued by lighthouses for numerous years and have captured images of these structures not only in Rhode Island, but literally around the world. Most of the modern images found in this book are mine. Historic images were found primarily in three sources which any interested researcher can access. The National Archives in College Park, Maryland, is a national treasure, with substantial images, plans, and supporting documents regarding lighthouses. To all those individuals on the third and fifth floors who provided assistance, thank you. Another resource that proved invaluable was the United States Coast Guard Historian's Office in Washington, DC. Scott Price and Chris Havern provided direction and assistance that proved most helpful; thank you. A third major resource was the Coast Guard Heritage Museum in Barnstable, Massachusetts. Bill Collette, Jack McGrath, and all the other retired "Coasties," thank you for all your help.

To all the guides, historians, and escorts at the lighthouses and museums around the world that I have visited who answered my questions and provided guidance, thank you. To Carol for all her help, both in traveling to all these locations as well as reviewing, editing, and discussing the final document. To Tony Pane, as always, for trying to teach me the finer aspects of the written English language (I hope I get there), thank you. To Salty Dog, my best friend, and a companion for many of these trips to lighthouses, hopefully more treats for the next book.

BIBLIOGRAPHY

Adams, W. H. Davenport, *Lighthouses and Lightships, A descriptive and historical account of their mode of construction and organization,* T. Nelson and Sons, London, England, 1878

Bachand, Robert G., *Northeast Lights Lighthouses and Lightships, Rhode Island to Cape May,* New Jersey Sea Sports Publications, Norwalk, CT, 1989

Davidson, Donald W., *Lighthouses of New England,* The Wellfleet Press, Secaucus, NJ, 1990

D'Entremont, Jeremy, *The Lighthouse Handbook New England,* Cedar Mill Press Book Publishers LLC, Kennebunkport, ME, 2008

D'Entremont, Jeremy, *The Lighthouses of Rhode Island,* Commonwealth Editions, Beverly, MA, 2006

Holmes, Richard, *Rhode Island Lighthouses: A Pictorial History,* Rhodeislandlighthousehistory.info Publishing, 2008

Snow, Edward Rowe, *The Lighthouses of New England,* Dodd, Mead, Quality Paperback, New York, NY, 1945, 1973

Thompson, Courtney, *Lighthouses of Southern New England, Massachusetts, Rhode Island and Connecticut, A Pictorial Guide,* Cat Nap Publications, St. John, New Brunswick, Canada, 2002

WEBSITES

There are numerous and varied websites regarding lighthouses both specifically about Rhode Island and some more of a general nature. The following websites are maintained about an individual station.

Block Island North http://www.new-shoreham.com/displayboards.cfm?id=7

Watch Hill http://www.watchhilllighthousekeepers.org/

Beavertail http://www.beavertaillight.org/

Sakonnet http://www.sakonnetlighthouse.org/index.html

Rose Island http://www.roseislandlighthouse.org/

Dutch Island http://www.dutchislandlighthouse.org/

Plum Beach http://www.plumbeachlighthouse.org/

Pomham Rocks http://www.lighthousefoundation.org/alf_lights/pomhamrocks/pomhamrocks_info.htm

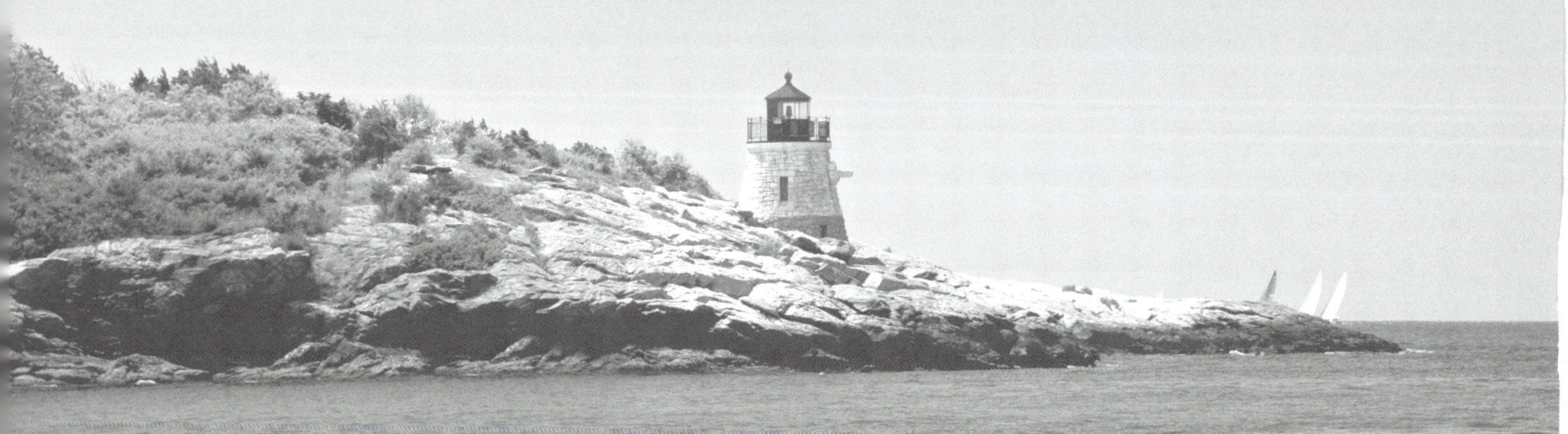

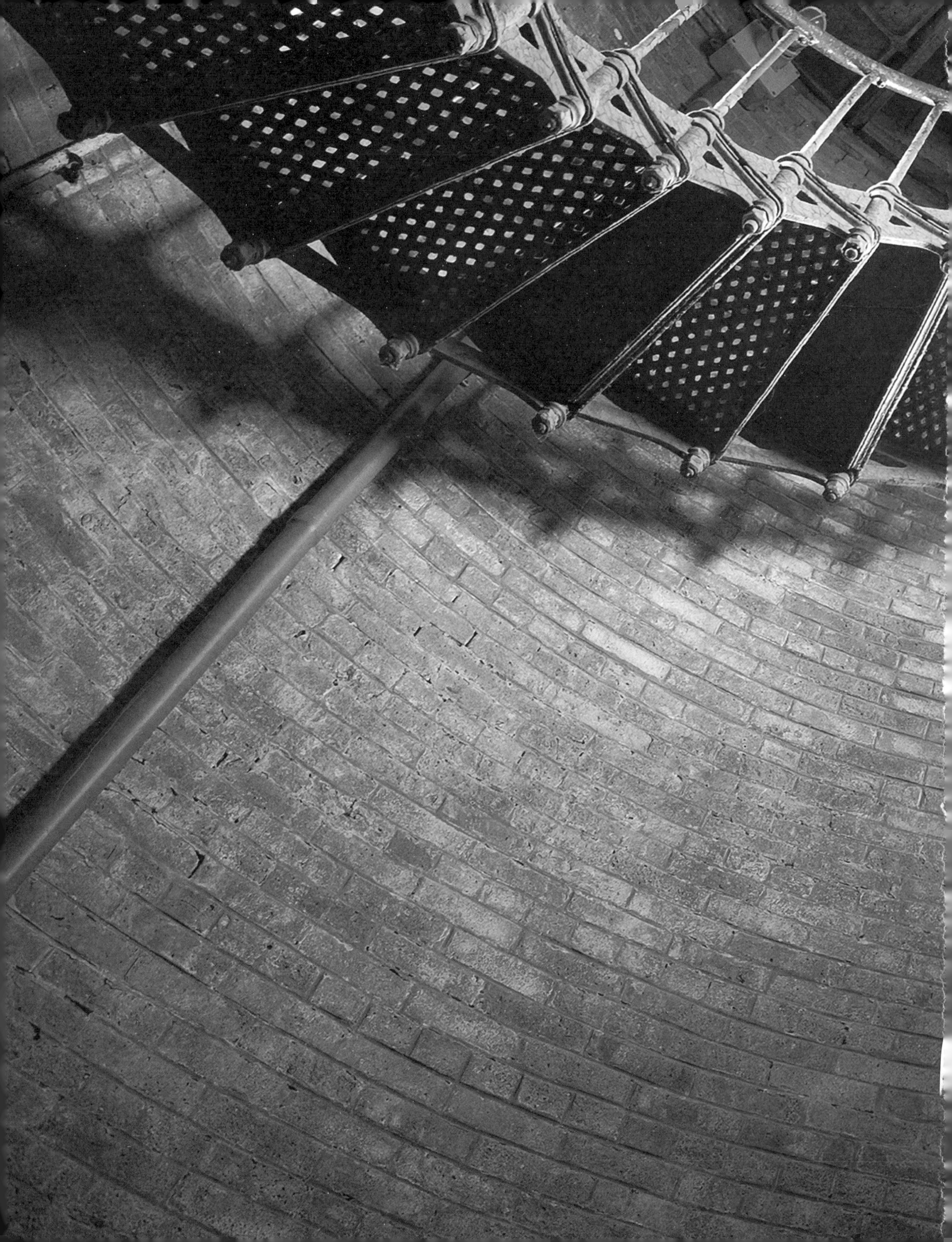